PORTFOLIO

BANDHAN

Tamal Bandyopadhyay is one of the most respected business journalists in India. He has kept a close watch on the financial sector for two decades and has had a ringside view of the enormous changes in the Indian finance and banking sector during this period. Tamal's weekly column, Banker's Trust, in *Mint,* is widely read for its deep insights, clarity and ability to anticipate and dissect major policy moves.

His previous books, *A Bank for the Buck* and *Sahara: The Untold Story,* have been bestsellers.

PRAISE FOR THE BOOK

'The transformation of Bandhan, a microfinance company, into a universal bank is as unique as the transition of Tamal from a business journalist to an author. As governor of the Reserve Bank, I had grown to respect Tamal for his passion for financial journalism, his enormous talent and endearing professional integrity. He combines all those attributes to tell the remarkable behind-the-scenes story of what it takes to overcome the challenges of last-mile connectivity in Indian finance'—D. Subbarao, former governor, RBI

'As an acclaimed journalist with decades of experience in financial markets, Tamal brings an intensity along with sincerity and integrity to his writing. In this book, he has woven a colourful canvas which draws the attention of the reader and makes him read, think and deliberate'—U.K. Sinha, chairman, SEBI

'The book is an ode to entrepreneurship and to microfinance. It is as much a story of financial inclusion and the building of an institution. Written with the perceptive eye of a seasoned journalist, the book is recommended reading for those looking for inspiration from role models in the new-age India'—Ashok Chawla, former chairperson, Competition Commission of India

'This is a fascinating story, deserving to be chronicled. And who better to do so than Tamal. It is a very revealing study—a must-read for those even remotely interested in this sector. The story is narrated by a person as well informed as a hands-on banker and has all the attendant nuances'—Vinod Rai, former comptroller and auditor general of India

'Bandhan, India's youngest bank, has a deep and long history behind it. First of its kind, the book takes the reader through India's journey towards financial inclusion. Tamal brilliantly captures a story of hope and what it takes to lift millions of Indians out of poverty'—Deepak Parekh, chairman, HDFC Limited

'Replete with fascinating anecdotes and containing perceptive pen portraits of some of the pioneers in the industry, the book makes for compulsive reading for all those who want insights into the growth of microfinance in India'—Y.H. Malegam, chairman of the RBI subcommittee set up to study MFI concerns

'Tamal's *Bandhan* is a must-read not only for those who want to relive Ghosh's entrepreneurial journey, but for anyone who wants the larger picture in Indian banking'—R. Jagannathan, *Swarajya*

'Tamal's journalistic expertise helps in making this book readable for anyone seeking inspiration. He is able to keep the reader glued'—Madan Sabnavis, *Financial Express*

'It's an earthy book for earthy people who can appreciate entrepreneurship at its finest'—V. Vaidyanathan, *Business Today*

'An engrossing tale of detail, of transformation of a simple not-for-profit activity into a full-fledged bank . . . It is a Bengal success story of entrepreneurship, passion'—V. Anantha Nageswaran, *Mint*

PRAISE FOR THE AUTHOR

'Tamal has set a new trend in the dissemination of knowledge'—Y.V. Reddy, former governor, RBI

'In a period of great financial illiteracy, it's refreshing to have a book written by somebody very literate about matters relating to finance'— P. Chidambaram, former finance minister

'Tamal is able to bring two sets of skills to bear on his writing. He obviously has deep domain knowledge . . . He also follows a critical journalistic principle, which is to never assume that you know everything about the subject you are writing on'—Subir Gokarn, former deputy governor, RBI

'Tamal's sharp reporting instincts as well as eye for detail help him paint a profile that accurately reflects the original'—T.N. Ninan, chairman and editorial director, *Business Standard*

'India's most-respected and well-sourced banking and financial journalist'— Raju Narisetti, senior vice president, strategy, News Corporation

'Bandyopadhyay does not pass judgments but lays open the issues and arguments of both sides. This balancing act is quite remarkable'— *Business World*

BANDHAN
THE MAKING OF A BANK

Foreword by **KAUSHIK BASU**

TAMAL BANDYOPADHYAY

PORTFOLIO
PENGUIN

An imprint of Penguin Random House

PORTFOLIO

USA | Canada | UK | Ireland | Australia
New Zealand | India | South Africa | China | Singapore

Portfolio is part of the Penguin Random House group of companies
whose addresses can be found at global.penguinrandomhouse.com

Published by Penguin Random House India Pvt. Ltd
4th Floor, Capital Tower 1, MG Road,
Gurugram 122 002, Haryana, India

Penguin
Random House
India

First published in Random Business by Penguin Random House India 2016
Published in Portfolio 2018

ISBN 9788184004984

Typeset in Sabon by Manipal Digital Systems, Manipal

Printed at Manipal Technologies Limited, India

MIX
Paper | Supporting
responsible forestry
FSC® C043100

This is a legitimate digitally printed version of the book and therefore might not
have certain extra finishing on the cover.

To my son, Sujan, aka Osho,
whose heart is in the right place

Contents

Foreword

*B*andhan: *The Making of a Bank* is a remarkable book. It is the story of the rise of Bandhan Bank from a cubbyhole, not-for-profit operation, giving microcredit to the poor, to a large for-profit bank with branches scattered all over India—all the while holding on to its founder's original motivation of combating poverty by lending to the poor, who would otherwise have to rely on extortionate moneylenders. Tamal Bandyopadhyay's book is also about much more. It is the personal story of Bandhan's founder, Chandra Shekhar Ghosh, who rose from the ranks, driven by an unusual combination of missionary zeal, entrepreneurial creativity and energy.

This book is primarily about finance and banking, the plumbing that underlies all economies and, partly, as a consequence of that, attracts attention mainly when things go wrong. It reminds the lay reader as well as the professional economist about the importance of this plumbing. It tracks some of the history of Indian finance, West Bengal's steady and steep fall from a position of dominance in Indian banking at the time of the nation's Independence in 1947, only to be reduced to a region with one of the poorest records of financial inclusion; and then it moves on to chronicle the recent stirrings and hope wherein Bandhan Bank plays an important role.

Tamal Bandyopadhyay is a gifted storyteller who combines the sharp vision of a finance expert with a journalist's skill for observation and narration. Bandhan began as an NGO, registered as Bandhan-Konnagar, and operated from the home of Ghosh's maternal uncle, Saroj Kanti Ghosh, at Uttarpara in Hooghly.

One of its first functioning offices, set up in 2002, was a four-by-six-foot cubicle at the home of a Sheikh Nazrul in Khirishtala, Howrah, a space rented for Rs 300 ($5) per month. Ghosh drew his inspiration from the sight of poor vegetable vendors in Kolkata's Shobhabazar taking loans of Rs 500 from the moneylender while paying him an interest of Rs 5 every day. The poor borrowers were quite unaware that this amounted to a compound interest rate of more than 700 per cent per annum.

Ghosh, familiar as he was with Bangladesh's success with Grameen Bank and BRAC, was determined to make his venture a success. In the early days of Bandhan, standing at a ramshackle train station, Ghosh predicted he would one day have a Bandhan branch office at each of the stations between Sealdah and Bangaon. There were twenty-two stations on that stretch. His forecast was way off the mark. Over the next decade, Bandhan would set up 2022 branches, spread over twenty-two Indian states. By 2007, *Forbes* magazine, listing the world's most successful microfinance entities, had Bandhan occupy the number two spot. Over the years, the microfinance entity has also shown an ability to use technology to improve efficiency; and its coming of age was signalled by its sale of stakes a few years ago to the World Bank Group's International Finance Corporation.

Apart from this central story, there are two other features that make this such an engrossing book. First, Bandyopadhyay has a fine understanding of the banking industry. So the underlying analytics of finance, and especially microfinance, is very well explained. The book is like a primer on microfinance explained with one extended example. In addition, we get a glimpse of behavioural economics in the vulnerability of the small traders and vendors, and the advantage that this creates for the unscrupulous moneylender. Much has been written on behavioural finance, a lot of it using formal statistical methods, including randomized control trials. Bandyopadhyay does not go into statistical methods, but his keen eye for detail captures some of the same ideas of modern behavioural finance in the form of tales and narratives, and, as such, this book is a wonderful complement to the more formal methods of research economists.

Secondly, even if this is no more than in short sketches of elegant prose, the reader gets a peek into India's banking and finance history, starting with the founding of the country's largest bank, State Bank of India, then called Bank of Calcutta, on 2 June 1806, with the original purpose of financing General Wellesley's war to subdue Tipu Sultan and the Marathas in central and western India. We also get an outline of the banking industry in West Bengal. In 1947, of the eighty-two scheduled banks in India, twenty-two were located in West Bengal, with Madras having the next biggest share with fourteen banks. But starting in the 1960s, greed and corruption, coupled with the proliferation of chit funds and clumsy regulation, brought Bengal's banking sector to a grinding slowdown.

What makes this a remarkable story is that Bandhan Bank started out from this rather dismal setting, but then succeeded against all odds, setting an example of how a for-profit bank can also be a model of corporate social responsibility and a powerful instrument of financial and social inclusion. It still has a great distance to go, and much will depend on how its story unfolds over the years. Regardless, this is an important tale, with implications for not just finance and banking, but also poverty eradication and development, and that is what makes this a book well worth reading.

Kaushik Basu
May 2016

Preface

I began closely tracking Chandra Shekhar Ghosh in 2010 while conducting a series of panel discussions for *Mint*, India's second-largest business paper, on financial inclusion. He was passionate about microfinance, but not necessarily the most articulate person in the room.

But this is what fascinated me: Bandhan was operating successfully in West Bengal, a state not too well known for its work culture. Entrepreneurship in the state was confined largely to running chowmein and momo stalls. But Bandhan was a highly efficient microfinance company based in Kolkata, employing 12,000 people.

In 2014, Bandhan got a banking licence, one of just two that had been handed out by Reserve Bank of India (RBI). A banking licence is a big deal in Asia's third-largest economy— in the sixty-eight years since Independence, only fifteen new banks have been set up, including Bandhan.

Obviously then, this was a big news story, and an evolving one. How would Ghosh turn the microlender into a bank? I was tempted to take a close look at the transformation and watch the birth of a bank from ground zero, having followed the banking and finance sector in India for about two decades, both as a reporter and as a commentator.

When Ghosh asked me to join Bandhan, I couldn't resist and signed up as adviser, giving up my day job at *Mint*, and becoming a consulting editor.

At this point, I would like to make it clear that while I have been a part of the Bandhan group since August 2014, this book is an independent project. It is not sponsored by Bandhan.

Also, this book is not so much about the new institution but about how Ghosh set up the microfinance business, and how he and his team implemented the changes that were needed to make it a universal bank—a transformation that I watched from a ringside seat.

As for my role in Bandhan, let me borrow an analogy from cricket. If commentator Harsha Bhogle were asked to join the administration of the Indian cricket team, he would probably see his job as analysing the playing style of each member, crunching the data, delving into cricketing history and offering a broader perspective, besides having his own insight into the dressing room by virtue of the personal relationships he had cultivated.

As an insider, I wasn't very sure whether I would write a book about Bandhan, though. In fact, when I signed the agreement with Penguin Random House for writing a book on finance, the subject was different. The thought first occurred to me when my column on the launch of Bandhan, in August 2015, drew close to half a million hits online—it seemed there was great demand for information on Bandhan.

There have been many books on microfinance, in India and overseas. Most of them have been written either from the point of view of the borrowers—how microfinance has changed their lives—or are academic studies on how such entities work, different models of microfinance, risk management, etc. This book is different—it is written from the point of view of the organization. It's about how a microfinance structure is built, and about entrepreneurship. It does not project Ghosh as a messiah of the poor, or as an agent of change, but as an entrepreneur who seems to have hit upon a magic formula—running a profitable business and at the same time benefitting the poor.

The book is broadly divided into three parts.

The first ten chapters are on Bandhan, its history as a microfinance company, the making of the bank and what the future holds for it.

The second part has two chapters on two key personalities in the Indian microfinance industry: Vijay Mahajan of the Basix Group, and Vikram Akula, the ousted promoter of SKS Microfinance Ltd, Asia's first listed microfinance company.

The last part is the appendix, which traces the history of microfinance in India, its trials and tribulations, the crisis of 2010 that nearly killed off the industry and its subsequent resurrection.

The first chapter starts with the launch of the bank and what it signifies for the industry, and particularly for eastern India, where the last bank was born before Independence, in 1943. The second chapter cuts back to the birth of Bandhan, the microfinance entity, with two branches in Howrah and Hooghly districts of West Bengal. Chapter three is on its growth, expansion to other parts of the east as well as other Indian states, its transformation from an

NGO to a for-profit microfinance company, the use of technology to increase efficiency, and the sale of stakes to Small Industries Development Bank of India (SIDBI) and the World Bank's International Finance Corporation (IFC).

The next chapter is on the hurdles that it faced, while chapter five takes a look at the first ten employees of Bandhan who are still with Ghosh.

Chapter six details what makes Bandhan a success story: its obsession with discipline. Chapters seven and eight capture the complex preparations for becoming a bank—the business plan, structural changes, technology and the arrival of new investors. The next chapter is on Ghosh himself, and chapter ten outlines what lies ahead.

The book is my attempt to tell a story about Bandhan, which, more than being a financial intermediary, is a way of life, both for the organization as well as for its millions of borrowers.

As with my previous books on finance, this one too is a journalistic exercise, based on extensive research and interviews with hundreds of people. There is, however, a critical difference: I am somewhat of an insider at Bandhan, and naturally face the dilemmas such a status entails.

I have consciously stayed away from areas where there is a conflict of interest. But being an insider has its advantages too. For instance, during one visit, I saw monkeys chewing on VSAT wires at a bank branch in Uttarakhand. Another time, a zonal manager told me how a borrower tried to push in actual pins at an ATM that had asked for a PIN to enable cash withdrawal.

The objective was not to write a coffee-table book to flatter Bandhan; rather, it was to take a close look at its business model and ethos to understand what makes it successful. Is it the scale? Does it have to do with austerity? Or is it an earthy, common-sense approach that has eluded others?

As a microfinance company, Bandhan has been enormously successful, combining profitability and inclusive financing. Will it be able to replicate this in its new avatar as a universal bank? That's another story. This is a story of a microfinance entity written with passion but from a dispassionate, objective point of view. It is a compelling tale, dear reader, and I hope you like it. If you don't, the failure is entirely mine.

Happy reading!

1

In the Beginning, There Was Only Chaos

On the evening of 31 August 2015, exactly a week after India's finance minister, Arun Jaitley, inaugurated Bandhan Bank Ltd at Kolkata's Science City auditorium, about a dozen senior executives of the bank were called to the boardroom on the eighth floor of its headquarters at DN 32, Sector V, Salt Lake City.

Gobindo Banerjee, Ashoka Chatterjee and Narayan Chandra Ghosh, who were on the seventh floor, were the first to arrive. Soon, Tarunava Sarkar, S.K. Giri, Amitava Goswami, Sundeep Bhan, A.K. Mohanti, S.K. Mitra, Ronendra Chowdhury, Arpita Sen, Somiran Ghoshal and four zonal heads of the bank—Sujoy Roy, Tapas Das, Nand Kumar Singh and Sourav Kar—joined them.

Chandra Shekhar Ghosh, the founder, MD and CEO of Bandhan Bank, called each of them personally over the intercom. That was his style. He would dial the intercom number and simply say, 'Can you come over to the eighth floor?' For a few, he would even add 'dada' (used to address an elder brother, in Bengali) or 'sir'. For instance, he would tell Narayan Chandra, former inspector general of West Bengal Police, and now the bank's chief vigilance officer, 'Naran sir, *ektu asben* (will you come for a little while)?'

More often than not, such meetings were called at short notice and with no fixed agenda. Senior executives of Bandhan Bank were used to it. Small groups of executives were typically called to Ghosh's room on the eighth floor, and if the group was big, the boardroom was the meeting place. For larger groups, the venue was the meeting room on the ninth floor. Ghosh would discuss an idea to see how others reacted, seek suggestions and, at times, make announcements.

However, this meeting was different. In the week following the bank's inauguration, Ghosh had hardly been seen at the headquarters during office hours. He would visit branches across the city to get a feel of how they were working and the problems they faced. Like smart politicians on election campaigns who break the security cordon to shake hands with the voters, Ghosh would get out of the circle of his colleagues in a branch to mingle with prospective customers. Some would bend and touch his feet as a mark of respect. They believed that Bengal had not produced an entrepreneur like him since Independence. He had been a familiar face on TV channels and newspapers in West Bengal ever since Bandhan got the banking licence.

West Bengal has a chequered history in banking. It was in Kolkata—then Calcutta—that the country's first deposit-taking bank was founded, in the early 1770s. Alexander and

Co., a British agency house, or a diversified conglomerate, launched Bank of Hindostan in partnership with local moneylenders (indigenous bankers called shroffs, or *banian*s,[1] in those days). Ramdulal De Sarkar (1752–1825), who rose from penury to become Bengal's first millionaire by wagering on the wreck of a ship, was one of the leading banians.

Of course, the first bank of a joint-stock variety in India was Bank of Bombay, established in Mumbai—then Bombay—in 1720. A joint-stock company is an entity that falls between the definitions of a partnership and a corporation— an association of individuals in a business enterprise with transferable shares of stock, much like a corporation, except that stockholders are liable for the debts of the business.

Many more banks were launched in the late eighteenth century in Bengal, but all of them collapsed because of excessive speculation and trading by their founders.

Bank of Hindostan survived three panic runs until it eventually went under in 1832, along with Alexander and Co. The General Bank of Bengal and Bahar, which came into existence in 1773 after a proposal by Governor General Warren Hastings, was successful and profitable, but did not live beyond 1775.

In 1806, Bank of Calcutta—one of the forebears of today's State Bank of India (SBI)—was established by a government charter. It was risk-averse and wouldn't lend for more than three months, and hence local businessmen—both British and Indian—continued to launch private banks.

---

[1] Not to be confused with banias, a community of merchants, bankers, moneylenders, dealers in grains or spices.

An RBI study called 'Evolution of Banking in India'[2] attributed the mushrooming of banks in eastern India to the fact that trade was concentrated in Kolkata after the growth of East India Company's business and administration. With this grew the requirement for modern banking services, uniform currency to finance foreign trade, and remittances by British army personnel and civil servants.

Many banks failed and the most-talked-about failure was that of Union Bank (1829–48), set up by Prince Dwarkanath Tagore (poet Rabindranath Tagore's grandfather) and a few others in partnership with British companies. When it collapsed, De Sarkar's sons, Asutosh (popularly known as Satubabu) and Pramathanath (Latubabu), picked up the tab for its bankruptcy. While their father remained a banian, they had become shareholders of Union Bank. Tagore's interests spanned coal, tea, jute, sugar refining, newspapers and shipping. He was the first Indian to become the director of a bank.

A Reason to Celebrate

After more than a century, the people of Bengal—known for their culture, intellectual acumen and aversion to business—had found a reason to celebrate: Ghosh and Bandhan Bank.

In the week following the inauguration, Ghosh would drop in at the bank's headquarters late in the evening before visiting Pekon Building on X 1/9 EP-GP Block, Sector V, Salt Lake City, which housed the central processing unit or CPU, the

[2] RBI Annual Report, Chapter 3, September 2008.

A BANK IS BORN: (From left) H.R. Khan, deputy governor, RBI; Chandra Shekhar Ghosh, founder, Bandhan Bank; Arun Jaitley, Union finance minister; Amit Mitra, finance minister, West Bengal; Ashok Lahiri, chairman, Bandhan Bank; at the launch in Kolkata on 23 August 2015.

back office of Bandhan Bank. He would begin his branch visits every day at 8 a.m. The only person who knew his whereabouts was Shyam Sundar Kamath, better known as Shyamlal, his driver of thirteen years, who ferried him all day in his Toyota Fortuner.

In a white full-sleeved shirt and black trousers, Ghosh looked relaxed. The day before—a Sunday—he had made surprise visits to four branches in Kolkata—two of them were open all through the week. The employees of the other two branches, which were supposed to be closed on a Sunday, were also seen hanging around, wearing Bandhan T-shirts and looking for customers. That had made him happy.

In the very first week, the bank had received about 5,50,000 applications from people seeking to open accounts. But not every account could be opened in such a short time. Ghosh was slightly annoyed with the rate of rejection—not all forms were complete with every detail. That made him visit the CPU repeatedly to check if the scanning machines were working properly and to get to the root of the problem. Out of curiosity, he also visited the cheque truncation centre at the back office regularly.

At the meeting, Ghosh read out the balance sheet of the bank as on 29 August 2015. Deposit collection was Rs 265 crore, and 97 per cent of this was retail deposits. Bandhan Bank's loan book was Rs 10,151 crore. In the first week, loan repayment collection was to the tune of Rs 415 crore, and fresh disbursement was Rs 60 crore.

The loan portfolio is a legacy of the microfinance company that existed till 22 August 2015, but the deposits were fresh. In India, the banking regulator does not allow a microfinance company to collect deposits. Of the 250 ATMs the bank planned to open by 31 March 2016, thirty-two were operational within the first week of starting operations, and the cash stashed in these ATMs amounted to Rs 1.2 crore. There were long queues at some of the ATMs in North Bengal: at Dhupguri in Jalpaiguri and at Cooch Behar. The bulk of the money raised in the form of deposits was placed in the interbank market, and the branches kept Rs 26 lakh each to meet customer demand.

Ghosh also briefed the senior team about his talk with RBI deputy governor H.R. Khan, the regional director in Kolkata, Rudra Narayan Kar, and the chief general manager, Sudha Damodar, who handed over the licence to him on 17 June 2015. 'You should be very careful about KYC and FATCA.

No compromise on these two issues . . . I don't care how much deposits we are collecting. Check, check and check again the colour of money,' Ghosh said.

While global anti-money-laundering and know your customer (KYC) norms had existed for a long time, the rules have become stricter to tackle global tax evasion. The Foreign Account Tax Compliance Act (FATCA) came into being in 2010 to provide the United States' tax authorities with an increased ability to detect those US tax evaders who conceal their assets in foreign accounts and investments. The non-US entities are now encouraged to comply with a new set of tax information reporting.

FATCA ensures that bank customers are properly classified, and US citizens report whether they own an account directly or indirectly through a foreign entity. To make this happen, foreign financial institutions across the globe (including Bandhan Bank) need to collect the appropriate statements and documentary evidence from their customers, and validate and store them.

'You know, on Friday, there was some problem . . . Saibal Gon, who was working at the CPU, had to come from Dunlop at 12.30 a.m. as no one else had the password to open one file . . . It was an opportunity to work together, to get to know each other; we never looked at the watch. We never knew how the time passed,' Ghosh told his colleagues at the meeting. Dunlop, which is situated in the northern outskirts of Kolkata, is twenty-seven kilometres from Salt Lake. Tired after spending many nights at the office, Gon had left for home late that evening, leaving his jacket on his chair. Ghosh had called him on his mobile presuming he was around.

Monkeys Playing Spoilsport

None of his senior colleagues reacted. They all knew what was happening. Being a new bank, there were problems but nothing was unexpected, at least for Ghosh. The biggest of these was the network issue—the links were slow and the servers, in some cases, inadequate. Many of the 501 branches that opened on the first day were in unbanked rural pockets. At some of the branches in Uttar Pradesh and Uttarakhand, monkeys were playing spoilsport by chewing up the VSAT connections.

Incidentally, monkeys have derailed Indian Prime Minister Narendra Modi's plans of making Varanasi Wi-Fi-enabled by regularly chewing optical fibre cables. A *Down to Earth* cover story in August 2015 pointed out that monkeys had been causing crop damage, to the extent that some Indian states even ordered their culling. In 2010, farmers in two of Bihar's worst-affected constituencies—Chainpur and Saharsa—formed an association, Bandar Mukti Abhiyan Samiti, to pressurize politicians to act.

When Bandhan Bank opened its doors, Ghosh was all smiles, beaming with confidence. But instead of gloating over the success of the launch of the bank—the first in eastern India after Independence—he chose to list his concerns. The objective was to keep his executives on their toes.

In the early days, managing cash was a problem. Keeping too much cash in a branch does not make sense as idle cash does not earn interest. On top of that, it also creates security issues. Other banks can be requested to step in but it is a tricky business as notes have to be sorted out. Typically, banks charge a fee—could be Re 1 or Rs 2 for every Rs 1000—and they also enjoy the 'float' as they keep the money with them for a few days. Float refers to the money in the banking system that remains briefly with a bank due to delays in processing cheques.

There were also issues about closing the daily balance sheets: debits and credits, matching outflow and inflow of money. Many of the branches and doorstep service centres (DSCs) were struggling to achieve the so-called 'day end', or matching the debit and credit at the close of business hours in the initial days. However, Ghosh seemed to be in total control. The bank started with a modern technology platform but that did not mean that operations would be completely hassle-free from the first day onwards. Besides, the employees would also need to learn the use of technology.

Despite extensive dry runs, there were issues. For instance, if one keyed in the customer code—which runs into several digits—instead of a cash deposit of a few thousand rupees, the entire calculation would go for a toss. Ghosh was aware that such things could happen. And he knew how to rectify them.

By 8 p.m., the office boys would start handing out pouches of puffed rice and *alur* chop (potato fritters), accompanied by a green chilli, to Ghosh and his senior executives. Bandhan employees have been enjoying this popular evening snack for the past one and a half years, ever since they started staying late in office to prepare for the bank to open its doors. It was only a week after the launch that Ghosh left for home at 8 p.m., telling himself he would have an early dinner with Angshuman, his son, and Nilima, his wife, and sleep well—something his driver, Shyamlal, too was craving for, having gone without sleep for days while travelling with Ghosh.

The D-Day

The event to mark the launch of the bank at Science City auditorium was unlike anything Kolkata had seen in decades. The 2200-seat auditorium was packed to capacity. There were senior bankers, captains of industry, regulators and about 300 women borrowers of Bandhan Financial Services Ltd (BFSL), the microfinance avatar of Bandhan Bank.

When Ghosh, 5'9", rose to speak, he often broke into Bengali—deviating from a written English speech—to address the women borrowers as 'ma o bonera' (mothers and sisters), a few of whom had turned small entrepreneurs, backed by Bandhan for over a decade. He also assured them that the organization would continue to serve them at their doorstep.

He ended his speech saying, 'We are a universal bank and we will have equal respect for all our customers, big and small. Today, all of us in the Bandhan family are rededicating ourselves to fulfil the demand of every Indian: banking as a fundamental right. You can trust us when I tell you we are committed to usher in a new era in Indian banking.'

Nobody knew that Ghosh had not had a wink of sleep the previous night, was running a high temperature and had terrible body ache. At one point, he had even thought that he would not be able to make it through. He probably fell ill because of all the excitement.

After all, in the history of Indian banking, nobody with his kind of background had ever got the regulator's nod to float a bank. There have been individuals who have got a banking licence to either set up new banks or convert their non-banking finance companies into banks—such as Uday Kotak (of Kotak Mahindra Group), Rana Kapoor (Yes Bank Ltd), Ramesh Gelli (erstwhile Global Trust Bank Ltd) and Dev Ahuja (20th Century Finance Corporation Ltd, which promoted Centurion Bank Ltd), but Ghosh is unique and cannot be compared with any one of them. The son of a sweet-shop owner in Tripura, speaking in English does not come naturally to him.

At the launch, when it was Union Finance Minister Arun Jaitley's turn to speak, he talked more about entrepreneurship than banking. 'The launch of Bandhan Bank will not just boost the growth of Bengali entrepreneurs, but signify the return of entrepreneurs to West Bengal,' he said.

Jaitley also made a political statement when he commented: 'When I came to this great city yesterday, I saw a pleasant change. With Bandhan Bank written, the whole city has been almost painted blue [the new bank's billboards have a blue backdrop]. I recollect my days from younger years when I used to see this city painted red. When it was painted red, of course, new institutions were not being born. The existing ones were shifting out.'

Jaitley continued, 'West Bengal was known not for producing many entrepreneurs but certainly known for producing intellectuals,' pointing at his panellists, 'even Ashok Lahiri and Amit Mitra had shifted out. I do hope this change of colour has brought back both of them . . . What is most important is the birth of a Bengali entrepreneur, which is of utmost importance for the revival and growth of the fundamentals of the state of West Bengal.'

Both Lahiri, chairman of Bandhan Bank and former chief economic adviser to the Union finance ministry, and Mitra, finance minister of West Bengal, shared the dais with Jaitley.

BANKING IS A FUNDAMENTAL RIGHT: At the launch of Bandhan Bank, Ghosh said his bank would have equal respect for all its customers—big and small. Here, he is holding a press conference after the launch at the Science City auditorium on 23 August 2015.

It was three days before the launch, on 20 August 2015, that the last 'Go Live' presentation was conducted by Deloitte Touche Tohmatsu India Pvt. Ltd, the consultancy firm engaged by Bandhan to handhold the organization in its transformation from a microfinance entity to a universal bank. That day, Sanjoy S. Datta, the firm's senior director, said, 'On Day One, we will not be perfect but Bandhan Bank will not disappoint you; we will be proud of what we have achieved.'

Datta also assured the senior management that he had made surprise visits to Kolkata, Mumbai and Delhi the previous week and found that Bandhan employees were fully conversant with the bank's products. Out of 501 branches that were to go live on the first day, 475 were up and running. The remaining twenty-six were a bit volatile but Datta did not specify which branches he meant. He did, however, warn that electricity was an issue and the UPS would not be able to handle all the branches and there could be breakdowns.

Three board members were present at the meeting: Bhaskar Sen (former chairman and managing director of United Bank of India), Pradip Kumar Saha (former chief general manager of SIDBI) and Sisir Kumar Chakrabarti (former deputy managing director of Axis Bank Ltd).

They were extra cautious. Chakrabarti insisted that a plan B must be ready and the employees should be prepared to work manually if the technology platform did not work because of connectivity issues. 'How many days will the bank take to open an account?' he asked. Sundeep Bhan, the head of the back office, said, 'A new account will be activated within seventy-two hours and the kit will be delivered to the account holder's house in a week.'

'Under-promise, Over-deliver'

Ghosh told Bhan a week was too long; it should be brought down to three days. Chakrabarti smiled. His advice was, 'Under-promise and over-deliver.' It was decided that random phone calls would be made to branches to check their preparedness and one banker on a motorbike would cover five branches every day to check if everything was running smoothly. A five-member quick-response team was formed under Tarunava Sarkar, the head of the corporate centre.

Nobody was willing to take any chances. After a little more than a decade, a new private bank had been born in India. A new bank is always welcome, as a large chunk of India's 1.2 billion population does not have access to formal banking services.

After India embraced economic liberalization following a severe balance-of-payments crisis, RBI opened the doors to a set of new banks in January 1993. It had received 113 applications, many from large industrial houses. Economist-bureaucrat Sharad Marathe, the first chairman of the erstwhile Industrial Development Bank of India (IDBI), reviewed the applications. Nine new banks were set up and one cooperative bank was allowed to convert itself into a commercial bank.

These were Global Trust Bank Ltd, ICICI Bank Ltd, HDFC Bank Ltd, UTI Bank Ltd (renamed Axis Bank Ltd), Bank of Punjab Ltd, IndusInd Bank Ltd, Centurion Bank Ltd, IDBI Bank Ltd, Times Bank Ltd and Development Credit Bank Ltd. Not all have survived. Times Bank was merged with HDFC Bank; Global Trust Bank was forced to merge with Oriental Bank of Commerce; and Bank of Punjab was acquired by Centurion Bank to form Centurion Bank of Punjab Ltd, which was later taken over by HDFC Bank.

In January 2001, RBI issued guidelines for a second set of new banks. A three-member committee consisting of

I.G. Patel, former RBI governor; C.G. Somiah, former comptroller and auditor general of India; and Dipankar Basu, former chairman of SBI, scrutinized the applications.

Later, two licences were issued. One was for the conversion of a non-banking financial company into a bank—Kotak Mahindra Bank Ltd; and the other was for Yes Bank Ltd, a new venture.

In 1994, the capital requirement was Rs 100 crore; in 2001, it was Rs 200 crore, to be raised to Rs 300 crore in three years. In the last round, it was fixed at Rs 500 crore.

In the past, RBI's stated objective behind giving licences had been to introduce competition in the banking sector which was largely dominated by state-owned banks. This time, its objective was to bring about greater financial inclusion in a nation where only 35 per cent of adults had access to formal banking services, according to a 2012 World Bank working paper.

In 2010, then finance minister Pranab Mukherjee announced that a new set of banks would be set up. Three years later, in February 2013, RBI released the final guidelines on licensing norms and applications were received till 1 July 2013.

A panel headed by former RBI governor Bimal Jalan sifted through the applications. Former Securities and Exchange Board of India (SEBI) chairman C.B. Bhave, former RBI deputy governor Usha Thorat, and RBI board member Nachiket Mor were the other members of the panel.

In order to be eligible for a banking licence, candidates needed to have a ten-year record and should never have been under the scanner of any regulatory, enforcement or investigative agencies. Twenty-six companies applied, but the Tata group later opted out.

The list of serious applicants included corporate houses such as Aditya Birla Nuvo Ltd and Anil Ambani–led Reliance Capital Ltd; financial intermediaries such as LIC Housing Finance Ltd and L&T Finance Ltd; the microfinance institution Janalakshmi Financial Services Pvt. Ltd; and public sector undertakings like India Post and Tourism Finance Corporation of India Ltd.

In the past, when RBI had opened doors to new banks, they were set up in the north, the south and the west, but not in the east. Incidentally, RBI was set up in Kolkata but its headquarters was shifted to Mumbai in 1937.

SBI, the nation's largest lender, originated as Bank of Calcutta on 2 June 1806 with a capital of Rs 50 lakh, primarily to fund General Wellesley's wars against Tipu Sultan and the Marathas. It was renamed Bank of Bengal on 2 January 1809 and opened branches at Rangoon (1861), Patna (1862), Mirzapur (1862) and Benares (1862).

In 1823, the government, which picked up 20 per cent stake in the bank and enjoyed the power to appoint its directors, gave Bank of Bengal the right to issue currency notes. This bank and two other Presidency banks—Bank of Bombay (set up in 1842 with a capital of Rs 52 lakh) and Bank of Madras (July 1843, Rs 30 lakh)—were merged on 27 January 1921 to form Imperial Bank of India. This was made State Bank of India on 30 April 1955 after RBI acquired a controlling stake in Imperial Bank of India.

Imperial Bank of India acted as a central bank till the establishment of RBI in 1935, performing three functions:

commercial banking, central banking and acting as a banker to the government. The Presidency banks were governed by royal charters and issued currency notes till the Paper Currency Act of 1861 was enacted, giving the government the right to issue currency.

Kolkata was also the first port of call for major foreign banks in India. Standard Chartered Bank started its Indian operations by opening its first branch here in April 1858, a year after the first war of Independence, in which sepoys of the British East India Company rebelled against the rulers.

The origin of Hongkong and Shanghai Banking Corporation Ltd (HSBC) can be traced to October 1853 when Mercantile Bank of India, London and China was founded in Mumbai, with an authorized capital of Rs 50 lakh. By 1855, Mercantile Bank had offices in London, Chennai (erstwhile Madras), Colombo, Kandy, Kolkata, Singapore, Hong Kong, Guangzhou and Shanghai. It was acquired by HSBC in 1959.

Citibank NA began its India operations in 1902, in Kolkata, and ABN AMRO Bank NV, which came to India in 1920, had its first branch in Kolkata too.

Kolkata Chromosome

Currently, three banks are headquartered in Kolkata.

Allahabad Bank, the oldest of the three, was set up in Allahabad on 24 April 1865 by a group of Europeans. By the end of the nineteenth century, it had branches in Jhansi, Kanpur, Lucknow, Bareilly, Nainital, Kolkata and Delhi.

In 1923, three years after P&O Banking Corporation acquired Allahabad Bank with a bid price of Rs 436 per share, the bank shifted its headquarters to Kolkata for operational convenience and business opportunities. P&O Bank was started by Peninsular and Oriental Steam Navigation Company to develop its private banking business. It opened for business in London in June 1920, and in the following month started operations simultaneously in Kolkata, Mumbai and Chennai. In 1927, Chartered Bank of India, Australia and China acquired P&O Bank, but Allahabad Bank continued to operate as a separate entity. On 19 July 1969, it was nationalized, along with thirteen other banks.

United Bank of India has its origin in United Bank of India Ltd, formed in 1950 with the amalgamation of four banks: Comilla Banking Corporation (founded by Narendra Chandra Dutta in 1914 in Bangladesh), Bengal Central Bank (founded by J.C. Das in 1918 as Bengal Central Loan Company), Comilla Union Bank (founded by L.B. Dutta in 1922) and Hooghly Bank (founded by D.N. Mukherjee in 1932). All four had suffered runs in December 1950 after the failure of Nath Bank, leading to their merger. At the time of nationalization, United Bank had 174 branches.

Set up by Kshetra Nath Dalal in 1926 in Noakhali, Bangladesh, Nath Bank shifted its headquarters to Kolkata after Partition, but could not survive for long.

UCO Bank was set up after the historic Quit India movement in 1942, by eminent industrialist Ghanshyam Das Birla, with a paid-up capital of Rs 1 crore. It started as United Commercial Bank, with fourteen branches across India. After the Second World War, it rapidly expanded overseas: Rangoon (1947), Singapore (1951), Hong Kong (1952), London (1953) and Kuala Lumpur (1963). In 1985, it was rechristened as UCO Bank after a bank with a similar name was set up in Bangladesh in 1983.

The east and the north-east are the most underbanked regions in India. According to RBI data, of around 1,26,000 bank branches in India, as on 31 March 2015, the east accounts for 16 per cent, and the north-east only 2.6 per cent. West Bengal, the fourth-largest state in India by population, where Bandhan Bank has its largest branch network, accounts for 5.62 per cent of bank branches, 6.22 per cent of deposits, 4.67 per cent of credit, and for every Rs 100 the banks mobilize in this state, Rs 58 is given as loans.

Bandhan Bank also has many branches in Bihar—the third-largest Indian state by population, which accounts for 4.78 per cent of the branch network, 2.44 per cent of deposits and 1.05 per cent of credit, and where the credit-deposit ratio is 33.26 per cent. This is the ratio of how much a bank lends out of the deposits it has mobilized. In this case, it broadly means that for every Rs 100 deposit collected by the banks, only one-third of the amount is given as loans. In other words, the region is being used by banks to collect money but they are not giving money to people in the form of loans. It could be either of the two cases: reluctance of banks to lend money, or lack of demand for loans among the borrowers.

Barring Odisha and Assam, bank branches in all other states in the east account for less than 1 per cent of deposit and credit. These branches offer loans to the extent of one-fourth to one-third of the deposits they mop up.

Bandhan began its operations as a universal bank with 501 branches, thirty ATMs and 2022 DSCs across 35,000 villages in twenty-two states. The plan is to have 632 branches and 250 ATMs in twenty-seven states by the end of the fiscal year 2016. It started with 1.43 crore accounts and a loan book of around Rs 10,500 crore. Over 71 per cent of the branches are in rural India and at least 35 per cent in unbanked rural pockets.

Statewise, West Bengal has the highest number of branches: 220, followed by Bihar (sixty-seven), Assam (sixty), Maharashtra (twenty-one), Uttar Pradesh and Tripura (twenty each) and Jharkhand (fifteen).

RBI's licensing norms require a new bank to have a capital of at least Rs 500 crore. Against this, Bandhan started with a Rs 2570-crore capital, which would be ramped up to close to Rs 3052 crore once the new investors' money came in. This translates to 44.54 per cent capital to risk (weighted) assets ratio (CRAR) for the new bank, almost three times the requirement, signifying its robustness. CRAR, a prudential norm also known as capital adequacy ratio, is the ratio of a bank's capital to its risk. Going by current norms, existing banks are required to have at least Rs 9 as capital to give loans of Rs 100. For new banks, the requirement is Rs 15. In Bandhan Bank, for every Rs 100 loan it gives at this point, it has a capital of Rs 44.54.

Despite Bandhan being a universal bank, Ghosh does not want it to have a finger in every pie of the banking business. It will continue to give small loans. Many of its bank branches will raise deposits to support the credit portfolio, but more importantly, Bandhan will also collect deposits from small savers who are often taken for a ride by so-called shadow banks. These are financial intermediaries over which there is no regulatory supervision.

West Bengal has more companies raising money illegally from the public than any other state. Going by a SEBI report, 104 of 194 companies against whom the market watchdog took action between mid-2011 and August 2015 for raising money by issuing debentures and equity are from this eastern state. Madhya Pradesh is a distant second with twenty-seven companies, and Odisha is third, with fourteen companies.

Shadow Finance

In an article in *Economic and Political Weekly* (EPW),[3] Subhanil Chowdhury, assistant professor of economics at Institute of Development Studies, Kolkata, quoted an RBI working paper.[4] According to the paper, West Bengal had one of the lowest ranks in financial inclusion in the country. Financial inclusion is making financial products available to all sections of society at an affordable price, with clarity and transparency, by the mainstream financial system. Excluding Kolkata, all other districts of the state had very low

---

[3] Subhanil Chowdhury, 'The Political Economy of Shadow Finance in West Bengal', *Economic and Political Weekly* 48, no. 18 (4 May 2013).

[4] Sadhan Kumar Chattopadhyay, 'Financial Inclusion in India: A Case Study of West Bengal', Reserve Bank of India Working Paper, Vol. July 2, No. WPS(DEPR): 8/2011

financial inclusion, based on data on penetration, availability and usage between 2006 and 2009.

The index of financial inclusion (IFI) constructed by this RBI paper had a maximum value of 1. Most of the districts in the state had an IFI value of less than 0.1, with some like South 24 Parganas having a value of 0.01. No wonder that most of the people in the state are outside the net of organized financial institutions; they prefer to park their savings in shadow finance institutions that promise a rate of return much higher than that offered by commercial banks.

The *EPW* article cited several reasons for the low rate of financial inclusion in West Bengal. Quoting the RBI working paper, it said the main reason why people did not keep their money in banks was that their income level was not sufficient to open and operate bank accounts. It stated:

There is a lack of awareness about banking facilities and the benefits that banks offer. Since most of the people do not have a collateral against which they can take loans, they borrow from the rural money lenders and carry on their banking transactions in the informal sector. While all these factors are important in understanding why financial inclusion has lagged behind in West Bengal, the change in banking policies with the introduction of liberalisation should not be underestimated. With the advent of economic reforms in the early nineties, there has been a decline in the bank offices opened in the rural areas (from 35,360 in 1993 to 31,667 in 2009), while the number of offices in the urban areas has increased significantly. Moreover, there is a huge concentration of both credit and deposit in the urban and metropolitan areas, which account for 77 per cent of the deposits and 80.4 per cent of the total credit provided by the scheduled commercial banks in 2009.

A news report by Manish Basu and Romita Datta in *Mint*[5] also dealt extensively with the phenomenon of rapid expansion of deposit-taking companies in West Bengal. India's capital market watchdog had fought protracted legal battles against two such companies—MPS Greenery Developers Ltd, and Rose Valley Real Estates and Constructions Ltd—in West Bengal, to stop them from collecting public deposits under collective investment schemes (CIS).

Despite issuing cease-and-desist orders a number of times, SEBI could not stop these firms from raising money from the public. The collapse of Saradha Group, a consortium of at least 200 companies that raised money from around 1.7 million people, in April 2013, is a case in point. Going by a few news reports, the group collected anything between Rs 20,000 crore and Rs 30,000 crore before it collapsed in 2013. The state government instituted an inquiry commission to probe into the collapse; it also created a Rs 500-crore fund to protect the poor investors who had lost their money in the scam.

West Bengal's finances have been indirectly impacted by the growth of deposit-taking companies because it was receiving a much smaller amount than earlier as a long-term

[5] Manish Basu and Romita Datta, 'Deposit-taking Companies Make Hay in West Bengal', *Mint* (28 March 2013), http://www.livemint.com/Money/HC4O6cOffE8tQnRxJ93PcM/Deposittaking-companies-make-hay-in-West-Bengal.html.

loan from the government's small savings collections, the *Mint* article pointed out.

All states receive 80 per cent of incremental small savings deposits (net of redemptions) every year in the form of a twenty-five-year loan that comes with a five-year moratorium.

West Bengal, which has traditionally had a high savings rate, used to receive in excess of Rs 6000 crore every year as loan from small savings deposits. Because of the moratorium on repayments through the first five years, this loan was invaluable for cash-strapped states such as West Bengal, though in the long run it also increased public debt.

Dealing with the slide in small savings deposits, the *EPW* article said:

If we look at the savings portfolio of the household sector in India, we find that between 2000–2005 the financial assets consisted of 12.8 per cent of GDP, while the physical assets accounted for 12.9 per cent. However between 2005–2010, the financial assets increased to 15.6 per cent of GDP, while physical assets declined to 11.8 per cent. In other words there was a greater degree of financialisation of savings [savings in financial instruments like bank deposits] in the second half of the last decade. If we further analyse the financial savings data, we find that bank deposits account for the largest share—increasing from 37.8 per cent in 2000–2005 to 51.6 per cent in 2005–10. The share of life insurance fund and that of stocks and debentures also witnessed a significant increase. However, there was a drastic fall in the share of claims on government—mainly the small savings schemes[6]—which declined from 19.5 per cent in 2000–05 to 2.6 per cent in 2005–10. This drop in small savings holding is because of two reasons: (a) decline in the interest rates of the schemes on offer, (b) the availability of other financial instruments in the market made possible by economic liberalisation.

West Bengal has been particularly hit hard by the fall in small savings deposits. The net collection from small savings was Rs 6,238.93 crore in 2006–07. This increased to Rs 8,985 crore in 2009–10, marginally declined to Rs 8,409 crore in 2010–11 and then subsequently declined to (-) Rs 987.22 crore in 2011–12. Therefore, within two years, approximately Rs 9,000 crore did not go to small savings schemes. The question is where did this money go? This money, which was earlier mobilised by the small savings scheme, must have been invested in financial instruments which promised a higher rate of return than that provided by the small savings schemes. Therefore, the shadow financial organisations like Saradha became an obvious choice for the small investor.

According to a note from West Bengal Savings Development Officers' Association, the corpus, as of November 2012, was minus (-)Rs 210 crore.[7]

---

[6] Small savings schemes provide safe investment options to the public through post offices and mobilize resources for development.

[7] Saugata Roy, 'State Govt Loses Benefit of Small Savings Fund', *Times of India* (22 January 2013), http://timesofindia.indiatimes. com/city/kolkata/State-govt-loses-benefit-of-small-savings-fund/ articleshow/18126963.cms.

What spawned the growth of these firms? The *Mint* article linked it to RBI's decision to stop Peerless General Finance & Investment Co. Ltd from managing small savings. Peerless was a residuary non-banking company, like Sahara India Financial Corporation Ltd, which used to raise money from the public and invest in RBI-mandated instruments.

The banking regulator first took on the Kolkata-based company and later Sahara India Financial. RBI's decision made Peerless's 60,000 field agents redundant, and most of them founded or became part of the collection network of the deposit-taking companies that have flourished in the past few years. They took advantage of poor bank penetration in the state's rural areas and a lack of understanding among savers about financial markets.

Large-scale Bank Failures

Proliferation of shadow banks is only one side of the story of banking in this part of India. The other side is the large-scale bank failures due to individual imprudence and mismanagement, fraudulent manipulations by directors and managers, and lack of expertise. Going back in time, the world wars and inflation too contributed to bank failures.

In 1930, there were 1258 banks in India. Of these, 919 were in Bengal. They were indigenous banks, *nidhi*s and loan companies. A nidhi belongs to the non-banking finance sector and its core business is borrowing and lending money only among its members. According to the

Indian Central Banking Enquiry Committee, 1930, they 'transact all kinds of businesses . . . including the issue of pass books and cheque books'.

In 1947, the year of Independence, India had eighty-two scheduled banks, and just over one-fourth of them—twenty-two—were in West Bengal, followed by Chennai (fourteen) and Mumbai (thirteen).

The partition of the country dealt a blow to the banking industry, and West Bengal bore the brunt. Of the thirty-eight banks that failed in 1947, seventeen were in West Bengal.

Until 1960s, many more banks in West Bengal went belly-up because of greed, corruption and lack of regulation.

Ghosh, fifty-five, has his task cut out. Bandhan is a break from the past. The burden of West Bengal's redemption from an inglorious banking legacy is on him.

Ghosh is now the chief of a bank, but before starting on his journey he learnt a valuable lesson from the women who sold vegetables at Shobhabazar in north Kolkata.

2

A Bottle of Mustard Oil,
for Training NGOs

In the late nineties, Ghosh came back from Dhaka where
he had worked with BRAC, the largest development
organization in the world dedicated to alleviating poverty.
He then started a knitting unit at 9, Hara Chandra Mullick
Street, Shobhabazar, in north Kolkata.

Four people used to work at Brajananda Knitting Factory,
handling fourteen small and two relatively large interlock
knitting machines. Hosiery makers for brands such as Rupa,
Lux and Amul would give them yarn for knitting woolicot
and clothes for vests and underwear.

The income was not enough for Ghosh to manage a
family, especially with a toddler—his son, Angshuman aka
Setu. So he started conducting training workshops for many
NGOs on developmental activities and capacity building
in and around Kolkata, earning between Rs 100 and

Rs 200 a day, except for Sri Mayapur Vikas Sangha, Nadia, an organization for poverty alleviation and healthcare. This organization would pay him Rs 1000 a day. He was a motivational speaker, and even spoke at blood donation camps. For most of the NGOs that Ghosh worked with, a fee of even Rs 100 was unaffordable. There were occasions when he would receive a bottle of mustard oil in return for holding a training camp.

THOSE WERE THE DAYS: In the late 1990s, Ghosh used to conduct training workshops for many NGOs on developmental activities and capacity building, in and around Kolkata, earning between Rs 100 and Rs 200 a day.

Each day, Ghosh would leave home early in the morning after eating rice, mashed potatoes and ghee, and would return late at night. The family could not afford even an egg for the child. There were days when there wasn't even enough rice at home.

Ghosh was getting restless. Vaskar, his brother, who was helping him manage the knitting factory, would often find him missing. Ghosh would leave home early morning and hang around Shobhabazar sabzi market, watching people.

One day, he saw a burly man in a red T-shirt riding a Royal Enfield Bullet. When the gentleman stopped at the entrance to the market, half a dozen women rushed to him. In fact, they had been waiting for him to arrive. To each of them, the man gave Rs 500 and collected Rs 5 simultaneously. He came back late in the afternoon, this time wearing a blue T-shirt. The same women—who were vegetable sellers in the market—returned the money, Rs 500 each.

Ghosh watched the ritual with curiosity for a few days. Every morning, the women would buy sackfuls of cauliflowers, tomatoes, brinjals and spinach outside the Sealdah railway station from the farmers who would come mostly from Lakshmikantapur in South 24 Parganas and Barasat in North 24 Parganas.

One evening, when those women were about to leave the market after settling the moneylender's dues, he could not resist asking them why they were paying so much interest to this man. His calculation was fairly simple: on Rs 500, they were paying Rs 5 as interest for half a day. This translated to 1 per cent interest for half a day, and 730 per cent a year!

But the women told Ghosh a different story. They were not paying any interest; rather, they were just buying a cup of tea for the moneylender. Moreover, they were earning enough to afford this. 'Will a bank give us money?' the group of women asked him in a chorus. How else would they get money without documentation and a guarantor? Besides, they were saving time and travel cost as the money was being given to them at their doorstep (in this case, the market).

The Eureka Moment

To use a cliché, this was Ghosh's eureka moment. He figured out what he should do. But how did Bandhan happen? For Partha Pratim Samanta, the first employee of Bandhan, this is where it all started.

Samanta was working with an NGO called Village Welfare Society, which had recently started dabbling in microfinance, or the business of giving small loans to poor people. One lazy afternoon in April 1999, Samanta saw a tall and dark gentleman, wearing blue jeans and a white half-sleeved shirt, with his young nephew in tow. The man and the child entered the Village Welfare Society office at F3, Gitanjali Park, Ariadaha, North 24 Parganas, and inquired about Ajit Maity, the boss. The NGO had advertised in local newspapers looking for credit officers, and the age limit was thirty-five. Samanta had a close look at this man and told him that he would not be considered for the job as he seemed to be over thirty-five. The man still insisted on a meeting and, after about forty-five minutes, he left smiling.

About a month later, at a training workshop at Pancharul, a remote village in Howrah, Samanta found the man sitting on the trainer's seat. They got talking at the breakfast table the next morning, where Ghosh quizzed him about the panchayat structure.

'He was extremely smart. It was as if he knew everything and was only testing my knowledge, but I found that he was taking notes,' Samanta told me.

By the time the three-day training period got over, they had struck up a relationship which was going to last a lifetime.

Ghosh joined Village Welfare Society as head of operations, at a salary of Rs 5000 a month. At his recommendation, Samanta was made a regional manager. Samanta was also given a motorcycle for supervising branches, for which Rs 400 was deducted from his Rs 1700 salary every month. Ghosh was living in Dunlop then, and would commute to the office on his black Bajaj Boxer. Often, Samanta would go to his house (his motorcycle was also a Bajaj Boxer, but the colour was red) and discuss India, poverty and how to expand microfinance.

One day in 2001, when Samanta was working in Raipur, Chhattisgarh, expanding Village Welfare Society's microloan operations, he got a call from Ghosh's wife, Nilima, saying, 'Your dada has resigned.' By that time, Bandhan had already been born in the shape of an NGO, registered under the Societies Registration Act. Apparently, Maity got to know this and confronted Ghosh in the Village Welfare Society office. Ghosh resigned on the spot; the resignation letter was ready in his drawer.

How did Maity get to know about the formation of Bandhan? There are two versions of this story.

An NGO, CARE India, had advertised in local newspapers, looking for trainers. Both Village Welfare Society and Bandhan applied for the assignment, and two names were common on both lists—Ghosh and Samanta. A confused

CARE India CEO asked Maity what Bandhan was, and the cat was out of the bag.

According to Maity, he got to know this at a seminar at Moulali Yuva Kendra, on AJC Bose Road in Sealdah in 2002. Suryakanta Mishra, then panchayat minister of West Bengal, was speaking at the seminar. Maity found a leaflet on Bandhan. When he asked Ghosh whether he had formed a parallel NGO, Ghosh's cryptic answer was: 'Yes, sir.'

Incidentally, Sushil Roy, executive vice president of ASA, the largest microfinance institution (MFI) in Bangladesh, known for its cost-effective business model, met Ghosh at that seminar and offered technical support to Bandhan.

After resigning, when Samanta met Ghosh at his residence in Dunlop, he told Samanta, 'If I can make both ends meet, you too will be able to do so.'

However, the journey was far from easy. There were times when a frustrated Ghosh thought of committing suicide —he was worried he would not be able to return the money that he had borrowed from his relatives to start the business of giving small loans to poor people. There was a demand for money but he did not have the resources, and no bank was coming forward to help him.

How did he finally manage to convince the lenders? More details on this later.

The Birth of Bandhan

Now to the story of the formation of Bandhan, the NGO and the original avatar of Bandhan Bank (it had undergone two transformations: first, from a not-for-profit NGO to a for-profit non-banking finance company, and finally, a bank).

Even before he watched the 'spectacle' of people borrowing money at a whopping interest rate of 730 per cent, Ghosh knew that there was a huge market for small loans, but nobody had looked into it seriously. The NGOs, including BRAC, where Ghosh had spent thirteen years, would never borrow money from banks for business as they did not look at this as business. For them, it was a sort of corporate social responsibility (CSR) activity—taking donations and distributing money to the poor as a one-time contribution. But if one wants to change the lives of poor people and make them entrepreneurs, it is important to be able to scale up lending operations. Essentially, this means the tap of money should not dry up as the poor need continuous support in terms of loans, and the amount must increase every year as their businesses grow. This is not possible unless one approaches this as a commercial activity.

Since these organizations were not scaling up, the borrowers too could not scale up their businesses. They would not get into expanding their business as they were not sure whether the lender could support them. The beneficiaries of small loans cannot have a vision in isolation—the visions of both the borrowers and the lenders are interlinked. As there was no assurance on the grants, the NGOs were not certain about continuing the project of giving money to the poor. So, what was the future of the customers?

While working with Village Welfare Society, Ghosh was also associated with scores of NGOs as a trainer and motivational speaker. He advised the NGOs to scale up but they would not listen. At that time, one Kartik Mirdha, of Human

Development Centre, a non-profit organization, told Ghosh to set up his own NGO.

Once, Ghosh was with Mirdha at a Rotary Club function at Esplanade in Kolkata. After the event, Mirdha took him to Todi Mansion at India Exchange Place Extension, where the office of the registrar of firms and NGOs was located. The office explained all that he would need to know to set up an NGO. Ghosh discussed the idea with his wife, and with Samanta.

Considerable time was spent discussing the name of the organization. Nilima suggested Setu—the nickname of their son, Angshuman—meaning 'bridge'. In Bengali, *setu* and *bandhan*—meaning 'bond'—are often used together. Keeping the meaning intact, they decided on naming the NGO Bandhan, which means bonding—the organization would be a bridge between the so-called haves and have-nots.

After finishing the paperwork, Ghosh rushed to Todi Mansion the following week. The entity got registered as Bandhan-Konnagar on 11 April 2001 under the West Bengal Societies Registration Act 1961. Its registered office was at 99 H/B, Haran Chandra Banerjee Lane, Konnagar, Uttarpara, Hooghly—the residence of Ghosh's maternal uncle, Saroj Kanti Ghosh.

The memorandum of association of Bandhan-Konnagar says the society aims for the following: welfare of the people; helping the aged, the sick, the helpless; working for the happiness of the needy, for their education, food, clothes; helping needy students; setting up a library; helping the needy at times of wedding, funeral and cremation; offering relief during flood, famine, pestilence and other calamities caused by nature or man; cultivating the spirit of culture;

and anything else conducive to the attainment of these objectives.

THE FIRST STEP: The memorandum of association of Bandhan-Konnagar.

'The income . . . of the society . . . shall be applied solely towards the promotion of the objects' and no member would get dividends or part of the profits.

Saroj Kanti was president of the society, and Biplab Sarkar, husband of a councillor at Konnagar municipality and a neighbour, was vice president. Ghosh was its secretary, and Samanta, the assistant secretary. One Ramesh Saha Poddar was the treasurer. And there were four other members— Manoranjan Ghosh, Tapan Bhattacharjee, Satyajit Ghosh and Bula Paul.

Even though the memorandum of association did not mention it, the regulations of Bandhan-Konnagar, under the affairs of the society, included microcredit. It said that the executive committee would supervise its activities such as borrowing, taking loans and grants for operations like thrift savings[8] and microcredit through promotion of self-help groups; and channelize borrowed funds and get refinanced by different government and non-government organizations for helping people to build training centres. The seeds of Bandhan were sown.

The first annual report of Bandhan-Konnagar was more direct in its objective. It clearly set the goal of the organization: 'To create an enabling atmosphere for poverty alleviation and empowerment of the poor of India through microfinance.'

Among other things, the objectives were: empower women by organizing them through self-help groups; ensure sustainability for the beneficiaries as well as the organization through microfinance; provide effective credit delivery system for establishing micro-entrepreneurship development; and develop a network among MFIs in West Bengal.

---

[8] Technically, there is no difference between savings and thrift, but when one uses money extremely carefully and saves despite difficulties, it is called thrift savings. Typically, it is done in small amounts.

The objectives were fine but running an organization was not easy, and Ghosh understood that very early on. He used to hold meetings at a building owned by the president, which was rented out for weddings. At its third meeting, highly agitated over some trivial issues, Poddar, its treasurer, started abusing everyone. The president was determined to quit, but the crisis was averted as Poddar himself resigned after a week.

'Let's Do It Ourselves'

The initial idea was to develop a string of NGOs supporting each other to broad-base operations. This would be an effective way to meet the demand of growing borrowers.

If they could develop ten NGOs which could finance one lakh families each, then small loans would reach one million households. But when Ghosh realized no NGO was willing to scale up, he told the members, 'Let's do it ourselves.'

That was the time when Maity of Village Welfare Society found out about the plan and Ghosh quit his organization. Nilima was in tears and could not sleep that night. When Ghosh called up his brother-in-law, Swapan, in Tripura, he too was not convinced about the idea of quitting a steady job. However, he volunteered to offer monetary help to Ghosh who was now set to start his venture. Ghosh's life savings amounted to Rs 2 lakh and Swapan chipped in some money. Bandhan had started operations.

But it was not that simple. There were intense debates on the location of the first branch. Ghosh suggested Konnagar, in Hooghly, where his uncle, Saroj Kanti, was living. Samanta's preference was Bagnan in Howrah, where some of his relations were staying.

Fatik Bera, Bandhan's second employee, too was keen on Bagnan as he knew the place well and was quite popular there by virtue of having been a student leader at the local college. They agreed on both the locations. There was also a conscious decision to avoid any locality where Village Welfare Society or any other MFI was present.

A place was taken on rent in early 2002 for the Bagnan office—a four-by-six-foot cubicle under a staircase on the ground floor on High Road, Khirishtala, at Sheikh Nazrul's house, for Rs 300 per month. A table and two chairs were bought. The daily collection data used to be entered into a register at a tea stall.

THE SEEDS WERE SOWN: Bandhan's office at Bagnan, Howrah. In this photograph taken in November 2003, Ghosh (second from right) is seen along with Saneesh Singh (fourth from right), then with SIDBI. On the extreme right is Fatik Bera, Bandhan's second employee.

Later, in August 2002, the office moved to a new place near Bagnan railway station—a flat with three rooms and a dining hall—for Rs 2500 per month. At the first meeting with Bandhan, when the landlord insisted that every month's rent be paid in advance, Samanta emptied his collection bag on his table—Rs 1800 in coins and the rest in cash. This was the mode of payment of rent every month.

The Konnagar office was almost on the railway track. Ghosh used to comb the outskirts of Kolkata every weekend in search of locations where Bandhan could set up its branches. Pritish Saha, one of the zonal heads in the microbanking division of Bandhan Bank, and an early employee of the group, told me that every Saturday and Sunday, his landline at Chakdaha, Nadia, would ring at 10 a.m. sharp, and Ghosh would be on the line. Saha was working for another NGO, South Asia Research Society (SARS) then.

Ghosh would spend the entire day with Saha, talking about building an organization. He would take a local train from Belgharia in north Kolkata (where he was living at that time), on the Sealdah–Krishnanagar line, and after a one-and-a-half-hour journey, he would take a rickshaw from the station to Saha's home. After lunch, Saha would ride his Hero Honda Splendor with Ghosh on the pillion seat to survey where branches of his dream organization—Bandhan was not registered then—could be opened. They would roam around Shantipur, Haringhata, Nagarukhra, Bishnupur, Ranaghat and Phulia—small towns and villages in Nadia.

One Sunday at Kalinarayanpur, Nadia, it rained heavily. They managed to find shelter but both of them were drenched to the skin. Even so, Ghosh went on with the day's work.

THE EARLY DAYS: In the run-up to the formation of Bandhan, Ghosh would roam around small towns and villages of West Bengal on his bike every weekend looking for opportunities to set up branches.

'Help Us to Help You'

Samanta prepared a leaflet and distributed it among the poor people at Bagnan and Konnagar. It said: 'Help us to help you.' They started collecting Rs 5 per day for forty days from shopkeepers and vegetable vendors, and once it became Rs 200, they would give a loan of Rs 1000. In a very short time, they got 130 borrowers in Bagnan and sixty-five in Konnagar. One needed to first become a member of a group to borrow money. So, there would always be more members than borrowers.

STIFF TARGET: The goal for Bandhan employees in the initial days was three members per day. A blackboard at the Bagnan branch in July 2003 shows how many members four Bandhan employees had enrolled.

Bera used to manage the Bagnan branch, and Manoranjan Ghosh handled Konnagar; Samanta was the coordinator. There were many who wanted loans, and since they had already saved for forty days, it was difficult to say no when they started asking for money. But where was the money to lend? Once Samanta and Bera landed up at Ghosh's residence and told him that they were finding it extremely difficult to face the members who were chasing them for money. Ghosh managed the situation by borrowing Rs 30,000 from a moneylender at 7.5 per cent interest per month, but it was difficult to sustain operations.

He started approaching banks for loans, but no bank was willing to give him money. Somebody suggested that if he could organize a fourteen-day training programme for MFIs, Grameen Bank of Bangladesh would give him the seed fund from some grants. He did that, but still didn't get the money. Apparently, Grameen Bank had given some money to three such groups in West Bengal, but none of them had actually worked, hence the apprehension.

A desperate Ghosh started knocking at the door of the regional office of SIDBI, on the eighth floor of Constantia Building at 11, Dr UN Brahmachari Street, Minto Park, opposite La Martiniere for Girls school. He would go there often, and on many a day would not be able to meet anybody. After waiting for an hour or so, Ghosh would walk down to Esplanade to catch a bus to go home, eating puffed rice and peanuts as an afternoon snack.

Around this time, as a technical resource person, Ghosh led and arranged a microfinance exposure programme for a few West Bengal NGOs in Bangladesh, co-sponsored by SIDBI and CARE (a US agency, which has been working in India since 1946, undertaking developmental activities). During this trip, he got familiar with ASA, known for its sustainable microfinance model which claims to make a branch self-reliant within a year. The meeting with ASA seemed to be a clincher, as a technical collaboration with them played a key role in convincing SIDBI to give money to Bandhan.

This is how senior officials of SIDBI and ASA narrated it:

Saneesh Singh, forty-seven, who had worked with SIDBI, is now the managing director of Dia Vikas Capital Pvt. Ltd, a subsidiary of Opportunity International Australia, a non-profit philanthropic organization and social investor that invests in institutions providing small business loans and savings, and training poor people to work their way out of poverty.

Singh has roots in Kolkata; his maternal grandfather, Charu Chandra Chatterjee, was related to the famous Bengali litterateur Bankim Chandra Chatterjee. Charu Chandra, a barrister, embraced Christianity and first moved to Allahabad, and later Barabanki, in Uttar Pradesh. During his childhood, Singh was influenced by his grandmother who believed in a saying from the Bible: 'Whoever is generous to the poor lends to the Lord, and He will repay him for his deeds.'

At SIDBI, which he joined in Lucknow in 1991, Singh was involved in small- and medium-sized enterprise (SME) lending, bank refinance and, subsequently, microfinance. This activity of SIDBI later gave birth to the SIDBI Foundation for Micro Credit (SFMC) in 1999, for channelling funds to the poor. Singh was closely involved in the launch and operations of the National Microfinance Support Programme—the SIDBI-implemented poverty-alleviation and income-generation projects of the Department for International Development (DFID), UK, and the International Fund for Agricultural Development (IFAD), Rome.

In 2000, when Singh was transferred to Kolkata, he hated it as, on the very first day that he walked into the SIDBI guest house in Lake Town, all his belongings and cash (brought for his daughters' school admission) were stolen. The next day, he had to borrow a shirt from a colleague and money from another to pay the taxi fare when he reached the office on Dr UN Brahmachari Street.

Singh first met Ghosh at the SIDBI office some time in 2001 when he came along with Maity of Village Welfare Society, where he was working then. Later, Singh met Ghosh at a training programme that he was conducting at Kotalipara Development Society, a small NGO in Barasat. 'I was impressed with Ghosh's passion. I told him, why can't he bring ASA to support the start-up? He agreed as he knew the ASA people well,' Singh said.

Singh also visited Bandhan's Konnagar office for the so-called due diligence. The office was 'created' by Samanta and Nilima overnight in treasurer Biplab Sarkar's drawing room, with posters on savings and microloans, registers and files. The third member of the team that set up the office was one Sabari Sarkar, who was working for the NGO Seva Sangha at that time. Sarkar, who later joined the Bandhan board, knew 'Shekhar da' as a trainer, and was an admirer of his go-getter attitude. They bought a table and a couple of chairs for Rs 2200 to complete the office.

Ghosh's 100-page spiral-bound proposal got a lukewarm response from SIDBI's Kolkata head, B.K. Maity, but Singh somehow persuaded him to send it to the headquarters in Lucknow for 'intervention'. For a few months, there was no response. When Ghosh and ASA's Roy went to Lucknow for a presentation, Singh also went there on a personal visit. The day Bandhan's proposal was discussed, Singh was summoned to the headquarters.

That was, in fact, Bandhan's second attempt to meet the SIDBI top brass in Lucknow. The first time that the Ghosh–Roy duo went to Lucknow on 10 June 2002, SIDBI cancelled the meeting at the last moment as the then finance minister

Yashwant Singh was to visit the institution that day. A new date was fixed after a month and, after much persuasion, Roy once again came from Bangladesh to Kolkata and took a train to Lucknow.

Going by the prevailing SFMC checklists, Bandhan did not quite qualify for any loan or grant. But Brij Mohan, SIDBI's chief general manager, who later became executive director, said, '*Usme dum hai lagta hai* (The proposal does hold weight),' and asked Singh, 'How convinced are you?' He also said if the money was not recovered, Singh would lose his provident fund. 'Are you ready?' 'Yes,' Singh answered.

The proposal was approved the following week. It was the beginning of a permanent relationship between SIDBI and Bandhan. Over the next few years, Bandhan received several hundred crores as support from SIDBI, both in the form of loan as well as equity, and kept expanding at an amazing pace.

Singh was in Kolkata until April 2007. By that time, Bandhan had opened its hundredth branch.

Brij Mohan, seventy-two, chairperson of RGVN (North East) Microfinance Ltd, which has got the RBI's 'in principle' approval to set up a small finance bank, was part of the team which set up the SIDBI head office in Lucknow.

When Ghosh came to Lucknow with his proposal, the microfinance initiative in India was highly skewed in favour of the southern states, especially Andhra Pradesh. The scenario was rather weak in eastern and central regions, and SIDBI was asking established players such as SKS Microfinance Ltd, Share Microfin Ltd, Spandana Sphoorty Financial Ltd and Bhartiya Samruddhi Finance Ltd (BSFL) to go there.

'We Compromised on Our Policies'

'We liked three things about Bandhan: Ghosh has invested his own money; it is the first such venture in the east; and it is fully backed by ASA of Bangladesh. In fact, Ghosh came with an ASA executive,' Brij Mohan told me.

'We compromised our policies on three important things. Bandhan did not qualify for a SIDBI loan as it did not have a three-year track record; Bandhan was not rated; and Bandhan also did not have the minimum client base of 5000.'

'Yet, we cleared the proposal as we were keen to help Bandhan. SIDBI was desperate to be in West Bengal. ASA gave us comfort. And we had a gut feeling that this man could do it—he looked sincere,' Brij Mohan said.

Bandhan had asked for Rs 15 lakh as loan and Rs 6 lakh as capacity-building grants. But the norm was that the grant could not be more than one-third of the loan amount. So, Brij Mohan suggested that a fresh proposal be made for a Rs 20-lakh loan and Rs 5.45-lakh grant. The money was disbursed in October 2002: a three-year loan at 9 per cent interest.

Roy, Md Enamul Haque, chief operating officer (COO) of ASA International NV (its global arm), and Md Azim Hossain, its director, investment and treasury, narrated the following story.

In 1978, at Shivalya Thana in Manikganj, 64 km northwest of Dhaka, the seeds of ASA were sown when Md Shafiqual Haque Choudhury, who had quit civil service before completing his probationary period, bought a two-anna (12 paise) notebook and wrote its resolution.

Its MFI programme, which started in 1992, simplified, standardized and decentralized the system of record-keeping, loan delivery and the collection process. It also standardized the loan appraisal process—taking a leaf out of the readymade garment business. A tailor stitches a shirt after measuring each individual but machine-made shirts typically have four sizes—small, medium, large and extra large—and they fit all. ASA developed its processes with a similar approach.

It went for round-figure disbursements and round-figure collection. For instance, a Rs 1000 loan will have a weekly instalment of Rs 25 for a year. It used to be called *hazare phachis*—Rs 25 for Rs 1000.

Every ASA branch would have four loan officers, one branch manager and 1000 clients; there would be groups of twenty each, all women. The collection would be at doorsteps, between 8 a.m. and 12 p.m., and disbursement of loans would be at branch offices, after lunch. The collection registers would have two columns: debit on the left, and credit on the right, intelligible to all.

Three Models

Bangladesh, which had seen the emergence of microfinance much ahead of India, has essentially three models. The Grameen Bank model of Nobel laureate Muhammad Yunus is centralized and well structured; it follows a hierarchical approach and the branches take a longer time to break even.

BRAC, on the other hand, has a holistic credit-plus approach, which covers social and financial services—credit and savings, insurances, environment, health, education, training and research.

THE FOUNDATION: Working with BRAC in Bangladesh, a development organization dedicated to alleviating poverty by empowering the poor, Ghosh (second from left) experienced poverty in its starkest form, and power structures in a village. That helped him pick up skills to motivate people, analyse human behaviour and resolve conflicts.

ASA is the most cost-effective, simple, innovative and decentralized entity, and it is not overly hierarchical. Its branches achieve break-even faster. Incidentally, Roy of ASA used to work with BRAC as a trainer where Ghosh too had worked.

'We were very keen that someone should replicate the ASA model in India. There were opportunities for hard-core microfinance in India, but nobody was willing to take the plunge. The ASA model was a great success even in Africa and the Middle East, ruled by Sharia laws, but there were no takers in neighbouring India. I committed technical support to Shekhar even before consulting my boss,' Roy said. He was looking after the technical support programme at ASA at that time.

Roy could not attend the meeting at the ASA headquarters at Shyamoli, Sher-i-Bengali Nagar, Dhaka, where the memorandum of understanding (MoU) for a technical support agreement between Bandhan and ASA was signed in 2002. Ghosh, Ronendra Chowdhury (popularly known as Runu da; head of the microbanking division at Bandhan), Sohel Mahmud Sagar (executive vice president, accounts) and Md Enamul Haque, then executive vice president, operations, were present. The agreement also outlined that ASA would provide skilled staff to train Bandhan employees.

After it was signed, Ghosh took the entire team out for lunch at City Garden, next to the ASA headquarters. There, Ghosh took out a small notebook and kept on taking notes over the next two hours while the others were eating chicken tandoori and tiger prawns.

Roy was inducted into the Bandhan board. Between 2002 and 2008, over eighty ASA employees were associated with Bandhan under an exposure programme.

Two ASA managers—Fazle Rabbi Raihan (who is currently working with ASA Philippines) and Nahid Khan (currently working with ASA Myanmar)—worked at the Konnagar and Bagnan branches. Samanta and Khan lived in the Bagnan branch where Samanta would cook and clean the vessels, and they would often fight over food.

On 10 July 2002, the first day at the Bagnan branch, Samanta bought a kerosene stove and cooked rice, dal and mashed potatoes for dinner for the three of them—Ghosh, Khan and himself. There was only one cot which was offered to Khan to sleep on; Samanta and Ghosh slept on the floor.

The ASA training started, as part of the technical support, on 1 July 2002 at Bagnan. The branch operations had begun before that in April 2001, with sixty-five members, all of them shop owners selling vegetables, tea, paan-biri, etc.— at a tough time when there was widespread panic over chit funds. At Nuntia, Bagnan, a ten-member group called Golap, which means 'rose' in Bengali, was formed. The first loan was given in October: Rs 1000 each to ten members. The loan amount was raised to Rs 3000, and by December 2002, there were 1200 members.

Along with Konnagar and Bagnan, Nilima tried to form a group at Dunlop. While the local women were convinced, the husband of one of them walked in one day and threw Nilima out, calling Bandhan a chit fund. Nilima also started a school there with two others—Ranjana Dutta and Jesmita Dey—under Dunlop Bridge. The school lasted for a year.

The system was such that the 'members' of the groups would save Rs 10 every week, and after twelve weeks, when the savings would amount to Rs 120, a member would be eligible for a loan of Rs 1000. However, to avail herself of that, she would need to put in Rs 80 on the day the loan was disbursed. Simply put, one would need to save 20 per cent of the loan amount. Till the loan was given, the 'compulsory savings' remained with the group members. The interest rate—then called 'service charge'—was a flat 17.5 per cent, even as 5 per cent interest—then called 'incentive'—was given on their savings.

The target for a handful of Bandhan employees those days was three members per day. Ghosh would call almost every day to check on the progress, ask every branch manager how many members he had been able to enrol.

Kalyan Kundu, who was attached to the Chakdaha branch in Nadia, said that every evening at 7.30 p.m., 'Sir' would call one Bishnu's house, which was next to the branch. Bishnu's father, a police constable, was mostly not at home. His mother would take the call and yell for Kundu to come over quickly. While Kundu would run to take the call, his colleague, Sudhanya Nopti, would follow him with the register which had the data. On the phone, Ghosh would inquire about the target.

If a branch had three employees, the target would be nine per day, and fifty-four a week. 'Sir was always precise and logical in his questions,' Kundu said.

Accounts Department in the Kitchen

At the Bandhan headquarters, then on the first floor of BA 74, Sector I, Salt Lake City, there were only three workers—Ghosh, Anirban Sarkar and Maneeta Rathore. It was a 600-square-foot one-bedroom flat, with the landlord living on the second floor and keeping a close watch on what was happening there. The ground floor was occupied by a laundry.

The bedroom was Ghosh's office; Sarkar was in the kitchen, running the accounts department; and Rathore would sit in the hall. Her official designation was programme assistant, but she would do many other things, including taking phone calls for Ghosh and managing his appointments.

There was no water dispenser in the office, and the employees were expected to bring drinking water from home. Sarkar would become nervous if anyone opened the kitchen tap, fearing that the accounts books would get wet. There was no service staff. Everybody was given a duster to clean their own table and computer.

Ghosh would come from Dunlop, taking a local train to Ultadanga, and from there he would walk to the office. He was always the first person to reach the office, latest by 8.45 a.m., and open it.

Often, he would go to the field carrying a big black Motorola handset that featured a monochrome display and an extendible antenna: a gift from his cousin, Deepak Ghosh. He would flaunt it while launching every branch and give everybody his phone number. Every branch of Bandhan would display his mobile number in bold on the noticeboard. Ghosh would take every call, greeting the caller with a 'namaskar'. This tradition continues even today, after Bandhan has become a bank and has about 20,000 employees on its roll.

By 2004, Bandhan had ramped up the branch network to ten: Bagnan (Howrah), Konnagar (Hooghly), Begampur (Hooghly), Birshibpur (Howrah), Shyampur (Howrah), Kolaghat (East Midnapore), Chakdaha (Nadia), Haringhata (Nadia), Shimurali (Nadia) and Chandapara (North 24 Parganas).

One day in 2001, before Bandhan started, Runu da stayed back late at Ghosh's residence, discussing the future of the organization. Around 1 a.m., when he was leaving for home, Ghosh offered to drop him at the Belgharia station from where he could catch a train to go home.

When they reached the station, there was hardly anybody around. The last train had already left and the platform was deserted. There were a few beggars who were fast asleep, and some stray dogs. They had no option but to turn back.

Standing on the platform, Ghosh said that one day there would be a Bandhan office at every station between Sealdah and Bangaon. The 76.5-km stretch was dotted with twenty-two stations, all located in the northern suburbs of Kolkata, going up to the last station between India and Bangladesh.

He got it wrong. In the next decade, Bandhan set up 2022 branches in twenty-two Indian states—something even Ghosh had not dreamt of.

3

The Big Bang

In the financial year 2002, its first year, Bandhan had two branches and 512 borrowers. It had disbursed loans worth Rs 3,50,000, operating out of the residence of Ghosh's uncle at Konnagar, Hooghly.

Thirteen years down the line, in August 2015, when Bandhan metamorphosed into a bank, the number of branches from where small loans were given (called DSCs) was 2022, with 6.7 million borrowers, and it had a loan book of Rs 10,500 crore.

By any yardstick, this has been a phenomenal growth. How did this happen?

In the second year of its existence, in 2003, there was no expansion in the Bandhan branch network, but the number of borrowers increased to 1143 and the outstanding loan amount was Rs 21,80,000. The amount of the first loan given to a borrower was anywhere between Rs 1000 and Rs 3000, and the second loan to the same borrower, after she cleared the first loan, would be Rs 1000–2000 more than the first loan. However, by that time, the requirement for compulsory savings was brought down to 10 per cent and the time taken between one's admission into a group as a member and disbursement of the loan cut down from twelve weeks to ten.

Three factors were taken into account for giving the second loan: past repayment record, future potential of the client's income-generating activity, and whether the first loan generated the expected income. As the interest rate was a flat 17.5 per cent, and the loans were repaid weekly, for a Rs 1000 loan, one needed to pay Rs 25 every week for forty-seven weeks.

Bandhan also created an 'in-house' insurance product—a premium of 2 per cent was charged on the loan amount, and in case of the death of a borrower, her successor would not need to pay back the money. Using the premium, Bandhan created a corpus of 'risk fund'.

By 2004, it had ten branches in five districts of West Bengal, and 5734 borrowers with an outstanding loan of Rs 1,20,37,872. In the same year, it also made a business plan for the next three years, up to 2007.

Exceeding All Targets

The target was to have eighty branches, 436 employees, 81,600 borrowers and a loan book of Rs 22.38 crore by 2007. The plan was wide off the mark. By 2006, Bandhan exceeded its three-year business targets in all aspects. The branch network was ramped up to 155, with 1,49,886 borrowers, and the outstanding loans amounted to Rs 37.11 crore. That year, Bandhan covered fourteen out of nineteen districts of West Bengal, and opened fifty branches in five districts of North Bengal—a new territory comprising Cooch Behar, North Dinajpur, Jalpaiguri, Darjeeling, Malda and Murshidabad.

Incidentally, Micro-Credit Rating International Ltd, popularly known as M-CRIL, found the projections too ambitious and impossible to achieve. Ghosh had a tough time convincing the rating agency that Bandhan would be able to achieve the projected growth. In one particular month in early 2005, it opened forty-four branches.

By that time, it had started getting funds from banks; apart from SIDBI, Ford Foundation and Friends of Women's World Banking (FWWB), three banks gave money to Bandhan to be on-lent to its borrowers. They were HDFC Bank, ICICI Bank and United Bank of India. In 2006, ABN AMRO Bank and UTI Bank (later renamed Axis Bank) also stepped in.

Enthused by the willingness banks showed to fund Bandhan and, of course, after gaining operational efficiency, Bandhan slashed the interest rate from 17.5 per cent to 15 per cent in July 2005, and announced that it would cut it further to 12.5 per cent from May 2006 onwards.

Md Shafiqual Haque Choudhury, founder and president of ASA, was quoted in Bandhan's 2006 annual report as saying, 'It is faster than the fastest-growing ASA. If it can maintain this growth, Bandhan will be the market leader in India.' It did so, and became just that.

In fact, in December 2007, *Forbes* released its listing of microfinance entities in the world, featuring Bandhan in the second spot. ASA topped the list and Bangladesh's Grameen Bank was ranked seventeenth.

This was the magazine's first-ever list of the world's top fifty microfinance institutions, chosen from among 641 microcredit providers. The list was prepared by Microfinance Informal Exchange, under the direction of *Forbes*. It looked at four parameters: scale, efficiency, risk and returns. To qualify, the institutions had to make available their audited financials and pass the review by a *Forbes* panel of advisers. Seven Indian MFIs featured on the list, including SKS Microfinance (ranked forty-fourth).

As the growth was better than expected, Bandhan revised its business plan, and went wide off the mark, yet again! In 2006, it had chalked out a five-year strategic business plan with the help of MicroSave, an international financial inclusion consulting firm, at a three-day workshop in a Kolkata suburb, to have 1300 branches, 8142 employees, 2.72 million borrowers, and a Rs 1616.5-crore loan book by 2011.

The actual figures for 2011 were 1553 branches, 8813 employees, 3.25 million borrowers, and a loan book of Rs 2503 crore.

As the growth engine revved up, Bandhan started expanding beyond West Bengal: first to the north-east and then to other parts of India. It converted itself from a not-for-profit organization to a for-profit non-banking financial company (NBFC), and embraced computerization.

The rating agencies were convinced that Bandhan would not be able to replicate its growth story in other parts of India, but Ghosh was determined to prove them wrong.

Before expanding to other states, Bandhan got a system audit done by Deloitte Haskins & Sells in 2005, the first by

any MFI in India. It even approached S.R. Batliboi & Co.,
the audit arm of Ernst & Young in India, for its audit, but
Ernst & Young did not find the proposal exciting enough as
Bandhan was too small then.

Later, in 2010, the three other firms of the so-called
Big Four—KPMG, Deloitte and PwC—were keen to get
the mandate for auditing Bandhan. Ernst & Young got the
mandate.

As Ghosh was convinced that the only way to scale up
operations was to approach the business as an NBFC and
not as an NGO, Bandhan decided to convert itself into a for-
profit organization. SIDBI and the lending banks also wanted
Bandhan to shed its NGO garb and become an NBFC, as they
too thought that was the way to go.

However, it was not easy as, under RBI norms, an NBFC
needed to have equity of Rs 2 crore: a big sum for Bandhan in
those days. It did not have that kind of capital. So, it started
looking to acquire an already existing NBFC. Kolkata-based
Ganga Niryat Pvt. Ltd was available. It had a capital of
Rs 39.2 lakh. Bandhan lapped it up in May 2006, and did
not even have to pay that much. By March, its capital rose to
Rs 66.5 lakh, with profits being ploughed back.

Ganga Niryat was renamed as Bandhan Financial Services
Pvt. Ltd (BFSPL), and commenced operations in Tripura from
June 2006. Till 2009, two parallel entities worked under the
Bandhan fold in the microfinance space: Bandhan-Konnagar,
as an NGO operating in West Bengal and Assam, and BFSPL,
as an NBFC in other states.

In April 2009, when the entire MFI portfolio was
transferred to BFSPL, and Bandhan-Konnagar became its CSR
arm, Bandhan was present in eleven states with 675 branches,

4118 employees, 1.45 million borrowers, and a loan book of Rs 703.5 crore. That year, Bandhan raised Rs 815 crore from banks to grow its loan book.

This was significant as the formal banking system, globally, was shaken in the aftermath of the fall of US investment bank Lehman Brothers Holding Inc. The interbank market collapsed as banks stopped trusting each other and recession gripped the world.

But the world of microfinance remained unscathed. By that time, Bandhan had already entered Tripura, Assam and Jharkhand, and, in 2008, it moved to Mumbai, Delhi and Patna in quick succession.

First Branch in Delhi

The first branch in Delhi was opened on 19 July 2008, giving Rs 1,83,000 of loans to nineteen women. Within a year, Delhi had eighteen branches in six districts, reaching out to 9259 borrowers and lending Rs 6.7 crore.

From the north, it moved back to the east, opening two branches in Patna only two days later, on 21 July 2008; Rs 2,65,000 was disbursed to twenty-nine borrowers. Ahead of that, it had opened a branch at Kishanganj, on the border of West Bengal and Bihar, as a pilot project.

By the end of the year, Bihar had thirty-two branches in four districts, covering 17,955 borrowers, and had disbursed Rs 11.74 crore as loan.

The next port of call was the west. Bandhan disbursed Rs 7 lakh to seventy-two borrowers across four branches in Mumbai, on 16 September 2008. By the end of the year,

Maharashtra had eighteen branches in Mumbai and Pune, covering 7300 borrowers and with a loan book of Rs 3.9 crore.

The growth also led to a four-tier operational structure. At the lowest level was the branch, consisting of a maximum of 3000 borrowers; six to seven branches formed a region, which was headed by a regional manager; five to six regions formed a division under a divisional manager; and five to six divisions formed a zone. The zonal teams were based at the headquarters, headed by an assistant general manager.

By April 2010, Bandhan's branch network crossed 1000, its borrowers numbered 2.5 million, and the loan

A MILESTONE: The inauguration of Bandhan's 100th branch on 11 August 2005 at Behala, Kolkata. A. Vikraman, then SIDBI's chief general manager (sitting fourth from left) is seen with Ghosh (extreme right). Third from left is Brij Mohan, then retired from SIDBI.

portfolio almost touched Rs 1500 crore. A few months before that, in December 2009, SIDBI picked up a stake in Bandhan for Rs 50 crore, making it the biggest investment by any government-owned institution in the microfinance sector. Incidentally, in October 2008, SIDBI had acquired close to 1 per cent of Bandhan through the conversion of a Rs 1-crore loan into equity. With the latest round, its stake rose to 10.92 per cent.

SIDBI's first investment in the MFI space was in Vijay Mahajan's BSFL—worth Rs 18 crore for a stake of just a shade under 10 per cent.

R.M. Malla, then SIDBI chairman and managing director, was the architect of the deal. N.K. Maini, the then executive director of SIDBI, explains, 'We were convinced about Bandhan because of its focus on the backward areas of the east and the profile of its borrowers. Ghosh has microfinance in his blood. The promoter's credibility is of utmost importance when we make an equity investment. Ghosh had remarkable clarity of what he wanted—a domestic investor, when private equity funds were making a beeline. He did not want to risk his mission.'

According to Maini, who retired as deputy managing director in 2015, SIDBI was the first institution to lend to Bandhan, and it was logical that it would take forward the momentum. He saw Ghosh as a tough negotiator. 'He did not treat us differently because we had been with Bandhan since its beginning. He was very particular about the terms and conditions and told us that Bandhan would use 5 per cent of its profit for CSR. We had no problem as it gels with our philosophy of sustainable development.'

Bandhan expanded to four more states that year—Gujarat, Madhya Pradesh, Rajasthan and Uttarakhand—and introduced high-value Samriddhi loans for micro, small- and medium-sized enterprises, of Rs 1–3 lakh. Following nearly a decade of association with Bandhan, some entrepreneurs' credit demand rose, and the new product was created to meet that demand. The idea was to create employment, and only those borrowers who had created at least two employments were eligible for the Samriddhi loan. Unlike the microloans which were given to borrowers after they formed a group, to avail themselves of the Samriddhi loan borrowers did not need to be part of a group. Typically, in microfinance, groups are formed to create moral and social pressure for repayment of loans even though the group is not responsible if an individual defaults.

Bandhan was growing at breakneck speed, even in the financial year ending March 2011. This year witnessed the gravest crisis in the microfinance industry when the Andhra Pradesh government promulgated a state law severely restricting their activities, following many suicides by borrowers, provoked by alleged coercive loan-collection practices by MFIs. Of course, Bandhan had the advantage of not being present in Andhra Pradesh, or for that matter, in the entire southern part of India then.

Most large MFIs at that time had substantial exposure in Andhra Pradesh, including the then lone listed entity, SKS Microfinance. While their loan books shrank dramatically, Bandhan grew by leaps and bounds. By 2011, Bandhan was present in eighteen states, with 1553 branches, 3.25 million borrowers and a loan book of Rs 2503 crore.

The very next year, when Bandhan completed a decade of existence, it had 3.6 million borrowers and a loan book of Rs 3730 crore. Convinced about the growth story, IFC, the private investment arm of the World Bank, after one and a half years of negotiation, pumped Rs 135 crore into Bandhan, picking up a 10.93 per cent stake.

While SIDBI had paid a premium of Rs 50 on a Rs 10 share, IFC paid almost two and a half times the amount: a premium of Rs 117. This was IFC's third attempt to buy a stake in Bandhan. Initially, it had offered to pay a premium of Rs 5, and later, as much as SIDBI had paid. Ghosh had held roadshows in Mumbai and Delhi, and had met three dozen investors, some of whom were willing to pay more than IFC.

One day, Brij Mohan, who by that time had become Ghosh's informal adviser, got a call from him: 'Brij Mohan sir, I am under pressure. So many investors want to invest (in Bandhan) . . . I am lost . . . What should I do? Please help, come to Kolkata.' Once Brij Mohan was at the Bandhan headquarters, Ghosh laid down all the proposals on the table.

There were extended discussions for two days with directors and senior employees of Bandhan, and rules were formed: Bandhan would be a pro-poor social organization; only development institutions would be allowed to invest so as to ensure that its objective was not compromised; Bandhan would look for more and more money without ceding control—this meant that the valuation would have to go up. Finally, this would be done in stages.

Even though there were takers for Bandhan who were willing to pay more than IFC, Brij Mohan's advice to Ghosh at that point was: 'You will grow big and must have a good parentage.'

The growth story continued till Bandhan got the RBI nod to transform itself into a universal bank. The collapse of a Ponzi scheme run by the Saradha Group, a consortium of at least 200 private companies that were believed to have collected Rs 20,000–30,000 crore, rocked West Bengal in 2013, but Bandhan did not feel the tremors because of its solid foundation.

Catching a Flight to Work, for the First Time

Bandhan's employees remember its 'invasion' of Tripura when a small team, led by Samanta, its first employee, took a flight—the very first in Bandhan's history. That was in June 2006. Before that, in 2005, Bandhan had only expanded to North Bengal.

At a meeting of regional managers at its headquarters, Ghosh asked them to raise their hands if they were willing to steer Bandhan's expansion in North Bengal. They all raised their hands but Ghosh chose divisional manager Satyajit Ghosh for the job—he had not participated in the exercise as he was not a regional manager. His colleague Swapan Saha accompanied Satyajit.

In June, when they stepped out of the Siliguri station, the first thing that attracted their attention was huge hoardings of chit funds, promising high returns. Swapan opened six branches in Siliguri, and Satyajit seven in Cooch Behar, all within a fortnight.

In 2008, Satyajit was asked to go to Delhi to set up Bandhan branches. That was his second visit to Delhi. For three days, he stayed at a hotel in Paharganj, close to New Delhi Railway Station, at a rent of Rs 3500 per day. On the fourth day, he moved to Sultanpuri in west Delhi, and opened sixteen branches there in two months.

On his very first day, Satyajit bought a map of Delhi and began familiarizing himself with the city. The language was a big problem for him. When he rented a house, it was not easy for him to buy a cot and a mattress as he could not explain in Hindi what he wanted. Somehow, he managed the word *gaddi*, and bought a cot at Panditji Timber at Mangolpuri, in north-west Delhi. Food was also a big problem as he was used to eating rice, sometimes even thrice a day, starting with breakfast. He had to change his food habits drastically.

Language, however, was never a problem for Runa Parven when she was sent to Delhi in 2009 as a divisional manager to look after the seventy-eight Bandhan branches spread across Delhi, Uttar Pradesh, Haryana and Uttarakhand. Later, she was posted in Mumbai and Patna too.

Parven was well versed in Sanskrit, and could read and write Hindi with some effort. For Marathi, she took the help of local employees, wrote down numbers in a notebook to check bus numbers, and watched TV whenever she could.

Satyajit used to travel in buses—from Delhi to Pilibhit, Dehradun and Nainital in search of locations to open branches.

Ghosh typically used to pick people for expansion activities outside West Bengal at meetings where he would ask them to raise their hands if they were game for some adventure. He followed the same formula in 2008 when he planned to expand in Mumbai, Delhi and Patna. Satyajit was chosen for Delhi, Samanta for Patna, and Pritish Saha for Mumbai.

The next afternoon, Saha was at the Howrah station along with another colleague, Sujit Biswas, to catch the Gitanjali Express to Mumbai, carrying Rs 20,000 in his pocket. They deboarded at Dadar, hailed a taxi and asked the driver to take them to a cheap hotel. The first hotel they were taken to was charging Rs 3500; after a long search, they settled for a guest house in Sion at Rs 800 per room.

It was booked for ten days, but Saha ended up spending fifty days in Mumbai. Those days, Bandhan employees' salaries were not credited to their bank accounts; one would need to come to the office to claim the salary. This meant that when one was out for months, one could not get the salary.

That was Saha's first visit to Mumbai. He used to walk around, get a feel of the place, and look for ideal sites to open Bandhan branches. The first location he identified was at Chembur, and then Vikhroli, Sion, Kalyan, Thane, Dombivli and Saki Naka. Overall, fifteen areas were identified.

Once the first twelve branches were identified, twelve employees were ferried from Kolkata to Mumbai to run the show. All of them moved into a place in Thane where a branch was in the making. Lunch was being cooked, and just as they were getting ready to eat, the landlord walked in with two police constables in tow, and threw them out as he suspected that they were running a militant outfit.

The entire contingent had to move out, leaving the food behind. They shifted to Everard Nagar, Sion East, near Somaiya Hospital, where another house had been taken up that morning for the purpose of opening a new branch.

In October 2008, Kalyan Das took a train to Bihar to replace Samanta who had already spent three months doing the groundwork. Danapur Express used to leave Howrah at 8.35 p.m. and reach Patna at 7.15 a.m. the following day. He tried to pick up as much Hindi as he could while on the train, but was still at sea at the Patna station as he realized that most people were speaking Bhojpuri.

The summer heat was a problem; he also missed his favourite fish curry. Das used to ask his parents to deposit money in his bank account so that he could withdraw it from ATMs when he needed to.

'First, we would identify a house that could be turned into a branch, check the locality, pay an advance and open the office. That was our formula,' he told me. Of course, prior to that would be an extensive survey of the locality, based on the financial needs of the people there.

Sudhanya Nopti, who is now part of Bandhan's insurance unit, explained his formula of an ideal branch location. 'Always start at a crowded place. Look at shanties, markets . . . strike conversations with women. It could even be a tube well or a municipality water tap where women have gathered to fetch water.'

From Non-profit to For-profit

Bandhan could not have grown had it remained a non-profit organization. Ghosh's theory has all along been that an MFI needs to scale up and approach the entire philosophy of bringing in change in society by making money available to those at the so-called bottom of the pyramid as business, and not as charity.

There were other issues as well. Bankers were comfortable giving loans to Bandhan as it had negligible bad assets (never more than twenty basis points or 0.20 per cent of the loan portfolio) and also had close monitoring, and systems and processes in place. However, they had reservations about increasing their exposure to Bandhan since they felt that, as an NGO, Bandhan was not required to maintain adequate capital and it was not a regulated entity. They were constantly insisting on its conversion into a company registered with RBI.

Capital is an important factor for the growth of any business. In the form of an NGO or a society, there were only two sources of capital for Bandhan: grants and internal accrual. Capital in the form of a grant was difficult to manage, particularly when the figures ran into crores, since regulation does not allow paying back the money invested. Society regulations also ban the distribution of dividend to the providers of capital. Under these circumstances, the only way for Bandhan to attract investors and fuel growth was by turning into a for-profit company.

The first step towards this was the acquisition of an existing RBI-registered NBFC in April 2006, as previously mentioned. While Bandhan-Konnagar remained as a society and continued to give small loans in West Bengal, the newly acquired NBFC, rechristened BFSPL, entered Tripura in June 2006, and expanded to neighbouring states in the north-east. For two years, 2007–08 and 2008–09, parallel operations were on. All new employees were on the payroll of BFSPL, and the culture, values and ethics were the same across the group.

The challenge lay in converting the society into an NBFC. Bandhan-Konnagar, as a microcredit organization, never focused exclusively on the financial requirement of its borrowers. Its approach was holistic: credit plus health and education. It was decided that the microfinance activities of the society would be transferred to the NBFC, even as the rest of the developmental activities remained with Bandhan-Konnagar.

As a policy it was fine, but how would one transfer the capital fund of Bandhan-Konnagar—generated through microfinance activities over years—into the NBFC? If Bandhan-Konnagar invested in BFSPL, it would end up exercising direct control over the company. However, the law of the land does not allow an NGO registered under the Societies Registration Act to hold shares in a company. Ghosh did not want to lose his control over the company at that point. So Bandhan-Konnagar was made settler of the trust called Financial Inclusion Trust, which was instrumental in retaining indirect control over the NBFC.

V. Nagarajan of V. Nagarajan & Co., a renowned chartered accountant who specializes in transforming NGO microfinance entities into for-profit NBFC MFIs, created the structure. He has been associated with MFIs since the 1990s, when NABARD started the concept of self-help groups or SHGs, inspired by the Grameen model of Bangladesh. Abhijit Ghosh and Arpita Sen, two of Ghosh's trusted executives, had spent hours in discussions at Nagarajan's house at Palam Vihar, Gurgaon, over lunches and dinners.

Out of such discussions, the idea of forming a public charitable trust emerged. Bandhan-Konnagar, in the capacity of settler, formed a trust for the benefit of the public at large. It became the beneficiary.

The thought behind forming this trust was to invest the trust property in the for-profit company and generate dividend income, which would be utilized for the benefit of society in various fields of development, especially education. Once the trust was formed, Bandhan-Konnagar donated a part of its capital fund to it.

It was also decided that BFSPL would donate 5 per cent of its profit every year to Bandhan-Konnagar to carry on its CSR activities. This happened many years before the new company law in India made it mandatory for corporations to spend money on CSR activities.

From April 2014, every company, private or public, which either has a net worth of Rs 500 crore or a turnover of Rs 1000 crore or a net profit of Rs 5 crore, needs to spend at least 2 per cent of its average net profit for the immediately preceding three financial years on CSR. Bandhan had framed the rule of 5 per cent spending on CSR for itself five years before this came into effect.

In April 2009, the trust invested the funds it received from Bandhan-Konnagar in the equity capital of the NBFC and, at the same time, Bandhan-Konnagar transferred its microfinance assets and liabilities to the NBFC directly. That's how the journey of Bandhan in its NBFC avatar began.

There were two trusts for the infusion of the capital fund: Bandhan-Konnagar Financial Inclusion Trust and North East Financial Inclusion Trust. Neither of these trusts took

any money from Bandhan's borrowers or the public at large.
Also, the Bandhan Employees' Welfare Trust was created out
of the bonuses that Bandhan gave to them.

Nagarajan has been involved in the transformation of
almost all trusts into NBFCs in the microfinance space. 'Each
case is different; you need to be innovative,' he says.

For instance, in the case of Mahajan's BSFL, soft loans
given to the holding company by Ford Foundation and
Swiss Agency for Development and Corporation (SDC)
were converted into equity as the promoters did not have
the money. In SKS Microfinance, the trust gave loans
to its members and they used the money to invest in the
NBFC.

Under the Indian Trusts Act 1882, there are two types of
trusts: charitable trusts and private trusts. The mutual benefit
trusts (MBTs) are a subset of charitable trusts. The Bandhan
model was different; it had accumulated a surplus (for a non-
profit organization, profit is called 'surplus') of around Rs 50
crore at that time.

Yogesh Chandra Nanda, former chairman of NABARD,
never met the Bandhan founder during his tenure there. Later,
in the summer of 2008, Ghosh came to Nanda's residence in
Gurgaon and requested him to be a trustee of the Financial
Inclusion Trust which would later invest in BFSPL. That
day, both went to Nagarajan's office and, once the formal
paperwork for the formation of the NBFC was done, they
had lunch at a Chinese restaurant.

Later, Nanda came to know that the trust deed mentioned
that he would be the first chairman of the trust and the tenure
would be five years. 'Ghosh did not even mention this to me,'

Nanda said. Other trustees were Vijayalakshmi Das (promoter and managing director of Ahmedabad-based Ananya Finance for Inclusive Growth Pvt. Ltd, which supports socially responsible enterprises; she is now the CEO of FWWB), and Jayanta Choudhury (now an assistant professor, department of rural development, Tripura University).

Networking Remote Branches

As Bandhan grew, the need to computerize its operations was increasingly felt, particularly when the industry started creating a credit bureau to keep a tab on multiple loans given by the MFIs in certain states. Ronti Kar has been the architect of the home-grown technology platform.

Ronti got to know Ghosh even before Bandhan was born, in 2001, when he was working as a consultant for a start-up called Syscon Solutions, which had its office in Salt Lake City, close to Bandhan's office. Ronti's colleague Anup Kumar Mondal introduced him to Ghosh. In 2003, Ronti left that office to join Cognizant Technology Solutions, but occasionally he would get a call from Ghosh seeking solutions to technical problems.

In 2007, 'Shekhar da' called Ronti to his office. He wanted to build a computerized system to run his business (at that time Bandhan had 318 branches and 4,49,304 borrowers). He asked Ronti if he could help him develop a solution quickly, as the lending banks were insisting on automation. Ronti was ready to lead a team to develop a simple web-based solution to start with, provided connectivity was ensured.

Ghosh promised connectivity, without taking into consideration the pathetic state of infrastructure in remote villages where many of the Bandhan branches were located. Ronti recruited two graduates (one of whom, Sudip Mahapatra, is still with Bandhan) and started the work, but he soon discovered that poor connectivity in the remote areas would not support this kind of solution.

Knowing well that building a disconnected solution and synchronizing the data would be too complicated, Ronti had his concerns. To address that, Ghosh got in touch with technological experts in Bangladesh who were involved in building the microfinance solution for BRAC. They promised to customize their product in sync with Bandhan's need in no time.

This was done, but in October 2008, Ghosh called Ronti again as the system was not working. At that point, Ronti decided to develop a software application with the help of some of his colleagues and even appoint a couple of people for its maintenance. He explained to Ghosh the commercial aspects and, after getting a go-ahead, started designing a solution which would work both offline and online. At the same time, the framework would have to be flexible enough to accommodate requirements in the future.

That was the most challenging part of the entire project. Besides, the cost would have to be low. That's how Micro-Finance Solution (MFSol) was born.

Ronti was doing this while working for Cognizant. Naturally, the pace was slow as he could work only after office hours and over the weekends. In October 2009, Ghosh called Ronti home and asked him to join Bandhan as the head of its IT department.

It was not easy to leave the security of a corporate job to join a start-up, but at the same time, Ronti was tempted to head its IT division. He asked for a 75 per cent pay hike and a package for developing the application framework. Ghosh, a hard negotiator, convinced him to join at a 40 per cent pay hike. By that time, Ghosh's younger brother, Dibakar (whom Ronti knew well), had come back to India from Canada, and joined Bandhan. He is a computer engineer with knowledge of software development and skills in networking and hardware.

Ronti joined Bandhan in December 2009 with an understanding that the software application would be ready in the next six months. It was a difficult task as there was no proper local area network (LAN) that enabled a group of computers to share a common communications line. Also, not all branches had computers. The credit officers who used to collect loan instalments from the borrowers hardly had any exposure to computers.

Getting approval for buying something was next to impossible in Bandhan those days. 'The most important thing I learnt in Bandhan was that before asking for anything, try to best utilize whatever you have. And that, I realized later, was one of the key factors behind its success,' Ronti told me.

Dibakar, Ronti and his BTech batchmate, Shyamlal Madhu, who started his career in Tata Consultancy Services, started work in a room at AB 48, Sector I, Salt Lake City, Kolkata, where Ghosh used to sit till he moved to a new office at EC 76. Outside the room, there was an IT team of eight people; most were operations guys trained to do IT support. Madhu is still with Bandhan, 'married to IT'.

Bachelor Madhu, in his late forties, does not carry a mobile phone. He is the first to reach office at 7.20 a.m. every day. Every year in April, during his performance appraisal, Ghosh tells him to get married if he wants a raise; 2016 was no exception.

About 100 branches then had computers and those branches were called Bandhan Data Conversion Centres (BDCCs), handled by specialized data-entry operators—IT credit officers (IT-COs). Employees of other branches would come to these centres with manual registers for data entry.

From these BDCCs, they used to export data on CDs to the headquarters. There, the IT support team would consolidate the data, correct it (there were many mistakes) and prepare reports every month to meet internal needs and provide data to the regulators.

Ronti realized that the conventional screen design would not work; the field employees would need a screen that looked like their registers. Apart from developing the new application, there was another big task—migration of the data from the existing system. The old system was developed in an unstructured manner, without following any design rules and, because of this, the data was inconsistent.

While Ronti was handling the technical part with help from Dibakar, a team led by Kalyan Kundu helped him implement it. Saibal Gon, Mrityunjoy Mondal, Biswanath Dey and Pritam Mondal were in Kalyan's team, looking after four zones.

On 14 May 2010, MFSol was launched. The first demo was given to a group of thirty IT-COs for their feedback. It caused quite a flutter among them as they had not seen this kind of application before. By July 2010, all branches migrated to the new system. However, the manual system still continued. Data entry for an entire day's work used to take forty minutes in MFSol.

The next challenge was building an automated system for consolidating the data of each branch that used to come through a file transfer protocol (FTP) server on a weekly basis. Every Saturday, data captured in the local system at the branch level was sent as a data file to the data centre at the headquarters, using data cards. The system that was initially built appeared to be very slow once the data volume started growing. So, Ronti had to redesign the architecture to bring down the consolidation time.

Only after feeling confident about the new system did Ghosh provide computers to each branch, by February 2011. There was intense debate on whether the branches should have desktops or laptops. Ronti was in favour of giving laptops to the field employees because of severe power shortage, but Ghosh ruled that out saying laptops would be prone to theft and the staff might mishandle them.

Training the branch managers and credit officers in the use of the software was not an easy task. It was done at Bandhan's training centre at Rajpur, a southern neighbourhood of Kolkata. Most were reluctant to touch the computers; they were afraid that they might mess things up. At the same time, the IT-savvy employees who were doing the data-entry job thought that they might lose their jobs if others were trained.

Lifting the Mouse in the Air

There were instances when the branch employees were directed over the phone, from the headquarters, to move the mouse up, and they lifted the mouse in the air. Once, when a support officer asked one user who was facing some problem in entering data to clear the screen (there was a 'clear' button which he had to click), the user cleaned the monitor with a wet cloth. Many would also keep the computer inside the cupboard and lock it before leaving the office.

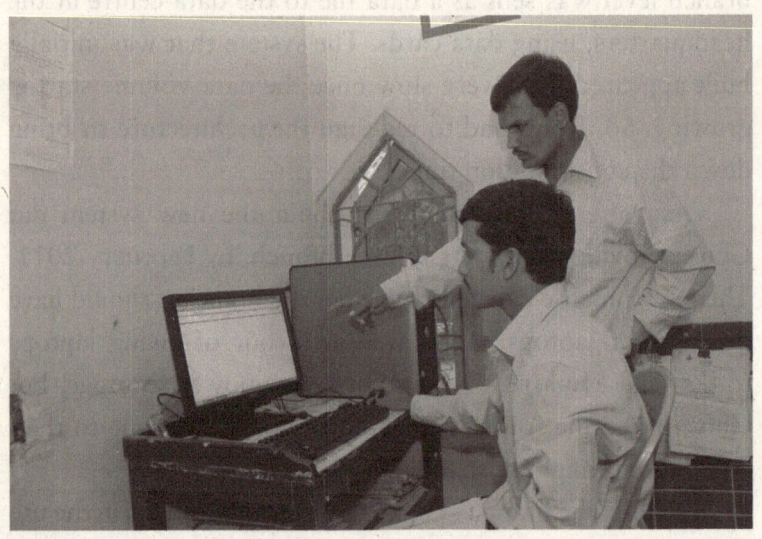

NO EASY TASK: Most credit officers were reluctant to touch the computers; they were afraid that they would mess things up.

The software had to be tweaked again in March 2011. A committee headed by noted chartered accountant Y.H. Malegam—set up after the Andhra Pradesh crisis that led to a law that severely restricted MFI activities in the state—recommended that interest must be charged on reducing balance of such loans instead of a flat interest rate.

Till that time, Bandhan was charging a flat interest rate. It was fairly simple: every borrower had to pay a fixed number of weekly instalments. It did not matter whether she was paying early or late. For example, for a loan of Rs 10,000, on a flat interest of 10 per cent, a borrower had to pay forty-four weekly instalments of Rs 250 each (which comes to Rs 11,000, i.e. principal + interest). It didn't matter whether she was repaying in thirty weeks or sixty; she had to pay forty-four instalments. But when the rules changed, interest was charged on decreasing balance. So, in the first month, it was charged on Rs 10,000; in the second month, it was charged on Rs 9750, and so on.

When this rule was brought in, the software had to be changed. Ghosh gave Ronti's team three months for this job. By that time, the then finance minister, Pranab Mukherjee, had already announced that the banking regulator would give licences to private banks for financial inclusion. Even though the guidelines were not ready, Ghosh knew that if Bandhan wanted to transform itself into a bank, it would not happen without the right technology.

The IT department was the first to move into Bandhan's new headquarters at DN 32, Sector VI, Salt Lake City, even before the building was ready. It occupied the fifth floor. For six months, there was no elevator and only the server room had air conditioning.

Initially, the users of MFSol were taking their own time to send in the data, and unless all the data was in, it was not possible to consolidate it and produce the MIS reports for the entire organization. (MIS, or management information system, broadly refers to a computer-based system that provides managers with the tools to organize, evaluate and efficiently manage departments within an organization.) Although almost 90 per cent of the branches were sending the data on time, there were problems with the rest since, in many places, there was no electricity for days.

Also, the data cards did not always work properly. The staff of some of the branches had to travel 30 km to the nearest cyber café to send the data. Then, there were instances of hard disks crashing owing to virus attacks.

An exasperated Ghosh gave Ronti a firm deadline and bluntly told everyone that he was losing his patience and would not wait beyond 30 May 2011 for the MIS. To make it happen, the IT team had to live in the office for a month. Anybody walking into the department before 9 a.m., when the working hours began, would find *gamchha*s, or thin towels, hanging there, and mats and pillows on tables, while the floor of the toilet would be wet as somebody would have just finished his bath.

By 5 June 2011, all data for the month ended May 30 was received, and things started stabilizing. The balance sheet for the fiscal year 2011 was drawn out of the manual data as the system had not been stabilized till then. From 2012, the balance sheet was prepared out of the MFSol data.

By July 2011, the Bandhan data centre had six servers. Data at the branches was still entered offline, and was sent weekly and monthly to the servers using FTP, but the old system of getting the data at the headquarters in hard copies and entering them in Excel sheets to get the MIS reports was stopped. The data flowed to the centralized server database without any manual intervention.

The Proof of the Pudding

The proof of the pudding lies in the eating. Bandhan could claim to have changed the lives of millions of people, but how would one check the veracity of such a claim? In 2010, Bandhan approached Indian Institute of Management Ahmedabad (IIM-A) for an impact study of its microfinance activities and related development programmes on the lives of the underprivileged. The study was led by Prof. Samar Kumar Datta.

Random samples were taken from five carefully selected, representative clusters in West Bengal, out of 1050 households.

One finding of the report was a reasonably high level of customer awareness on the terms and conditions of loans and interest rates, indicating that information was being disseminated to the borrowers in a transparent manner.

More importantly, it was found that the average annual net income of a household from all sources increased by Rs 13,231, representing a 13.81 per cent rise. This rise in income did not come at the cost of increased risk exposure for households, as measured by fluctuation of monthly income over the past three years.

The borrowers' families increased their ownership of non-farm business assets by Rs 15,588 on average, and could also generate, on average, 35.82 man days per annum of full-time employment for family members.

Another study, carried out by Prof. Abhijit Banerjee and Prof. Esther Duflo of the Massachusetts Institute of Technology, on Bandhan's CSR programme for the poor—Targeting the Hard Core Poor Programme—in Murshidabad,

West Bengal, found a 15 per cent increase in household consumption, and positive impacts on other measures of household wealth and welfare, such as assets and emotional well-being. Here, the sample size was 1000 ultra-poor households.

Bandhan was a success story. Down south, SKS Microfinance and other microlenders were doing even better. But their dream was to be shattered. How would Bandhan remain unscathed?

4

How to Jump the Humps, Move Past the Roadblocks

In October 2010, forty-eight hours after the Andhra Pradesh government promulgated the ordinance which nearly killed the microfinance industry, the then West Bengal finance minister, Asim Dasgupta, called an emergency meeting at Writers' Building, the state secretariat, to take stock of the situation and the impact of the Andhra law in the eastern state.

Dasgupta was worried. He had heard stories about the alleged coercive collection practices of MFIs that had led to many suicides in Andhra Pradesh.

Bandhan was quite big by that time. It had 1050 branches across fifteen Indian states even as around 50 per cent of its operations were in West Bengal and 70 per cent in eastern India. It had 2.5 million borrowers served by 6765 employees, and a loan book of close to Rs 1500 crore. By that time,

SIDBI had already picked up an equity stake in Bandhan, infusing Rs 50 crore—its largest investment in the MFI sector. Naturally, Ghosh was under tremendous pressure. Had Dasgupta decided to go the AP way, it would have been the death knell for Bandhan.

The meeting was attended by Rekha Goswami, minister for self-help group and self-employment; finance secretary C.M. Bachhawat; senior executives of RBI, NABARD and SIDBI in West Bengal; Ashok Kumar Das, managing director of West Bengal Infrastructure Development Corporation Ltd; and Narayan Chandra, then director, economic offence cell, finance department (who would later join Bandhan), among others.

Goswami had reservations about the high interest rates charged by the MFIs in West Bengal, but others briefed Dasgupta that the ground realities in West Bengal were not comparable with those of Andhra Pradesh. The MFI growth in the state was relatively slower and there were no multiple lendings—the root cause of the AP crisis. They showed statistics to strengthen their case.

By the time the three-hour meeting got over, both Dasgupta and Ghosh were relaxed—for different reasons, though. Dasgupta was convinced that there would not be any political fallout as MFI borrowers were not over-indebted in West Bengal, and Ghosh, who was not present at the meeting but was briefed about it, heaved a sigh of relief that it would be business as usual for Bandhan.

Five days after the Andhra Pradesh law was promulgated, on 15 October 2010, then finance minister Mukherjee inaugurated Bandhan's 1551st branch at Kirnahar, in the Bolpur subdivision of Birbhum district in West Bengal. That sent a strong signal to the outside world that everything was well with Bandhan.

THE MASTER STROKE: Five days after the Andhra Pradesh law was promulgated, then finance minister Pranab Mukherjee inaugurated Bandhan's 1551st branch at Kirnahar, in the Bolpur subdivision of Birbhum district in West Bengal.

Ghosh could isolate Bandhan from the AP crisis as it did not have any presence in the southern state, or, for that matter, anywhere else in south India; but it was not easy to avoid the ripple effect. He knew that banks would soon clamp down on giving loans to MFIs, and if the source of money dried up, Bandhan would not be able to give fresh loans.

The borrowers of MFIs need money continuously, otherwise they cannot grow their businesses; any disruption kills their business and the ability to pay back, and default rises. Bandhan had a Rs 400-crore sanction from IDBI Bank at that time. In normal circumstances, it would have drawn the money later when the demand for loans picked up.

But Ghosh did not want to lose time; he lifted the money overnight, along with another Rs 110 crore from other banks, even if that meant booking losses as Bandhan had to keep the money with another bank in the form of a fixed deposit, the returns from which were less than what it had to pay to the lenders.

It also used the crisis to put the brakes on its fast and furious growth, and consolidate. The senior team was told not to add any new branches and customers. Even when the existing customers were looking for new loans after clearing the existing loan, there was close scrutiny and, in the process, the sanctions were deferred. The idea was to keep Bandhan liquid, as banks had started recalling loans from other MFIs.

Those days, all MFIs operating in West Bengal used to meet every Saturday at 2 p.m. at the Bandhan office to exchange information and take stock of the situation. At those meetings, they decided not to adopt any coercive practice for loan collection, even if that meant a rise in defaults; to avoid conflict with the borrowers at any cost; and to have no interaction with the borrowers in the evenings.

That was the biggest crisis the Indian microfinance industry has ever faced, but there have been many minor hurdles that Bandhan has experienced which have not been reported by the media. Most of them were local in nature, but had they not been handled with care, they could have blown up the organization.

Fighting the Chit Funds

The most critical issue that Bandhan had to tackle in its early days was the mushrooming of chit funds and collective investment schemes (CIS) through which hundreds of big, medium and small companies used to raise money from the public in West Bengal and other eastern states, offering very high returns. Many of these companies had employed the agents of Peerless,[9] which pioneered the technique of collection of small savings in this part of the country. RBI forced Peerless to stop taking public deposits in 2006, and that might have spawned the growth of unregulated deposit-taking companies in West Bengal and other eastern states.

As an MFI, Bandhan was in the business of giving money and not taking deposits, but it was not easy to convince people that the borrowers had nothing to lose; it was Bandhan which was taking the risk as it would not get back its money if the borrowers defaulted. Almost everywhere, it had to fight the shadow of chit funds and the might of moneylenders. And of course, getting the right kind of people with skills was always a big issue.

Bandhan's 2005 annual report talks about some of the stumbling blocks:

- Lack of skilled staff at the field level: Since MFI was a relatively new entity in West Bengal, it was extremely difficult to get staff; they could not be brought from other states as language would be an issue.
- Lack of awareness of the public about MFIs: Often, Bandhan employees were mistaken for moneylenders. This is why borrowers were reluctant to take loans; in fact, when they were approached, they were not elated—they were petrified.
- Expectations of cheap loans: The poor borrowers would always expect to get the loans at subsidized rates. This is

---

[9] As stated earlier, Peerless was a residuary non-banking company, like Sahara India Financial Corporation Ltd, which used to raise money from the public and invest in RBI-mandated instruments.

because of various government schemes. It was difficult to convince them that small loans are always more expensive because of higher operational costs and risks, since they are not backed by securities or collateral.

- Opening bank accounts: Bandhan also had to open bank accounts for smooth transaction of funds required for operations at the branch level, but banks were not willing to open accounts.

Of course, there had been sporadic cases of defaults and, if not tackled properly, they could have spread and created a big hole in Bandhan's balance sheet.

Bandhan's first crisis broke out in 2005 at Payradanga, Nadia, where some of its borrowers had sold the land and property of another Bandhan borrower who had taken money from them as well. Local politicians stepped in and the news spread far and wide, painting Bandhan as the villain. The employees were even hauled to the Ranaghat police station.

Pritish Saha, now a zonal head at Bandhan Bank's microloan unit, rushed to the police station, and Satyajit Ghosh, another zonal head, was in touch with Ghosh through the night, briefing him every half an hour, using a Siemens mobile phone with an antenna, which the Bandhan boss had gifted him a few months back. All the TV channels in West Bengal were reporting it from the field, describing Bandhan as a chit fund. Satyajit managed to get his colleagues out of the police station the following morning, and appeared on TV channels to tell the real story.

Kalyan Das, another old employee, remembers a default case in Bagnan in 2004. Overnight, the team was changed, new employees were brought in, and field visits intensified. The new team worked for one year at Bagnan, and recovered the bulk of the money.

Criminal Infiltration

Das also recollects a problem at Bhadohi, the carpet city of Uttar Pradesh, which was an epicentre of rising defaults in 2009. A team of six on motorcycles was sent for counselling and collection even as criminals infiltrated the Bihar operations around the same time. Arun Kumar, the branch manager of Bihar Sharif, misappropriated Rs 9,33,000.

At Sitamarhi, another branch manager, Vinod Kumar, ran away with Rs 6 lakh.

There was fraud at the branches of Siwan district where people from one particular village were managing operations at nine branches. They ganged up and took the organization for a ride. FIRs were lodged and six of them were arrested. They could not get bail for two and a half months. Once they were out on bail, all six of them were dismissed from work.

There was action, and punishment was meted out to the culprits promptly. This was combined with intense counselling and training to bring back normalcy. Bad loans, which rose to 2 per cent, dropped to 0.2 per cent, or only twenty basis points, in the loan book in Bihar by 2011.

Law and order problems are typically managed by two gentlemen in Bandhan: Narayan Chandra, former IG of West Bengal, who was also director, economic offence wing, in the finance department of West Bengal, and Sanjit Mallick, former deputy superintendent of police, North 24

Parganas. Mallick joined in June 2006 and was an adviser when Bandhan turned into an NBFC. Narayan Chandra, currently the chief vigilance officer of the bank, joined in July 2011. As director of the economic offence wing, he was looking into tax evasion, and also authored a report on chit funds.

Both of them recollect many incidents of trouble. For instance, at Rampurhat, Birbhum, in 2007, a credit officer was beaten up by moneylenders. The initiative to free him was taken by the borrowers of Bandhan who surrounded the police station.

The local administration of Rampurhat, the superintendent of police and subdivisional officer, and even the district magistrate of Birbhum, were all under the impression that Bandhan was a chit fund. Only when it was explained to them that Bandhan was not collecting deposits and, in fact, it had given Rs 3 crore in loans, Balvir Singh, divisional commissioner of six districts—Bardhaman, Hooghly, Birbhum, Purulia, Bankura, East Midnapore and West Midnapore—arranged a meeting of district magistrates and assured all help.

Similarly, in 2008, when Bandhan employees were roughed up in South Dinajpur, the district magistrate asked what Bandhan was. By that time, Bandhan had already featured in the *Forbes* list as the world's second-largest MFI.

Narayan Chandra remembers many incidents of fraud in different parts of Odisha; Surat in Gujarat; Raiganj in North Dinajpur; and also Siliguri in West Bengal. After joining Bandhan, he started employing retired police officers in all troubled pockets. Barring stray incidents such as what happened in East Midnapore, he did not see much of a political interference, but there had always been pressure for donations (which, in Bengali, is known as *chandar julum*).

Considering the size of Bandhan, the incidents of fraud have not been too many and, in most cases, there has been early detection and settlement because of a bunch of dedicated employees and even borrowers. There have been stray cases where credit officers, after collecting weekly instalments from the borrowers, went home with the money instead of returning to the office. Many times, branch managers reached the homes of the credit officers before they could run away with the money, as borrowers alerted the branch office after they noticed the credit officers cycling on a different path back.

Income Tax Raid

Bandhan, one of the biggest taxpayers in Kolkata, also had to face the nightmare of an income tax raid. One fine morning in March 2013, police officers surrounded the Bandhan headquarters. It was a search operation by the income tax authorities. They had come to investigate the taxable status of Bandhan-Konnagar, the group's CSR arm, as they claimed that Bandhan-Konnagar had never filed its income tax return.

Bandhan-Konnagar was housed in the same premise as BFSL, the group holding company. The income tax officers were looking for unaccounted cash on the office premises, carrying sacks and ropes along with them to carry the cash back to their office. But there was nothing to carry as the cash lying in the office tallied with the books of accounts of BFSL.

The income tax officers had conducted searches at the premises of five other companies before trooping down to the Bandhan office that day—all were popular chit funds in West Bengal. There were parallel raids at the Bandhan headquarters, a few other Bandhan offices, including its training centre at Rajpur, and the residence of its chairman and managing director, Ghosh, that morning.

The contention of the income tax officials was that the activities of Bandhan-Konnagar were not charitable in nature, and it should not get any tax benefit. It took two years for the income tax authority to uphold the charitable status of Bandhan-Konnagar and give the group a clean chit.

Separation from ASA

The separation from ASA has also not been a happy story. By 2007, when Bandhan was going great guns, ASA wanted to take over Bandhan. It wanted to own 75 per cent of Bandhan, asking Ghosh to keep the rest.

When Ghosh did not agree to the proposal, ASA started its operations in West Bengal by buying out Dilkusha Hire Purchase Pvt. Ltd, a Jalandhar-based NBFC.

To run it, ASA started offering jobs to senior Bandhan employees. The first to leave Bandhan was its director of administration, Kalyan Mitra. He was made the CEO of ASA India. An upset Ghosh told ASA to decide whether it wanted to continue raiding Bandhan, and if the answer was in the affirmative, the organization should quickly decide on which employees to tap. He also promised to release those employees within twenty-four hours.

Ghosh had also said that he was grateful to ASA for the technical support, but if Bandhan collapsed, ASA would have to take the blame. That stopped the raid. Ghosh even had a frank chat with Runu da (the second in command in Bandhan), who was wooed by ASA to make up his mind on whether he would like to put in his papers and join that organization.

Sushil Roy, who had been instrumental in forging the technical support agreement with Bandhan, was the COO of ASA International at that time. He stayed away from this deal to avoid any conflict of interest.

By that time, Bandhan had built tens of thousands of skilled staff and did not need any assistance from ASA. Though the institutional relationship between ASA and Bandhan has snapped, there is no lack of warmth between the employees. A framed photograph of the ASA founder, Choudhury, still adorns Ghosh's corner office at Bandhan. In earlier days, the framed photograph used to be on Ghosh's table.

Love Your Borrower

There had been incidents of Bandhan employees falling in love with borrowers and their daughters, though not too many.

In 2006, there was a crisis at Jalpaiguri, North Bengal. A branch manager, one Biswas, allegedly molested a woman borrower, the wife of a leader of the Kamtapur Liberation Organization (KLO), a militant organization based in North Bengal and Assam, whose objective is to carve out a separate Kamtapur state. The KLO would settle for nothing short of Biswas's head.

With the help of the local panchayat chief, Dilip Barman, a meeting was arranged at the borrower's house, with an implicit understanding that Biswas would get a mild thrashing. It was a big risk to take as nobody was sure what the KLO would do, but the gamble paid off. After a few tense moments, a settlement was reached—the borrower's outstanding loan of Rs 5000 was waived off, and Biswas, besides being slapped repeatedly, was fined Rs 5000.

He was transferred overnight to Manikchak, Malda, and an internal inquiry was initiated. But even before the inquiry could be completed, Biswas, a married man with a child, eloped with the daughter of the cook of the residential branch where he was staying.

There had been conflicts with self-help groups too, developed by local administrations in different parts of West Bengal, even though it was not as big a movement as Andhra Pradesh had witnessed. In Dinhata, Cooch Behar, when many borrowers broke away from SHGs to join the Bandhan fold, the Dinhata municipality chairman issued a diktat to stop this.

The district collector, Kamal Kanti Banerjee, also tried to stop it. He called Bandhan a chit fund which was giving loans at that time, but would raise deposits later. By that time, Rs 25 lakh had already been disbursed.

A local primary school teacher, Dilip Chowdhury, who used to run a bookstore, Chowdhury Library, explained to the local administration that Bandhan was there to give loans and not collect deposits.

In the Mathabhanga subdivision of Cooch Behar district, the wife of a local CPI(M) leader was a borrower but she never came for the weekly meetings, although she would pay her instalments. When she was repeatedly marked 'A' (meaning 'absent') on her passbook, the party got upset. Its student wing, Students' Federation of India (SFI), took out an anti-Bandhan morcha, and a local politician, who was also a minister in the state, asked Bandhan to down its shutters as it was scaring poor people who could never pay back the money they were taking.

Almost all incidents were local in nature and none of them spread or affected Bandhan's operations in a big way. This was primarily because of the training of its employees. They were taught how to tackle the troublemakers—be they politicians, moneylenders or local dadas—sweet-talk them, respect them and build relationships with them. A panchayat member would always be greeted with a namaskar.

The troublemakers would often come and provoke Bandhan employees, but the latter never argued, challenged or tried to establish Bandhan's superiority over the moneylenders.

Collecting and carrying cash had also not been easy. There were attacks on Bandhan employees, and money was stolen—but such incidents were few. Typically, the borrowers' meetings took place at a fixed time every week at the same venue, and the employees took the same route to go back to the office carrying the weekly repayments. It would have been fairly easy to track them and steal the cash.

The employees were taught how to carry cash on different parts of their body, including socks. Women employees stitched pockets to their petticoats. They changed routes, and if they sensed danger, the borrowers accompanied them. They tried every trick to keep the money safe, but they were told not to risk their lives. In Bandhan's history two employees lost their lives and a few got injured while trying to stall a theft. The organization paid compensation to the deceased persons' families and took care of the treatment of the injured.

How to Keep Trade Unions at Bay

Bandhan could also be a case study on how to keep trade unions at bay. It had 14,500 employees as an MFI, and they were not unionized. This is significant, particularly because the bulk of its operations have been in West Bengal, a state known for its militant trade unionism until recently.

Efforts to prevent union formation include identifying the potential troublemakers, seeing to it that they don't get together on a regular basis, isolating them, and even resorting to transfers; in the latter case, in several instances, the transferred employee has quit. At the same time, the non-performers are also continuously counselled and motivated by their seniors to do better.

Another deterrent factor was the incentives given to the employees to be a part of the institution by investing in its equity shares at par value. This option was open till December 2009, when SIDBI invested in Bandhan at a premium of Rs 50. A large segment of the employees has invested in the company through the Bandhan Employees' Welfare Trust.

The ultimate reason behind the employees not forming unions is that Bandhan has changed their lives. In the bleak employment scenario of West Bengal and other eastern states, they would not have got jobs had Bandhan not been there.

The employees also have a unique way of managing the quality of assets. Generally, unless it is a case of fraud, the defaulters are not confronted; Bandhan does not ask for money. The employees counsel the borrowers, engage them in conversation, praise their children and talk about everything under the sun but the repayment of the loan instalments. They exude empathy for them, and their storytelling has a cathartic effect on the borrower. At the end of it, the borrower either puts the money in the credit officer's pocket or arranges to pay for it in the next few days.

Debasish Mandal, one of the early employees of Bandhan, narrated the story of Halima Begum of North Bengal. Halima took Rs 3000 but could not repay. She stopped attending the group meetings; one would not even find her at home during the day. Once, Mandal stayed put at her home from 11 a.m. to 6 p.m., but she did not return. Her two children had to starve because there was no food at home. Mandal took them to the branch office, offered his lunch to them and dropped them back home.

That night, somebody knocked at the branch office door. Mandal was too scared to open it till he heard Halima's voice. Accompanied by her husband, she had come to pay her instalments and bless Mandal.

5

The Ten Commanders and the Girl from Basirhat

What is the key to Bandhan's success as the world's largest microfinance company? Former RBI deputy governor Usha Thorat, who is passionate about financial inclusion and has tracked Ghosh's journey as a regulator, says Bandhan's founder knows the language of the poor.

This could be said of many of his employees too, particularly those who had joined him in the early days. They came from a background very similar to that of Bandhan's borrowers, which is perhaps why they felt empathy towards them. Like their borrowers, they have grown with the organization and are doing well today. But in 2002 and 2003, when Bandhan had started with just two branches at Bagnan in Howrah and Konnagar in Hooghly, they could not have known that one day they would be called bankers, earn a decent salary and even drive their own cars. They were all very simple folk.

Here's looking at Bandhan's first ten employees.

1. Partha Pratim Samanta

Zonal head, microbanking division

Samanta, Bandhan's very first employee, joined on 1 July 2002. He oversees 500 DSCs today.

He comes from a family which owned land and, at the same time, dabbled in business in a village called Uttar Harishpur in Howrah. His father owned a rice mill and ran a decorator's business, putting up pandals for weddings and local festivals in the neighbourhood. However, the business did not do well and his father turned into an alcoholic. In his schooldays, Samanta, the eldest of three brothers, often had to intervene to stop his father from beating up his mother.

To earn money, Samanta resorted to selling eggs during his college days. Selling one egg fetched him 20 paise; so, by selling around 200 eggs, he could make Rs 40 a day. But selling 200 eggs a day was not easy; it was hard work. By the time he joined the Purash-Kanpur Haridas Nandi Mahavidyalaya in Howrah for an undergraduate course in commerce, Samanta grew ashamed of his inebriated father, who often needed to be picked up from the road and carried home.

It was only natural that Samanta would try his luck when Village Welfare was looking for people for its 'training rural youth for self-employment' (TRYSEM) programme. Village Welfare Society provided skill development training for the youth, to generate employment opportunities in carpentry, agro-machinery repairing, electrical wiring, radio repairing, two-wheeler repairing, handloom weaving and zari embroidery, among other things. He applied for the nine-month course which, in 1991, promised Rs 300 as stipend every month through the local panchayat body. Incidentally, Maity, chairman of Village Welfare Society, was a distant cousin of Samanta's father.

Next year, Village Welfare offered him a job, with Rs 500 as salary. The project, funded by Germany's Karl Kübel Stiftung (KKS), aimed to distribute ducklings among the poor. Samanta's job was to clean duckling excreta from the cages and distribute the young ones. Later, he got a promotion and a salary of Rs 700 per month, and became the second in command after Shyamal Chowdhury, who was then running the project.

THE FIRST EMPLOYEE: Partha Pratim Samanta used to sell eggs during his college days. Selling one egg fetched him 20 paise.

By 1994, Village Welfare decided to start a microfinance business. The only other entity which was into microfinance in West Bengal then was South Asia Research Society (SARS), a council of microfinance practitioners and associations. One Bijoy Krishna Gharami of Bangladesh's Grameen Bank started training Village Welfare employees even as it was forming women's SHGs—the bedrock of the microfinance business. At SHG meetings, they would talk about income, savings, loans, and social issues such as dowry and the oppression of the girl child.

Samanta was selected as one of the four managers to run the show. His salary went up to Rs 900 a month, and he shifted to Dakshineswar, where the microfinance office was located at Village Welfare boss Ajit Maity's residence, near the famous Dakshineswar Kali Temple. Over the next two years, he started overseeing MFI branches at Nimta, Beliaghata and Birati in north Kolkata, and North 24 Parganas.

After Ghosh joined Village Welfare as head of operations in 1999, they got to know each other and struck up a friendship which has lasted a lifetime. Once, at Samanta's house, Ghosh told his mother, 'I will make your son's future,' even though at that time, he could not think of leaving Village Welfare.

Both of them were dreaming about setting up a microfinance organization but it was not easy for Ghosh to woo Samanta from Maity's fold. He succeeded in doing so through relentless persuasion and even playing a trick which made Maity doubt Samanta's commitment to Village Welfare.

Ghosh resigned from Maity's organization when Samanta was in Raipur, Chhattisgarh, to expand Village Welfare's reach. Immediately, Samanta too resigned and joined

Bandhan. Maity tried hard to convince him to stay back but did not succeed. After Samanta's resignation, Ghosh told him, 'If I can make both ends meet, you too will be able to do so.' At that time, Samanta's salary was Rs 3500. He settled for far less at Bandhan.

When Bandhan expanded to Tripura, Samanta led the team that set up branches in the north-eastern state. They took a flight from Kolkata in June 2006—the first flight taken by any Bandhan employee for official work. The entire office came down to see them off at the door. Samanta bought a new wheeled suitcase for this.

2. Fatik Bera

Cluster-in-charge, audit

Responsible for the audit of 200 branches, Bera has fifteen members in his team. He joined Bandhan on 10 July 2002.

Fatik, thirty-eight, was the youngest of nine siblings—six brothers and three sisters. His father was a farmer in Tajpur, Howrah, and had a landholding of about 10 acres.

Fatik completed his BSc at Bagnan College in Howrah in 2000, and also received a diploma at an Industrial Training Institute (ITI). In his college days, he was a leader of the SFI, and a member of the CPI(M) district committee.

Like Samanta, he too came through Village Welfare, which he joined in 2000. As a credit officer meeting borrowers at different places, he was entitled to a bicycle. However, one evening, soon after getting the bicycle, it was stolen from Ariadaha, Dakshineswar. Fatik was too scared to come back to the office as he had been given a loan of Rs 1200 to buy the cycle. He quit the job after barely two months and, in fact, never took any salary for that time.

One day in October 2001, Samanta bumped into Fatik at a bus stop in Howrah where he was selling pumpkin seeds, green gourd, cauliflower, spinach and radish. The moment Fatik saw Samanta, he wanted to run away as he had not returned the cycle! He thought Samanta was still with Village Welfare and was chasing him for the cycle. Samanta assured him that he was not looking for the cycle; in fact, Ghosh was looking for him—he had opened an NGO and Fatik could join him.

Fatik was excited as he knew Ghosh—he had met him at a training session at a Mahila Unnayan Sangha in Bangalpur, Bagnan. Without losing time, the very next day Fatik headed to Ghosh's residence at Dunlop, near Baranagar railway station. By the time Fatik reached his house, Ghosh had finished his lunch. There was only some rice left, which a hungry Fatik devoured with onion and green chillies.

Ghosh offered him the job and asked him to go to Konnagar, Hooghly, but Fatik instead suggested Bagnan, where he was quite popular by virtue of having been a student leader.

With a Rs 10,000 kitty, which Ghosh gave him to start operations, Fatik moved to Bagnan and formed Golap a ten-member group at Nuntia. His first salary was Rs 1000, and after a few months, it was raised to Rs 1500, but initially, he hardly had any money as he had to chip in from his pocket to take care of the defaults. He started getting a regular salary of Rs 2500 only from September 2003. Samanta was earning a little more—something Fatik did not like. How could a science graduate get less money than a commerce graduate, he wondered.

THE BICYCLE MAN: Fatik Bera (third from left), Bandhan's second employee, quit his first job at Village Welfare without taking his salary after his cycle was stolen.

When Bandhan entered North Bengal in 2005, and opened forty branches in Alipurduar and Cooch Behar, Fatik was part of the team that drove the expansion. Since 2010, Fatik has been associated with the audit wing. On weekdays, he travels extensively across West Bengal, but weekends are reserved for his family: his wife and two sons.

The journey in Bandhan was not all fun for Fatik. There were many unsavoury incidents. Once, when he was posted at Rabibhag, Howrah, he was taking photographs of a Bandhan borrower, a woman, and asking her to sign on the loan application form. But her husband mistook him for a human trafficker, and ran after him with a machete.

3. Satyajit Ghosh

Zonal head, microbanking

He joined on 19 November 2002.

A cousin of Ghosh, Satyajit was born in Dhaka in 1969, but was brought up in Jalpaiguri, North Bengal, by his grandmother and a police officer uncle. After graduating from Ananda Chandra College of Commerce at Jalpaiguri, Satyajit, along with three friends, set up a firm to distribute medicines. That didn't do well, and during one of his trips to Bangladesh in 1987, he joined BRAC, where Ghosh was working at that time. In fact, Ghosh was instrumental in getting him the BRAC job. Initially, Satyajit was involved in the development programmes, later moving to credit programmes.

In 2000, he came back to India and joined Village Welfare as a branch manager at Udaynarayanpur, Howrah. Later, he was made the area manager in Hooghly district. Satyajit did not find Maity, the Village Welfare boss, very ambitious; he was rather happy with half a dozen branches and a few thousand borrowers for his microfinance operations.

Satyajit was part of the first team at Bandhan. While Samanta was an assistant secretary of the society, Satyajit was a member, but he continued to work with Village Welfare till November 2002 as a supervisor of community organizers (COs) at the Konnagar branch. Along with Rabbi Raihan and Purnendu Goswami of ASA, Satyajit prepared Bandhan's first cash register, for which they spent one whole night at the makeshift office, eating roomali rotis and chicken curry for dinner.

NUTS AND BOLTS: Satyajit Ghosh (second from left), Bandhan's third employee, was instrumental in preparing its first cash register.

In 2004, when Bandhan's tenth branch was opened at Chandapara, Gaighata, North 24 Parganas, Saroj Kanti Chakrabarty, a school teacher and the editor of a local newspaper *Jamunamoti*, interviewed Satyajit and reported on the loan disbursement by this branch. This was Bandhan's first appearance in the media.

When accountant Sumit Banerjee resigned at the Bandhan headquarters, Satyajit was made accountant. Later, he opened Bandhan's audit division.

In 2005, when he was made a divisional manager, Bandhan had fifty-four branches, under two divisions and four regions. At a meeting at Bandhan's headquarters, Ghosh asked the regional managers to raise their hands if they were willing to steer Bandhan's expansion in North Bengal. As a divisional manager, Satyajit did not participate in the exercise, but Ghosh picked him and Swapan Saha for the job. Later, he set up Bandhan's Delhi operations, opening sixteen branches in two months.

4. Amalesh Sharma

Member of the accounts division

Sharma joined on 2 December 2002.

A commerce graduate from Ranaghat College, he was born in 1975 at Kalinarayanpur, Nadia. His father was a daily wage earner.

While working as a data entry operator and managing MIS at SARS at Hingalganj, South 24 Parganas, Sharma got to know about Bandhan from his boss, one Dasgupta, whose first name he cannot recall. When he sought a job, Ghosh was only too happy to offer him a CO's position at the Bagnan branch managed by Samanta and Purnendu Mullik of ASA.

Sharma replaced one Piyush Roy, who, in the few months he spent at the branch, had become familiar with the women borrowers. Sharma's first acid test was to convince these borrowers to interact with him. They were not willing to trust a new person. 'Your elder son is going away but the younger son will take care of your needs,' he told them, and won them over.

HE KNOWS HIS ONIONS: Amalesh Sharma (extreme right), Bandhan's fourth employee, focused on the prevention of defaults.

Sharma was shy with women, but he tried hard to get over this. 'My efforts were to prevent defaults. When a woman's husband fell ill and was hospitalized, another woman chipped in and I remained the guarantor,' he told me. He also remembers one incident where a woman borrower's baby died but she still paid up, saying, 'My child is dead but I cannot ignore my duty of paying back the money.'

From the field, Sharma came back to the headquarters in 2006, first to the audit division and then to accounts. He got married to a colleague in Bandhan, Debjani Kundu, but it was an arranged marriage.

5. Debasish Mandal

Team member, audit (microbanking)

As a cluster-in-charge, he is responsible for the audit of 200 branches, and has fifteen members under him.

He joined Bandhan on 16 June 2003.

Debasish was born into a poor farmer's family in a small town in Diamond Harbour, South 24 Parganas. His father, a farm worker, suffered paralysis in 1998 when Debasish was studying BCom at a local college. His brother worked in a jewellery shop; the family of two brothers and a sister, besides the parents, did not have any other source of income.

Debasish started giving tuitions and making paper packets at home from old newspapers to sell to provision stores and sweet shops. He was desperately looking for a job after graduation, and the Bandhan offer at the Bagnan branch came as a godsend.

He still remembers his first interaction with residents of a remote village, Ghoraghata, in Howrah, where he had gone to form a new group. People mistook him for a chit fund

THE RECOVERY MAN: Once, the angry husband of a defaulter attacked Debasish Mandal (third from left), Bandhan's fifth employee.

agent and confined him to a house, till Samanta rushed there with official documents proving his identity and rescued him. Debasish went on to form four groups there.

He has an equally interesting story about loan recovery. At Akubhag in Hallyan, Bagnan, a gentleman had two wives who happened to be sisters—Sahanara and Jahanara. Both of them took loans, but Jahanara was not paying back the money, while Sahanara was regular in her repayment schedule. When Sahanara's loan was repaid fully, the husband asked for a new loan but it was denied on the grounds that his second wife Jahanara's loan had yet to be repaid. The angry husband attacked Debasish with a knife. Had the members of a group of borrowers not come to his rescue, the situation could have taken a serious turn.

6. Sudhanya Nopti

Part of the insurance division

Nopti is responsible for all claim settlements.

He joined Bandhan on 15 July 2003.

An MSc in physics, Nopti, fifty-one, had worked with Grameen Bank in Bangladesh for about twelve years and was conferred the Muhammad Yunus award—consisting of a citation and 5000 Bangladeshi takas—for his 'five star' performance in collecting savings, managing groups, overseeing sanitation programmes, keeping high outstandings and the quality of loan assets. He left Grameen Bank in 2001, frustrated with the stagnation in his career—there had been no promotion for years.

His first port of call in India was the SARS headquarters at Jodhpur Park in Kolkata. Nopti had visited SARS in 1997, when he had come down from Grameen Bank on a tour. He joined SARS in June 2001 as a regional manager with six branches under him but left in December 2002 as he was not happy with the way the organization was being run.

Nopti shared his concerns with Ghosh, who had come to the Phulia branch of SARS in Nadia to impart training to the branch staff.

After a brief training session at Bagnan, Nopti opened the Chakdaha branch with Kalyan Kundu, Mrinmoy Mondal and an ASA employee. He still remembers the struggle to open Bandhan's ninth branch at Shimurali, Nadia, where the landlord refused to give the place to Bandhan on rent as he was convinced that it was a chit fund.

'INVADING' TRIPURA: Sudhanya Nopti (third from left, standing), Bandhan's sixth employee, was part of the team that set up the Tripura operations in 2006.

The story of the eighth branch at Haringhata, also in Nadia, is no less interesting. Here, the branch manager was caught in the act with the sister-in-law of the landlord. He was sacked immediately, and the situation was brought under control quickly with the help of the members of a local club.

Nopti was part of Samanta's team that in 2006 set up operations in Tripura, where Bandhan had to once again face the allegation of being a chit fund. From Tripura, Nopti was transferred to Howrah, and finally, in July 2011, he moved attached to the insurance division. From the microfinance borrowers, he used to collect a premium of Rs 1.51 for every Rs 1000, and an additional Rs 3.10 for the spouse, making it Rs 4.61. In case of death, the loan would not have to be repaid; on top of that, the borrower would get Rs 10,000. According to him, the claim ratio was 59 per cent as the mortality rate in this segment of borrowers was very high.

Every time Ghosh landed in Kolkata after a landmark event such as Bandhan getting a big award, one person sure to rush to the airport with a garland to receive him was Nopti.

7. Mrinmoy Mondal

Zonal team member

He takes care of at least 150 branches.

Mondal joined Bandhan on 24 July 2003. He graduated in arts from Shantipur College, Nadia. After doing a technical course in engineering at ITI, Kalyani, in 2000 he joined Hindustan Motors Ltd as an apprentice at its Uttarpara factory in Hooghly, where the company began production of the iconic Ambassador.

His friend used to run a stationery shop at Dunlop from where Ghosh used to buy chocolates for his son. Mondal's uncle used to work with BRAC and knew Ghosh well. Mondal had visited Ghosh at his Dunlop residence on the floor above Ashoknagar Dental Clinic, near Baranagar railway station ticket counter, with his uncle, but not to seek a job.

In fact, he was happy with his agency of Central Dairy of Haringhata, selling its products. Ghosh's cousin Pravakar used to buy milk from him. Ghosh too would often drop by his kiosk but not to buy milk; he would keep on asking him to join Bandhan, and Mondal would refuse. He was working hard; he would start collecting milk (unless the quantity was 40 litres, milk pouches would not be supplied to his shop) at 5 a.m. and work till midnight. Late in the evening, a visibly tired Ghosh would walk by his shop. 'I was working hard but this man was working even harder . . . That attracted me,' said Mondal.

He surrendered the agency and joined Bandhan for a salary of Rs 2000. He was earning more at that time and was dreaming of being an entrepreneur, running a dairy business.

Ghosh told him to go to Konnagar, and to carry a mosquito net along. After a three-day pre-service orientation, he was posted at Chakdaha (Nadia), Haripukhur branch, which opened on 18 July 2003. A woman called Sukriti was supposed to join the branch but she did not turn up; Mondal replaced Sukriti and got her bicycle. When an extremely upset Mondal complained to Ghosh that he had been given a ladies' bicycle, Ghosh asked him to show where it was written on the bicycle that a man could not ride it. Mondal used it for two years.

After four months, Mondal was made team leader. Purnendu Goswami of ASA cautioned him against going to Gangnapur, Nadia, where people used to make acid bombs using old car batteries. Not paying any attention to his words, Mondal went there, met people who were into making cane baskets, and got eleven customers. The recovery rate at that place was 100 per cent.

ROMANCE IN THE OFFICE: Mrinmoy Mondal (fourth from left, standing), Bandhan's seventh employee, fell in love with a colleague and proposed to her within a fortnight, after hearing her sing a Rabindra Sangeet.

From Chakdaha, Mondal was to go to Machlandapur in North 24 Parganas; Bina Majumdar was to replace him. She sang

Rabindra Sangeet when she came for her interview. Of course, Bandhan was not a place for song and dance, but ASA's Rabbi Raihan, a trainer, asked her to sing a song during the interview and she obliged. Within a fortnight, Mondal proposed to her. Bina was Bandhan's first female employee.

Their wedding, in February 2005, was not attended by anyone from Bandhan. There was a whip against it as marrying a colleague was a taboo then. Bina left her job after two years.

8. Kalyan Kundu

Team member, IT

Kundu oversees networking and hardware-related issues at various branches with a team of forty people. He joined Bandhan on 11 August 2003.

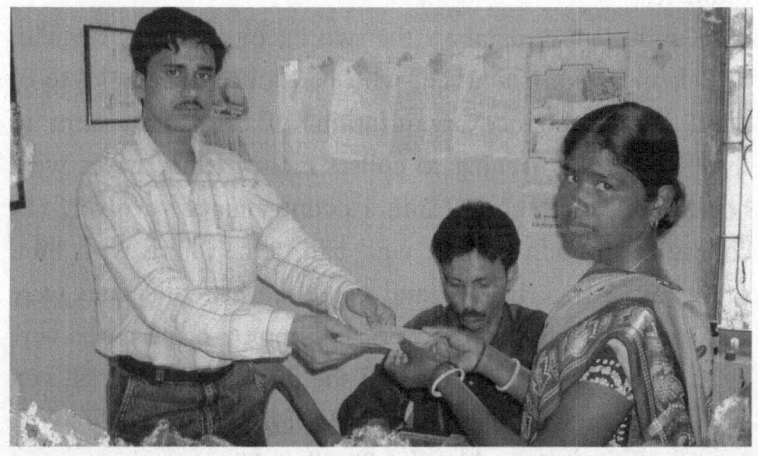

ALL ABOUT COMMITMENT: Kalyan Kundu (standing), Bandhan's eighth employee, did not take a day off even when his father died.

Kundu hails from Kandi, Murshidabad, a small subdivisional administrative headquarters, which boasts one of the oldest municipal bodies in India, formed in 1869. His father, a graduate, had never worked, and the family lived on farming and selling plots of land to meet any exigency. One of four children, and a commerce graduate from Raja Birendra Chandra College of Commerce, Kundu knew one Chandan Mishra who used to work for Bandhan.

He came to the BA 74, Salt Lake City office seeking a job. When Ghosh asked him when he could join, Kundu said he could start that very day. He was offered a monthly salary of Rs 2000. The very next day, he was sent to Bagnan, the centre where all old Bandhanites got trained. A month later, he was transferred to Chakdaha, along with Debasish and Nopti.

Chakdaha turned out to be the best branch, with 4000 customers and no overdues—a benchmark for other branches.

Kundu still remembers the two dacoits, Elai and Malai, at Beldanga, Murshidabad, who had killed an employee of another microfinance organization. When Kundu went to their house one evening to collect money (their wives were borrowers), Elai showed him a country-made revolver. His colleague, Subodh Nandi, who had come along with him, ran away. Struck by fear and panic, all his colleagues were waiting outside in the darkness for him. On being asked why he had come there, Kundu told the duo, 'I will not tell you who I am, you will beat me up . . . Everybody is scared of you. I am a poor man, working for Bandhan.'

They spoke for three hours and ultimately paid one instalment. 'Allah will help you, love people . . . Send your dog every week, we will pay,' Elai and Malai told Kundu.

At Bongaigaon, Assam, in 2009, Muslim women helped him and his colleagues get out of a mess by dressing them up in burqas.

In 2009, when Bandhan was computerized, a non-technical, operational team was formed with four members: Mrinmoy Mondal, Saibal Gon, Biswanath Dey and Pritam Mondal. Kundu was made its leader. They would come up with ideas and Ronti Kar, the technology head, would develop the software. Nobody knew anything about keyboard, CPU, mouse or any other part of a computer.

In 2010, Kundu steered a fifteen-day project on balance sheets. He would bathe on the terrace and go to bed at four in the morning after sending a text message to Ghosh on the progress of the work.

He never took a long holiday. For his wedding, he stayed away from office for no more than three days. When his father died, he did not take a day off. Now, he is planning to take a week off and go on a honeymoon, which has been overdue for years.

9. Sanjib Kumar Das

Leader of a three-member team at the logistics division

Sanjib joined Bandhan on 13 August 2003.

A BCom graduate from Surendranath College, Kolkata, Sanjib was born in Dankuni, Hooghly. His father, who used to work in a paint factory, died of kidney failure at the age of fifty-five.

Sanjib worked with Village Welfare for about a year but lost his job when he refused to take a transfer to Chhattisgarh. When he called Ghosh for a job, the latter obliged. Sanjib's first salary was Rs 1500 a month.

After a three-day stint at Konnagar, he was asked to report at the Begampur branch, Bandhan's third after Bagnan and Konnagar.

At Bagnan, his bicycle was stolen; at Mathabhanga, North Bengal, high on the local brew *haria*, locals attacked him as the menfolk were upset that

NO REGRETS: Sanjib Kumar Das, Bandhan's ninth employee, could have taken up a job at a paint factory where his father used to work. He chose to join Bandhan for a monthly salary of Rs 1500.

Bandhan employees were approaching only women. They also thought Bandhan was a chit fund. Sanjib visited their homes in the evening and explained to them that Bandhan gives—and does not take—money.

At Kamakhyaguri, North Bengal, he slept on the floor on newspaper sheets as there was no furniture at the time of the branch's launch. From a local decorator, he hired a sofa set for the launch.

After his father died, the paint factory where he was working offered Sanjib a job but he declined the offer. There are no regrets. He looks up to Ghosh, who calls him Sanju, just as his father did.

10. Kalyan Das

Zonal team member in charge of close to 150 branches

Kalyan joined Bandhan on 1 September 2003.

Eldest among three brothers and one sister, Kalyan, a graduate, hails from Jaipur, a village in Howrah. His father used to work in a factory, repairing gearboxes of trains.

Kalyan's first job was at Village Welfare, where he worked for a year as an entrepreneur organizer, giving loans and collecting savings. He did well, expanding the market in different parts of Howrah, but got bogged down by a severe liver ailment. His monthly salary rose from Rs 1100 to Rs 1950 within a few years, but he was finding it extremely difficult to continue with the field job. His branch manager, Sudarshan Pal, and colleague Sushanta Haldar asked him to get in touch with 'Ghosh Babu' who gives money only to women. The idea sounded funny to Kalyan Das.

However, he dropped in at the Bandhan office, at BA 74, Salt Lake. Aditi Chatterjee, the lady who used to look

THE PRANKSTER: Kalyan Das, Bandhan's tenth employee, would ride the branch manager's bike and, after the ride, using a stick, get the meter back to its old reading, but the fuel tank would show as empty.

after administrative matters, opened the door. There were
three persons in the office, including a lean, tall, dark man on
the computer. He called Kalyan into a room and said, 'I am
Ghosh Babu.' He asked Kalyan to go to Bagnan and offered
him a monthly salary of Rs 2000. Kalyan was excited at the
prospect of getting Rs 50 more than his usual salary, but did
not turn up for a month.

When Kalyan finally went to Bagnan, carrying a Village
Welfare diary, he met Samanta. There were three days of
training—essentially field visits with his colleague Amalesh
Sharma.

Once, at Bagnan, Kalyan's senior colleague Haripada
claimed to have bagged a role in Tollywood. As was his
wont, Kalyan slapped him in jest and disbelief. All hell broke
loose. An office circular was issued saying nobody would be
called 'dada' any more—a practice prevalent till then—and
all seniors would be addressed as 'sir'.

After this episode, Rabbi Raihan (of ASA), till then
Kalyan's Raihan da, a short, fair and stocky man, would tell
him for days on end in a Bangladeshi dialect, 'Your job is
hanging by a thread.'

In 2004, defaults at Bagnan were rising; the epicentre was
Kacharipara, NH 6 (Bombay Road for most in West Bengal),
a place which always had law and order problems. It was
said that people were murdered elsewhere and their bodies
dumped there.

Three groups were involved in the default. The leader
of one of them, Angura Begam, whose nickname was Mara,
had created fake identities and managed to raise Rs 3,63,000
(given to sixty-three women who did not exist). With a rise in
defaults, the Bagnan branch was shrinking.

Overnight, the team was changed: Samanta, the branch manager, was demoted to the post of CO, and a new team consisting of Kalyan Das, Sanjib Das, Kartik Bittar, Tapas Maity and Biplab Saha was brought in.

Field visits to collect money intensified. Short and boyish-looking, Kalyan used to be sent to Begam's house. There he would wait for the *khala* (maternal aunt in Urdu) to appear, chewing paan, while the others hid somewhere. Kalyan would wait till evening when the *azaan* was recited in the local mosque.

The day he collected Rs 1475, everybody hugged him, and all of them celebrated by eating fritters and tea. The five-member team worked for one year at Bagnan and recovered most of the money; Rs 82,800, however, remained to be collected.

Kalyan also remembers those fun days when he and Kartik would ride the branch manager's bike and, after the ride, using a stick, get the meter back to its old reading, but the fuel tank would show as empty.

11. Runa Parven
The first female senior divisional manager

Parven had two states under her jurisdiction in 2010–11.

One of the five daughters of a bicycle shopowner, Parven hails from Basirhat, North 24 Parganas. Her father died in 1994, when she was still in school, and her sister supported the family. An MA in Sanskrit from Rabindra Bharati University, Parven also has a diploma in work education.

While doing her post-graduate programme, she joined Katiahat B.K.A.P. Girls' High School in North 24 Parganas

on the other side of the Ichamati River. At that time, Swapan
Kumar Saha, a senior at Basirhat College and an employee of
Bandhan, introduced her to Ghosh.

On 1 December 2004, Parven was interviewed at Bandhan
and sent to the Baruipur branch in South 24 Parganas as a
community organizer (the old avatar of credit officer) for pre-
service orientation.

In the school, her salary had been Rs 800 per month.
Here, it jumped to Rs 1850. From there, she was sent to
Chakdaha when Bandhan was just about twenty branches
old, and by August 2005, she was made a manager in
Garia. By January 2006, she was a regional manager with
six branches under her. In one of the groups that she was
attached to, one woman borrower, Roza, did not turn up
one day as she was down with fever. Parven visited her home
to inquire about her health. At this, Roza, started crying,
sharing that even her next-door neighbour had not bothered
to come see her.

In two years, Parven was made a divisional manager
and she raised the number of branches from twenty-seven to
forty-eight.

In April 2010, she was sent to Delhi as divisional manager
to look after seventy-eight branches in Delhi, UP, Haryana
and Uttarakhand. The Haryana branches had a tough time
getting customers, as moneylenders were ruling the roost
there. Closer home, at a village in Howrah, Parven had to
spend half a day hiding in a cowshed as a group of Bandhan's
borrowers thought her life could be at stake as violent fights
broke out between rival political parties.

Parven also worked in Mumbai and Patna. She is now assistant manager, operations, and looks after 113 branches: forty-nine in Hooghly and sixty-four in Murshidabad, with around 750 employees.

Parven tours extensively during the first three weeks of every month. In the last week, when she comes to the headquarters, typically, she catches the 5.30 a.m. train from Basirhat, reaches Barasat around 6.45 a.m., where she changes trains

ALL ABOUT EMPOWERMENT: Runa Parven, Bandhan's first female senior divisional manager, has built her own house and drives a Zen Estilo.

and reaches office by 8.15 a.m. She leaves office by 6.30 p.m., catches a train from Ultadanga and reaches home by 9.30 p.m.

Parven loves Bandhan for its work culture and fast-track promotions. She has built her own house and drives a Zen Estilo.

6

The Bandhan Pathshala

_____

Somebody who has been associated with a large microfinance organization in Bangladesh once told me that Ghosh could have sent truckloads of branch managers and credit officers anywhere in West Bengal. There was no need for any feasibility study; the market was as fertile as it could be and there was almost no competition for microfinance.

He was both right and wrong. Indeed, there has been virtually no competition as most Indian banks do not see any business opportunity at the so-called bottom of the pyramid. However, merely unloading sackfuls of money to the credit-starved poor cannot help them in the long run. The capital has to be accompanied by an extremely tight monitoring system, which is what Bandhan ensured.

The key to Bandhan's success as an MFI was its 2003 manual, which was the bedrock of its operations. The first edition of the manual, called 'Programme Strategy and Operational Guidelines', was published in April 2003, when Bandhan's headquarters was a 550-square-foot, one-bedroom flat at BA 74, Sector I, Salt Lake City, where the hall was the reception area, the kitchen housed the accounts department, and the bedroom served as Ghosh's office. The manual was in Bengali.

Even before that, Ghosh had circulated a slim version, a few cyclostyled pages stapled together. The five-page draft, a summary of a few Bandhan circulars distributed among the field workers on the dos and don'ts of the MFI business, was dictated by Ghosh and written by Nilima. Ghosh himself typed it out. Both BRAC and ASA working norms were reference points for those circulars.

Ghosh was the editor of the first official manual, developed by ASA's Roy and a few others, including Runu da, Samanta, Satyajit and Bera.

The manual laid down every rule of Bandhan, ranging from what kind of furniture a branch could have to the process of appointing employees and their promotion, and the guidelines for forming a team of borrowers and giving loans.

Let's take a close look at the manual. It says that a branch would have three to four COs, a peon-cum-cook, and a branch manager for overall supervision. Every CO would handle 360–400 group members. This meant every branch would have 1440–1600 members.

In the early days, it was a three-tier structure. A CO was responsible for 360–400 members, a branch manager for 1440–1600 members, and a regional manager for five to eight branches.

The regional manager, however, would not have a dedicated office; he would be attached to one of the centrally located branches that came under him.

The office time for branch employees was between 7.30 a.m. and 3.30 p.m., Monday through Friday; for field visits, the same hours but with a one-hour lunch break, between 1 p.m. and 2 p.m. On Saturdays, the branch would remain open till 1.30 p.m., without a lunch break.

For the head office, there was no half day. The office functioned from 9 a.m. to 6 p.m. every day, with half-an-hour lunch breaks. Every branch would have two registers: one for recording attendance and another, called 'movement muster', to keep tabs on employee movement while he or she was away from office.

Attendance is something that has remained sacrosanct at Bandhan, even after it became a bank. In the first week of August 2015, barely three weeks before the bank's launch, Ghosh made a surprise visit to a Bandhan branch at Survey Park near his house. He was there at 8.55 a.m. and watched the branch manager walk in at 9.15 a.m. Ghosh asked him where he lived. The branch manager came from Baghajatin, in the southern part of the city, about a half-an-hour commute from Survey Park.

Ghosh gave the branch manager two choices: one, he could quit his job and stay at home; two, he could be transferred to Krishnanagar, in Nadia. If he were not coming from home, surely he would be punctual in reaching the office. The manager begged him for a last chance.

The branch manager's job is to meet five customers and call up another ten. By meeting them personally, the branch manager would know if there was any communication gap between his colleagues and a prospective customer, in which case, he could step in to rectify it.

Discipline is the key, and Ghosh does not compromise on this for anything. Maneeta Rathore, now communications head of Bandhan, who joined the group in June 2004, vouches for it. A student of South City College, Rathore was looking for an avenue to engage herself after her BCom final exam. She had also enrolled herself for a diploma in public relations at Bharatiya Vidya Bhavan, in Salt Lake City. She saw an advertisement from Bandhan in the *Telegraph*, seeking an office assistant.

About a dozen girls were interviewed. There were very few chairs and only one table; the candidates had to take turns to write an essay on 'Your Life'. Ghosh and another gentleman interviewed Rathore. It went well, and Rathore, fairly sure that she would bag the job, mustered the courage to ask Ghosh whether she could come a little late to office. The office hours were from 9 a.m. to 6 p.m. The Bharatiya Vidya Bhavan class would start at 7 a.m. and end at 9 a.m. She was seeking a ten-minute grace period. But Ghosh's response was curt: 'At Bandhan, nine means nine, but six can become seven.'

That's how the interview ended, and Rathore thought she had messed up her chances. However, a few days later, Swapan Saha, who was looking after HR at that time, called at her house to tell her the job was hers. She was offered

Rs 3500 per month. When she dropped in at the office to collect her appointment letter, Rathore haggled for another Rs 500, but Ghosh was firm—she could take it or leave it; a pay hike could come only after six months.

Even if someone reaches the office one minute past 9 a.m., it is counted as being late, and three such instances lead to losing a day's salary. Initially, it was a ten-minute grace period, but soon, 9.10 a.m. became the de facto official time as people started reaching after nine. So Ghosh removed the grace period. Then, employees started running, begging autorickshaw drivers to speed up, and tumbled over each other to come in by 9 a.m.

Walking on the pavement near Bandhan's office in Kolkata—it has changed four addresses in the past fifteen years before moving to the current headquarters at DN 32, Salt Lake City—around 9 a.m. was always a risk for others, as Bandhan employees would sprint to be on time.

There were some smart people who would hoodwink the system—they would come late but sign the register and enter the right time; there would also be some overwriting. But Ghosh was even smarter. At Bandhan's third headquarters at AB 48, Salt Lake City, he introduced the card-punching system for employees. And at DN 32, CCTVs were installed, apparently to detect theft, but that was an excuse. He wanted to keep a close watch on his employees.

Ghosh would have a monitor on his table showing who was doing what. Suddenly, one department head would get a call via the intercom from Ghosh: 'Doesn't your team have any work? Get out of your workstation and look at what's happening around,' he would say.

He also played other tricks. For instance, he would come earlier than 9 a.m. and wish 'good morning' to a senior employee, a habitual latecomer. After this, the man would be so embarrassed that he would never come late again.

Through the CCTVs, Ghosh would watch everybody—how much time they spent gossiping and doing things other than work. Reading newspapers and magazines during office hours was not encouraged in the MFI. There was no television except in Ghosh's room. Smuggling in newspapers was tough, and only the communications division was allowed to read newspapers.

Of course, there was an annual picnic for employees of the headquarters, which would be a family affair. For this, every employee would contribute towards the food, and Bandhan would hire a bus. Many a time, they went to Shantiniketan—a university town near Bolpur in Birbhum district, approximately 160 km north of Kolkata, established by Rabindranath Tagore.

Between December and February, every Sunday would see many such picnics, organized by each division of Bandhan. Till recently, Ghosh would attend every picnic, on certain days even attending two or three, having starters at one place, lunch at another and tea at yet another. He used the picnics as an opportunity to reach out to every employee directly. At all such picnics, there would invariably be quiz competitions to test the employees' knowledge of the

Bandhan way of work. One would have to read the manual thoroughly to win the contest.

'Give Me Your Sundays, I'll Give You the Future'

The picnic would always be on a Sunday, because Ghosh would never allow anybody to lose a working day. In fact, he would tell all his employees: 'Give me your Sundays, I will give you the future,' à la Netaji Subhas Chandra Bose's famous slogan, 'Give me blood, I will give you freedom.' Those who stayed back at Bandhan (and most of them have done so) today find those words prophetic.

Until recently, no Bandhan employee, however senior, was allowed to go directly to a railway station to catch a train or the airport to take a flight for office work, unless the train or the flight was early in the morning. The person would need to drop in at the office first and sign the register, and only then proceed to the station or airport.

He would also identify the troublemakers and post him or her at such a place that the person would be forced to quit. However, as a CEO, he does not believe in firing people. He tries out the person in every department till he or she fits in.

Ghosh does not like people taking leave. For any leave, one would need to inform him in the morning before office hours, even if he is overseas. He would listen to the person and then hang up. The next two days, he would not even look at the person. He would ignore them for a few days and would not call them to meetings in his room. This was his way of showing displeasure.

However, this would last for a few days, after which it would be business as usual. Also, he does not like people leaving at 6 p.m. If anyone left the office at 6 p.m., Ghosh would politely ask him whether he had not been keeping well. Till about a few years ago, it was mandatory for everybody to bid him 'bye' before leaving, every day.

In the initial years, he also did not like Bandhan employees getting married to each other, but there have been instances where he was instrumental in getting people married off. Of course, there's logic behind his dislike of marriage between two Bandhan employees. 'I wanted people to show dedication to their work and develop skills. They can earn a decent salary to support a family only if they work hard and get promotions. If they get married early in their careers, they will find it difficult to do that,' he says.

There have also been instances where credit officers stopped supporting their own parents. In such cases, Ghosh stepped in and struck deals, whereby a fixed sum from an employee's salary would be given to his parents. This would be done through intimate counselling.

Ghosh may be a strict disciplinarian, but he doesn't believe in sacking people unless there are issues of integrity or sexual harassment. If someone is not good at something, he tries placing him or her in other departments to retain the person and get the best out of him for the organization.

The List of Furniture

Talking about the MFI branches, the list of furniture that a Bandhan branch could buy in 2003 makes for interesting reading.

One 'half secretariat' table (whatever that means) of 4 feet by 2.5 feet, either made of steel or wood, for Rs 2500.

One wooden 'long table', 6 feet by 3.5 feet, for Rs 4500.

One 'standard size' plastic chair with armrests for Rs 1500, and eight chairs, without armrests, costing Rs 550 each. The chair with armrests was for the branch manager while the other chairs were for COs.

Between two and four long wooden benches, for Rs 700 each, for the borrowers to sit on.

A plastic stool for the peon for Rs 300.

Besides, there would be a blackboard (Rs 700), an information board (Rs 1500), a steel cupboard (Rs 4500) and a four-drawer file cabinet (for Rs 3500) for the office.

Then, there would be five cots (Rs 1200 each), one almirah and two wooden clothes stands. The kitchen would have a meat-safe (Rs 1500), a water filter (Rs 500), six tea cups and saucers and a tray (Rs 500), a flask (Rs 225), and vessels and other utensils required for cooking (Rs 1600).

Each branch would have three ceiling fans (Rs 1600 each) and two hurricane lamps (kerosene lamps), in case the power went out.

The regional manager would have the half secretariat table, two chairs (one with armrests and another without armrests), one steel almirah or file cabinet (even the thickness of the steel is mentioned in the manual, along with its size and price).

Each office would have a guest room, equipped with a wooden cot (Rs 1500), a clothes stand (Rs 1000), a quilt with a cover (Rs 650), a bedsheet (Rs 250), two pillows with covers (Rs 250 each), a towel (Rs 125), a mosquito net (Rs 300), a few plates and glasses, and a jug for water.

leave without pay; at the second, a six-month suspension; and at the third, sacking.

If anybody is absent without applying for leave, at the first instance, a warning would be issued, coupled with double the number of days marked absent as leave without pay; at the second, a three-month suspension; and beyond that, sacking.

If someone smokes in the office, he would be warned the first time, transferred the second time, and suspended the third time.

Similarly, if the signboard is not fixed properly and the office premises are kept untidy, the punishment would start with warning and could go up to losing an increment.

Employees were also punished if they furnished fake travel bills, signed on blank cheques or made false allegations against a colleague. For such offences, the punishment varied between penalty and leave without pay to missing an increment, a demotion and even sacking.

Bicycle, Raincoat and Calculator

Finally, if somebody takes an interest-free loan but does not buy a bicycle, raincoat or calculator within fifteen days, the person would need to return the money, with Rs 500 as penalty.

The Bandhan manual also lays down norms for selecting the members of groups who would eventually borrow money. Typically, they would be daily wage earners, belonging to the so-called weaker section of society, and their monthly income would be less than Rs 2000 (in 2003). On an average, a group should have twenty members; at the initial stage, it could start with six, and later the number could go up to fifteen or even twenty-five. Only women could become members and not more than one person from a family could join. They should belong to the age group of eighteen to fifty-five.

Under no circumstance can an unmarried woman become a member; a divorcee or a widow could, but after extensive due diligence. It was noticed that unmarried women, after getting married, moved to another village to stay with their husbands. This made loan collection from them difficult. The only exception to this was relatively older unmarried women who ran their own businesses. The chances of them leaving their village were slim.

The manual suggests that the groups could be named after flowers or rivers, but there should not be two groups of the same name attached to one branch.

Each group would have a president, a secretary and a cashier, for a term of one year. At most, a person could be nominated for a second term. Non-refundable entry fee for the members was Rs 10, and they would need to bring in two copies of passport-size photographs, one of which would be pasted on the application for the loan, and the other on the passbook.

Each group would meet at a particular time, on a particular day and in a particular place—typically the courtyard of a member's house. The group members would have to arrange for the mat on which they would sit.

To start with, every member would have to save at least Rs 10 every week, on which they would get 5 per cent 'incentive', annually. If somebody wanted to save more, the amount would have to be in multiples of five, such as Rs 15, Rs 20 or Rs 25.

After eight weeks of savings, one would be entitled to apply for loans.

The first loan could be between Rs 1000 and Rs 3000. For a loan of Rs 1000, one would have to keep a 10 per cent security; and for Rs 2000, 15 per cent. It would be disbursed by the branch manager in the presence of the CO and other group members.

In 2003, the interest (Bandhan called it service charge) was a flat 17.5 per cent. This means, for a loan of Rs 1000, one would have to return Rs 1175—forty-seven weekly instalments of Rs 25 each. If a borrower was unwell and hospitalized, she was exempted from paying the weekly instalments for three weeks. Bandhan also offered life insurance, at a premium of Rs 20 for a cover of Rs 1000.

In case of default, the manual asked Bandhan employees to look for the reasons behind the default and seek the help of village elders and the borrowers' neighbours.

In April 2003, when this manual was released, Bandhan had two branches, 135 groups, 2021 members and 1118 borrowers, supervised by six COs. The average loan size was Rs 2458, total loans disbursed Rs 27,48,500, and loans outstanding Rs 21,80,000. It had savings of Rs 5,74,356.

By April 2010, Bandhan had 1050 branches in fifteen states. There were 1,29,229 groups, 25,24,935 members and 23,01,433 borrowers. By that time, it had disbursed loans of Rs 4929 crore, and the outstanding was Rs 1495 crore.

Despite the phenomenal growth, the 2010 manual was as detailed, and a dossier for micromanagement, as it had been seven years earlier. Writing the preface to the fourth edition of the manual in 2010, Ghosh, its chairman and managing director, said, 'The previous editions of the manual should be preserved with utmost care.'

The fourth edition is in English. The previous two editions—in July 2005 and July 2007, released after the first formal manual in April 2003—were in Bengali.

By this time, the community organizers were called credit officers and a new tier was created below them: junior credit officer (JCO). Similarly, there were assistant branch managers below branch managers, and senior branch managers above them but below regional managers. Above regional managers, there were associate divisional managers, divisional managers, senior divisional managers, assistant general managers, deputy general managers, general managers in charge of operations and risk management and internal audit, below the chairman and managing director.

Bandhan had, by that time, also introduced different types of loan products. For instance, 'Suchana', a microloan of Rs 1000 to Rs 15,000, was for twelve months for first-timers. 'Srishti' was a microenterprise loan of Rs 16,000 to Rs 50,000, for two years. And 'Samriddhi' was a micro, small- and medium-sized enterprise (MSME) loan of Rs 51,000 to Rs 3 lakh, for twelve, eighteen and twenty-four months, respectively. There was also 'Suraksha', a microhealth loan of Rs 1000 to Rs 5000, for twelve months.

Since RBI was no longer allowing the collection of savings, Bandhan started asking for an upfront payment of 10 per cent of the loan amount as security.

The appointment conditions for entry-level employees had also changed by then. The JCOs would undergo a six-month probation. Payment would depend on qualifications: a JCO who had passed class XII would get Rs 3800, and a graduate or postgraduate JCO Rs 4130 per month. A graduate JCO could apply for a CO's job after a year.

Maternity Leave

The 2010 manual also speaks about a twelve-week maternity leave, which did not find mention in 2003, when there were hardly any women employees at Bandhan. Any employee who has spent six months with the organization is entitled to maternity leave twice in her career, provided there is a three-year gap between the two pregnancies. The sanctioning authority for maternity leave is the chairman and managing director, while all other leaves are sanctioned by the immediate boss of the employee.

There are still not too many women in Bandhan. In the field force, women account for about 10 per cent; Assam leads, with one female employee for every two males. In the initial days, Ford Foundation, which used to support Bandhan with funds, insisted on greater participation of women in the organization. All job advertisements would carry this line: 'Women are encouraged to apply.'

There had been at least one advertisement looking for only women employees. It was for Bandhan's all-women branches, of which it had quite a few. The nature of the job, however, does not excite women as it involves working long hours and riding a bicycle to meet borrowers in villages.

The 2010 manual also mentions that the organization will pay Rs 500 to a cook in every branch. This amount is raised by 10 per cent after six months of 'good service'.

It talks about seventy-nine types of misconduct related to irregularities in loan sanctioning, and the related punishments. For instance, if a branch keeps Rs 1000 as cash without proper reason and planning, the branch manager will be fined Rs 100 per day of keeping the money. If more than one loan is given to the same family, and the money involved is more than Rs 15,000, then the concerned CO will have to go on leave without pay for three months; the branch manager too will be fined Rs 1000.

In case of instances of 'moral turpitude', the punishment is a three-month leave without pay for the first time, temporary suspension for the second time, and sacking for the third time. If one writes an anonymous letter to the higher authorities against a colleague, alleging misconduct that cannot be proved, the writer, if identified, will face temporary suspension. Not keeping bedsheets, pillow covers and towels properly in the cupboard of the guest room also attracts a penalty!

By this time, the quantum of interest-free bicycle loans rose to Rs 2500, to be repaid in twenty-five monthly instalments of Rs 100 each, and the cycle had to be bought within twenty-four hours of taking the loan. In case the cycle is stolen, another Rs 2500 will have to be given, without interest.

For motorcycles used by regional managers, one has to pay forty-eight monthly instalments of Rs 350 each. Bandhan would pay Re 1 per km in the first year, Rs 1.15 between the first and second years, and Rs 1.5 after two years towards the cost of maintenance and fuel. While riding the motorcycle, one must wear a helmet (as also the person riding pillion), shoes (not sandals), and the speed limit is capped at 40 km per hour. He or she cannot ride with a person 'unknown' to the organization, and any personal errand, if not mentioned in the logbook, would attract a fine of Rs 500.

Around this time, Bandhan had also become somewhat liberal with the use of office stationery. For instance, every staffer would get three or four pens a month. Except for the refund or withdrawal of loan security, which had to be written in red ink, blue pens were to be used. For buying pens, paper, envelopes, rubber bands, pins, etc., the monthly budget was Rs 20 per employee. After four years, a cupboard could be repainted, but the cost could not exceed Rs 500 (transportation cost extra).

A Way of Life

The 2010 manual also lays down the norms for buying furniture for branches and the budget for each piece, ranging from 'long table' to blackboard and ceiling fan. It also gives a list of kitchen utensils—frying pan, spoons and plates, besides a grinding stone and containers for salt and spices. Collectively, their cost is capped at Rs 2150. Similarly, furniture and other things such as mosquito nets and towels for the guest room should not cost more than Rs 4275.

The manual continues to specify the size of the signboard to be displayed outside a branch. Its size has remained the same—3 feet by 2 feet—and the cost has also not risen after seven years: Rs 800. This time around, the branches were encouraged to put up a couple of arrow boards on the road, indicating the location of the office if it was not visible from the main road.

I have visited a few such branches on the outskirts of Kolkata. Spending time with the employees there, what I found was that more than being a financial institution, Bandhan is a cult—a way of life. In one branch, seven employees ate their breakfast—rice, dal and mashed potatoes—and five of them, credit officers, went on their bicycles to different villages to meet groups of borrowers and collect their weekly instalments.

They all came back by 1 p.m., counted the notes again and again, kept them in the chest in different bundles (based on the denominations of the notes) tied with rubber bands. The office table turned into a dining table where they ate their lunch consisting of rice, dal, one vegetable and fish. By the time lunch was over, there was a queue of borrowers outside the office.

While the repayment instalments are collected from the borrowers' doorsteps, fresh loans are given at branches, in the presence of everyone. Once this exercise got over, one credit officer carried the extra cash of the day (the residual money after giving fresh loans from the day's collection) to the nearest bank branch to deposit in Bandhan's account, even as the branch manager was seen keying the data into a computer.

The residential facility gives a sense of security, particularly to the wives of the field workers who feel assured that their husbands are not whiling away their time playing cards, smoking or drinking while not working, as such things are not allowed at residences-cum-branches. Living there inculcates discipline and a sense of austerity, which would not have been possible had they lived on their own or had commuted from home.

The system did not change even after Bandhan became a bank—the same monitoring and personal touch: meeting a borrower once a week, fifty-two times a year. The credit officers are now collecting deposits too from the same customers who have been borrowing from Bandhan. Also, instead of making an entry in a notebook and later keying the data into a computer, the credit officers now carry handheld devices which are connected to a central server for real-time data collation.

In July 2015, after a tiring day in Patna, when a group of Bandhan executives planned to return to their hotel late in the evening, Ghosh decided to visit the local MFI branch at Anishabad, the oldest in Bihar, set up in 2008. At the branch, all the employees touched his feet. The first thing he did was check the register.

There were mistakes; some papers were not signed. He asked the branch manager how much cash he had in the chest and checked if the amount tallied with the entries in the register. He found that this particular branch had withdrawn a small amount from the bank the previous day.

Why did the branch manager do it? He withdrew from the bank because he did not consider the cash in hand. Ghosh sat him down and explained to him why one should be meticulous in keeping tabs on everything—daily collection, cash in hand, deposits into and withdrawal from banks—to make a branch successful. The branch manager ought not to compromise on this.

In my view, the MFI business is a simple one, where the products are standardized. You don't really need detailed credit appraisal of loans to individuals. All one needs to do is keep the amount small and get the group right, keep the supervision of the groups tight, and the repayment will come.

Here, risk management is all about keeping the loan amounts small, forming a good group and carrying out strong supervision. The costs are primarily for group formation, giving the members financial education, very close supervision, and keeping the operations near the borrowers. Credit appraisal, which is a major cost for banks, is not a very important cost for MFIs. Ghosh's understanding of these is unquestionable.

Eight Training Centres

To keep the employees updated on and familiar with operational norms, Bandhan has eight training centres across six states—West Bengal, Assam, Tripura, Bihar, Maharashtra and Haryana. Another is coming up at Rajpur, which already houses the oldest training centre of the organization. A group of thirty-four in-house trainers, and many hired from the market, has been busy giving thousands of hours of training to the employees every month.

CAPACITY BUILDING: Ghosh laying the foundation stone of Bandhan's ninth—and latest—training centre, at Rajpur, West Bengal, in May 2015.

The idea of training the employees continuously is as old as Bandhan itself. In the early days, when there was no training centre, Sunday was the day of training. The venue was the Pragyalaya auditorium at Auxilium Convent School in Barasat, North 24 Parganas. Bandhan used to take the hall on rent for nine hours, from 9 a.m. to 6 p.m., but would invariably end up continuing the training till 9 p.m.

The father in charge of Auxilium Convent School would come at 6 p.m. and ask them to vacate the hall, but Ghosh would somehow convince him to let them stay longer. The father would tolerate this once in a while, but on many Sundays, he would shoo them away, and Ghosh would stand under a tree and carry on with the training.

Another venue for training was a Christian missionary centre at Baruipur, South 24 Parganas. FWWB India used to finance the training programmes.

The focus was always on organizational discipline and how to bring in social and economic change. The biggest challenge for Bandhan was creating the right kind of work culture in a state not known for it. 'We never felt we were working; we were serving the people. We wanted to change people's lives—through training, workshop, discussions, sharing . . . We would eat, sleep, walk, talk Bandhan,' said Runu da.

Training is the key to building capacity in its employees. Periodically, the organization brings in resource persons—ranging from former governor of the Central Bank of Bangladesh, Atiur Rahman, to RBI deputy governors, economist Abhijit Vinayak Banerjee, and many more experts in MFIs, banking and management—to interact with the employees and teach them the nuances of the business.

As part of the training, there have been monthly meetings at different tiers—senior executives, branch managers and

COs—where every circular was dissected and its message percolated to the bottom. Ghosh believed that blind implementation of the norms would not work; every employee had to understand why a particular norm was laid down, the logic behind it and what it brought to the table.

All such meetings culminated in staff conferences in every state where Bandhan was present, every year, typically on Sundays. This was a platform for close interaction between the employees and the senior management.

If training is the heart of Bandhan, picnics are its lifeline, and the manual is its backbone. None can escape from it. At every level, there have been periodic tests on one's awareness of the norms laid down in the manual, and refresher courses were arranged if needed.

From these training sessions, Ghosh also gets his ideas on delicate HR issues. One day, in the run-up to the launch of the bank at the Rajpur training centre, he found piles of shoes outside all classrooms except one. Instantly, he knew that the microfinance employees were being trained in all those classrooms with the shoes outside, and the one room which did not have shoes piled outside was being used to train bank employees. That was a cultural problem, and Ghosh knew how to tackle it.

7

On the Way to Becoming a Bank

Typically, after six every evening, employees queue up near the lifts on the higher floors of the Bandhan headquarters in Salt Lake City to leave the office. Many come to work from faraway places. They leave home early in the morning and commute for long hours to reach the office by 9 a.m.

The evening of 2 April 2014 was different, though. It was past 6 p.m., but nobody was in a hurry to go home. They were not busy with work either, even though everybody was glued to their computer screens, which displayed the RBI website. Impatiently, they kept refreshing the website.

A few minutes after 6 p.m., Pappu Banerjee of Bandhan's communications division screamed, 'We got it.' Instantly, Chandan Mukherjee, an accountant, lifted him up on his shoulders and started running. There was a loud cheer on the fourth floor where the communications division, and a few others, run their offices.

'WE GOT IT': On 2 April 2014, all Bandhan employees at the headquarters were celebrating after RBI announced that it was giving in-principle banking licences to Bandhan and IDFC.

Arpita Sen, deputy general manager, institutional finance team of Bandhan, rushed to the seventh floor, where Ghosh was holding a meeting with a few senior executives, and broke the news: 'Sir, *aamra peye gachi* (We got it).'

From a list of twenty-five applications, RBI gave its nod to two—IDFC Ltd and Bandhan—to set up universal banks. It was an in-principle approval, and both would need to set up the banks within eighteen months, which would be subject to the banking regulator's final nod.

By the time all the senior employees rushed to the eighth floor, where the boss sits, Ghosh was in no position to talk to them. He was juggling two mobile phones—reporters from newspapers and television channels were calling—and his two landlines were ringing non-stop.

MAN OF THE HOUR: Ghosh was juggling two mobile phones, taking calls from newspapers and television channels after RBI gave an in-principle licence to Bandhan, surprising many. Poulami Datta, part of Ghosh's secretariat, can also be seen.

Piyali Ghosh, his secretary, soon took charge and stopped passing most phone calls on his landlines as an excited Ghosh walked up and down the office, talking to the media.

Company secretary Indranil Banerjee soon started calling the board members and Bandhan's investors to give them the news. It went on till midnight, and by the time the senior executives left office, it was 1 a.m.

The next morning, they were greeted by a band which Runu da had hired to celebrate. The band moved in and around Salt Lake, blaring popular Hindi songs, and some of the Bandhan employees, led by Runu da, danced all the way. Of course, it was not easy to arrange the band party. Narayan

Chandra had put his foot down as he thought this would not go down well with the neighbours in the locality.

Ghosh addressed all employees in the conference room on the ninth floor, and asked them not to work that day and enjoy the moment. Sweets were distributed at the head office as well as on the field; there were flowers and gulal all over, and the nine-storeyed building was lit up in the evening. The euphoria continued for the next couple of days, until the weekend.

At the meeting, Ghosh highlighted the HR issues which would come up on the way as Bandhan transformed into a bank. He made it clear that banking would be a different ball game, and that the existing Bandhan staff neither had the qualifications nor the experience to steer the organization through this phase. It would need to hire bankers, and the staff should welcome them as teachers.

Also, some of the MFI employees could upgrade themselves and become bankers, provided they took up the challenge and developed competence. Capacity-building has all along been Ghosh's pet theme; he used the meeting to focus on that once again to prepare the employees for the transformation.

32 kg Excess Baggage

The conditional licence closed a cycle which had started on 1 July 2013, the day Bandhan submitted its application for the same. Sen had to pay Rs 3800 to Air India for 32 kg of excess baggage in the cargo on her flight from Kolkata to Mumbai.

As Ghosh was attending a microfinance event in Hyderabad, organized by the lobbying group Microfinance

Institutions Network (MFIN), Sen carried the application to Mumbai the previous day, 30 June, which happened to be her birthday. Two sets of applications were to be submitted, seeking the licence to commence a banking business under Section 22 of the Banking Companies Act 1949.

Each application had 336 pages, but the annexures ran into thousands of pages as they contained, among other things, Bandhan Financial Services Pvt. Ltd's memorandum and articles of association, financial statements, credit facilities from banks, annual reports, loan portfolio, ratings, audit reports, various studies undertaken to assess the impact of microloans on borrowers, and everything else to illustrate the group's ten-year track record.

Sen had to seek the help of others at Kolkata airport to put the big box in the scanner, and finally to take it to the baggage counter. There was curiosity about what it contained. After landing in Mumbai, Sen's biggest challenge was picking up the big box from the conveyor belt and putting it on the trolley.

From the airport, she headed to Ramee Guestline Hotel on Kohinoor Road, opposite Swaminarayan Temple, at Dadar East. By that time, Ghosh had already checked in.

The following morning, Monish Shah, a partner at Deloitte Touche Tohmatsu India Pvt. Ltd, joined them. On their way to the RBI headquarters at Fort, they went to the Siddhivinayak Temple at Prabhadevi to offer prayers.

As they reached RBI a bit early, the trio spent a few tense minutes over coffee at the Starbucks outlet in Horniman Circle. Around 10 a.m., Shah and Sen carried the box lying in the lobby of the RBI building to the lift. The destination was the thirteenth floor, the office of Sudha Damodar, chief

general manager, department of banking operations and
development (DBOD).

They had to wait as another applicant was already with
Damodar. After a little while, the trio was ushered into a
conference room even as two gentlemen were getting out of
it, carrying a suitcase each. N. Sara Rajendrakumar, general
manager, was with Damodar.

As the Bandhan team kept the box on the table in the
conference room, they were offered pouches of apple juice.
Ghosh introduced himself, and Sen and Shah, to the central
bankers. Sen opened the box and took out the application, a
spiral-bound book and a CD.

There was a brief interview. Damodar's questions were on
why Bandhan wanted to become a bank, Ghosh's vision for
it, whether it would face any problems in terms of meeting the
RBI norms of priority loans and other reserve requirements,
the number of employees on its roll and its business model as
a bank.

While they were leaving the RBI premises, they saw a long
queue outside the gate, where the managing director and vice
chairman of IDFC, Rajiv Lall, and senior executives of L&T
Finance Ltd and Janalakshmi Financial Services Ltd, among
others, were waiting with bagfuls of applications.

Three years after the February 2010 Union budget
announced that licences would be issued to new banks for
financial inclusion, RBI released the final guidelines on
licensing norms on 22 February 2013. Work at Bandhan had
started even before that.

On 1 January 2013, Ghosh formed a six-member team to
steer its banking project. Runa Mallick, Soumyajit Dutta and

Sen were picked from Bandhan's existing staff, and senior bankers Dipankar Das, Soumen Chakrabarty and Malay Basu Mallick were hired from different banks. Sen and Basu Mallick were made the joint coordinators.

The challenge in this phase was to present a credible application to the banking regulator, supported by a solid business model.

By April, Bandhan engaged Deloitte to handhold it for the preparation of the application, and later for its transformation from an MFI into a bank. Around that time, S.K. Giri, chief operating officer, core banking solutions, NABARD, came on board. He replaced Basu Mallick as the coordinator.

Ghosh had also formed a twenty-member team for undertaking a geo-mapping exercise of prospective bank branches. The team suggested 825 locations. They were revisited, the potential of each location was analysed, and the team finally zeroed in on ideal locations for 691 normal bank branches and 816 ultra-small branches.

There was an advisory committee too. Headed by Ghosh, the committee had a mix of bankers and non-bankers as its members—Gobindo Banerjee (retired general manager of Punjab National Bank), Ashoka Chatterjee (retired general manager of Indian Overseas Bank), Partha Sarathi Basu (retired deputy general manager of Indian Bank) and Narayan Chandra.

Around the same time, Bandhan's internal research and development wing, headed by Piyali Bhattacharjee, conducted a study on potential deposit mobilization from the micro-borrowers and non-borrowers, titled 'The Voice of Customer'.

The team which was formed to do the geo-mapping exercise continued its work even after the banking application was submitted to RBI.

Those days, there were intense discussions for long hours on products, processes, interest rates and financial projections, and they were often inconclusive. A project management office (PMO) was set up to manage the activities.

The Third Floor

The Bandhan office had moved into the DN 32 building in 2010. Since then, all floors of the ten-storeyed building were occupied, except for the third floor. It was Ghosh's dream that the third floor would be used when Bandhan finally got its banking licence.

Once his dream came true on 2 April 2014, new departments were formed and workstations allocated on the third floor. Ghosh himself supervised the seating arrangements. Banerjee, company secretary, and Abhijit Ghosh, deputy general manager, finance and accounts, sat side by side, as they needed to oversee the legal and regulatory work. In the same cubicle, the business development head, Giri, and Sen were offered seats. These four were running the PMO.

THE QUARTET: (From left) Arpita Sen, Indranil Banerjee, Abhijit Ghosh and S.K. Giri were running the PMO for the transformation of the MFI into a bank.

The PMO created different functional units on the third floor to oversee HR, branch premises, products and process, and IT. The Deloitte executives were also on the same floor. Almost every evening, Ghosh would drop by and discuss strategies and processes until it was late, till the office boys came with packets of puffed rice and potato fritters.

The first query from RBI came on 5 September 2013. The central bank asked many questions related to operational issues. A fortnight later, Banerjee got a call from Ghosh, asking him to come to the boardroom. By the time Banerjee reached, Bandhan's senior executives had already assembled there, and the RBI queries were on the screen.

They were asked to give their views on the issues raised by the regulator. This was the first of many letters that RBI would send to Bandhan, asking questions and seeking information. Each time, Deloitte drafted the reply with inputs from the senior executives after extensive brainstorming sessions. On occasion, it took weeks to answer as one needed to dig into old records.

RBI also wanted a firm commitment from Bandhan that the public shareholding in the company would be brought up to at least 51 per cent, a necessary precondition for the licence.

In early 2014, RBI inspected Bandhan to check its preparedness, though not officially. It was a routine inspection which the regulator had been doing for the NBFC, but this time all questions were related to the banking licence.

A fortnight before the announcement on 2 April 2014, a couple of senior RBI officials had visited the Bandhan headquarters and grilled the senior management on several issues, including capital, products, processes, governance, IT and risk. The RBI officials had also gone to the field to do a recce on Bandhan's preparedness.

Around that time, there had been intense speculation in the media on the prospective new banks. Bandhan had not figured anywhere.

Restricted Area

The real work started after getting the in-principle licence as Bandhan had to get ready to be a bank within the next eighteen months. The third floor got the tag of 'Restricted Area' where a group of thirty executives, handpicked by Ghosh, was working.

Ghosh was keen to open the bank on 15 April 2015—the Bengali New Year's Day. A countdown timer was put up on the third floor. On every successive day, the number of days left for the launch got reduced, but nobody knew who was in charge of changing it. Many suspect that Ghosh himself used to do this every morning before the others came in.

There was intense discussion every day on the likely model of the bank and everything else, but progress was slow as the discussions were often inconclusive. The team members fought hard with different ideas, raised issues, but in most cases they were unable to take decisions, and Ghosh had to step in. His message was clear: Don't just discuss problems; if you raise one problem, offer three solutions. Even the structural model that Bandhan Bank has adopted—'hub-and-spoke'—was Ghosh's idea. More on this later.

The promoter of a new bank was required to set up a holding company for the bank as well as all other financial services companies it owned, which were regulated by RBI

or other financial sector regulators. Called non-operative
financial holding company (NOFHC), it does not have any
other activities. It is to be registered as a non-deposit-taking,
non-banking, financial company with the department of
non-banking supervision (DNBS) of RBI, but its regulatory
and supervisory frameworks are governed by another
department—DBOD.

And, of course, it would have to be set up under the
Companies Act 2013, after the repeal of the Companies Act
1956.

Deepak Kumar Khaitan, a practising company secretary
in Kolkata, was chosen to guide Bandhan on the
incorporation of the entities. One of the conditions of the
in-principle approval of the banking regulator was that the
memorandum and articles of association of the NOFHC
and the bank would need to be approved by RBI before their
incorporation.

Looking at the complexity of the legal requirement, it
was decided that a reputed legal firm should be engaged to
handhold Bandhan on the legal and regulatory issues. Three
firms—Amarchand & Mangaldas & Suresh A. Shroff & Co.,
AZB & Partners and Khaitan & Co.—were considered, and
Amarchand & Mangaldas was selected for the job.

Saurya Bhattacharya, then a senior associate, was deputed
to advise Bandhan with his team, under the leadership of
Vandana Shroff, a partner at the firm.

The Deloitte team made the first draft of the memorandum
and articles of association, of the NOFHC and the bank,
respectively, and Amarchand & Mangaldas reviewed it. They
were finalized after several rounds of meetings and conference
calls.

The papers were submitted to RBI in August 2014. After raising a few queries, the banking regulator cleared them on 20 October 2014, with a few modifications, leading to a revision in the drafts. Both the entities could not be incorporated at the same time. As the bank would be a subsidiary of the NOFHC, the NOFHC had to be incorporated first and it would subscribe to the shares of the bank.

For Banerjee, Abhijit and Deepak Khaitan, many Sundays were working days at that time. On 14 November 2014, relevant forms were uploaded on the website of the ministry of corporate affairs. All three were apprehensive, as it was an incorporation under the new Companies Act, and they were not aware of any entity that had been incorporated ahead of it under this Act.

To their relief, no questions were asked and the NOFHC—Bandhan Financial Holdings Ltd—was incorporated on 17 November 2014, completing the first legal step for the setting up of the bank.

The next stage was the incorporation of Bandhan Bank. The document was already cleared by the RBI, and the team by that time had gained confidence with the experience of incorporating a company under the new Companies Act. So, within a week of the incorporation of the holding company, it applied to the registrar of companies (RoC) seeking the availability of the name 'Bandhan Bank'. It was granted on 24 November 2014.

Within three weeks, on 16 December 2014, it moved the RoC, seeking the bank's incorporation. But it was not easy to convince the RoC, which felt that RBI had given its in-principle approval to Bandhan and not Bandhan Bank, and so it should not give its nod for the incorporation of an entity called Bandhan Bank.

It took rounds of discussions to convince the RoC of the complex licensing norms of RBI. Finally, the certificate of incorporation was issued on 23 December 2014. Ghosh was eating a late lunch of masala dosa at Balaji Restaurant outside Mumbai airport before catching a flight to Kolkata when Banerjee called to give him the news. A teetotaller, Ghosh ordered a Coke to celebrate and wash down his dosa.

Now, the bank was born as an entity. The next stage was the registration of the NOFHC as an NBFC. The company secretary went to the RBI central office in Mumbai to submit the application. The certificate would be issued by the RBI Kolkata office where DNBS has historically been located.

Banerjee, Abhijit and Bandhan Bank's chief financial officer, Sunil Samdani, were in constant touch with RBI's Kolkata office, but the DNBS officials were convinced only after they were given satisfactory clarifications by the central office in Mumbai. It was cleared on 2 June 2015, but the certificate of registration was not issued on that day. On the afternoon of the following day, 3 June, DNBS Kolkata called up and asked Bandhan to collect it. Ghosh rushed there with half a dozen colleagues, grinning ear to ear, and collected it in the evening. Another hurdle was crossed.

The Biggest Challenge

The next, and the biggest, challenge was the increase in public shareholding, which could be done through fresh equity infusion. Under RBI norms, the public shareholding in

Bandhan, the holding company of the NOFHC, would have to be at least 51 per cent.

IFC and SIDBI held 10.93 per cent and 9.63 per cent, respectively, aggregating 20.56 per cent stake (SIDBI's stake marginally came down from the original investment because of fresh equity infusion by IFC). The existing investors had pre-emptive rights and hence, if Bandhan wanted to bring in any new investor, the existing ones would have to be given an option to subscribe to new shares. Only if they declined to do so could a new investor come in.

Bandhan needed an investment banker to handle it. Kotak Mahindra Capital Co. Ltd (the merchant banking arm of Kotak Mahindra Bank), JM Financial Institutional Securities Ltd, Axis Capital Ltd and a few others were consulted. Kotak was selected to conduct the deal even as Amarchand & Mangaldas was there for legal guidance.

The Kotak team was led by T.V. Raghunath. Bandhan's team had four members—Abhijit, Sen, Banerjee and Giri. Ghosh himself was leading the team. Two more young executives of Bandhan supported the team, working round the clock—Amit Sarkar and Anindya Banerjee.

This was the most difficult part of Bandhan's journey towards becoming a bank. Invitation letters were sent to IFC and SIDBI, in accordance with the pre-emptive rights they enjoyed, while Kotak prepared the teaser, or the document that typically gets circulated to potential buyers of a specific security that may be offered for sale in the future.

It was decided that the first round of discussions would be done with SIDBI. The Bandhan team, along with Deloitte's Sanjeev Shah (legal expert), Shah (project leader) and Anshuman Jaiswal (Amarchand & Mangaldas), went to

Lucknow on 17 June 2014. On their way to Howrah railway station to catch the Rajdhani Express, they were caught in a massive traffic jam on Howrah Bridge and almost missed the train. That was not a good omen.

There was an hour-long presentation, and another couple of hours were spent answering questions from SIDBI executives Pradeep Malgaonkar, U.S. Lal, Vivek Malhotra, R. Raman and A.R. Samal. By lunchtime, it was clear that SIDBI was doubtful of investing further in a company which was going to transfer its business to a subsidiary.

The Bandhan team tried to convince SIDBI that ultimately it would hold its stake in the bank through this route, and had they gone for a direct holding in the bank, they would have had to pay more as the bank's valuation would be higher. SIDBI suggested that Bandhan come up with a revised proposal, with more details.

IFC, which was initially excited about the idea of Bandhan becoming a bank, developed cold feet and was lukewarm to the idea of raising its stake.

When rounds of discussions did not yield any result, Bandhan asked Kotak to look for prospective investors.

Once the teaser was circulated, more than a dozen investors from across the globe started showing interest.

KPMG did the financial due diligence, while legal due diligence was conducted by Khaitan & Co. (it replaced Amarchand & Mangaldas for this assignment). That was quite a job. The entire organization was shaken up by the amount of information asked for the due diligence.

A development finance institution of the UK, a private equity fund, and GIC Special Investments Pte Ltd, a private equity and venture capital firm specializing in direct investments and fund investments, were willing to invest at a valuation of around 2.9 times of the price to book, a valuation ratio typically used by investors—something Bandhan was expecting. That would have pegged the price of Rs 10 per share of Bandhan at around of Rs 330, which would make it a premium of Rs 320. In 2009, SIDBI had paid a premium of Rs 50 while buying a stake in Bandhan; and in 2012, IFC had paid nearly two and a half times the amount: a premium of Rs 117.

Armed with this, Bandhan approached IFC and SIDBI again and asked them whether they would like to invest at this valuation, or else Bandhan would ask the new investors to step in.

Ghosh was in a hurry. He knew that the original deadline for opening the bank (15 April) could not be met, but he maintained his calm as the date was not sacrosanct, and he had time till October 2015 when RBI's eighteen-month window would close. IDFC, the other entity that got the licence, had already said that they would start their bank in October.

While SIDBI wrote to Bandhan asking for a revised proposal, IFC started negotiations. An IFC team visited Bandhan's Kolkata office twice. Mengitsu Alemayehu, director, South Asia, IFC; Swapnil Neeraj, principal investment officer and microfinance lead for Asia; Nilesh Srivastava, head of the financial sector investments portfolio in South Asia; and Abhishek Girish Gupte, an investment officer of IFC, were keen to know the entire process of setting up the bank. They assured all sorts of support, guidance and consultancy for the successful launch of the bank.

The negotiations continued for almost two months but did not go anywhere as IFC was asking for a lower valuation.

GIC and the other two prospective investors wanted similar rights as those enjoyed by IFC and SIDBI. Among the three, the private equity fund was the most stringent, but the valuation offered by it was the best. After comparing the terms and conditions of all offers, Ghosh and his team felt that the next round of negotiations could be done with the development finance institution and GIC. Accordingly, the team instructed the investment bank.

The head of South Asia at the development finance institution had several rounds of meetings with Bandhan's senior management team, but as the discussion progressed, it kept on adding new terms and conditions. When it prepared the detailed term sheet, there were many things which the initial non-binding term sheet did not contain. These changes did not excite the Bandhan team to take the discussion forward. The managing director, debt and financial institutions, of the UK entity, could not conceal the fact that he was upset.

A term sheet is nothing but a brief document which a prospective acquirer submits to the target company, indicating the price and conditions under which it offers to acquire the company. This is a precursor to an actual acquisition agreement, and legally not binding. A draft of the term sheet is usually circulated among the parties and their attorneys for changes to be negotiated before the final version is signed.

By that time, IFC and SIDBI were turning positive towards the valuation given by others. IFC agreed to invest at a valuation which Bandhan was expecting and to invest both in the BFSL as well as the bank, up to the limit permitted by the regulator.

Even as the development finance institution's terms and conditions did not find favour with Bandhan, discussions with GIC were progressing well. Pankaj Sood, senior vice president and head, director investment, at GIC's private equity wing in India, who was earlier with Kotak's investment bank, and Holger Michaelis, senior vice president at GIC Special Investments Pte Ltd in Singapore, along with Gaurav Jain and Kushal Chand, made several trips to the Bandhan office in Kolkata to demonstrate their eagerness for investing in the company.

The financial and legal due diligence reports of KPMG and Khaitan & Co. were shared with all three—IFC, SIDBI as well as GIC—for review. Around this time, Desai & Diwanji, GIC's legal counsel, came into the picture. The law firm's team, led by Toral Desai (two members of the team were Jolly Abraham and Monika Deshmukh) camped at the Bandhan office for several days, interacting with the senior management and reviewing legal issues. In all, they had 750 questions. The answers were given in phases.

IFC's legal counsel, AZB, was relatively conservative in raising queries and relied mostly on the due diligence report prepared by Khaitan & Co., Bandhan's legal adviser.

The Seventh Floor

At that time, the scene of action shifted from the third floor—which was being renovated—to the seventh floor. The cabins on this floor were all occupied by senior Bandhan executives, but there was an open meeting area. The quartet of Banerjee, Abhijit, Giri and Sen would sit at a round table, and there would be an extra chair for Ghosh, who would frequently drop in and join the discussions.

Once he was there, nobody knew how long it would take and there was no question of lunch or dinner, even if it was late afternoon or close to midnight. Of course, there would be rounds and rounds of tea and the different kinds of biscuits stored in Bandhan's pantry in the headquarters. Ghosh would sip on green tea, while the others had either black or regular tea, with milk and sugar.

Ghosh and the team also made a trip to the GIC headquarters in Singapore to present the bank's business plan. The GIC managing director and president, Tay Lim Hock, was very impressed, and he committed to investing in Bandhan.

The lunch at Annalakshmi, a south Indian restaurant in Central Square, was also a novel experience for the Bandhan team. There was no fixed price for the meal: one could pay as much or as little as one wished to. Buying stakes in a bank, that too a bank with Bandhan's unique profile, was very different. The buyers couldn't simply pay what they wanted. There was hard bargaining, even though both GIC and IFC were convinced that Bandhan was an entity worth betting on.

To reiterate his commitment, Hock led a team of GIC senior executives to meet Ghosh and his people at the Taj Mahal Hotel in Mumbai.

The venue where the four teams of GIC, Bandhan, Desai & Diwanji and Khaitan & Co. would dissect the term sheet was the boardroom on the ninth floor. Sen was made the coordinator of the Bandhan team. Toral of Desai & Diwanji, a hard-core professional, was not ready to concede anything, even if her client, GIC, agreed.

Naturally, progress was very slow. There were moments when Ghosh was either upset or furious over certain observations or comments made by the other side. But he would give vent to his feelings only within his close circle. On the discussion table, he would always be smiling and charming; inside there was a steely resolve that he would not be cowed down by any pressure; and he would not compromise on anything to get the deal done. At times, he would even risk the deal being abandoned.

The IFC term sheet was relatively benign and, without losing much time, Bandhan accepted it. The same thing happened with GIC too, but after rounds of gruelling discussions. Once both were in place, Bandhan was ready to submit its application for the final licence. Ghosh went to Mumbai with Giri and Sen.

The ritual was the same that had played out on 1 July 2013. This time around, of course, there was no payment to the airline for carrying documents in the cargo, as the package was much lighter—only 250-odd pages, stowed away as cabin luggage. However, there was another problem. At night, they discovered that the pages had been bound upside down. Giri and Sen had to work for hours through the night, unbinding and then rebinding it using the spiral wire. On 21 January 2015, the team submitted it to RBI, after praying at the Siddhivinayak Temple at Prabhadevi.

The application was supported by the term sheets which made it evident that three investors—IFC, SIDBI and GIC—would pick up stakes in Bandhan. However, that was not enough. The regulator wanted Bandhan to submit a certificate by a chartered accountant saying that the public shareholding in Bandhan had indeed risen to 51 per cent and its share capital had increased. This meant some work was still left. And that was the most difficult part—the official closure of the deal.

In any such deal, the first step is to prepare a non-binding term sheet which contains mainly the investors' backgrounds, valuation of the company, the investment amount, the percentage of stake to be taken and the key rights.

At the next step, the binding term sheet captures the number of shares to be purchased, the price, the percentage of holding, the process of the board and shareholders' meetings, including board seats, various kinds of rights, restriction on share transfer, dispute resolution, etc.

Only after this, at stage three, are the share subscription agreement and the shareholders' agreement signed.

Finally, after the funds flow in, the amendment of the article of association reflects the rights of the investors.

The next few weeks saw intense negotiations, and the writing and rewriting of many draft agreements by the legal firms for share purchase, but it was not progressing the way Ghosh would have liked it to. His target date for the opening of the bank was 15 April, even though no announcement had been made. By that time, he knew it would not be possible, even though work was in full swing in terms of preparing the logistics of a new bank: branches, technology and other operations.

A month after the final application was submitted, on 23 February 2015, the Bandhan team and their legal counsel went to Delhi to sort out all issues and close the deal at the IFC office, where representatives of GIC and SIDBI too would be present.

Bharat Anand, a partner at Khaitan & Co., accompanied the Bandhan team. Anand, with his precision in arguments and articulation, added a lot of value to the discussion which lasted for several hours. On the first day, it went on till 11 p.m. It had started at 9.30 a.m.

Dinner at 2 a.m.

The Bandhan team booked Hyatt Regency, Gurgaon, during their Delhi visit. They left the IFC office at the Maruti Suzuki Building on 1, Nelson Mandela Road, Vasant Kunj, at midnight and by the time they reached their hotel, it was 1 a.m. When Abhijit called room service for rice, dal and some vegetables, he was greeted with 'good morning, sir', and dinner was served around 2 a.m.

Ghosh had to catch a flight to Kolkata at six in the morning that day. Nobody slept that night; they assembled in Ghosh's room and spent the next few hours chalking out the strategy for the next day's meeting till Ghosh left for the airport. He did participate in the meeting, though, through a conference call. Wiser after the previous day's experience, the team changed hotels, and shifted to Jaypee Palace, close to the IFC office in Delhi.

Exactly a month later, on 23 March, the team flew down to Delhi once again, to iron out the last few issues—there were not too many, but they were critical in nature—as, by that time, most of the issues had been resolved through conference calls and the continuous exchange of emails. This time, the Bandhan team had a new member—Sunil Samdani, the CFO of the bank. Before joining Bandhan, Samdani had been the CFO of Karvy Financial Services Ltd, in Mumbai.

The next stopover was in Lucknow, at the SIDBI headquarters. After many more meetings, conference calls and emails—polite and not-so-polite—and a normally cool Ghosh losing his equanimity occasionally, the agreement was frozen on 22 April 2015. The curtains were drawn on the six-month-long, arduous negotiations.

It was signed on 24 April in Bandhan's boardroom. Most senior executives were present there. Wearing a crisp white shirt, Runu da looked relaxed as the pilot project of handheld machines for the microfinance credit officers at Rajpur was a great success. Runu da had been under stress, as the project had a critical bearing on the bank's success. The field staff working at the DSCs, who had been collecting and disbursing loans manually, would now do it in real time through handheld devices connected to a central server.

Ghosh thanked the team and said, 'It has been an excellent learning experience for us.' At 6.42 p.m., he signed the agreement with a new Klipper pen bought specially for this purpose. The entire exercise continued till 1 a.m.

IFC's stake in BFSL rose to 16.44 per cent, and SIDBI's went up to 8.13 per cent, even as the new investor, GIC, picked up a 16.70 per cent stake.

SEALING THE DEAL: On 22 April 2015, Ghosh signed the agreement for equity sale with a new Klipper pen.

In the bank, IFC was going to pick up a 4.93 per cent stake, GIC 4.99 per cent, and SIDBI 0.33 per cent.

It was decided that the money would flow in on 8 May. The GIC money hit the Bandhan account at Kotak Bank first, and then the SIDBI funds flowed in. Later in the afternoon, the IFC money was also credited to the account. A board meeting was called the same day, and shares were allotted.

GOODBYE, MFI: Ghosh (middle) signing the last balance sheet of the MFI in Bandhan's boardroom in May 2015. With him are Sunil Samdani (left), the CFO of the bank, and Indranil Banerjee (right), the company secretary.

Pankaj Sood and Gaurav Jain of GIC came down to Kolkata to collect the share certificate; the same was sent by courier to IFC and SIDBI.

Around three in the afternoon, Subrata De of De & Bose Chartered Accountants, Kolkata, mailed the certificate to RBI, saying that the deal was complete, the money had flowed in, and shares had been issued to new investors. The last hurdle was crossed for the acquisition of the banking licence under Section 22 of the Banking Regulation Act, 1949.

RBI issued it on 17 June 2015. At noon, Damodar handed it over to Ghosh. One of Ghosh's colleagues wanted to take a photograph on his mobile but Damodar, the central banker, did not allow him to do so.

Ghosh, however, did not escape being photographed with the final licence. As he was walking out of the RBI central

HERE IT IS: Ghosh with the author outside the RBI headquarters in Mumbai on 17 June 2015, after receiving the banking licence.

office, Suryakant Niwate, a photographer with *Business Standard*, clicked him.

From there, Ghosh rushed to Trident Hotel at Nariman Point to hold his first-ever press conference in Mumbai, to announce that the bank would be launched on 23 August. Even before the press conference started, the *Business Standard* website flashed Ghosh's photo, holding the licence outside the RBI building.

Finally, Bandhan had crossed the regulatory hurdles on its way to becoming a bank. But there were operational issues. It was not a cakewalk.

8

Building the Backbone

Simply put, the job at hand was to build an inclusive bridge to connect the credit-starved masses that had so far eluded India's mainstream banking system. For that, technology was the key.

On day one, Bandhan Bank started its operations with 501 branches—a record in the banking industry, globally. However, it did not set up so many branches to create a record—it was a necessity.

Bandhan's microfinance avatar had 2022 branches, offering doorstep services to its 6.7 million borrowers. The credit officers at these branches used to collect weekly repayments from the borrowers at their doorstep even as the loans were disbursed at the branches, using the collection money. After the disbursement of fresh loans, if there was surplus cash, it was deposited with the nearest bank branch, public or private, in Bandhan's account.

Even after transforming itself into a bank, the business of giving small loans would continue. So, where would the microfinance branches (rechristened as doorstep service centres—DSCs) keep the excess cash? At the branches of Bandhan Bank.

Naturally, the bank would need all these branches. The plan was to adopt a 'hub-and-spoke' model where every branch (hub) would be linked to four or five DSCs (spokes). While the DSCs would continue to give loans (and also collect deposits from the borrowers of small loans), the bank branches would predominantly be liability centres, collecting deposits, at least in the initial years.

Technology played a critical role in making this plan a success. There had been intense debate on which core-banking solution (CBS) would be best suited for the bank ever since the submission of the application to RBI for the banking licence, but without any conclusion.

There were many reasons behind this. Not too many senior executives of Bandhan were technology savvy, and many of them were overwhelmed by the technological complexity of running a bank vis-à-vis a large microfinance company.

Besides, in India, there has been no reference architecture of connecting a bank with customers in the remotest pockets of the country. The last-mile connectivity has always been elusive. So, every discussion would invariably end with which bank was using which CBS, and anecdotal stories of how customers of a certain bank were taken for a ride despite the successful implementation of core banking.

CBS is a networking of branches with a single centralized database, which enables customers to operate their accounts and avail banking services from any branch of a bank on the CBS network, regardless of where they maintain their accounts. Once the CBS is in place, the customer of a branch no longer remains just that: she becomes the customer of a bank.

The points to note are:

- CBS is an application for facilitating only transaction.
- The network connectivity is separate from the CBS.
- CBS addresses about 10 per cent of the banking operations, while a large number of other applications are required to run a full-service bank.
- System integration—creating a technology environment with network connectivity, application software, integration with external agencies as well as interfacing multiple applications—is a specialized job.
- Project implementation is a difficult job and it requires a large IT team.
- Finally, one needs to work out the complete functionality requirements carefully to assess what is required and who is best suited to deliver it.

As the original plan was to start the bank on 15 April 2015, the pressure was mounting to identify the right technology partner even as big, small and unheard-of IT companies were making a beeline to sell something or other to Bandhan. The consensus was that Bandhan should assign the task of IT implementation to a capable firm which had a good reputation, experience and financial strength.

Deloitte, the consulting firm that Bandhan had hired for helping it in its transformation into a bank, prepared the request for proposal (RFP) to invite bids from various companies. An RFP is nothing but a solicitation, often made through a bidding process, by an agency or company interested in the procurement of a commodity, service or an asset, to potential service providers.

Given his background in technology implementation in cooperative banks under the aegis of NABARD, S.K. Giri was put on the job, along with Ronti Kar, general manager (IT), and Dibakar Ghosh, additional general manager (IT). Incidentally, the NABARD project, headed by Giri as chief operating officer (of CBS), was probably the first instance of complete technology outsourcing in Indian banking.

The conventional approach to technology adoption in a bank, so far, had been the asset-acquisition model by which assets such as hardware, software, application software and networking equipment are acquired by the bank on capital expenditure basis, popularly known as the Capex model.

While most banks have been acquiring technology through the Capex model, some of their more enterprising peers tried the new concept in bits and pieces. Bank of India was the first big bank to outsource the IT services under the build, operate and transfer (BOT) model. A few others followed it with a more refined approach and larger scope. In its latest avatar of complete outsourcing, the first example is probably that of a NABARD-sponsored outsourcing programme for over 200 state and district cooperative banks.

Technology Fault Line

Even under the Capex model, system integration and implementation are usually sourced from specialized IT firms, but their management and maintenance are either done by the banks themselves or outsourced. The first-generation banking technology experts in India are more familiar with this model, even as the next generation of experts are more inclined to full outsourcing, given its quick turnaround time as well as single-point management control—a trend that has been emerging slowly but steadily. Caught at the crossroads, Bandhan Bank faced the question of how to avoid the probable technology fault line.

The decision, endorsed by Ghosh, was to outsource the IT services in a big way. It was due to the fact that Bandhan had neither the required skill set within the organization nor the time to experiment.

For any large, complex project, an RFP is considered to be the heart and soul of the procurement. While preparing the RFP in May 2014, all top IT companies—TCS Ltd, Accenture Services Pvt. Ltd, Hewlett-Packard India Sales Pvt. Ltd, Wipro Ltd, FIS Payment Solutions & Services India Pvt. Ltd and Polaris Financial Technology Ltd—were asked to make presentations on the appropriate solution for Bandhan.

The idea was to collect as much information from as many sources as possible and, at the same time, create awareness within the organization about all the emerging trends in banking technology. It familiarized the bank's senior management with the technological vocabulary, and made them aware of the complexities involved.

A few technical experts chipped in while the RFP was being framed. Prominent among them were Nabankur Sen, former chief information security officer of Axis Bank, and P.A. Kalyansundaram, former general manager (IT), Bank of India, apart from the technology experts from IFC, Washington.

They pitched in with their comments and observations on various technology pitfalls such as talking about uninterrupted connectivity without considering the size of the bandwidth or focusing on the size of the bandwidth without taking into account the prospective number of users or the projected volume of transactions, etc.

These things could inadvertently creep into the RFP and potentially become a permanent source of dispute between the service providers and the clients. The RFP incorporated their suggestions to make the service obligations of the prospective service providers bulletproof.

The target technology architecture of Bandhan Bank posed a significant challenge, particularly in view of connecting its existing 2022 DSCs, catering to 6.7 million customers. Any future technology needed to factor in this aspect, as Bandhan had decided that, while converting into a bank, these outlets would need to be linked to the main core banking system in real time unlike the old model of MFSol, which had only been working as an offline database aggregator.

The Biggest Challenge

There were some 12,000 credit officers who used to collect weekly repayments from the borrowers in rural pockets.

Shifting from an offline, distributed system to an integrated real-time system was, perhaps, the biggest challenge.

Keeping this in mind, the network architecture envisaged at least 600 bank branches located in proximate areas that these 2022 microcredit outlets could be linked to. The linking was important from the point of view of hassle-free cash management as well as bringing other banking services such as deposits, remittances and insurance products to the hinterland.

The 401-page RFP, which Bandhan Bank circulated among the interested technology companies, laid down the rules of the bidding process, the disclaimers, and the rights and obligations of the bidders and the bank; outlined the major aspects of business strategy and the framework of engagement; and detailed terms and conditions of the engagement, among other things.

The document was uploaded on Bandhan's website on 9 June 2014. The deadline for submitting the bids was 30 June, which was later extended to 10 July, as many IT firms had pleaded that three weeks were inadequate to respond to such a complex proposal.

Before that, all the companies had sent their representatives to the pre-bid meeting in June. The meeting, which lasted for several hours, discussed all queries raised by the vendors, a few of whom were apprehensive of whether Bandhan would be able to pay for the high-value technology it was looking for. They, in fact, wanted to put up minimal architecture to keep the technology cost as affordable as possible.

With this kind of scepticism, four companies took a deep breath and put up bids. They were HP, Wipro,

FIS and Polaris. Even with an elaborate pre-bid exercise to keep the functional framework same for all, the responses were as different as chalk and cheese. Yet, one thing was strikingly similar: they all used the 'financial inclusion' solution model, featuring an intermediary server to capture large microcredit transactions, either offline or online, synchronizing with the central database at the end of each working day.

Bandhan Bank was determined to connect all its field-level credit officers through handheld devices, with a GSM network. The idea was to ensure that all transactions were synchronized with the central database on a real-time basis, barring a normal level of downtime, typically experienced in mobile phone connectivity. That was important from the viewpoint of managing a huge operational risk across 12,000 weekly instalment collectors in remote locations.

The final evaluation of the bids was done on a score-based, parameter-driven model. Pravir Vora, former IT head of ICICI Bank, was consulted to judge the efficacy and suitability of the proposals. However, the parameter-based score did not make much difference from a technical point of view.

The core-banking application was standard—both HP and Wipro had put up Finacle, a core-banking product developed by Infosys Ltd, even as FIS and Polaris lined up their own solutions. As far as IT infrastructure was concerned, HP and Wipro both had a name in IT system integration and management, and had emerged very strong contenders. Polaris had partnered with HCL, again a strong combination, but FIS had preferred to go solo.

At this stage, Bandhan's own evaluation team, along with representatives from Deloitte and Vora, went on site visits to assess the capability of service delivery on the ground. The team went to Bangalore to do a survey of FIS facilities at Whitefield, as well as collect customer feedback at ING Vysya Bank Ltd (now merged with Kotak Mahindra Bank), which was using the FIS software. It also looked at the Infosys facilities to get a feel of the product functionality, and interacted with the HP and Wipro management teams.

Wipro chairman Azim Premji invited the team for a private dinner at his office on Sarjapur Road, where Wipro is headquartered, to send the message across that Wipro was serious about the engagement even as Infosys had arranged for a morning meeting with Kris Gopalakrishnan, its former executive vice chairman.

At the HP office in Electronic City, the Bandhan team was greeted with a ceremonial lamp-lighting.

From there, the team moved to Chennai to take a look at Polaris. They met the Polaris head, Arun Jain, and the senior technology team, over an authentic south Indian lunch at his office. While the Polaris solution was perceived to be suitable for a small bank, it was found to be a little ahead of the curve in terms of an app-based solution. However, that did not clinch the deal even though the team knew that very soon, such a solution was going to catch the imagination of the banking community worldwide. There were many other technical issues to be considered.

Back in Kolkata, the team got down to combining the technical scores with the site-visit scores. This exercise gave no major results as there was no significant technical difference. Therefore, all four firms were called to the price negotiation table. However, the preference was for an original equipment manufacturer (OEM)—a system integrator which has a core-banking product of its own—to take up the lead vendor role. Such a vendor playing the role of a lead system integrator is perceived to bring in better value for its customer since it has a higher stake.

Spotlight on FIS and Polaris

That effectively put the spotlight on FIS and Polaris, as they were the only vendors which had their own core-banking application; HP and Wipro were merely implementers. For obvious reasons, prices quoted by the pure system integrators were a tad higher than the OEM vendors. After twelve gruelling sessions of tough negotiations, finally FIS was picked and Polaris came a close second. FIS, the US-based software provider, did not have a large presence in the Indian market. It had worked with only two banks—ING Vysya Bank and a fledgling Bharatiya Mahila Bank.

The next round—negotiations for the final contract—was even tougher. Bandhan's internal team of IT professionals, company secretary and head of the banking transformation project were supported by an external legal counsel, Khaitan & Co, since it had no law officer who was an expert in IT matters. Often, the discussion went on for several hours, well into the night. It took an intense tug-of-war of wit between the two teams for nearly a fortnight to finally find a common ground.

Typically, the vendors try to draft the terms in such a way that their deliverables are somewhat reduced to an extent that is possible. FIS was no exception. For instance, it fought hard to get Bandhan to agree to a clause that after the clearance of the user acceptance test (UAT) and commencement of banking operations, every single request for change would be addressed by the vendor strictly on a commercial basis. Had the bank accepted this, it would have opened a continuous source of additional revenue for the vendor.

FIS, in fact, agreed that all changes—whether regulatory, tactical or business-related—would be supported by it on a continuous basis during the seven-year agreement period, without any additional cost to the bank. The contract was signed on 30 September 2014.

After signing the contract, FIS hosted a lunch for the Bandhan IT team and Ghosh at Hyatt Regency in Kolkata. Over a traditional Bengali meal, both teams buried all their differences and committed to creating a unique architecture in Indian banking to reach the last mile.

While the agreement was for providing banking technology, including hardware, applications, network connectivity and maintenance, Bandhan bargained hard for a few critical things to bring down the cost:

- building capability to meet all regulatory reporting in the next seven years; designing and building an application for handheld devices; and networking for 2022 DSCs, alongside the bank branches;
- the IT cost was linked to per bank branch on a monthly basis at a fixed cost for the next seven years. It also followed a step-down rate formula. This meant that there would be a threshold number of bank branches to be covered by the IT infrastructure,

and when it exceeded, the rate would reduce for the incremental outlets;

- all 12,000 handheld devices used by the credit officers of DSCs would be connected to the central server; FIS would design and build a software application for the 2022 DSCs;

- services would be available at 99.5 per cent level on a 24/7 basis;

- in a disaster recovery situation, services would resume within 120 minutes;

- when a bank employee is on his computer, the system should respond within five seconds; and FIS would also provide a 16/6 (from 7 a.m. to 11 p.m., between Monday and Saturday) helpdesk for supporting banking operations for all its outlets.

After the contract was signed, Bandhan brought on board Ananta Kumar Mohanty, an IT expert who had earlier worked for SBI and Central Bank of India, to head its IT operations. He had the most onerous task of implementing the project to help the bank meet the target date.

A New Solution for Microbanking

Since the new bank would continue with the business of giving small loans, developing a solution for this business was imperative. Could the MFSol, the existing application, be integrated with the core banking? The answer was 'yes'. Did it match up to the banking product requirements? The answer was 'no'. This is simply because MFSol was capable of handling only a single product—giving loans—and not taking deposits.

So, FIS had to develop a new solution for the microbanking segment, keeping in view the existing business process, the banking needs of the new-generation customers and the real-time operations facilitated through the handheld devices.

The UAT was an exhausting phase. Also known as beta testing, application testing or end-user testing, UAT is the last phase of the software delivery process, when the actual users test the software to make sure it can handle required tasks in the real-world scenarios, according to specifications. With requirements frequently changing, both Bandhan and FIS had a tough time in configuring the system appropriately to be able to pass the testing hurdles.

It took six failed attempts to migrate the data from the existing system to the new core-banking platform, over nine months, to develop the solution. Finally, BCore replaced MFSol.

For both FIS and Bandhan, it had been a roller-coaster learning process, dotted with many acrimonious sessions between the two, but finally the system was put in place. Ghosh and Runu da spent many sleepless nights watching the data migration at the branches in different parts of West Bengal and in other states, as well as at Pekon Building in the next lane, which housed the back office of the bank. There were days when customer transactions would be over by 7 p.m., but often it would take past midnight and even early hours of the next day to close the books.

Technology was a critical issue, but there were many others. Even the final licence of RBI was not enough for any entity to start a bank. It needed at least forty-three registrations with and approvals from various agencies, including the banking regulator. They could vary from opening a current account with the deposit accounts department of RBI's regional office to getting a membership for joining the negotiated dealing system of the central bank, as well as the approval of National Payment Corporation of India for Aadhaar-enabled payment system and membership of the Deposit Insurance and Credit Guarantee Corporation, the Foreign Exchange Dealers Association of India and Clearing Corporation of India Ltd.

And even after getting the approvals, a bank could not use any of them before its launch. During the trial period, ten days before the launch of the bank, a senior Bandhan Bank employee checked his balance in an IDBI Bank account using a Bandhan Bank ATM. This could have generated an income of Rs 8 as transaction fee for Bandhan Bank had it been officially running at the time. But that was not the case. The system could not recognize the test transaction as Bandhan Bank did not have the clearance for such a transaction. This brought the day's settlement for the entire banking system in India to a halt for more than an hour.

Other Critical Issues

Bandhan Bank did not start from scratch. It had a legacy of 6.7 million borrowers, 2022 DSCs and a loan book, or asset base, of Rs 10,500 crore. While the customer base and the loan book gave such a bank a head start, the legacy also had its pitfalls. Bandhan's peer, IDFC Bank, too, started with an asset base much larger than that of Bandhan. Historically,

Kotak Mahindra Bank, which got the banking licence in 2003, had also started with an asset base, as Kotak Mahindra Finance Ltd, the group's flagship company, converted itself into a bank, the first non-banking finance company in India to do so. Its loan book was smaller than Bandhan's.

The bulk of the money disbursed as loans to small borrowers was given to Bandhan by India's commercial banks. Under the banking law, 40 per cent of a bank's loan book must be given to certain segments such as agriculture and small businesses, among others. Such loans are called priority loans.

Since most banks do not have the infrastructure to reach out to such borrowers, they give money to the microfinance companies to be on-lent to this segment of borrowers, and this is considered as the banks' exposure to priority loans.

At least thirty-six banks had given a Rs 8000-crore loan to Bandhan for this purpose; they got the priority sector benefit. Bandhan did not need to pay back the money to the banks as soon as it became a bank itself; it was allowed to return the money as and when the bank loans would mature. That was a reprieve, but there was a problem on another front. Even though all loans given by Bandhan fall into the category of priority loans, they did not count towards its priority-sector lending requirement, as RBI cannot allow both the commercial banks who had lent to Bandhan as well as Bandhan Bank to enjoy the same benefit.

After discussions with the banking regulator, a solution was found—Bandhan Bank would need to adhere to the priority loan norms only on its new loan portfolio after netting off the loans which had been given out of funds taken from other banks. Its capital and deposit collection would back the new loans.

The banks would not recall their loans to Bandhan overnight as they would continue to get the benefit of priority loans. Besides, where else could they earn 12 per cent and more interest? Corporate credit growth for the banking system in the fiscal year 2015 in single digits was at an eighteen-year low, and investment in government papers would not give a return of even 8 per cent.

Even then, the consensus was not to take any chances and build a war chest by tying up with banks for thousands of crores in a line of credit and bringing down assets through securitization—the financial practice of pooling various types of loans and selling their related cash flows to third-party investors as securities.

Then, there was the issue of maintaining the statutory liquidity ratio (SLR), or the compulsory buying of government bonds. When Bandhan was starting its operations, banks were required to buy government bonds to the extent of 21.5 per cent of their deposits. The limit is not fixed; it is changed from time to time. The bond-buying requirement is also applicable to the money that one bank borrows from another.

By that logic, Bandhan Bank would have needed to keep an SLR on its bank borrowing of around Rs 8000 crore, which is not a small sum. But the banks which had lent to Bandhan from their deposits had already fulfilled the bond-buying obligation on such deposits. So, the question was: could the SLR be counted twice—once by the lending bank, and a second time by Bandhan Bank?

Bandhan Bank also had to face the rating issue. Rating is necessary for a commercial bank to be able to borrow from peer banks and access other money market instruments. Since the small loans are not backed by any collateral, the rating agencies typically would not give a good rating to such unsecured loans.

Indeed, the quality of such loans has been impeccable, as they have virtually zero default (Bandhan's bad loans were 0.20 per cent of its total loan book) but the rating agencies go by the rule book. For them, the presence of collaterals or securities to back such loans is more important than the quality of loans.

Building a War Chest

The consensus was to build a war chest by tying up with banks for thousands of crores in a line of credit and bringing down assets through securitization.

To ensure the flow of deposits from the very first day, Bandhan also decided to distribute clay piggy banks to its 6.7 million borrowers where they could save money. They did so. And broke their piggy banks on 23 August 2015, the day the bank was launched, offering their savings to open deposits.

And, of course, in order to become a bank, Bandhan needed to have bankers on board. Even before it received RBI's in-principle approval, Ghosh started employing reputed retired bankers, primarily from the public sector, as consultants to advise him. Immediately after receiving the conditional nod of the regulator, it advertised in the *Economic Times* and the *Telegraph*, looking for people.

The advertisements invited applications from experienced professionals to lead different divisions of the 'proposed Bandhan Bank' such as credit, deposits, retail banking, treasury, compliance and risk management, among others, as well as branch heads and assistant branch heads. Picking the right people was not an easy job as there were close to 39,000 applications.

While division heads were chosen from among the applicants, as well as candidates recommended by head hunters and selected by various committees consisting of sector experts, around 700 professionals were appointed to run the branches. A few thousand microfinance employees, selected from the in-house pool through tests, supplemented the professional bankers in the branches. They were given extensive training before their migration from the DSCs to the branches.

Two Internal Meetings

A peek into the internal meetings that used to be held every week in the run-up to the launch of the bank will give a fair idea of the obstacles faced and how Bandhan found ways to overcome them. While the account of such meetings is as true as it could be, I am refraining from naming the senior professionals except for Ghosh, who was leading from the front.

A review meeting held on 20 December 2014, in the ninth-floor conference room, was jam-packed with employees sitting in three rows behind the first row, which was occupied by the senior management team.

Ghosh: How many days are left for the launch?

Almost everybody, in chorus: 116. (At that time, the target date for the launch was 15 April 2015.)

Ghosh: How many days minus Sundays?

Again, in chorus: 100 days.

Ghosh quickly got down to work, asking how many lease deals for bank branches had been signed.

The executive in charge of premises: 168.

Ghosh: What was the target?

The executive in charge of premises: 350.

Ghosh: Why couldn't we achieve the target? I want all 600 deals to be signed by 15 January. Now, let us know the status of the premium locations.

The executive in charge of premises: In Kolkata, we have done ten agreements, and another ten are expected to be closed next week. The (cost of) rental is the issue; because we are in a hurry, the landlords want to take advantage . . . In Mumbai, the rental is very high. They are asking for Rs 6 lakh per month and Rs 36 lakh as advance. The branches will not make money in the first two years.

Ghosh: We need to look at selling third-party products to generate income. Get the right place for the branches, and the right people to run them. No compromise, please.

Another gentleman, at this point, said, 'Sir, we should look for those locations where the Bengali population is very high in Mumbai and Delhi.'

Ghosh curtly replied, 'We are a pan-Indian bank; not for any community. By the way, how has the handheld-device pilot project at Ultadanga been working?'

A gentleman associated with the project said, 'Sir, it's extremely slow. Our boys can't download even though the devices are connected to the server.'

Ghosh, looking terribly agitated, said, 'Don't confuse me. Our system is not working . . . No supervision, no monitoring . . . Success depends on the process . . . My fourteen years of management experience in Bandhan has taught me that complaints must be accepted and solved; don't give excuses. The department heads must accept responsibility . . . You asked me for people, I have given them to you. It's your responsibility now. You accept the fault and rectify . . .

'The bank is my life. I can't compromise with life . . . I can compromise with my people. I will fire them; sign the termination letter.

'Talk to FIS and sort this out quickly. We must start the next pilot projects at Canning (South 24 Parganas) and Hasnabad (North 24 Parganas). Let FIS manage them.'

Then he started explaining the model of the bank.

'A few DSCs will be attached to each branch. Every DSC will have five credit officers, looking after twenty-five groups of 3000 customers. The distance between a DSC and a bank branch will be 2 km. The DSCs will start work at 7.30 a.m., and the first group meeting will be held at 8 a.m. The credit officers will be back at the DSCs by 2 p.m.

'The bank branches and the DSCs will be two channels of the bank.

'Fifteen bank branches will form a cluster. There will be three operational heads to help the cluster head manage. They will look after five branches each, and will get motorcycles to commute.

'In the microloan channel, six DSCs will have one regional manager, and six regional managers will have one divisional manager. The DSCs will report to the branches but will have dotted-line relationships with the regional managers and the divisional managers, who will monitor them.

'DSCs will have the power to sanction loans up to Rs 1 lakh. The branches and DSCs will complement each other. Any questions?'

Nobody had any questions.

Ghosh ended the meeting, telling the microloan business head that 67 lakh KYC forms must be distributed among the borrowers by the end of December.

'Let's put in more effort. We cannot build a bank working from nine to six. You all are leaders, not managers.

'We need to move fast with as many branches as possible as more small banks will start soon . . .'

(The RBI gave in-principle licences to ten small finance banks on 16 September 2015, three weeks after the launch of Bandhan Bank. Eight of them are microfinance companies. They will have to be operational within eighteen months of receiving the conditional licence.)

No to Fair-weather Friends

Another meeting was held on 1 August 2015.

The weather was bad; there was a depression over the Bay of Bengal, and heavy rain had led to major waterlogging at Salt Lake City Sector V. Attendance in the office was low. The depression over the north-east of the Bay of Bengal intensified into the cyclonic storm 'Komen', with the meteorological department forecasting heavy to very heavy rains in Gangetic West Bengal. Chief Minister Mamata Banerjee had cut short her visit to the UK by a day and was coming back to Kolkata that evening. The state government had sounded a high alert in all south Bengal districts. As many as forty-eight people had died thus far in West Bengal, and the state had called in the army for rescue operations.

Ghosh started by saying, 'In bad weather we have reached office. I don't see too many of you . . . No excuse till 23 August. No leave till 23 August. I will assess people who are with me in times of stress, not good times. Please tell your family, this is an emergency.'

The legal department suggested a six-page document for loan sanctions. Ghosh rejected it outright, saying, 'I want a one-page document. More paper will push up the cost; the borrowers will get confused and bad loans will rise.'

Ghosh asked his secretary, Piyali, to bring the file of dummy forms. Since Piyali could not locate the file, Ghosh asked her to get all the files that were on his table.

Then he asked the premises department head whether the soft board had reached every branch. While the concerned executive was groping for an answer, Ghosh called up the branch located on the first floor of the Bandhan headquarters on DN 64, Sector V, Salt Lake City. The response was: 'It's not there.'

Then the discussion was on the timing of the bank branches. One senior executive suggested that Bandhan branches should remain open for an hour extra compared to other banks. Ghosh loved that suggestion.

Promptly, he said, 'The branch timing will be 9.30 a.m. to 4.30 p.m. Anyway, the second and fourth Saturdays are a holiday, but don't give leave, use these two days for training.'

Then he turned to the head of one of the zones that was lagging behind in terms of preparedness of branches. 'The bank is totally target-based; if you lose business, the bank will lose business. Why should I keep you?' he asked.

Done with him, he asked how many branches were ready and the status of mock runs in branches.

The executive in charge of branches reeled out the data: West Bengal had 274, Bihar seventy-seven, Assam sixty-three, Maharashtra forty, Uttar Pradesh thirty-one, Madhya Pradesh twenty-three, Tripura twenty-two, Rajasthan and Chhattisgarh seventeen each, Odisha and Gujarat sixteen each, Jharkhand fifteen, Uttarakhand ten, Delhi and Telangana two each, Andhra Pradesh, Kerala, Mizoram, Meghalaya, Nagaland and Sikkim one each.

At that point, Ghosh chose to underline the challenges that the bank could face on the first day.

One challenge was filling in cash in ATMs on a Sunday (23 August was a Sunday). Even if the bank wanted to fill in cash with new deposits collected on the first day, it would not happen in the first half. Besides, who would count the cash and sort it out?

One suggestion was to get the money from DSCs and fill the ATMs, but that would not work as DSCs had been asked not to keep any cash on 23 August. It was decided that either the ATMs would be closed on the first day or a very few of them would operate in metros.

Distribution of welcome kits among the depositors was another issue ahead of the launch. India Post would pick up the packets from Kolkata, and Blue Dart Express Ltd worked only at 229 pin codes. So, First Flight Courier Ltd also got a share of this job.

A bigger challenge was cash management. Every day, beginning 24 August, the DSCs would generate cash, about Rs 6 lakh per centre. If one centre got looted, it would destroy the bank's reputation.

Such amounts were not new to the DSCs, but they were not in the limelight before. With Bandhan becoming a bank, everybody got to know how these centres worked, and they could be targeted. Ghosh did not want to take any chances. His advice was: involve all police stations and write to the district magistrate and the superintendent of police in every district. And, of course, involve other banks for cash management.

Finally, he asked everybody to wear formal clothes on 23 August to signal the change—Bandhan was no more an MFI, it was a bank—and requested his colleagues to get haircuts. To this, one of the women executives retorted, 'We can go to the parlour only if we have time, sir.'

Ghosh chose to ignore her comment and told the premises department head to change the banner at every branch from 'Opening shortly' to 'Opening on 23 August'.

By the time the meeting got over, it was 4 p.m.

Before leaving the room, Ghosh asked: 'Are we ready?'

All executives present there said: 'Yes, sir.'

Ghosh: 'How many days to go?'

All: Twelve and a half days.

Ghosh: 'How many hours to go?'

Nobody was expecting this, but Ghosh had the answer. It was like a military parade.

The exercise went on till 20 August when Deloitte presented its last 'Go Live: Readiness Review Report'.

Even in the last twelve and a half days, something happened which could have derailed the bank's launch. President Pranab Mukherjee was to launch the bank. His wife, Suvra, died on 17 August and, naturally, he could not make it to the launch.

In fact, his office had informed Bandhan a few days earlier that she was critically ill. By that time, invitation cards had been printed and the minute-by-minute schedule of the programme was sealed, a requirement for any event graced by the President.

There were three options before the bank: one, to postpone the launch; two, to postpone the event but make the bank operational on 23 August; and three, to look for another chief guest who would launch the bank.

Ghosh called an emergency meeting with a few senior executives in his room on the day the President's wife died. Piyush Pandey, national creative director, India, and vice chairman of Asia Pacific at Ogilvy & Mather (O&M), which was looking after the branding of the bank, joined the meeting over the telephone, from Mumbai. His suggestion was that the bank should go ahead with the launch function. It could be done in a unique way, by two of its customers: one representing microbanking, and another, general banking. One borrows money from the bank, and another keeps deposits.

After hearing them out, Ghosh wanted to be left alone in the antechamber attached to his room, his mobile phone switched off. Finance Minister Arun Jaitley had already been invited for the function but his office had not confirmed his presence till then. Time was fast running out.

At that point, Bandhan Bank's chairman, Lahiri, stepped in. Ghosh took a flight to Delhi and accompanied Lahiri to his meeting with Jaitley. New invitation cards were printed two days before the launch but there was no time to send them to the guests who were flying down to Kolkata from other cities. They got their cards either at the airport or at the hotels where they were staying.

With the final data migration taking thirty-six hours, the bank's website went live at 11.30 a.m. on 23 August 2015, minutes before Jaitley lit the lamp to mark the inauguration of Bandhan Bank.

It went live, with CBS, full networking of 501 bank branches, 2022 DSCs, thirty ATMs, remittance facility through RTGS/NEFT, and image-based cheque-clearing facility available at the branches on the first day.

One could not have asked for more.

9

A Man with Uncommon Sense

At one of the management committee meetings of Bandhan Bank at its headquarters in Kolkata a few months before its launch, Ghosh narrated a story: 'A gentleman was seen standing on a railway platform, asking the station master many questions. His first question was, what time will the Poorva Express come from Delhi? And the next, what time will Toofan Express go to Delhi? Do you know why he was asking such questions?'

Nobody in the senior management team had the answer. 'He wanted to cross the railway track,' Ghosh quipped, adding, 'We cannot do that.'

'Have you ever seen the driver of an ambulance being questioned by the traffic police? We need to behave like an ambulance . . . Of course, there will be problems but we will find solutions and move ahead. Don't brood over problems. Let's solve them.'

This is quintessential Ghosh—an entrepreneur who believes in action, more a doer than a thinker—a doer driven by a strong, earthy common sense.

In another such meeting, I heard him say, 'There are no words like "if", "by chance" in my dictionary.' 'Why not do it today? Let's start. We have not the time,' is a typical Ghosh expression to convey his sense of urgency. This may prompt many to brand him as a risk-taker. He is probably that, but not a gambler. There is logic behind every risk that he takes.

Enamul Haque of ASA International told me that Ghosh did not pay attention to one of ASA's key suggestions. 'We wanted him to go slow on expansion but he was going ahead at breakneck speed; he is a risk-taker but has performed very well, beyond our assumption.'

Brij Mohan of SIDBI too has the same impression of Ghosh. Once, at the SIDBI guest house in Lake Town, Kolkata, when Brij Mohan impressed on him the chances of tripping if he ran very fast, Ghosh did not defend himself. He accepted the well-meant advice, but put forward his arguments to address Brij Mohan's concerns in terms of investment in manpower, systems and quality control.

On the spot, he explained the measures he had put in place, including very strong internal audits. 'I was convinced that he was aware of the pitfalls and had taken adequate steps,' Brij Mohan said.

ASA's Sushil Roy, who was instrumental in the technical support agreement, found in 'Shekhar' a young leader who was willing to face any challenge. Unlike many others in the microfinance space, Ghosh did not have any 'mindset' problems, he told me.

Ghosh approaches most things in a different way. In June 2015, an O&M team led by Pandey showed Ghosh the rough cuts of the ad films that the agency had made for Bandhan Bank. Television spots for the films had already been booked by media-buying agency Madison World, owned by Sam Balsara.

The senior executives of the bank were happy with the films, but not Ghosh. He called for his driver Shyamlal, and Samiran Das, who served tea on that floor. He wanted them to watch the clips. Only when he was convinced that the message was clear to Shyamlal and Samiran did he smile.

Next month, when the O&M team trooped down to the Bandhan headquarters again to show the final product, they also showed a film that the agency had made for a steel company, which had received many awards. Ghosh watched that film, which was rather long, and quipped, 'I don't want an award-winning film. What is there for me? My bank? My products?'

As a matter of fact, Ghosh doesn't care about frills. That, however, does not mean he does not have a heart. He has quite a large one. But, before we delve into those aspects, let's understand his background first.

The Origin

The roots of the Ghosh family were in Sonargaon, Dhaka, from where West Bengal's longest-serving Communist chief minister, Jyoti Basu, hailed. Before Independence, Ghosh's father, Haripada Ghosh, moved to Comilla, about 100 km south-east of Dhaka, which was a part of Greater Tripura then. Ghosh's great grandfather, Nabin Ghosh, started a sweet shop at Comilla, which was about five hours by boat from Sonargaon, but close to Tripura.

Ghosh was born in Bhattapukur, Agartala, in west Tripura, in 1960. His mother, Suchitra Ghosh, was from Bikrampur, Dhaka, but mostly lived with her uncle, Chittaranjan Ghosh, a Congress leader, at Collins Street, central Kolkata.

In his early days, Ghosh led a nomadic life, constantly changing places in search of a stable life and education. He had spent his childhood at Sonargaon, but went back to Tripura in 1971, after the liberation of Bangladesh. Soon, he went to Mariani, Assam, a town near Jorhat city, on the border of Nagaland, famous for the Hoollongapar Gibbon Sanctuary, to stay with his uncle, Sadananda Ghosh.

Sadananda used to sell snacks on a pushcart at the railway junction to make his living. From there, he shifted to Siliguri in North Bengal, where one of his maternal uncles used to stay.

His father tried his hand at running a restaurant at Bagdogra, part of the Greater Siliguri Metropolitan Area in Darjeeling, even as Ghosh dropped out of school and started selling milk to neighbours to help his father run the family of four sons and two daughters.

Even in Siliguri, he did not settle down; he went back to Bangladesh, where he graduated from Narayanganj's Tolaram College, staying at a Ramakrishna Ashram, with his grandmother (father's aunt) taking care of two meals a day. When he was doing his post-graduation in statistics at Dhaka University, Ghosh lived at the Brajananda Temple on the university campus.

One day, his bicycle got stolen from the university campus. Borhannbhai (Borhann Uddin, a statistics professor) lent him his old Phoenix cycle, which brought back the smile on Ghosh's face. Until recently, he was driving a Toyota Fortuner; now he has a Land Rover Discovery in his garage.

By the time Ghosh completed his MSc in statistics in 1985, his father died of liver cancer at fifty-two.

His first choice at the university was, however, physics. Benu Sharma, CEO of Asian TV in Dhaka, a classmate of Ghosh's at Dhaka University, fondly remembers 'Shekhar' as someone who was always willing to help others. Those days, Ghosh's used to sing Assamese singer Bhupen Hazarika's popular song, 'Manush manusher jonno' (Humans are for humanity).

Around that time, BRAC—formerly known as the Bangladesh Rehabilitation Assistance Committee, and later as the Bangladesh Rural Advancement Committee, a development organization dedicated to the alleviation of poverty and empowerment of the poor—advertised for a programme organizer. Ghosh applied and got the job.

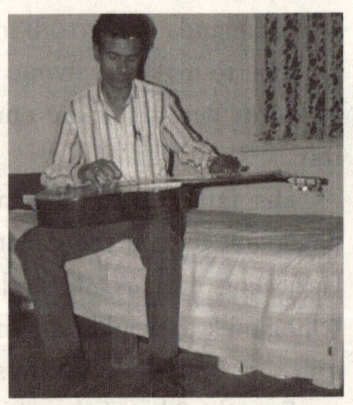

THE SOUND OF MUSIC: In his university days, Ghosh used to sing Assamese singer Bhupen Hazarika's popular song, 'Manush manusher jonno' (Humans are for humanity).

His first posting was at Gaibandha, a disaster-prone northern district of Bangladesh, affected by frequent floods, cold waves, nor'easters, tornadoes and *monga* or seasonal food crisis.

His job was to form groups of men and women—on the lines of self-help groups—and mobilize them against corruption in the government and establish their rights. He used to meet women in the morning and men in the evening, and travel extensively on a bicycle. His initial salary was 1000 taka per month (INR 860, in February 2016), which was later raised to 1600 taka (INR 1384).

'I used to consider myself quite wealthy when I saw families starving for days and eating mashed potatoes after selling advance labour for 15 taka when the daily wage was 75 taka,' he told me on a flight from Kolkata to Delhi.

The BRAC concept was to make these people aware of their rights and let them decide what they wanted to do. While there was an outreach programme meant for that, there was another project to give them training and microcredit. At some point, the two different programmes got merged into one rural development programme.

Working with BRAC, Ghosh experienced poverty in its starkest form. He also got a sense of the power structure in a village. That helped him pick up skills to motivate people, analyse human behaviour and resolve conflicts. He also learnt patience and humility. As a university student, he was quite hot-headed and impatient, but looking at abject poverty, he often asked himself how he could get angry with these people.

The BRAC assignment also taught him that human capital cannot be built without training; education without discipline is meaningless. The most critical piece of learning which helped him a great deal in creating Bandhan was that poor people don't care much about money if it's given free. Only when they are charged for the money do they deploy it, earn on it and pay back. From a programme organizer, he was promoted to the position of a manager and, finally, became a faculty member training MFIs across Bangladesh. By the time he left BRAC in 1997, his salary was 10,000 taka.

His return to Kolkata followed his marriage with Nilima, whom he fondly calls Nili. To Nilima, he is 'Sir' in the presence of others but 'Shurid' (friend) in private.

The sixth of eight children (five sisters and three brothers), Nilima comes from a wealthy family in Bishalgarh, Agartala, Tripura. Her father, Haridas Ghosh, was a transport operator who also owned a hardware shop.

In 1985, the year Ghosh completed his post-graduation from Dhaka University, his brother, Vaskar, met Nilima's elder sister, Poornima, as a prospective bride for his elder brother. But Vaskar liked Nilima more than Poornima. Much later, in 1993, once again Vaskar dropped in at Nilima's five-storeyed massive house in Tripura, bride-hunting for his elder brother. This time, Ghosh and a few of his friends were in tow. By that time, Poornima had already got married and Nilima was doing her graduation.

Nilima entertained them by singing a Rabindra Sangeet:[10]
'*Chokher aloy dekhechilem choker bahire*'
Roughly translated, it means:
The world I had seen,
A world of images, was outside.

---

[10] By convention, a Bengali woman used to entertain the prospective groom by singing a Rabindra Sangeet in those days.

Now, as darkness draws a screen,
I turn to my heart for a vision.

When her mother asked Nilima whether she liked Ghosh—a tall, dark and handsome young man—Nilima made it clear that she found him 'uncultured' as he kept mum while his friends did all the talking. When the two of them were left alone in a room, Ghosh confided in her that he was running a high temperature and was in no position to talk.

Nilima gave her nod for the marriage, but on one condition—that she must be allowed to complete her post-graduation. When they got married in August 1993, Ghosh remained in Dhaka, working for BRAC, and Nilima in another part of Bangladesh, doing her MA in public administration from Chittagong University. Only after she completed her studies in 1996 did both of them come back to West Bengal, and their son, Angshuman, was born the following year.

Ghosh had been feeling uncomfortable in Bangladesh—there was social unrest, and attacks on minorities. But life was not smooth in West Bengal either. Income from the knitting factory that he was running with Vaskar was not sufficient to support the family. Also, there was frequent labour trouble in the Left-ruled state, which was not exactly known for its work culture. He also did not find professionalism among NGOs; they were not willing to scale up the business of small loans.

He was a restless soul doing many things to manage a living, roaming around, networking with people and doing the groundwork for the birth of Bandhan. Occasionally, he was seen crying in the puja room of his uncle Manoranjan Ghosh's residence at Konnagar, where the couple was staying. He often told Nili that he was always praying to God

not to give them another child as he would not be able to
financially support another member in his family.

A Fairy Tale

What followed seemed like a fairy tale. Bandhan was registered
as a trust in April 2001, and the next year it opened two
branches, at Bagnan and Konnagar, to start its microfinance
operations. By 2014, when it got the in-principle approval
from India's banking regulator to set up a bank, it had
2022 branches across twenty-two Indian states, and at least
14,000 people on its roll. There were 6.7 million borrowers.
Many large corporations as well as established financial
intermediaries were among the twenty-five entities that had
applied for a banking licence, but only two could make it.
Bandhan was one of them.

How did he build this empire?

Those who know him well say he is modest. Underneath his
apparent naivety, there is a wise, even wily, man. He is a man
with uncommon common sense. 'He looks very simple, but he
is very sharp. People often misjudge his wisdom by looking at
his simple exterior and he uses this to his advantage,' says Brij
Mohan of SIDBI. A central banker who met Ghosh at the RBI
office in Kolkata (it was 'love at first sight') was completely
taken in by his simplicity. 'He lacks articulation but knows
the language of the poor. He could instantly strike a chord as
he has enormous empathy for them,' says this gentleman who
does not want to be identified, as he is a regulator.

Another central banker who had worked in RBI's
Kolkata office claims to have done nothing for Ghosh

except for introducing him to people at various functions since 'he did not know his way'. Ghosh has brilliantly built on those introductions. This person too has reservations about being identified. 'Everybody talks about poverty alleviation through MFIs but very few people know this like Chandra Shekhar . . . He understands what poverty is; what the borrowers need and how much they can pay back. He would not give them one penny extra to ensure that no money was wasted and every rupee was paid back.'

To illustrate Ghosh's success, this central banker refers to the Differential Rate of Interest (DRI) scheme that was introduced by the government in March 1972. Under this scheme, in 2009, a borrower whose annual family income from all sources did not exceed Rs 18,000 in a rural area, and Rs 24,000 in urban and semi-urban areas, and landholding did not exceed one acre of irrigated land or 2.5 acres of non-irrigated land, was eligible for Rs 20,000 of housing loans and Rs 15,000 of other loans at 4 per cent interest rate.

No collateral was required for such loans, and repayment was to be done in five years, including a moratorium period. The overall target for loans given under the DRI scheme for the banking system was 1 per cent of the total advances of the previous year, but most could not meet the target as they found no takers. On the other hand, in Bandhan's early days, it gave loans as small as Rs 1000.

A Relationship Man

Ghosh used to keep the executives of RBI, even remotely connected with rural credit, informed of every step he was taking, even though he was not required to do so. He would send a monthly progress report to all of them, even though they might not read those and would give feedback only occasionally.

This illustrates his extreme sincerity, clarity of purpose and uncanny knack for building relationships with everybody who matters. Indeed, he is very much a relationship man. ASA International's Haque told me that every time his team came to Kolkata, Ghosh called them home for dinner and served simple, home-cooked food, thereby forging stronger ties.

Saneesh Singh of SIDBI, who played a key role in Bandhan getting its first loan from the development finance organization, is also hugely impressed with Ghosh, who he found was 'extremely receptive to ideas'. 'He is very innovative and hard-working. He has a very strong rustic common sense and is street-smart. He is always at the right place at the right time, meeting the right people and willing to explore ideas. He is an entrepreneur who is willing to take risks,' Singh said.

One thing, however, Singh could not understand—why Ghosh was resisting technology. 'He was happy with the manual operations of Bandhan.'

Initially, Ghosh was guarded, but later they became friends and used to discuss the vast financial needs of the poor in the hinterland and the enormous possibilities. Once, Ghosh brought some chocolates to Singh at the SIDBI office in Kolkata from one of his overseas trips, but Singh politely declined to accept them. From that day onwards, a greater intimacy developed between the two, and Chandra Shekhar became 'Shekhar' to Singh. 'We were buddies though I could not put my arms around him because of the institutional framework between us,' Singh said.

Y.C. Nanda of NABARD, who had been on the board of BFSL, the non-banking finance company which got the banking licence, since 2008, says, 'Initially, I would advise him frequently, tell him what BFSL should do, and he would listen to me quietly and would never argue. But I stopped advising him after I found he knew much more than I did. His assessment and judgement were far superior to mine.

'I had only managed NABARD, but he has created an institution. For me, it was easy to manage a strong, very well-established institution, but creating an entirely new organization of this size is a great achievement. I would say Bandhan is entirely Chandra Shekhar's creation. The board's contribution is that it did not stop him from doing what he wanted to do; it did not interfere too much. That's the only credit the board should get.'

Ghosh has the uncanny ability to see things differently. When the logistics and premises team of Bandhan Bank was finding it difficult to close the property deals for the Kolkata branches—and only eighteen of thirty-five locations had been finalized—he asked the team why they were so slow. One of them pointed out that the rentals were an issue. With particular reference to one branch at Kankurgachi in north-central Kolkata, the team member said, 'Sir, it's a question of who will blink first. The Gupta Brothers [a restaurant chain] is offering Rs 190 [per sq. ft] but the landlord likes a bank as a tenant.' Ghosh's curt answer was, 'I like the bank but that does not mean I don't like money . . . Pay more than Gupta Brothers and take the premises.'

A Disruptive Management Style

In some sense, Ghosh's management style is disruptive. At least one senior banker who has joined Bandhan recently finds him a 'benevolent dictator'. He does not believe in hierarchy, and that often creates parallel management. He reaches out to employees of almost every level. He gives them direct access, and this keeps the information flow continuous, something which he had learnt at BRAC.

He does not believe in allowing people to do their jobs without any supervision, particularly when they are dealing with money. 'Poor people dealing with money always tend to deviate and hence they should be kept under strict supervision,' has been his management mantra while building Bandhan, the microfinance company.

Runu da does not see this as a negative point. According to him, 'CMD-Sir is always with people. He has direct contact and loves to hear from them. He knows where they are lacking and how to nurse them and cover up their weak points; he recognizes people's worth; he always thinks of how to develop the employees' futures.'

Ghosh's style of micromanagement is of course changing now. Those who have been with him for the past fourteen years vouch for the change. Some of them were shocked when, after the first board meeting of Bandhan Bank in July 2015, Ghosh announced that the bar was open at a party he had thrown at the Novotel Hotel for the senior management. Single malt Glenlivet was served there. In Bandhan's fourteen-year history, alcohol had never been served at any party.

His crisis management strategy has been unique. When SKS Microfinance was flourishing and everybody else in the industry thought all other MFIs would be wiped out, he kept his calm and held on to his nerves. After watching closely, he introduced a new product in 2007: education loan at 12 per cent—10 percentage points less than the cost of other loans at that time.

Why did he do that? There were a couple of reasons. First, to gain social equity as nobody else was giving education loans; second, he was running the risk of losing some customers who had been paying 22 per cent. The education loans were offered only to these customers. He thought it would be better to offer a subsidized loan than lose an income of 22 per cent and acquire new customers.

Similarly, in 2014, after getting RBI's in-principle approval for a bank licence, he was not sure whether commercial banks would continue to give money to Bandhan. So, he wanted to rein in the loan growth, which was not easy as the customers would get nervous if they felt that Bandhan did not have money to lend.

He started looking at technicalities and found some reason or other to call for close scrutiny of books in certain pockets where the loan demand was too high. Following this, he either cut down the size of disbursements or put them on hold. Nobody suspected anything but his purpose was served. Later, when he was convinced that banks would not stop giving money to Bandhan, it was not difficult to resume giving loans, and the loan growth in the second half of the fiscal year 2015 was phenomenal.

In May 2010, ahead of SKS Microfinance's initial public offering (IPO), the first by any MFI in India, and much before the crises that engulfed the industry in the aftermath of Andhra Pradesh promulgating a state law, Ghosh slashed interest rates by 5 percentage points, to 18.97 per cent, creating a new benchmark. 'That was a master stroke which prevented the government of West Bengal from going the Andhra Pradesh way and clamping down on Bandhan,' says Brij Mohan.

All these people have seen Ghosh as the Bandhan boss. Nilratan Haldar is someone who had watched Ghosh as his boss, at BRAC in Bangladesh, as a senior programme manager. 'A job given to him was done. I had around nineteen trainers working under me but nobody could match Shekhar in resource mobilization,' Haldar told me.

He also mentioned one of Ghosh's traits that used to irritate him. 'He would pick up handbills, papers, interesting articles in magazines, and keep them in his folder. If he came across a saying like "The most important word in human relationship is 'we' and the least important word is 'I'" on a piece of paper on the road, he would immediately pick it up and keep it in his bag. We always wondered why he did this. In fact, if we lost any piece of paper, we used to say, search Shekhar's folder.'

Haldar told me that once Ghosh was caught sneaking into BRAC's computer room, which also housed its library, a restricted zone for junior employees like him. After that, Ghosh changed his strategy. He would enter at midnight and keep the person who handled the photocopier on guard. There, he would read books on management and make his PowerPoint presentations for the next day's training. By the time he finished his work, it would be 4 a.m. He would get up at 7 a.m. for a walk, and by 9 a.m., he would be in the classroom.

Turning Adversity into Opportunity

'He can turn adversity into an opportunity. The Andhra Pradesh crisis illustrates that; he thrived after that,' says Nanda. The former NABARD chairman is also aware of Ghosh's cost-consciousness. In the EC 76, Sector I, Salt Lake City office, where Bandhan was headquartered till 2011, there used to be a wooden bench in his cramped cabin, on which he would sit and rest. There was no sofa.

'When I came to Kolkata to attend the first board meeting, I was put up at a guest house which did not have proper air-conditioning arrangements,' Nanda told me one evening in November over a cup of tea at his flat in Mumbai.

According to former RBI deputy governor Usha Thorat, tremendous consciousness of cost is the hallmark of Ghosh. He speaks the language of the borrower and is in total control.

'He keeps his cost low by not limiting the number of people he would need . . . He keeps as many people as he requires but may not give them a very high salary . . . I find his model very interesting . . . He has total control and at the same time he empowers people, and the result is phenomenal growth.'

Nanda also remembers Ghosh was earning a pittance— some Rs 8–10 lakh as salary after Bandhan became an NBFC.

The board forced him to raise his salary because otherwise it would have been difficult to get senior executives, as his salary would have capped their compensation. 'Even today, he travels economy class on flights. We have forced him to take business class at least on long international flights.'

ASA International's Haque had an anecdote of Ghosh's cost-consciousness. Ghosh once took a couple of senior ASA executives and Runu da in a taxi to Park Street. He wanted to show them around Kolkata. They got down from the taxi at Park Hotel and walked through New Market. Haque, who had not been to Hajj then, wanted to have beer at a Park Street restaurant. Ghosh entertained the three of them with a single bottle of beer.

Is it frugality or Ghosh's sense of humour? Singh of SIDBI also had a taste of his rustic humour. His Opportunity Fund at Dia Vikas Capital wanted to pick up a stake in Bandhan, but, as a policy, it could not pay a premium. Ghosh refused to offer the stake at a par value, saying, 'If the groom does not charge dowry, the bride's family thinks there is something wrong with the groom.'

Haque's final impression of Ghosh? 'Ghosh was (and is) at the right place, at the right time. He is an explorer; he gives the impression that he is a simple and innocent man but he is wise.'

Vijay Mahajan, a veteran in the MFI business, says Ghosh has seen the business, studied the predecessors well, and learnt lessons from others' failures. 'He went beyond copying to improvising—the Xerox is better than the original.'

Brij Mohan adds that Ghosh is good at reading between the lines and that makes him a tough negotiator with auditors, raters and investors. He also has the ability to see things from a different perspective. For instance, when everybody blamed the over-aggressiveness of the MFI industry for the Andhra Pradesh crisis, Ghosh held the banks responsible, as they were flooding MFIs with money. 'Had they not been pumping in so much money, how would the MFIs have managed to grow their balance sheet?' he asks.

According to Nanda, Ghosh's advantage is that he is not a banker and does not carry any extra baggage. He is driven by strong common sense. 'I remember when Bandhan started growing, there was pressure on him to get highly qualified people—CAs and MBAs—at higher cost, but he kept on saying he did not need tigers to catch rats; cats could do the job. He has tremendous understanding of the operations of microfinance,' he says.

Pritish Saha, a senior executive of Bandhan Bank, throws light on the softer side of Ghosh. Once, on a typical location survey for an MFI branch in South 24 Parganas, they felt hungry in the afternoon. Along with Ghosh and Saha, there was another gentleman, Robin Biswas, all three riding on one bike. Ghosh wanted to have bananas for lunch. Biswas got down from the bike and started bargaining hard with a roadside banana seller, an old lady. Ghosh quietly stepped in, bought a dozen bananas for the three of them at the price the lady asked for.

Maneeta Rathore, Bandhan's communications head, is familiar with a relatively unknown side of Ghosh: he is a gadget freak. He would change his mobile often and has a knack for understanding electronic gadgets. Every time he went overseas, he would buy a camera for the office. He believes in recording everything. He would ask Rathore to use the camera and record all events. And, of course, he would also pick up some souvenirs for all—chocolates, fridge magnets, earrings, bangles . . .

Ghosh would also never go on a foreign trip spending Bandhan's money. In the early days, each time there was an invitation, Rathore would send a mail asking the organization that had invited him to foot the bill. His first overseas trip was sponsored by PlaNet Finance, now called Positive Planet.

Only once did Rathore think of leaving Bandhan, when she got a job at a new private bank, but Ghosh persuaded her to stay back. He did not make a counter-offer but said that Bandhan would give her a lot of flexibility and she could follow her academic pursuits. She was convinced. 'Sir can always make you change your mind. In front of him, you're under a spell. He is a great motivator.'

Why don't people leave Bandhan? There is transparency in dealing with people, a clear-cut career path, fast-track promotion, and the employees get competitive salaries. Runa Parven, Bandhan's first female divisional manager, also swears by this. Ghosh had told her, 'You don't have to bother about your future, that's my responsibility. You just work.' Runa says, 'Sir has kept his word.'

In December 2014, there was a feast at Ghosh's son Angshuman's seventeenth birthday, at Neelkamal Building, Survey Park, Santoshpur, Kolkata. While others were busy having dinner, Ghosh was seen on a conference call with one of Bandhan's prospective investors at 9.30 p.m., in a park nearby.

Everybody heard him screaming. 'I know my job better than you, don't teach me how to run Bandhan.' Apparently, the prospective investor in Bandhan was pushing for a higher valuation by rejigging the business plan and jacking up the interest rate, but Ghosh put his foot down.

That's a different story, but this is Ghosh's style of functioning—even at social gatherings, he would attend a conference call or huddle around with his group of people and hold an important meeting. He would do it even at his own wedding anniversary and on his son's birthday.

He Teaches to Dream

He attends almost every Bandhan employee's wedding. At such gatherings, he often gives motivational speeches. He talks about the old days and how Bandhan has progressed. His obsession with discipline is claustrophobic, but people still stick with him because he teaches them to dream. When Bandhan was a small office in a one-room flat, he would tell its handful of employees that one day, Bandhan would have a ten-storeyed building. Now it has that, and plans to have a forty-storeyed headquarters in the coming years.

Giving training under a tree, on the pavement, after being thrown out of the hall that had been rented for the purpose, because they had exceeded the time for which the rent had been paid, he would say, 'One day Bandhan will have training centres.' Now, it has eight training centres across India and, at the time of writing this book, another one was being built.

He would also say that one day, 'Bandhan will become a bank.' Now it is.

Piyali Bhattacharjee, who heads Bandhan's research wing, finds in Ghosh a boss with a lot of humility. In the early days, the organization could not afford more than one service staff, and whenever he went on leave, Ghosh himself would carry glasses of water and tea from the pantry for his guests.

She remembers an incident at Bandhan's second office (CF 173, Salt Lake)—there were just two washrooms, of which one was reserved for Ghosh. On her first day in office, she ended up sharing the washroom with her male colleagues. Ghosh instantly understood the discomfort of the female staff. He walked into her room late in the afternoon, and asked the women employees to start using his washroom.

'He is completely a team person. He derives his strength from his team. He arrives at critical decisions through consensus. Any kind of news, be it good or bad, is shared with the team first.'

When Samanta, Bandhan's first employee, got married, he needed to spend Rs 25,000. Ghosh offered him Rs 15,000 as loan and accepted only Rs 7000 back, and gave Rs 8000 as a gift.

Samanta is amazed by Ghosh's zest for knowledge. Once, he dropped in at Ghosh's Survey Park residence early in the morning. His son opened the front door but he found the bedroom locked from the inside. He waited in the drawing room for over an hour. When the bedroom door opened, he saw Ghosh and his wife coming out along with another gentleman whom he did not know. Sheepishly, Ghosh told him that the couple had been learning how to speak English. They had been doing it once a week for three months then.

'Ultimately, it has been an act of God. Destiny . . . Nobody could have stopped it,' Nanda of NABARD says. According to him, people trust Ghosh, and his employees believe in his leadership. 'He has been surprising us all the time with his achievements. The entire MFI industry is terribly jealous of him. People kept on telling me that there was something wrong, perhaps the recoveries were fudged. So, when the NBFC was formed, I hinted that if any adjustments were needed this was the time they should be done. Ghosh laughed and said there was nothing like that to be done.'

An RBI official who had worked in Kolkata said there were allegations by Bandhan's peers that its financials were fudged, and the regulator had discreetly probed these allegations but nothing was found to be amiss. Brij Mohan of SIDBI too says Bandhan's fast growth and strong balance sheet year after year did not help Ghosh in winning many industry friends in the early years. He is simple; he would call a spade a spade and was not afraid of criticizing policies if they did not support MFIs. He is apolitical, not beholden to any ideology. Thorat wonders how Ghosh manages the political administration in a state like West Bengal.

He may not have too many friends, but even his worst enemy would probably find it difficult not to build a good relationship with him. Maity of Village Welfare, whom Ghosh had deserted to form Bandhan, finds him very aggressive but, at the same time, very level-headed. 'He is a relationship man. Even now, he calls me Maity Sir.' Thorat admires his modesty, and says success has not gone to his head; he is rooted in reality.

What takes the cake is probably his simplicity. In early August, about a fortnight before Bandhan Bank's launch, Ghosh was forced to go to Quest Mall at Park Circus in Kolkata, with his wife and three women employees—Poulami Datta, Arpita Sen and Bhattacharjee—to buy two sets of clothes: one for the launch of the bank on 23 August, and another for the networking dinner the previous night.

They first went to the Raymond outlet but it was one that only tailored suits and did not sell readymade ones. So, a Louis Philippe suit worth Rs 50,000 was chosen along with a white shirt that cost Rs 5000, and a red tie. After a 40 per cent discount, the bill came to Rs 39,080. Ghosh toyed with the idea of buying a leather belt but chose not to as the shop declined to offer a 40 per cent discount on that.

There was no time to buy the second set of clothes for the dinner. Not happy with the idea of spending more money on clothes, Ghosh brought clothes from home and asked people around him whether they would suit the occasion. There were four shirts—Austin Reed, John Rich, Peter England and Pepe Jeans—all had been bought at discounted prices. Two of them were half-sleeved shirts! It was difficult to convince him to buy a new one.

Finally, he bought a Van Heusen shirt, and the suit he wore that evening was a McGregor NY 1921, given to him by his brother who lives in Paris.

His driver, Shyamlal, has been with him since July 2003. From Bihar's Madhubani district, Shyamalal came to Kolkata in search of a job in his teens, and ran errands for customers at Sonagachi brothel in north Kolkata, Asia's largest red-light district. For him, his boss has not changed at all—except for his taste in clothes—he looks smarter now.

In May 2015, when Ghosh went to Narayanpur, North 24 Parganas, for a field visit, thirty-four-year-old Bebi Answari tripped while rushing to be photographed with him. There was nothing unusual about this. Many of Bandhan's women borrowers these days want to be photographed with Ghosh ever since Bandhan got the banking licence. The more savvy ones even take selfies. But there is a difference—Answari is blind.

Born into a Hindu family, she had lost her eyesight when she was in school and could not get married. A Muslim man married her but she was not accepted by his family. They were living in a shanty near the Kolkata airport, with her husband driving the trucks that carry PepsiCo bottles, till he fell seriously ill and lost his job in 2009. With a Rs 6000 loan from Bandhan, Answari started a business of plastic waste. Her latest loan is of Rs 34,000. Her husband, back on his feet now, has bought an autorickshaw from her income. With two children, the family is happy.

'I won't miss my eyesight as long as Sir is with us,' says Answari.

A SENSE OF SECURITY: 'I won't miss my eyesight as long as Sir is with us,' says Bebi Answari.

10

The Way Forward:
A Universal Small Bank?

A month ahead of Bandhan Bank's launch, after its first board meeting, Ghosh threw a party at the Novotel Hotel in Kolkata for its directors and senior executives. Addressing the executives before the bar was opened, Bhaskar Sen, one of the directors, narrated a story he had picked up on the Internet.

Einstein was once travelling from Princeton on a train. When the conductor came down the aisle, punching the ticket of every passenger, Einstein reached into his vest pocket.

Not being able to find his ticket there, he reached into his trouser pockets.

It wasn't there. He opened his briefcase but he couldn't find it there either. Taking note of his plight, the conductor said, 'Dr Einstein, I know who you are. We all know who you are. I'm sure you bought a ticket. Don't worry about it.'

Einstein nodded appreciatively.

The conductor continued with his work. When he was ready to move to the next compartment of the train, he turned around and saw the great physicist down on his hands and knees, looking under his seat for his ticket.

The conductor rushed back and repeated, 'Dr Einstein, don't worry, I know who you are. No problem. You don't need a ticket. I'm sure you bought one.'

Einstein looked at him and said, 'Young man, I too know who I am but I don't know where I'm going. That's why I am searching for my ticket.'

Bhaskar Sen, former chairman and managing director of United Bank of India, wanted to send a message: that Bandhan Bank should know what it wants to be in the Indian financial system; it should know where it wants to go . . . its destination.

This is the biggest challenge before Bandhan Bank. In the past, there have been a few instances of non-banking finance companies becoming banks (Uday Kotak's Kotak Mahindra Group and Dev Ahuja's 20th Century Finance Corporation), but this is the first case of a microfinance entity turning into a universal bank. It is different from the others and it needs to maintain its unique identity. It wants to predominantly be a bank for those who otherwise do not have access to formal banking services—the so-called bottom of the pyramid, the segment of customers which Bandhan had been catering to as a microfinance entity. But, for a microfinance company, transforming into a bank is not easy, owing to at least two factors: one, banking is a highly regulated business, and two, unlike microfinance, which is a seller's market, banking is a buyer's market.

Structurally, in some sense, Bandhan Bank resembles Bank Rakyat Indonesia (BRI) which focuses on micro, small- and medium-sized enterprises. BRI has thousands of microbanking outlets, called 'Unit Desa', besides bank branches. Although both branches and units are part of the same organization, the Unit Desa system is clearly distinguished from the branch network in terms of target groups, services and mode of operation. The branches' commercial operations cater to wealthy, private and corporate customers in and around district towns, besides administering the government-sponsored loans, even as the units serve micro and small customers in rural pockets.

However, the similarity ends there. Among other differences, the employees attached to the units do not offer the doorstep banking services that Bandhan does; the customers come to them. The regulatory framework in Indonesia is also different, where depositors can be incentivized in various ways which RBI does not approve of. BRI is in the process of launching its own satellite for the efficient handling of fifteen to sixteen million electronic transactions per day. As Indonesia is an archipelago, fibre-optic communication systems don't work there; banks need to use satellites for communication.

Bandhan wants to stay away from corporate banking in its initial years and continue to do what it has been doing and is good at—giving small loans. During its microfinance days, it was sourcing money from commercial banks and giving loans to vegetable sellers, rickshaw pullers and tailors, among others. As it was supremely efficient, the microfinance entity could keep its operating cost low and make a decent profit. Now that it has become a bank, it will be able to raise money from the public in the form of deposits. This will bring down the cost of resources. And in due course, the bank will pass on the benefits to its customers.

Taking Conventional Banking Head On

The idea is unique. It is taking the conventional banking model head on. In India, most banks use the semi-urban and rural pockets as a catchment area for collecting deposits, and deploy the money in the form of retail loans and lend money to corporations. Bandhan Bank wants to raise deposits predominantly from urban India and lend in the hinterland.

If the early days are any indication, the bank is doing wonderfully well in raising deposits. But can it maintain the tempo?

In the initial phase, even bulk deposits, for which it has to pay relatively higher rates of interest, are fine. This is simply because even though such deposits cost more than other deposits, the bank can replace the money it borrowed from other banks at an even higher cost. As a microfinance entity, it used to borrow from banks at 12–12.5 per cent and lend to small borrowers.

Once that phase gets over and it repays all bank borrowings, the challenge will be to garner the current and savings accounts (CASA), which are low-cost deposits, the lifeline of a bank. For the success of any bank, cost of money plays a key role; the lower the better, because if the cost of deposit is low, it can earn more from loans and can also give loans at a relatively lower rate. This helps the borrowers to pay back without defaulting, as the interest burden is less. As a portion of total deposits, HDFC Bank has the highest CASA among banks in India and hence its cost of money is the lowest in the industry.

The microfinance borrowers will also turn savers and keep their money with Bandhan Bank, but the volume of such deposits will be very low, and transaction costs high, because these savers are expected to use their debit card to withdraw money frequently. Since such depositors will be large in number—at least 6.7 million to start with—and Bandhan Bank's ATM network will be relatively small in its initial years, they will end up using other banks' ATMs and the bank's cost will rise.

Besides, the existing microfinance employees of the bank have the expertise in giving small loans and ensuring the repayment of such loans; they do not have any exposure to collection of deposits. If the same set of employees is engaged in deposit mobilization also, it may end up diluting the risk management and credit collection standard, and that will lead to a rise in bad assets. The microfinance entity's bad assets were to the tune of 0.20 per cent of the loan book.

Indeed, government bodies, corporations and high-net-worth individuals (HNIs) could be a source of deposits, but the challenge will lie in tapping them, particularly when the bank is not willing to offer either corporate loans or high-value mortgages, car loans and personal loans. Will the HNIs be interested in keeping money with Bandhan Bank to earn a little more interest than what they get from other banks? The bank management strongly feels it will get money based on its positioning, which the bank's tagline explains: *Aapka Bhala, Sabki Bhalai*. This essentially means once you keep your money with Bandhan Bank, you will do good to others, because this will be used to give loans to people who are otherwise not entertained by the banking segment, even as your money will remain safe, liquid, and you'll earn interest—probably a little more than what other banks are offering.

This has worked in the initial days. Anecdotally, I have come across instances where people have withdrawn money from other banks to keep deposits with Bandhan Bank, but the real challenge will be when it scales up. Typically, a bank customer prefers to have all services from a single bank, and this works well for both the customers and the banks. Bandhan Bank will have to strive hard to attract retail deposits, at least in the initial years, as it will not offer a bouquet of services which can cater to all classes. It may not become the primary bank for many, particularly among the urban middle class and upper-middle class, to start with.

If it wants to offer many more products, it will end up competing with other banks that have better reach in this segment and also run the risk of diluting its core area or the unique selling proposition (USP)—that it is a bank for the unbanked. Can it compete with HDFC Bank or SBI in terms of products and processes today? If the answer is no, it should play to its strength. In banking, what one doesn't do is more important than what one does. The challenge before Ghosh is to refrain from doing too many things in the excitement of running a universal bank.

Even if Bandhan sticks to its core strength of giving small loans to those who remain outside the banking system and reaches out to small and medium units, there are many critical issues that it would need to tackle. For instance, the loans given by the microfinance entities are all unsecured, not backed by any collateral. Such loans affect a bank's rating and a relatively lower rating pushes up the cost of borrowing for the bank. Despite holding such unsecured loans on its books, Bandhan's bad assets were minuscule, but it will not cut ice with the raters. It is another matter that many banks with secured loans on their books have piled up bad assets.

Another point to note is that the microfinance entity had only women borrowers, and even though the loan disbursals are not based on a group model, the existence of a group helps a great deal to hedge risks as it creates peer pressure as well as cooperation. An individual is always ashamed of defaults while others are paying up regularly; similarly, for a genuine reason (say, a husband's hospitalization or a child's school admission), when a borrower is not able to pay her weekly loan instalment, group members step in to help her out. While the small loans will continue to be given in the same way, as a bank, Bandhan will also give loans to men and individuals, something it had not done before. If the microfinance employees are involved in assessing the risk profile of such borrowers, they will need reorientation.

Although the existing microfinance branches have been converted into DSCs, and Bandhan Bank will follow the hub-and-spoke model, many microfinance employees have been trained to understand the basics of banking transactions and are deployed in bank branches. Will they live up to the expectations? Is the Bandhan management overestimating their ability? I don't have the answers. Certainly, running a bank branch is very different from meeting borrowers at their doorsteps and collecting weekly instalments.

Two Banks under One Roof?

For all practical purposes, Bandhan will be running two
banks under its fold—a bank for Bharat (for loan assets) and
a bank for India (for liabilities or deposits). Simply put, it will
mobilize deposits primarily from the salaried class and HNIs
in urban centres, who have money, and give that money in
the form of loans to poor people, SMEs and MSMEs in semi-
urban and rural pockets. Of course, its existing borrowers too
will turn savers but the money collected from them in the form
of deposits will not be enough to serve their credit needs.

Indeed, the business model is challenging, but a much
bigger challenge is the assimilation of two different cultures.
In a sense, the microbanking division will play the role of
an in-house business correspondent, but Bandhan has not
created a separate subsidiary for this purpose—it is a division
of the bank.

In his first address to the senior microfinance employees
after getting the in-principle approval from the banking
regulator, Ghosh told them to accept the bankers who would
be hired to run the show as their teachers. Most of them have
accepted his advice in letter and spirit as they are fiercely loyal
and committed to the organization, and yet the HR issues are
real and cannot be swept under the carpet. These employees
have created Bandhan. It will be interesting to see how they
reconcile themselves to the fact that banking is not their
cup of tea and hence a set of new people will run the show,
and the bulk of the old employees will continue to do what
they were doing even as Bandhan is no more a microfinance
entity, but a bank. Getting the existing employees and the

new bank employees on the same boat is as easy or as difficult as any other large merger in India's banking history, as at least 20,000 employees are involved at the initial stage.

Headquartered in Kolkata, it may also find it difficult to attract banking talent, particularly when it is not offering top dollar. One way of tackling this could be by making the senior employees owners of the bank by offering them stock options, something which HDFC Bank has done. It did not offer attractive salaries to its employees but it could attract the best talent, mostly from foreign banks and from different geographies, by giving them ownership. The senior employees of the microfinance entity who have been with the group since its early days have been given stocks.

There are other issues as well. Connectivity is one of them. In many pockets where Bandhan Bank has gone, no bank has dared to go. It is equipped with technology but connectivity is uneven, and there will be a continuous struggle to find a solution. India has more mobile phone connections than bank accounts, but even if it wants to use the mobile platform as the dominant channel in rural pockets, it's not an easy task. Imagine a situation where you have too many trains but the railway track is still not adequate to ensure that all of them run on time.

A Broadband-deficit Country

India is still a broadband-deficit country. At the moment, we have about a billion mobile users, but call drops are endemic and Internet connectivity is weak. Why is this so? Both voice and data connectivity require a bandwidth, which is to be obtained from the government in the form of spectrum allocation at high auction fees. Once allocated, private companies are relatively free to decide on the use of the spectrum profitably. The use of the spectrum or bandwidth is essentially urban-centric.

India's telecom revolution has been ushered in through voice telephony, first in the urban areas and later in the hinterland. Indeed, progress has been made in rural telecommunications, but it is concentrated in voice telephony and not so much in the area of data transmission, which requires strong last-mile, fibre-optic connectivity and higher investments in increasing the density of tower infrastructure.

Besides, technology and innovation are, by and large, an urban phenomenon. Mobile technology has also made most of its growth story from urban centres due to greater demand and affordability.

In addition to bandwidth issues, even the so-called vernacular or local language Internet has not taken off in India. Almost all transactions are still happening on English-language sites, and e-commerce is largely the preserve of the English-speaking elite.

The growth of Internet technology in villages has been slow due to three reasons: the lack of literacy in the adult population, the overarching use of English, rendering it usable only for a few people and, more importantly, the lack of data and a delivery format suitable for catering to rural requirements. As there is relatively less demand, there is not enough incentive to invest in setting up the platform. Most payment wallets continue to be concentrated in urban India.

Now that the multilingual messaging facility is available, it remains to be seen how long we would need to wait for a technology solution that breaches the illiteracy barrier. The deciding factor for investment of big money in mobile technology in the banking space will be how many customers are using the mobile wallet on their own mobile phones.

India has got around four lakh towers now, and the number will probably rise to five lakh by 2020. The government's plan for setting up a national information highway is also on a rather slow-moving lane. Hence, we have more mobiles but less connectivity. Till India builds its own information highway, human interface will continue to play a critical role in achieving the last-mile connectivity. And to that extent, banking services will continue to be rendered in more traditional ways than otherwise.

Finally, the pricing of loans will remain a sensitive issue for a bank like Bandhan. As a microfinance entity, it was allowed to keep a spread of up to 10 percentage points for small loans over its cost of money. This means that if it is borrowing from banks at 12 per cent, it can charge a microborrower 22 per cent. Within the 10 per cent cap, it has to manage the operational cost to make a decent profit. A bank does not enjoy such a huge net interest margin, even though the transactional cost for small loans is very high. In fact, some of the private banks and foreign banks do charge 22–24 per cent or even more for small loans which are not backed by any security. But the high rates do not attract the attention of the regulator and the policymakers, as such loans form a minuscule part of the overall loan book of these banks. For Bandhan Bank, small loans will form a sizable segment of its loan book and hence at what rates such loans are given will attract public attention.

It may enjoy the benefit of charging higher rates at the initial stage, but after some time, pressure may mount on bringing down the loan rates. It would also need to pare loan rates to have a competitive edge over others, but that won't be a cakewalk, considering the terrain where it operates and the size of the loans.

Bandhan Bank also needs to keep in mind that competition will intensify. One small finance bank has already started operations and nine more will be launched by April 2017. They will be accompanied by at least ten payments banks. And as I read the proof of this book, RBI has released its draft guidelines for on-tap licensing of universal banks in the private sector.

Ghosh, its founder and now MD and CEO, has never failed in any initiative since he established the group in 2002. This is both good and bad. It's good as it gives him enormous confidence, but it also makes him vulnerable to even a small dose of failure. By nature, he is impatient. While climbing up, he always takes two stairs at a time. Is this to burn more calories? Once he was asked this question at an offsite of Bandhan. His answer was, given a choice he would have liked to climb four or even five at a time just to keep pace with the scorching growth of the MFI.

Research has not yet clarified whether there is any difference in the energy spent in climbing one step at a time as opposed to two. Many say that to burn the maximum number of calories when climbing a flight of stairs, the single-step strategy is better. Perhaps as a strategy, one step at a time suits a bank better. Speed pays in microfinance, which is all about discipline and monitoring of loans; banking is the game of a long-distance runner.

Bandhan Bank's biggest advantage is probably the fact that Ghosh is not a banker; he can see things from a different perspective. But can he compete with the ilk of Uday Kotak and Rana Kapoor or should he prefer to remain an entrepreneur and let others do the banking job?

Ghosh is a risk-taker but he would probably need to appreciate the fact that Bandhan Bank may not be able to emulate the growth graph of its microfinance avatar, as the field is different. Nobody in India knows better than him the psyche of a small borrower and the alchemy of doing business with the poor profitably. Bandhan will be a success story if it does not deviate from its chosen path—a bank for the unbanked, a 'universal small bank'.

11

Vijay Mahajan: A Tragic Hero

Vijay Mahajan set up Bhartiya Samruddhi Finance Ltd (BSFL), the first for-profit microfinance institution in India, in the form of a non-banking finance company, in 1996. It has many firsts to its credit: the first Indian MFI to access external commercial borrowing (ECB) in 1997; to get a bank loan in 1998; and to raise equity in 2000. It was also the first to get a rating from Crisil Ltd, a Standard & Poor's company, in 2003. The rating was FA-, the lowest notch in investment grade. Besides, it was also the first to offer microinsurance and weather-index-based crop insurance (in 2003), and integrate livelihood-promotion services with microcredit by 2009. And it was the first one to go bust.

BSFL is popularly known as Basix, the phonetic acronym of its holding company, Bhartiya Samruddhi Investments and Consulting Services Ltd.

Vijay Mahajan, or VM as he is popularly called in the
MFI circle, is a failed entrepreneur. BSFL, the flagship of the
group, was hounded by banks for non-payment of loans,
and by 2015, the company's loan book shrank to just 3 per
cent of its size in October 2010, with bad loans eroding more
than double its capital. VM features in the bank defaulters'
list along with his namesake Vijay Mallya, the flamboyant
chairman of the UB Group—known as much for his love
of the good life and the popular Kingfisher calendar as for
Kingfisher beer, India's largest-selling brew, and the grounded
Kingfisher Airlines Ltd.

Many call VM the Bhishma Pitamaha of the Indian
microfinance industry for his wisdom, integrity and deep
understanding of the field. In the epic Mahabharata,
Devavrata became Bhishma after he took the *bhishmapratigya*,
or terrible oath—a vow of lifelong celibacy so that his
father, Shantanu, the king of Hastinapur, could marry a
fisherwoman, Satyavathi, and their children could inherit the
throne. His father granted him the boon of *ichcha mrityu*, or
control over his own death.

VM's heart was in the right place. A gold medallist
from IIM-A and an electrical engineer from Indian Institute
of Technology Delhi (IIT-D), he chose the promotion of the
livelihood of the poor as his mission over high-paying corporate
jobs. But unlike Bhishma, he could not choose the time of his
death, metaphorically. He wanted to remain alive and thrive in
the livelihood-promotion field, but could not do so.

NABARD's Y.C. Nanda said, 'The failure of Basix is not
the failure of VM, it is the failure of MFIs in Andhra Pradesh

due to external factors, including the state and the regulator. I had suggested that he work in Bihar and promised all help from NABARD, but he said Hyderabad was the MF capital and that he had a start from there.'

He is a tragic hero who got trapped between two contradictory demands—his mission of doing good to the poor, and doing it sustainably. Unlike Ghosh of Bandhan, who saw business at the bottom of the pyramid and, at the same time, touched millions of lives that the formal banking system does not care for, and Vikram Akula of SKS Microfinance, whose concept of social business was probably hijacked by private equity investors, VM was caught in a dilemma—what comes first: alleviating poverty or sustaining the entity?

Too Broad an Agenda

As a tragic hero, his hamartia was taking on too broad an agenda. In order to promote livelihoods, he dabbled in too many things but ultimately could not manage them all. 'The Basix mission is to promote a large number of sustainable livelihoods, including for the rural poor and women, through the provision of financial services and technical assistance in an integrated manner,' a message on the group's website says. 'Basix will strive to yield a competitive rate of return to its investors so as to be able to access mainstream capital and human resources on a continuous basis.' This was crafted in 1996, and was possibly ahead of its time.

THE MAN WITH A MISSION: Vijay Mahajan (sitting second from left) at a dairy farmers' cooperative meeting in Nanded district, Maharashtra, in 2002.

VM was one of the victims of the controversial Andhra Pradesh microfinance law. BSFL collapsed under the burden of bad loans when borrowers in Andhra Pradesh refused to repay. 'We are unlikely to survive beyond the next two to three months if we don't get fresh funds,' VM had told me in a TV interview in August 2011, eyes moist.

We were at a TV studio in Mumbai after he had met his bankers in a five-star hotel in central Mumbai. To create the impression that the interview was recorded at some other time and not on the day of his meeting with the bankers, VM changed his kurta before facing the TV camera. At that time, BSFL's net worth was Rs 128 crore, down from Rs 230 crore in September 2010, just before the Andhra law was promulgated, and an accumulated loss of Rs 450 crore was threatening to make its net worth negative.

In October 2015, when VM dropped in at my residence in Bandra, Mumbai, after attending yet another bankers' meeting, he told me over dinner that the BSFL story was virtually over. It had a Rs 540-crore exposure in Andhra Pradesh, while in the rest of India it was Rs 1268 crore. After the banks stopped lending, Rs 540 crore of the Andhra Pradesh book and the Rs 110-crore loans given outside the southern state (overall, Rs 650 crore) had turned illiquid. The Andhra Pradesh loan portfolio was written off.

By January 2012, BSFL had repaid bank loans and interest to the tune of Rs 1266 crore, but Rs 652 crore was still due (with interest, it rose to Rs 683 crore), and this is why VM featured in the defaulters' list. BSFL lenders included SIDBI and eighteen other lenders, including Axis Bank.

At dinner, I found that VM had stopped having his Old Monk rum with soda and ice, almost a daily evening ritual for him for over two decades, even though he did not mind single malt occasionally. In fact, at an MFI conference in Delhi in 2014, when industry body MFIN gave him a memento recognizing his 'lifetime achievement', it also gave him a gift—a bottle of a single malt. I asked VM whether he had drunk during his *shodh yatra*.[11] He had not.

Soul-searching Journey

When he saw BSFL collapsing in January 2011, VM went on a sixty-day shodh yatra—a soul-searching journey across

---

[11] 'Shodh' stands for research, while 'yatra' stands for journey. Loosely translated, the term means a journey to understand the lives and livelihood of the poor.

India, seeking the truth—to reconnect with poor people and to learn from them what went wrong.

On 31 January 2011, at Sevagram, Wardha, he wrote on his blog:

> T.S. Eliot's lines come to mind and it metamorphoses into 'Here I am at the end of the way. Having had thirty years, thirty years largely wasted . . . The years of *les guerres de l'interne*'. I am about to reach Sevagram. Came here first in 1982 when I was working with a Gandhian NGO, the Association of Sarva Seva Farms, which worked to rehabilitate landless families who had received Bhoodan (land gift) under the campaign led by Vinoba Bhave, when he walked 40,000 km over 14 years (1951 to 1965) to appeal to landlords to give some of their land to the landless.
>
> Thirty years . . . largely wasted? Who can tell? Just emerging raw from the microfinance crisis. A field which has received a Nobel Prize for one of its pioneers, Dr Mohammed Yunus, and was widely praised till a year ago is now widely condemned—by people like Bangladesh PM Sheikh Hasina, and the former Reserve Bank of India Governor Dr Y.V. Reddy. What is real? The earlier assessment or the current one? What is real is what the people say.
>
> That is why this Shodh Yatra. An exploration of truth. Unable to match Gandhi, one can at least mimic him. So what leads me to begin this journey? A search for the truth, the wisdom that lies with the people . . . A grassroots enquiry into the lives and livelihoods of poor people.

It is a hybrid yatra—I will walk while in a village or a town, stopping by every once in a while to have a dialogue; and drive between habitations. I intend to do this . . . over a period of January 30, 2011 (today) till April 18, 2011. The beginning date and place are significant to me—today is Gandhiji's martyrdom day and I am starting from his Ashram in Sevagram, Wardha, near Nagpur. My Shodh Yatra will end . . . on April 18, 2011 (Bhoodan Day) at Pochampalli, a village about 50 km from Hyderabad, AP, where Vinoba Bhave started the Bhoodan Movement in 1951. . . . As I plan to take 2–3 days off after every 10 days, it is 60 days. At about 80–90 km a day, I expect to cover about 5000 km in 60 days.

VM, sixty-one, was born in Pune, Maharashtra, and brought up in Jaipur, Rajasthan. Youngest of four brothers, two of whom have been in the army and one in the air force, VM is the son of a civilian ordnance officer in the Indian Army. After a five-year bachelor's degree in technology, specializing in electrical engineering, at IIT-D, where Manvinder Singh Banga, or Vindi Banga, who went on to become the youngest chairman and CEO of Hindustan Lever Ltd, was his batchmate, VM joined Philips India Ltd as a trainee marketing executive. It was a top job in those days, other coveted employers being HUL, Telco (now Tata Steel Ltd) and Larsen & Toubro Ltd in the private sector. VM worked for four years in Kolkata and the North-east before going to IIM-A.

At IIT-D, Amit Mitra, now West Bengal's finance minister, taught him microeconomics; while at IIM-A,

C. Rangarajan, who later became an RBI governor, taught him macroeconomics. Interestingly, the younger brother of Vindi, Ajay Banga, the global CEO of MasterCard; Arvind Subramanian, the chief economic adviser to the ministry of finance; and Vishwavir Ahuja, formerly country head of Bank of America and, since 2010, CEO of RBL Bank Ltd, are all his batchmates from IIM-A. VM also studied economic development policy as a fellow at the Woodrow Wilson School of Public and International Affairs, Princeton University, in 1989, when Ben Bernanke, former chairman of the US Federal Reserve, was on the faculty.

A Decade of Disappointment

I asked VM: How did the son of an urban middle-class family who had been to an IIT and an IIM come to work in rural-livelihood promotion? VM said he turned eighteen in 1972, the twenty-fifth year of India's Independence. So he was a product of the seventies—a decade of disappointments and frustrations.

India had to host millions of refugees from East Pakistan in 1970, and a lot of people remained hungry; Bangladesh was born; then there was the Nava Nirman movement in Gujarat, where the middle class protested against inflation and corruption; the Naxalite movement in West Bengal, in which far-Left radical Communists supported the Maoist political ideology; and, finally, Jayaprakash Narayan's call for total revolution, which led to Indira Gandhi imposing the Emergency.

'I graduated from IIT-D just when the Emergency was declared, so that put an end to even trying for the IAS exam,'

VM said. 'I wanted to join a rural development institution. There were three options before me: the Gandhians, the Christian missionaries and the Leftists. Like a Trishanku, I found something appealing in each but could not accept any of them totally.' Trishanku refers to the state of limbo between one's goals or desires and one's current state or possessions. So, VM used his middle-class instinct, looking for safety in the Philips job, at least for the time being.

But the livelihood bug had already bitten him and, during his extensive travels in Bihar, Odisha and the North-east between 1975 and 1979, VM could not shake off his urge to do something for India's poor. So in 1979, he went to IIM-A, attracted by Prof. Ravi J. Matthai, its founder-director, who had stepped down and was running a rural development project at Jawaja, Rajasthan. It had started as an education project, but turned into a rural-livelihood project for weavers and leather workers. VM went for a summer internship at Jawaja at the end of his first year at IIM-A, and did several course-work projects in rural development during his second year. 'This was my way of preparing myself for a lifelong pursuit of rural development,' said VM.

By that time, VM was courting Savita Bhatla, a batchmate at IIM-A. A make-or-break conversation took place one evening at IIM-A, after they watched Satyajit Ray's *Apur Sansar*. VM was deeply moved by the poverty depicted in the film and told her that he would like to serve the rural poor all his life. 'I told him I had no problem with him doing that as long as he did not expect me to do the same. I wanted to have a choice of career. We agreed and, soon after, got engaged, while we were still in IIM-A,' Savita told me in Hyderabad, where VM lives.

The Trishanku

VM, the Trishanku, dilly-dallied, but ultimately chose to work in Bihar with a Gandhian NGO: the Association for Sarva Seva Farms (ASSEFA). Set up in October 1969 in Tamil Nadu by Subaiah Loganathan, it was working with landless poor households that had been allotted land under Vinoba Bhave's Bhoodan Movement. Between 1982 and 1985, VM worked with ASSEFA at Gaya, Jamui and Deoghar districts of Bihar on small projects to level the undulating land, make it cultivable, install borewells, irrigation pumps and pipelines, bring in seeds and fertilizers, and motivate the Bhoodan allottees to cultivate their own land. 'Within three years, the lives of very poor people were transformed in front of my eyes,' said VM.

With the help of Loganathan of ASSEFA, and another NGO leader, Aloysius Fernandez of MYRADA, VM started Professional Assistance for Development Action (Pradan). Deep Joshi, a young and idealistic programme officer at Ford Foundation in Delhi, supported him from the start and joined Pradan in 1986. Many young professionals out of IITs, IIMs and the Institute for Rural Management (IRMA) at Anand, a district in Gujarat, worked at the grass roots for Pradan, which, in Hindi means 'to give in exchange', as against *dan* which means 'to give in charity'.

By the end of 1988, when VM left on a year-long fellowship to study economic development policy in the US, Pradan was already known for its grass-roots professionalism. VM returned in mid-1989, and continued to work at Pradan, which by then was running livelihood-promotion projects around poultry, mushroom cultivation, tussar silkworm rearing, cattle-hide processing, handloom weaving, etc.

By 1991, when India faced its worst-ever balance of payments crisis and was forced to embrace economic liberalization, VM had left Pradan. 'I was looking for an answer on how to scale up its work manifold. I felt that there are two prime requirements for this: more capital and more policy support.'

Acharya Ramamurti, one of the Gandhians VM had worked with in Jamui, Bihar, became the mentor of then prime minister V.P. Singh of the Janata Dal (JD), and he pulled VM into the party as a young adviser on rural development. But the stint didn't last long. 'I was told by a seasoned JD worker that to be in politics one needs to have at least one of three Ms: money, muscle or mass base. I had none of these, so I petered out.'

Working with the Dalai Lama

During his year-long fellowship at Princeton in 1988–89, VM had made friends with Thomas Fisher, a young Britisher, and Geoffrey Onegi-Obel, a Ugandan. The three of them established a US non-profit agency called VikaSoko—a word synthesized from *vikas*, a Hindi word meaning 'development', and *soko*, a Swahili word meaning 'marketplace'. In 1992, VM and Thomas activated VikaSoko, offering consultancy and training in economic development. Their first client was His Holiness the Dalai Lama's Tibetan Government-in-Exile, in Dharamsala, and they worked together to produce the first integrated development plan for the 1,20,000 Tibetans in exile in India.

They also carried out a large eight-state, two-year study of the rural non-farm sector in India for SDC. This made VM realize how serious the credit constraint was for microenterprises.

During this period, he carried out two more studies—one for Ela Ben's SEWA Bank (Ben was then a member of the now-defunct Planning Commission) and another on financial services for the rural poor and women, for the World Bank. With a grant from Ford Foundation, VM formed a team of five, including his IIM-A batchmate Bharti Gupta Ramola, who was a partner at PricewaterhouseCoopers Financial Advisory; chartered accountant Nagarajan, who was an auditor at Pradan; Anoop Seth, a banker with interest in rural development; R. Balakrishnan, a general manager at NABARD; and Joe Madiath from Gram Vikas, an NGO in Odisha. They studied Grameen Bank and BRAC of Bangladesh, Bank for Agriculture and Agricultural Cooperatives (BAAC) of Thailand, BRI of Indonesia and ShoreBank of Chicago. Bharti and Seth would go on to join the Basix board.

The report done for the World Bank was circulated widely and sent, among others, to then RBI governor Rangarajan, and then finance minister Manmohan Singh. Impressed with the findings, Rangarajan formed a three-member committee—deputy governor R.V. Gupta (in charge of rural credit), Yashwant Thorat (RBI general manager at the rural planning and credit division), and NABARD chairman P. Kotiah—to visit BRI. From this germinated the idea of local area banks (LABs).

When they met the finance minister separately, Singh expressed his wish to set up a bank for the poor, like Grameen Bank. It did not happen as the Narasimha Rao-led Congress government was soon voted out of power, and Singh was no longer the finance minister.

VM persisted and met several financial sector bigwigs. One of them was S.A. Dave, then chairman of Unit Trust of India (UTI), the nation's oldest mutual fund. Dave was willing to help him start a microfinance division at UTI. VM also met the chairman of HDFC Ltd, Deepak Parekh; ICICI chairman N. Vaghul; National Dairy Development Board (NDDB) chief Verghese Kurien; and his international friends in Ford Foundation and SDC, in search of a sponsor. All of them expressed support for the idea.

Finally, he managed to convince Ratan Tata. In 1996, with a Rs 1-crore loan from the Sir Ratan Tata Trust, he set up a pilot microfinance operation in Raichur, Karnataka. VM was looking for loans and not a grant, as he wanted to demonstrate that microfinance was viable.

Learning from ShoreBank USA, Basics Ltd was established as a holding company and two operating NBFCs were set up under it: Sarvodaya Nano Finance Ltd (SNFL), for supporting women's self-help groups, and BSFL, for farmers and rural non-farm enterprises. At the beginning, in 1996, VM contributed Rs 8 lakh to the equity of the holding company, Bharti Gupta Ramola Rs 2.5 lakh, and Deep Joshi Rs 0.5 lakh—a total of Rs 11 lakh. Till 1996, NBFCs were allowed to take deposits. So, the two NBFCs also raised deposits.

But this ideal start did not last long. Within a few months, Chain Roop Bhansali's CRB Capital Markets Ltd, an NBFC, which had gotten an in-principle approval from RBI to set up a bank, went bust before it was given the final licence. Lakhs of depositors wanted their money back, but it did not have the money to pay them. That forced RBI to tighten the registration norms for NBFCs: now they would need Rs 25 lakh net-owned funds to start operations and maintain adequate capital for their loans as they grew.

Both BSFL and SNFL needed to be capitalized more if they were to grow bigger, but no one was willing to put equity into NBFCs lending to the rural poor. Nagarajan and Gupta Ramola advised VM to raise ECBs. An ECB is an instrument used in India to facilitate access to foreign money by Indian corporations and public sector undertakings. Ford Foundation stepped in with $3 million, and SDC gave Swiss francs 2.5 million (about Rs 15 crore in 1997). Basics Ltd then invested in the two NBFC subsidiaries BSFL and SNFL through soft loans, maturing in twelve to fifteen years, partly as equity and partly as debt. The equity investment was sufficient to fulfil RBI capital adequacy requirement.

In August 1996, then finance minister P. Chidambaram announced the idea of LABs in his mid-year budget speech. He also deregulated interest rates for loans given out by LABs and urban cooperative banks (it was capped at 12 per cent). 'I heard Chidambaram's speech on a transistor on my way to Banswara, Rajasthan, and cried with joy,' VM told me.

Basics was among the first three entities to get the approval for setting up a LAB. Its Krishna Bhima Samruddhi Local Area Bank Ltd covered three districts—Raichur and Gulbarga in Karnataka, and Mahabubnagar in Andhra Pradesh.

Overall, six LABs got the RBI approval, out of the 227 applications that were submitted to float such banks. Of this pack, Vinayak Local Area Bank Ltd at Sikar, Rajasthan, closed down in January 2002, and another, South Gujarat Local Area Bank Ltd, merged with Bank of Baroda in June 2004. Four of them still exist—Capital Local Area Bank Ltd in Jalandhar, Coastal Local Area Bank Ltd in Vijayawada, Subhadra Local Area Bank Ltd in Kolhapur and Krishna Bhima Samruddhi. Incidentally, the Jalandhar-based LAB converted itself into a small finance bank in April 2016.

The holding company Basics Ltd, by 1997, had four subsidiaries: the two microfinance NBFCs Sarvodaya and Samruddhi, KBS Local Area Bank and Indian Grameen Services (IGS), a non-profit Section 25 company for providing technical assistance and support services to borrowers and their SHGs.

Building the Team

With the corporate structure in place, VM began building his team. He hired B.L. Parthasarathy, his senior colleague in the rural credit studies he had done in 1992–95, and a former banker, to run BSFL's credit operations; and M.S. Sriram, from IRMA, to oversee finance. Sankar Datta, his former colleague from Pradan and then a professor at IRMA, was hired to run IGS for livelihood-promotion services.

Sriram and VM worked hard to raise money from banks, but no bank was willing to bet on BSFL. In 1998, Global Trust Bank gave the first loan of Rs 50 lakh to BSFL, and promised to give more. By that time, the ECB route was opened by RBI for

NBFCs, and VM managed to raise $2 million from Desjardins, a Canadian cooperative, itself funded by the Canadian International Development Agency, and a similar amount from a Dutch development agency, Cordaid.

Having lent out more than Rs 20 crore to 20,000 clients in six districts of Andhra Pradesh and Karnataka, BSFL faced a severe fund crunch. When Sriram left in 1999 to join IIM-A as a finance professor, VM hired Viswanatha Prasad, an experienced professional who has worked with the TVS Group and Karvy Securities. The focus was on raising equity, and in November 2000, the IFC was persuaded to bring in $1 million, while ShoreBank USA and Dutch Triodos Bank gave $0.50 million each. Among local institutions, ICICI Bank put in Rs 1 crore equity, and HDFC Rs 50 lakh.

The president of the World Bank and IFC, James Wolfensohn, came to Hyderabad to sign the equity agreement with VM, in a glittering ceremony at the ITC Grand Kakatiya Hotel.

'Mr Wolfensohn told us that, before the signing ceremony he had breakfast with the then chief minister of Andhra Pradesh, Chandrababu Naidu, who told him that the SHG model, which the AP government was running at that time for giving money to the poor, was a far better model than MFIs,' VM told me. I did not reach out either to Wolfensohn or Naidu to check the veracity of this. If this is indeed true, this conflict simmered through the years, leading to the 2010 Andhra Pradesh state law that killed BSFL. But let's not jump to the end of the story so soon.

The equity should have led to BSFL growing like a rocket. But like a Greek tragic hero, VM had his hamartia:

his livelihood-promotion mission. He wanted Basix to do aggressively what he had done in Pradan in small pilot projects—promoting livelihoods of the poor through skill training, capacity building and creating market linkages.

In 2002, on completing five years of microcredit, BSFL carried out an impact assessment study of its borrowers. It was found that only 52 per cent of the borrowers had had any significant increase in income, 25 per cent had reported no change and 23 per cent had actually showed a decline in income. 'That study left us devastated. The loan repayment rate was more than 98 per cent, but that was of no use as half the borrowers were not getting any benefit because of low productivity, high risk and lack of market linkages,' VM said, justifying what he had done.

The Boardroom Battle

After the study, he called for a strategic shift—financial services must be accompanied by training, capacity building and market linkages if the lives of the poor have to be changed. The Basix board did not oppose the idea, but wanted this to be done through the non-profit IGS and told him that BSFL should not be touched. He fought with the board. VM was always conscious of the tag attached to him: he was a messiah of the poor. 'We are not a financial enterprise. We are a new-generation livelihood-promotion institution,' he would say at every board meeting. Prasad, who had been appointed as the CEO of BSFL in 2002, tried to counsel VM time and again, but in vain.

By 2003, frustrated and tired of fighting with VM, Prasad decided to quit. Bharti and other board members tried to hold

him back but VM was adamant on internalizing livelihood
services in BSFL, which Prasad did not approve of. While
Prasad left to set up India's first microfinance fund, Bellwether
Microfinance Fund, VM took over again as the CEO of BSFL
to show how one could provide livelihood services and still be
profitable.

The problem with VM was that he knew his mission but
did not know how to run it as a business. After Prasad left, the
exodus of star credit officers began. Some left to join new private
banks looking to penetrate rural India, and a few others went to
the insurance sector. Kishore Kumar Puli left to join ICICI Bank
and later set up Trident Microfinance Pvt. Ltd, while Shubhankar
Sengupta left to set up Aarohan Financial Services Pvt. Ltd. Many
more left to join SKS Microfinance and other MFIs.

VM worked himself into a frenzy to establish a viable
revenue model for livelihood services. He led the expansion
of BSFL to the poorer parts of Maharashtra, Odisha, Madhya
Pradesh, Chhattisgarh, Bihar and Jharkhand, but that came
to a halt in September 2004 when he had a massive heart
attack. With a 95 per cent blockage in his left artery, he had
to undergo a bypass surgery at Hyderabad's Global Hospital.
He was out of action for six months and the board appointed
N.V. Ramana as the CEO of BSFL and S. Ramachandran as
the chief financial officer.

VM came back after a few months as the Basix group CEO
and tried to raise money to implement his livelihood strategy
by building revenue models for support services; he stopped
focusing on the microcredit business. Responding to the 2002
impact-assessment study, he decided to first deal with risk
mitigation through microinsurance, by offering coverage for

the lives of borrowers and their spouses, hospitalization, livestock death and microenterprise assets. Devarkona Sattaiah, who had joined BSFL as a field executive in 1996, led the insurance work and became one of VM's trusted lieutenants. The work on weather-index-based crop insurance with ICICI Lombard General Insurance Co. Ltd was widely recognized; Harvard Business School wrote a case study on it.

'This is where the hubris began to set in slowly. Having been named one of the sixty outstanding social entrepreneurs of the world at the Davos World Economic Forum in 2003, VM started seeing a halo around himself,' one of his disciples, who prefers to remain anonymous, told me. By 2005, VM was beginning to be sought after by many for advice. He was appointed by the government as a part-time member of the Insurance Regulatory and Development Authority of India; Rajasthan chief minister Vasundhara Raje Scindia invited him to design and run the Rajasthan Mission on Livelihoods.

Larger than Life

In 2006, he was invited to join the global board of CGAP, the World Bank's Washington-based microfinance policy body. The Government of India also nominated him as a member of the Raghuram Rajan Committee on Financial Sector Reforms, in 2008. He became larger than life. Tim Geithner, the US Treasury Secretary, met VM in Mumbai in 2010, and a photograph of the two at the meeting was published on the front page of the *New York Times*.

Ironically, during those five years, from 2004 to 2009, when VM was a rising star in the global MFI circuit, Basix was steadily losing ground. The microfinance landscape in India was also changing fast. MFIs like Share, SKS Microfinance, Spandana and Asmitha began to grow fast and attract equity capital. Private equity investors, after smelling profits, began pushing MFIs for growth, growth and more growth.

BSFL was overtaken and its capital adequacy fell to nearly 10 per cent, severely restricting its ability to raise more bank loans. As a result, Crisil downgraded BSFL from FA- to FB+, a non-investment grade, in March 2008. VM begged banks to disburse the loans they had sanctioned but only a few obliged him. The panic button was pressed. VM became impatient with Ramana, whom he had repeatedly told that, unlike other MFIs, BSFL should stay focused on the livelihood mission and grow slowly. After yet another argument one afternoon in July 2008, Ramana decided to quit BSFL.

For the third time in twelve years, VM took over BSFL's reins, but this time his board, bolstered by investor members, told VM to behave himself and focus on growth and profitability and catch up on lost ground. Keeping in mind that he was already fifty-five and had had a heart bypass, they also asked him to look for a CEO who was younger and had mainstream banking experience. In the meantime, to raise equity, VM knocked on the doors of those he had known for years: N.K. Maini at SIDBI, Rajiv Lall at Lok Capital and Vineet Rai at the Aavishkaar Goodwell Fund. They came to his rescue by pumping in Rs 50 crore of capital by the end of March 2008.

VM appointed Sattaiah as the chief operating officer, and together, they expanded BSFL from Rs 450 crore to Rs 1000 crore of loans outstanding in eighteen months, between April 2008 and September 2009. They also managed to integrate insurance and livelihood services into the offerings. By 2009, over half a million farmers were being served by BSFL.

As required by the BSFL board, within a year, VM had identified a CEO for BSFL: forty-two-year-old Sajeev Viswanathan, director of the global transactions services business of Citibank NA in London, who had also worked as the second-in-command at Citibank, Russia. Sajeev joined as CEO in November 2009. By that time, BSFL had a Rs 1000-crore loan book. The new CEO's mandate was to make it grow profitably, while following the livelihood strategy. Sajeev focused on growth and raising fresh equity. In early 2010, BSFL got one more round of capital—over Rs 140 crore from two private funds: Matrix Partners, and ironically, the India Financial Inclusion Fund, managed by BSFL's former CFO, Viswanatha Prasad.

The equity helped BSFL to borrow more, and by September 2010, BSFL had a loan book of Rs 1808 crore, 70 per cent of which was in eighteen Indian states other than Andhra Pradesh.

VM, who continued to be the Basix group CEO, declared that he would retire in April 2011, after completing fifteen years at Basix. But that was not to be. After a hugely successful IPO of SKS Microfinance in August 2010, MFIs in Andhra Pradesh pursued even more growth, causing overlending and distress among some borrowers who could not repay. Reports of suicides by some MFI borrowers fuelled the antipathy that bureaucrats and politicians had already developed towards MFIs.

On 15 October 2010, Andhra Pradesh promulgated an ordinance to control microlenders, after a spate of reported suicides following alleged coercive recovery practices adopted by some of them. The law, which restricted MFIs from collecting money from borrowers on a weekly basis, made it mandatory that government approval be obtained if a borrower takes more than one loan. Opposition leaders, including Chandrababu Naidu, made things worse by escalating the demand for a loan waiver.

While the repayment rate dropped to 5–10 per cent following the state law, commercial banks, which typically provided 80 per cent of the funds to the industry, stopped lending to MFIs. Inside BSFL, there was turmoil as one-third of its total Rs 1800-crore portfolio went sticky in Andhra Pradesh and the neighbouring states of Karnataka, Maharashtra and Odisha. When VM returned from his shodh yatra on 19 April 2011, Sajeev Viswanathan met him, and seeing the writing on the wall, conveyed his decision to leave BSFL. VM brought in Manmath Dalai, an experienced banker from SBI and BNP Paribas who had been the CEO of KBS Local Area Bank for three years.

From here on, the story unfolded quickly. SIDBI decided to support the four big MFIs each of which had at least Rs 1000-crore exposure to Andhra Pradesh (Spandana, Share, Asmitha and BSFL) and two small ones (Future Finance and Trident). It made use of the RBI-sponsored corporate debt restructuring (CDR) mechanism, under which a joint lenders' forum offers the stressed companies relaxation in the terms of loan repayment, including a reduction in interest rate, a repayment holiday and the stretching of the loan tenure.

While all other MFIs agreed, BSFL refused to participate in the CDR on the grounds that BSFL had lost more than its net worth and would need capital infusion, in addition to debt restructuring. BSFL investors, particularly IFC, Axis Bank and SIDBI, insisted that it should not default and should continue to repay its loans as scheduled, even if it meant shrinking its loan portfolio. VM was hoping banks would reward a good borrower and eventually agree to start lending, as his portfolio outside Andhra Pradesh was doing fine. IFC offered to put in more equity but it did not do so. Equity investors were waiting for assurances from bankers, who, in turn, were waiting for assurances from equity investors and regulators.

Liquidity Squeeze

Without getting fresh funding, BSFL repaid the creditors Rs 1064 crore and an interest of Rs 202 crore up to 31 January 2012. This led to a shrinking of the book outside Andhra Pradesh to just Rs 291 crore, over half of which became sticky, as the borrowers realized that BSFL was not making any fresh loans and held back the last two to three instalments. The deterioration of portfolio quality led to a severe liquidity squeeze, and BSFL could not service the debt to the banks any more.

Eventually, it approached its lenders for CDR in March 2012, and the forum approved a restructuring package. The loan-restructuring scheme outlined that, out of the outstanding loan of Rs 652 crore, Rs 500 crore would be turned into compulsorily convertible cumulative preference shares (CCCPS), and the balance term loan was given a moratorium till April 2014, to be repaid in the subsequent five years. CCCPS are preference shares which are to be compulsorily converted into equity shares after a stipulated time. Preference shares are quasi-equity instruments where the holder or investor is entitled to dividends before profits are distributed to common shareholders. It is a hybrid between debt and equity, often a lower-cost route to raise equity, compared to issuing common shares through an initial offer, rights issue or a follow-on public issue.

Holding company Basics, which owned over 34 per cent of BSFL, was required to bring in fresh equity to the tune of Rs 25 crore, 50 per cent of which was to be infused before the implementation of the restructuring package, and the rest by 30 June 2014. VM, as the majority shareholder of Basics Ltd, was also required to pledge his shares in the holding company as well as BSFL.

Basics Ltd was able to infuse Rs 12.5 crore before the implementation of the package, and a further Rs 1.25 crore on 31 March 2014, but the balance promoter contribution—Rs 11.25 crore—could not be brought in even after extensions granted by the bankers. In September 2014, the company approached the banks for a one-time settlement, which was still being negotiated at the time of writing. Out of the nineteen lenders, it was able to settle with thirteen. SIDBI and IDBI Bank approved of the settlement but closure had not yet taken place. Negotiations were on with the remaining four lenders—Punjab National Bank, Corporation Bank, Syndicate Bank and Andhra Bank.

The conversion of debt into CCCPS in the first stage of the CDR process was a precursor to what RBI eventually announced as strategic debt restructuring (SDR) in 2014. Had the CCCPS been converted into equity, as envisaged in the second stage of the CDR, the lenders would have owned as much as a 92 per cent stake in BSFL. But that's a technicality now, as BSFL has turned into a carcass; it had a performing loan book of Rs 61 crore on 30 September 2015. Exactly five years earlier, it had had a loan book of Rs 1808 crore.

While CDR, introduced in 2001, allows banks to recast the debt of a troubled borrower, cut interest rate and increase the time of repayment, in SDR, introduced in 2015, the banks can convert their loans into equity if the restructuring does not help.

VOICE OF REASON: Vijay Mahajan (second from left), Nachiket Mor (third from right), then with corporate banking at ICICI, Brahmanand Hegde (extreme right), then a manager in ICICI looking after the agriculture portfolio, at a kirana store in Raichur district, Karnataka, in 1999.

Incidentally, VM's colleagues, who had left him and floated their own companies, have not been doing a great job either. For instance, Kishore Puli's Trident was one of the five MFIs that were admitted to the CDR cell in mid-2011, to restructure Rs 130 crore worth of loans. Shubhankar Sengupta also had to sell a substantial portion of his stake in Arohan to

IntelleCash, a subsidiary of investment banking and advisory firm Intellectual Capital Advisory Services Pvt. Ltd.

Some people now say that VM did not understand the business of microcredit like his peers in the industry, such as Samit Ghosh (Ujjivan Financial Services Pvt. Ltd), P.N. Vasudevan (Equitas Micro Finance Ltd), Ramesh Ramanathan (Janalakshmi Financial Services Pvt. Ltd), Govind Singh (Utkarsh Micro Finance Pvt. Ltd) and, of course, Chandra Shekhar Ghosh of Bandhan. But they also acknowledge him as their guru in microfinance. Samit Ghosh calls Basix the 'university of microfinance'.

Hamartia and Hubris

Last year in October, VM said my way of looking at him as a tragic hero was not entirely wrong. He accepted that his hamartia was stretching himself too thin along the livelihood-promotion space, and his hubris was the thought that he could do so sustainably, but the solution he came up with did not last. Nobody can question his quest to do good to the poor but he failed to combine his idealism with business acumen.

VM does not mind the sobriquet Bhishma Pitamaha. 'Like Bhishma, I was with the Kauravas; I knew that not everything my peers were doing was right but I did not leave them. I fought for the MF industry and got a thousand arrows shot in my back.' VM's failure to curb the malpractices of some of his peers, in an industry which he had pioneered, and whose association (MFIN) he was the president of, had jeopardized the lives of borrowers, and that had led to political leaders stepping in and the Andhra Pradesh law killing BSFL. VM was aware of this and pleaded with RBI to regulate MFIs—something a banking regulator does in many countries. That, however, is a different story.

Basix also did not get a licence for a small finance bank which RBI gave to ten entities in 2015, eight of which are MFIs. VM said it was the final atonement for his being with the Kauravas. Possibly, he was referring to the MFIs' love for private equity investors who do not love the business of serving the poor as much as they love the money that it generates.

What will you do now, I asked him. Quoting Mark Twain, he said: 'The reports of my death are highly exaggerated.'

'While BSFL has been shrinking, the rest of the Basix group has been growing,' he claimed. 'Our financial inclusion company Sub-K today serves 1.2 million clients with a range of financial services, including microcredit, using mobile phones.'

He has an agricultural services company, Basix Krishi Samruddhi Ltd, a rural vocational training company, Basix Academy for Building Lifelong Employability, a solar energy company, Vayam Renewable Ltd—all have been growing. An urban solid-waste company, Basix Municipal Waste Ventures Ltd, and a rural logistics company, Connect India E-Commerce Services Pvt. Ltd, are coming up.

'Maybe in your next book you will cast me as Bhagirath, who brought his accursed ancestors to life by bringing the water of the river Ganga to this world. Meanwhile, I will choose when I die since you called me Bhishma Pitamaha and endowed me with ichcha mrityu.'

12

Vikram Akula: A Fallen
Angel or a Prodigal Son?

At a microfinance summit in Delhi in December 2014, Vikram Akula, once the poster boy of India's microfinance industry, and the ousted founder-chairman of SKS Microfinance Ltd, Asia's first listed microlender, was seen in a suit instead of his trademark kurta-pyjama. He had lost weight and looked lean. His new venture, Vaya Finserv Pvt. Ltd, a business correspondent that collects deposits and gives loans on behalf of banks in rural pockets for a fee, and SKS had moved RBI with applications, seeking licence for a small finance bank, along with seventy others, but neither could make it. Akula, chairman of Vaya, owns a 26 per cent stake in Vaya Finserv.

He could be associated with Vaya only after his three-year non-compete agreement with SKS ended in November 2014. The non-compete agreement did not allow him to enter into housing finance, lending against gold, insurance, business correspondent for any bank and any other field of business where SKS was present. The only exception was made for a mobile-banking pilot project with which Akula was associated at that time. He had to leave SKS in November 2011 after a bitter boardroom battle.

In 2013, Akula had made an abortive attempt to come back to SKS. Most investors in the company resisted his move and SKS Trust Advisors Pvt. Ltd (STAPL), the largest shareholder in the company, which was ramping up its stake in SKS by buying shares from the market to support Akula's move, had to give up. Later, the trust sold the shares and even relinquished its status as a promoter of the firm.

The question that everyone has been asking for years now is: Why did Akula have to leave? After all, SKS was his own creation, his blood, sweat and dream. Is he a fallen angel or a prodigal son? What led to his ouster from SKS—greed, obsession for control or, simply, lack of management skills?

Let's go back to November 2011. SKS Microfinance's managing director and chief executive officer, M.R. Rao, and chief financial officer, S. Dilli Raj, were seen leaving the firm's crucial board meeting in Mumbai on 23 November, a Wednesday, much before it got over.

From private equity fund Sandstone Capital Advisors Pvt. Ltd's office on the tenth floor, at Chandramukhi Building, where the board meeting was being held, the duo hopped across to the SBI headquarters on Madame Cama Road in Mumbai's business district, Nariman Point.

A meeting was scheduled with two managing directors of SBI to discuss SKS's new business strategy—conversion from an MFI to a multi-product rural financial services company. SKS wanted to play the role of an intermediary between banks and rural India, and earn fees. It had been talking to SBI and ICICI Bank for this.

The decision to change the business model had been taken in August 2011 at a meeting with Vinod Khosla, based in San Francisco, and some of the board members. Khosla, founder of US-based Sun Microsystems, is Akula's mentor and the first investor in SKS. Many say Akula had endorsed the decision at that time but he started opposing it later, even as he firmly maintained that he had never supported it.

Akula's ouster from SKS was as much the result of serious differences on strategic issues between him and other senior executives and/or the board as of a clash of personalities. The dramatis personae in this theatre of the absurd were Akula, Rao, Raj and former CEO and managing director of SKS, Suresh Gurumani.

Indeed, the independent directors of the SKS board, such as its chairman, P.H. Ravikumar, and others—Tarun Khanna, Geoff Woolley and V. Chandrasekaran—played a role in Akula's exit, but they did so only because of the aggressive initiative of two shareholders who were also directors—Paresh Patel, CEO of Sandstone Capital Advisors, and Sumir Chadha, managing director of WestBridge Capital.

NOT HIS CUP OF TEA? Vikram Akula has had many clashes with the senior management of SKS Microfinance.

Both saw massive erosion in the value of the firm because of the conflict between Akula and the Rao–Raj duo. The stock lost at least 90 per cent in the year after its listing in August 2010. Of course, the backdrop of the erosion in stock value was the Andhra Pradesh law which nearly killed the MFI business in the state where SKS had the greatest exposure.

The first time the independent directors of SKS found something amiss in the firm's corporate governance was when Infosys co-founder and billionaire N.R. Narayana Murthy's Catamaran Ventures was given a stake in the company at a price lower than what another investor (who had come in earlier) had paid.

Ahead of its IPO, SKS sold shares to hedge fund Tree Line Asia for Rs 60 crore, at a valuation more than double of what was paid by Murthy's Catamaran a month earlier. Tree Line was sold stock at Rs 632 per share while Catamaran was offered stock at Rs 300 apiece.

The company justified the deal on the grounds that even though the Tree Line deal was discussed ahead of the Catamaran transaction, it was sealed later. Apparently, Akula defended the pricing by saying it had been committed to earlier. The board ratified the sale, treating it as a one-off case because Murthy's integrity was unquestionable. SKS also instituted an advisory board headed by Murthy, which neither had any other member nor held any meetings.

The First of Many Clashes

The first clash happened when Akula, backed by Rao and Raj, wanted to throw Gurumani out in October 2010 after

SKS's blockbuster IPO. Gurumani was appointed as the CEO because the board did not find Rao fit for the top job. Rao himself had been instrumental in bringing Gurumani on board, but the two had fallen out later. The Rao–Raj combination and Akula did not find Gurumani adding much value to the company and claimed he was spending more time in Mumbai with his family than in Hyderabad, where the firm was based.

At least one independent director put his foot down against this, as Gurumani had helped steer the historic IPO. This director wrote a dissent note against Gurumani's ouster. He was persuaded to withdraw this by other members of the board, who pointed out that an on-the-record dissent note would weaken the company's case if Gurumani were to legally challenge his ouster.

In an interview with *Business Standard* in September 2013, Akula, however, said that it was a decision of the SKS board, and not his alone. 'A chairperson of the board has no such unilateral authority. I can also make a general comment that whenever a new CEO comes into an established organization with an incumbent management team, fierce political manoeuvring is often unleashed. And it is very hard for a board to sort through the corporate politics when it is not involved in day-to-day activities,' he said.[12]

With me, he was more candid, and said, 'MR [Rao] and Dilli [Raj] had long-standing grievances against Suresh [Gurumani]. They had also rallied to their side many of the senior

[12] Surajeet Das Gupta, 'I'd Love to Return to a Leadership Role in SKS: Vikram Akula', *Business Standard* (9 September 2013), http://www.business-standard.com/article/companies/i-d-love-to-return-to-a-leadership-role-at-sks-vikram-akula-113090900034_1.html.

management team, several of whom were former colleagues of MR from his previous company. I tried to address the concerns of MR and Dilli, but finally, in September 2010, they gave me an ultimatum—either Suresh goes or they do. It was a Hobson's choice. I took their ultimatum to the board. The board decided to exit Suresh, and MR became MD and CEO.'

Rao was made the CEO and managing director after Gurumani's ouster, but Akula continued to interfere in operations. SKS insiders say Akula had vision and passion, but lacked the ability to execute plans. They also claim that he became insecure about his role and position when he was not operationally in control.

As chairman, Akula tried to wrest control by setting up a committee of executives who would directly report to him, bypassing the managing director and CEO, but the independent directors scrapped this arrangement as they expected the chairman to be the guiding light of the firm and not a hands-on manager.

Staring at the Wall

Once the committee was dismantled and Rao was asked to oversee day-to-day operations, Akula found himself completely isolated. He used to come to the office and stare at the wall in his room. Almost nobody would talk to him.

Earlier, Rao and Raj had joined hands with Akula to throw Gurumani out, but after that mission was accomplished, the group split, with Akula in one camp and the duo in the other.

Akula denied that he was power-hungry and insecure. According to him, SKS was doing many things he did not approve of, and Rao, in fact, gave him (then chairman of SKS) his resignation on Friday, 22 April, a day after a leading business daily wrote about SKS's insurance fraud. 'I presume MR did so because for months he had been defending our insurance work, despite the fact that I had been persistently pointing out problems. I asked him to withdraw his resignation until I could establish a committee of senior executives that would assume day-to-day responsibilities. My idea was that once that committee was in place, he could then formally submit his resignation to the board. This would enable a smooth management transition.' However, Rao never re-submitted his resignation.

I reached out to the company for corroboration of the chain of events but it chose not to offer any comment.

Once the two shareholders' representatives on the board found the firm losing its value fast because of the infighting, they stopped supporting Akula, who, after the IPO, virtually did not hold any stake in SKS. The two directors increased pressure on Akula to quit when he asked for an extension to exercise the first tranche of his employees' stock option scheme.

Akula had been given two tranches of these schemes (18,52,188 equity shares under the 2007 options and 17,96,537 shares under the 2008 options), and sometime in August 2011, he was 'in money' for the first tranche. This means the market price of the stock was higher than the price at which the options had been given to him and he could make money by selling them, but he could not arrange for the money to pay for his stock option schemes and hence wanted more time to exercise it. He was allowed to do so after he committed to quit SKS.

Had he not quit, he would have run the risk of being sacked. The three-hour board meeting on 23 November 2011 in Mumbai was bereft of acrimony. The meeting took as long as it did because there were several formalities to be completed—for instance, Akula had to give back the company laptop and the minutes of past board meetings, credit cards, computers, cell phones, and everything else with the exception of two Blackberry Pearls and one laptop which were his own.

There was no severance package but he was entitled to receive a monthly payment of Rs 10,47,667 for the calendar years 2012 and 2013, in lieu of providing consulting services—for about twenty hours a month—to the company to ensure an orderly transition of his responsibilities to his successor.

The seventeen-page separation agreement was meticulously drafted. Akula's one-page resignation letter was accepted on the spot through a resolution passed by the board at 4 p.m. that day. Immediately, a media release was issued, saying 'Vikram Akula steps down as executive chairman of SKS Microfinance' and Ravikumar took over as the new 'non-executive chairperson-interim' of the company. The last sentence of the release quoted Akula: 'I will also cherish the memories of having been able to work with a committed team at SKS.'

At the time of leaving, Akula was drafting plans to expand to Sri Lanka, Nepal, China, Vietnam, Mali, Nigeria, Morocco, Egypt, Afghanistan, Peru, Colombia and even the US. Although the firm maintained that his exit was voluntary, differences between the founder-chairman and the top management played a crucial role in the order of events.

At the 2011 San Francisco meeting, Akula claims to have made his last desperate attempt to save the 'soul of SKS'.

Apparently, since 2009, he had not been comfortable with the quality of the new products. He was against retailing insurance and lending against gold.

'At the San Francisco meeting, there was a compromise proposal where we would take steps to get "back to the basics" of doing what was best for our customers, even if it meant being less profitable. In exchange, I was asked to resign as chair of the board and head a board committee for "client protection". It was not ideal, but I humbled my ego and accepted it because I thought it would help me protect the soul of SKS. But when we got back to India, there was immense pressure on me to resign from the board completely, and all the safeguards for client protection we had discussed in San Francisco never materialized,' he said.

Ernst & Young was appointed to conduct a forensic audit of SKS after Akula raised serious regulatory and ethical concerns, but its findings were never released.

Roots of Conflict

The differences were not restricted to the business philosophy alone. After the Andhra Pradesh government clamped down on microfinance in October 2010, Akula wanted to launch a mass agitation against the government, in which thousands of borrowers would gather and microfinance institutions would disburse loans to them.

He was also against the repayment of loans advanced to the MFI by commercial banks.

But the board did not approve of this as SKS, by that time, was a listed entity. The board felt that in financial services, once a default takes place, the stigma would be difficult to overcome. The board decided that SKS should not become a defaulter; it was better to shrink the balance sheet, recover money from customers and repay all loans. Besides, a listed company could not look for a political solution to the problem.

Of course, Akula had his own logic. 'One has to understand that my argument for a rally of borrowers against the AP MFI Act was made in the context that the MFI Act was part of a political attack on microfinance. We needed a response to show that borrowers wanted and needed the financial inclusion we were delivering. The politicians needed to know that we had the goodwill of the borrowers. Had we organized such a rally, the AP situation may well have turned out differently,' he said.

'In terms of prioritizing the disbursement of new loans to borrowers versus repaying banks, my logic was that in microfinance, the confidence of the borrowers is everything. If we slow down—or worse yet, stop—disbursements, and borrowers think the institution is about to fold, they will stop paying en masse. It is effectively the reverse of a run on the bank. In AP, for example, the MFI Act prohibited us from giving borrowers new loans, and sure enough, borrowers lost confidence in SKS, and our repayments in AP dropped from 98 per cent to 10 per cent in three months. It was game over. We had to write off Rs 1300 crore. In the rest of the country, I wanted to ensure continued disbursements to keep the confidence of our borrowers. In fact, I personally explained this to the MD of one of our banks, and he fully understood and agreed to accept a delayed payment, so that we could continue to disburse loans and maintain borrower confidence.'

The Andhra Pradesh government's clampdown was provoked by, among other things, indiscriminate multiple loans extended by MFIs and their alleged coercive collection practices that led to some suicides.

An investigation carried out by the Guardians Human & Civil Rights Forum and Third Eye, a private investigative agency, at the insistence of Akula (who was chairman then) and the company's CEO, Rao, without the knowledge of the board, found that in seven of the twenty-two suicide cases, SKS employees had played a role.

Referring to one particular case—Dullapalli Sita of Apparaopeta in Tadepalligudem—the investigative report said SKS 'resorted to intimidation, humiliation and other legal and immoral action against the victim and even after her death her family was subjected to harassment'. However, an investigation carried out by the state government exonerated the company from such charges in all cases except one.

The Andhra Pradesh law made government approval mandatory for every second loan to a single borrower, extended the repayment cycle and barred MFIs from approaching the customer's doorstep.

Loan write-offs in Andhra Pradesh, following a crisis triggered by the contentious state law, brought down SKS's net worth to Rs 390 crore in March 2013 from Rs 1795.9 crore in September 2010. By that time, SKS had written off loans worth Rs 1362 crore and pared its staff in the state to 1200 from around 7000. The firm scaled down the number of branches in Andhra Pradesh to 120 from 550.

In the run-up to his resignation, Akula made a presentation to the board in August 2011, titled 'Institutional Governance

Systems', and wrote it a long letter on 4 October 2011, in which he extensively dealt with the 'mission drift' of SKS.

Launching a scathing attack on the management's alleged abandoning of the 'core mission' and the 'core competence' of the company and entering new business lines such as gold loans and retail insurance which were not in sync with its mission, Akula wrote, 'I did not start SKS to get into pawnbroking and crass moneylending . . . While I recognize that a listed company needs to adapt and give value to all its shareholders, a dramatic turn in business objectives is, to my mind, unjustifiable.'

The letter also discussed a dilution of the training schedule and an incentive structure which was based only on growth parameters. It spoke about one particular drive undertaken between December 2009 and March 2010, where field employees were given consumer goods such as TVs, fridges, mixers, DVDs and ten grams of gold. The value of these items was ten times the monthly salary of a staff member.

Finally, the letter alleged that 'the MD appears to have created a hostile work environment' and the MD, the CFO and some of the board members kept him out of most important meetings even though his employment contract stipulated that his responsibility was the 'overall management of the company', including 'establishing the business objectives, policies and strategic plan of the company'.

Political Risk

Incidentally, Gurumani, former CEO, identified political risk as the biggest risk for SKS at a time when it was growing rapidly, raking in profits, and its borrowers were a big vote bank. It was only natural that it would attract the attention of politicians and things could go horribly wrong.

The microfinance sector was getting overheated, with private equity investors putting money in most companies involved in giving tiny loans, chasing growth as if there was no tomorrow, and microfinance institutions poaching each other's customers to scale up business.

So, industry body MFIN was created at the end of 2009; it was instrumental in promoting a credit bureau. A code of conduct was put in place, with limits on borrowing and the number of customers.

The objective was to alleviate political risk. Akula, however, was not too excited by the concept of a credit bureau to keep a tab on the MFI borrowers, as he was a staunch believer in the group model—in which a group of women is responsible for every individual paying back her loan.

Around April 2008, when Gurumani was heading Barclays Plc's retail operations in India, his former colleague Rao, then chief operating officer at SKS, approached him and offered him the CEO's job. Rao had worked with Gurumani at Standard Chartered Bank in 1995, where the latter was heading the auto loan segment and Rao, regional manager, north, auto loans, was reporting to him.

While working for Barclays, Gurumani was familiar with SKS's mobile-banking projects. He was tempted to consider the SKS offer since, by that time, Barclays had lost out on a bid for ABN AMRO Holding NV and had to be content with being a one-branch bank while SKS had 1400 branches.

Gurumani joined SKS in December 2008 as managing director and CEO, with the mandate of transforming SKS using better technology and processes. There was a plan to hit the capital market with an IPO in the first half of 2011, which was later advanced.

Ahead of the IPO, in December 2009, Gurumani, along with Rao and Akula, went to Mexico to study Compartamos Banco, the largest microfinance bank in Latin America, serving more than 2.5 million clients. Compartamos wanted to alleviate poverty by providing microcredit to small businesses, initially by offering loans to women at the base of the economic pyramid. It was incorporated as a for-profit company in 2000, and obtained a commercial banking licence in 2006. In 2007, Compartamos raised $467 million through its IPO.

While Akula and Rao had to leave Mexico in a hurry because of business exigencies, Gurumani stayed back to study the local model. His finding: microfinance is a business of making money and not eradicating poverty.

Back in India, he claimed to have advised Akula to change the mission of the company from eradicating poverty to empowering women. 'Let's say we are improving financial inclusion,' Gurumani apparently told him, but Akula refused to budge.

So, eradication of poverty remained the mission of SKS in its IPO prospectus filed with the capital market regulator, and Akula's email signature remained 'Vikram Akula, founder and chairman, SKS Microfinance—Empowering Poor'.

The political establishment did not take kindly to the stories of coercion by loan-collection agents and the suicides spread across Andhra Pradesh.

High Growth

In the run-up to the IPO, SKS's growth was spiralling out of control, and the private equity investors were averse to stemming the growth. It had 2200 branches and 22,000 employees at the time.

The company tried to focus on diversifying, slowing growth and building secured lending products, like mortgage and gold loans, but could not succeed. It also tried to sell health insurance, mobile phones, solar lights, etc., but they did not work either. Insurance distribution failed, as there were too many bogus claims, and policies were sold like a savings product.

Meanwhile, the valuation of the company was rising by leaps and bounds. SKS raised Rs 1653 crore through a share sale in July 2010 and the stock had a stellar listing on 16 August 2010, gaining 10.51 per cent to close at Rs 1088.58, as against an issue price of Rs 985. Three weeks later, Akula became the executive chairman, and Rao the deputy CEO. Around the same time, it was decided that Gurumani was not the right person to lead SKS. On 3 October 2010, SKS terminated the services of Gurumani as CEO, triggering a 6 per cent fall in the company's stock.

Gurumani had had a five-year contract from 1 April 2009 to 31 March 2014. Rao replaced him as the CEO of SKS.

A year later, when Akula was pushed against the wall and forced to quit, he desperately wanted Gurumani to come back to SKS to be by his side.

A Failed Attempt

Three years after his ouster from the company, Akula made an attempt to come back but did not succeed. This time too the place of action was Mumbai. SKS's annual general meeting (AGM) on 3 December 2013 was largely a tame affair with STAPL choosing not to press its demand for a board seat for Akula.

STAPL, however, forced the company to put all seven resolutions to vote at the AGM—four ordinary and three special resolutions—including the reappointment of its managing director and CEO, Rao. All resolutions were passed except one special resolution on employees' stock options.

The trust also wrote to the capital market regulator, seeking its intervention to withhold the results of the vote. It cited 'irregularities' in the conduct of the poll at the AGM and sought 'an independent enquiry'. Bikshamaiah Gujja, chairman and managing director of the trust, was quoted in the media as saying, 'We believe if the incomplete proxies were precluded from the valid votes as decided by the scrutinizers, the results may well have been different.'

STAPL had demanded a board seat for Akula in the microfinance institution but faced stiff resistance from the management. It dropped the proposal and suggested a seat instead for Ravi Reddy, one of the early investors in SKS and an associate of Akula, but the board declined to accept him too. The SKS board wanted the trust to nominate an independent director of repute who would be acceptable to all—obviously that was not Akula or a person associated with him.

Before the AGM, where Akula made the abortive attempt to come back, Khosla and a few board members met him at Taj Mansingh Hotel in New Delhi in September 2013. Apparently, the board was willing to welcome Akula at a later date without specifying any time frame, but Akula was in a hurry.

What provoked SKS Trust to put forward Akula as its nominee for a board seat at SKS Microfinance? There was, of course, Akula's stated wish to return to the company he had founded and nurtured. 'At my end, I would love to return to a leadership role at the company. After all, financial inclusion is my passion and I have spent nearly fifteen years building SKS,' Akula said in the *Business Standard* interview.

Another reason could have been the central government's decision to create India's twenty-ninth state by granting statehood to the Telangana region. Andhra Pradesh, Akula's home state, is where SKS took birth. Akula has deep knowledge of doing business in Telangana, and has political connections in that region.

Once Telangana was created, many hoped that the new state might repeal the 2010 law enacted by the Andhra Pradesh Assembly that made it difficult for MFIs to do business in the state. Led by Akula, 'a son of the soil', SKS could have started recovering bad debts and building new businesses. Akula was also well known to global investors; raising money from the international markets to support future loan growth could have been easier for SKS with him on the board.

But the SKS management had strong reservations about his return. For one, the company's board believed that a 'controversial' member, who wouldn't operate in harmony with the management, would not add value to the lender. The management resisted his re-entry as the company had started making profits again and Akula might rock the boat with his reservations against SKS Microfinance's business model.

The chorus within the company was that Akula was not the right person to run the business. The conflict had something to do with his personality—he did not seem to be able to get along with most people in SKS. 'He is impossible to work with. He lacks basic people skills. If things go well, he will take the credit; if things don't go well, he will blame others,' one investor in SKS told me on condition of anonymity.

Another investor said Akula was not qualified to run SKS because he lacked financial skills. Akula's knowledge of the MFI business dated back to a time when it was a localized phenomenon, with the focus on a borrower model and weekly repayment schedules. The model has since changed—it is distribution-led. An MFI also needs to ensure end-use, or utilization of money for the purpose for which it is advanced.

But there are others who point out that in 2008, when Akula stepped down from the CEO's position, the company had 2.5 million customers, 1000 branches, 9000 employees, and around Rs 2100 crore loans outstanding. They argue:

'Had he been so bad in people management, could he have built this empire?'

They also contest the allegation that he tends to blame others when things go wrong. In May 2011, at a press conference in Hyderabad, Akula took responsibility and admitted to procedural lapses after news of suicides by MFI customers in Andhra Pradesh made newspaper headlines.

People familiar with Akula refer to his attention-seeking behaviour and say he is obsessed with self-promotion. They also say Akula 'checks in' and 'checks out' at his convenience. For instance, in December 2008, he resigned as the managing director and CEO and became the non-executive chairman at a critical time, when the company was preparing for its IPO. He returned to the company as executive chairman in September 2010, after the highly successful IPO.

The Beginnings

SKS Trust chairman Gujja, a former director of Deccan Development Society—a non-profit organization working for India's poor through agricultural programmes, immunization drives and other social projects—gave young Akula his first job, at Rs 1000 a month, in 1990. Belonging to a backward caste, Akula was born in Hyderabad but brought up in the US where his father, Akula Krishna, a surgeon, settled in 1970.

Akula founded SKS in 1997, turned it into India's largest lender to the underprivileged, unbanked poor, and steered it through an IPO in 2010 that was subscribed almost fourteen times. Along the way, he became the poster boy for India's microfinance industry. Today, SKS has nothing to do with

Akula. Its website does not even mention him as its original promoter.

SKS was founded as a not-for-profit organization Swayam Krishi Sangam—a Sanskrit phrase which means 'self-work society'—in late 1997. It was in the business of giving tiny loans to underprivileged borrowers, mostly concentrated in Andhra Pradesh, which then was India's fourth-largest state by area and fifth by population. It disbursed its first loan on 28 June 1998.

In 2005, Akula converted SKS from an NGO into a for-profit, non-banking finance company with a minimum capital of Rs 2 crore. Sangam lent money to its 16,000 women borrowers to form the share capital of SKS. This was done through MBTs under the Indian Trust Act 1882; there are two types of trusts—charitable trusts and private trusts— and MBTs are a subset of private trusts. SKS gave loans to the members of the MBTs, and they in turn put the money back in the form of equity.

The five MBTs initially held a 99.5 per cent stake in SKS. The stake got diluted with the arrival of new investors. At the time of SKS's IPO in July 2010, the five MBTs collectively held a 16.1 per cent stake in it.

Ahead of the IPO, the company wanted to set up a new governance structure for the MBTs, to insulate SKS post listing from any adverse findings or developments at the SKS trusts. That paved the way for setting up STAPL in November 2009. Geoff Woolley of Unitus Inc., an SKS board member, was instrumental in getting this done. Unitus, formed by some employees of Microsoft, was one of the early-stage investors in SKS.

It was decided that STAPL would have independent directors on its board and be run professionally. Sandeep Farias, founder of investment fund Elevar Equity, and Robert Pavrey, his colleague, were appointed as directors. Later, Narayan Ramachandran, then with Morgan Stanley; Anu Aga, former chairperson of Thermax Ltd; and Gurcharan Das, former CEO of Procter & Gamble India, joined the board, and except for Das, who remained on the board for eighteen months as chairman, none of them stayed for long.

Akula, many in SKS say, was not willing to give up control of the trust but the private equity investors persuaded him to reconstitute it in the run-up to the IPO.

It was reconstituted, but Akula was not happy with the new structure. Woolley had to step down, and Akula got the freedom to deal with the trust structure and the trustees. It was decided that he would have the final say on where the trust money would go and the trustees would administer his plans. Unwilling to accept a lame-duck position, the trustees—all eminent and independent people—resigned, and Akula gained total control over the trust. This was the first of three attempts to reconstitute the trust.

After November 2009, amendments were made in March 2010, February 2012 and May 2012 to the trust deeds. All powers, including appointment and removal of trustees, approval of accounts and elimination of social audits vested with the settler—SKS NGO, the original not-for-profit organization. Akula was one of the seven members on its board.

People who are aware of Akula's side of the story of the trust's reconstitution say it is a private trust, but under Woolley's scheme of things, the plan was to run it like Ford Foundation, which Akula did not approve of. He found that women borrowers of SKS were not receiving benefits under the new trust structure, and there was a conflict of interest because at least one trustee was benefiting by taking financial decisions that were hurting the trust. And not all of them were 'independent' and 'professional', they say.

Not everybody, however, supports this point of view. SKS board members and many former SKS trustees have expressed concern about governance at the trusts.

Gujja was the chairman of the trust, and Nirup Reddy, a Supreme Court lawyer, was a trustee, but the settler has the power to appoint, remove and nominate trustees and approve its accounts.

One of the early investors in SKS was Reddy, through Kismet Microfinance. 'I had known Ravi for a long time—we're actually distantly related—and had hit him up for an initial donation in early 1997. At that point, he was interested in SKS, but he was working 24/7 on Think Systems and was not in a position to do anything substantial,' Akula wrote in his book, *A Fistful of Rice: My Unexpected Quest to End Poverty through Profitability*.

In 1998, when SKS began operations in Tumnoor village in Medak district of Andhra Pradesh, Reddy offered a $50,000 donation, the book says. Later, when SKS decided to migrate from a non-profit to a for-profit model, Akula again approached Reddy for assistance.

'Ravi had always been drawn to our for-profit vision for SKS, and he, along with his partner Sandeep Tungare, were eager to become angel investors. He also helped me identify other investors who might be interested in stepping up,' Akula wrote.

The trust was irked by the fact that relatively smaller shareholders like Paresh Patel and Sumir Chadha were given a board seat while the trust itself had not been given one.

In December 2013, when the five MBTs sought a board seat in SKS for Akula in their capacity as the largest shareholder in the company, it set the stage for the second round of an intensely intriguing corporate battle—the first round was waged in November 2011 when Akula was forced to leave SKS.

Control and Greed

While almost everybody within the company had indulged in the blame game when SKS was not doing well, no one can take away the credit from Akula for creating SKS Microfinance and nurturing it for a decade. Nonetheless, the story of SKS is probably also the story of its founder's obsession with control, and the investors' greed.

According to sources in the company, its investors and the Venture Intelligence Blog,[13] between March 2006 and November 2008, SKS received investments of $111 million from private equity, the largest by any company in this sector. The private equity investors in the company—excluding those who picked up shares in the pre-IPO placements—include Unitus, Sequoia Capital India, SVB Indian Capital Partners, an

---

[13] http://ventureintelligence.blogspot.in/2010/08/sks-microfinance-private-equity-story.html.

affiliate of Silicon Valley Bank, Sandstone Capital, Vinod
Khosla's Khosla Ventures and Kismet Capital.

It started in March 2006 when Unitus and Khosla Ventures
invested $0.5 million each for a total stake of 30.18 per cent,
pegging the company's valuation at $3.1 million. One year
later, in March 2007, Sequoia Capital India, Unitus, Khosla
Ventures, Kismet Capital and Odyssey Capital invested
again—to the tune of $11.7 million. The price was Rs 49.77
per share. Of this, Sequoia Capital India invested $6.2 million
for a 20.38 per cent stake; Unitus, Khosla Ventures and
Kismet invested $1.5 million for 4.95 per cent each; Odyssey
Capital invested $1 million for 3.35 per cent. The company's
valuation rose to $30.4 million.

In January 2008, Sequoia Capital India, SVB, Unitus,
Kismet Capital and Khosla Ventures invested $23 million for
a 28.86 per cent stake. Shares were issued at Rs 70.67 apiece.
Sequoia Capital India invested $10.4 million and Unitus
invested $4 million. SKS's valuation rose to $78.9 million.

In September 2008, Sequoia Capital India invested
$1.87 million for a 1.69 per cent stake by purchasing
8,18,069 shares from Akula at Rs 103.91 per share, leading
to a valuation of $99.3 million.

Two months later, in November 2008, Sandstone Capital,
Kismet Capital and SVB invested $75 million for 20.58 per
cent in compulsorily convertible preference shares (CCPS) (to
be converted to shares in December 2009). Also, equity shares
were allotted to Sandstone for $12.8 million (20,85,448
shares), Kismet Capital for $5.5 million (8,85,044 shares),
SVB for $0.5 million (81,383 shares) at Rs 300 per share. The
valuation zoomed to $401.1 million.

In July 2009, Sequoia along with SVB invested $9.8 million for a 3 per cent stake by purchasing two million shares from Unitus at Rs 240 per share. At the IPO in August 2010, the company sold 1,67,91,579 shares, over half of which (93,46,256 shares) were sold by existing shareholders, diluting 21.6 per cent of the company. Shares were issued at Rs 985 per share, valuing SKS at $1.51 billion.

Riding a Tiger

The private equity investors cared for the scale of the business as scale ramps up valuations. By 2011, Akula was riding a tiger he could not tame. Greed, obsession with control and the Andhra Pradesh state law made for a deadly cocktail that almost killed SKS.

In the *Business Standard* interview, Akula dissected what went wrong in SKS:

> My vision was to create a model of microfinance that could scale. It is estimated that India's unbanked population needs credit of about Rs 2.5 lakh crore. To get that quantum of funds for the sector, I believed we had to follow a commercial model that would be able to tap funding from capital markets, unlike a non-profit model that depended on donations. Donations are limited. On the other hand, funding from capital markets is virtually unlimited. That is why I set up SKS on a commercial model and pursued an IPO. It was not about making money.
>
> I thought it would be the best way to access the huge quantum of funds needed for financial inclusion. My goal was to blend philanthropy and capitalism, meaning I wanted to harness the power of the market—of private capital—to help bring about financial inclusion in rural India.

Having said that, I could have been more careful about the type of investors I brought in. I could have been more careful about the type of senior management I brought in. Somewhere along the road, I lost the ability to control the philosophical direction of SKS. Perhaps, if I had stayed on as CEO for those last two years, instead of returning to the US and moving to a non-executive board role, things would have worked out differently.

Hit by the Andhra Pradesh crisis, the microlender reported losses for seven consecutive quarters before registering a profit in the December quarter of 2012.

In a rare interview with me in February 2013, the company's CEO and managing director, Rao, and chief financial officer, Raj, were equally frank in admitting that the for-profit organization made the mistake of staking larger-than-life claims of empowering the poor and eradicating poverty. They also conceded that intense competition in the sector did not lead to a price war that would have benefited tiny borrowers and instead diluted the process of sanctioning loans.[14]

On being asked what went wrong at SKS and whether it was a victim of political risk, Raj listed the mistakes made by the company and praised the state intervention:

The AP crisis was definitely an external event. It was a state intervention but this is not to say that everything was alright with the sector in 2010.

---

[14] Tamal Bandyopadhyay and Dinesh Unnikrishnan, 'SKS Microfinance: The Inside Story', *Mint* (7 February 2013), http://www.livemint.com/Industry/hvWN2IbllrX5hXKj3keERL/ SKS-Microfinance-The-inside-story.html.

The first mistake was all of us started as non-profit organizations and we embraced for-profit model for good reasons—to achieve scalability and sustainability. What is the point in doing some good to some people if you can do more good to more people? But when we embraced the for-profit model, we should have discarded the larger-than-life claims and mission statements like empowering the poor and eradication of poverty. The for-profit model doesn't go with this.

When we had our initial public offer, people looked at our numbers, portfolio size and, most importantly, the individual incentive system like the ESOPS (employees stock options) and the salary levels. They were all relevant for a for-profit mainstream operation but the claim of eradicating poverty did not gel with that.

The second mistake at the sector level was that in 2009 and 2010, there was intense competition. There were 400–600 companies and even smaller firms were getting funds—be it debt or equity. If we go by the text book definition, intense competition should result in a price war but we had intense competition and no price war. Everyone was charging 31–32%.

The trouble was in the absence of playing the price card, process dilution became the selling proposition. Everyone was in the bar and all were drinking.

The customers also started playing one against the other on the processes and forced us to dilute them.

The state intervention put these things in the spotlight. In a way, we want to credit Andhra Pradesh government for the wonderful job of inviting nationwide attention on this issue. But for the intervention of AP government, the borrower would not have got the attention she is getting now.

When asked whom he blamed, the state law or himself, Rao's answer was equally candid:

It's mix of all factors. If you drive the car, you can look at the rear view but you can't be driving all the time looking at the rear view. Today, after two-and-a-half years, 9.2 million borrowers are defaulters and are cut off from the mainstream. They are the largest chunk of non-performing borrowers anywhere in the world. Let's bring them back to the mainstream. Allow us to do the incremental lending.

Speaking of Akula, Raj said:

Vikram is the founder—a visionary and a social entrepreneur who created scale and sustainability for the sector as a whole and let me use the phrase—a founder is a founder.

The final question was if Akula could be blamed for the Andhra Pradesh crisis, and Raj's answer was:

Absolutely not. Every single operator converted themselves to for-profit model and each one of them continued with the positioning of eradication of poverty. Let me repeat, everyone was in the bar and all were drinking. It's a matter of second guessing and no individual could have been any wiser.

On 5 September 2013, Akula made a brief appearance at the SKS headquarters at Kundanbagh in Begumpet, Hyderabad, but left after exchanging pleasantries with Rao and Raj. Possibly, he was certain that he would make a comeback. But the company was not ready to let this happen.

People familiar with SKS at that time told me that the era of celebrity promoters was over and it would not be easy for Akula to stage a return.

Akula has done what he could have—setting up a new venture and seeking a bank licence. Named by *Time* magazine as one of the 100 most influential people in the world in 2006 for his work in financial inclusion, and featured on the front page of the *Wall Street Journal*, Akula believes that microfinance is a core solution to the global poverty problem and yet it could be highly profitable—a balance all microfinance entities are struggling to achieve. I believe he is busy writing a tell-all book on his exit from SKS.

Can He Do a Steve Jobs?

Many believe he could do a Steve Jobs in SKS. In 1985, the Apple board voted to fire Jobs, but in 1997, with the company operating at a loss and Microsoft's Windows 95 flying off the shelves, Apple's board decided that the company needed Jobs. In August of that year, Jobs returned to Apple as its interim CEO. 'He had become a far better leader, less of a go-to-hell aesthete who cared only about making beautiful objects that made money,' wrote *Fortune*'s editor-at-large Peter Elkind of the co-founder's triumphant return.

When I asked him to describe himself, Akula said, 'Am I a prodigal son or a fallen angel? I am neither. I am an idealist who naively believed that all people wanted to do good, even greedy capitalists. I believed that greed could be harnessed for good. As a result of this faith in people and faith in markets, I let a handful of rapacious profiteers into SKS (some on the board and some in the management) and they destroyed the soul of SKS, which I had nurtured for more than a decade. And by the time I realized and tried to do something, it was too late. I had let the fox into the hen-house and could not get the fox out.'

WALKING THE TALK: 'Vikram is the founder—a visionary and a social entrepreneur who created scale and sustainability for the sector as a whole,' says M.R. Rao, CEO and MD, SKS Microfinance.

Meanwhile, on 4 April 2016, SKS Microfinance decided to change its name to Bharat Financial Inclusion Ltd, wiping out the last trace of its promoter Akula from its visage. A company release issued on that date said, 'Bharat Financial Inclusion reflects the new brand and its delivery capabilities as "Bharat", the Sanskrit name of India, emphasizes the company's unique distinction of having a formidable, predominantly rural network across the country . . . The corporate name-change decision has been taken in view of the fact that the company's core has undergone a transformation.'

Appendix

The Road to Hell Is Paved with Good Intentions

Good intentions, when acted upon, may have unforeseen bad consequences. Nothing can illustrate this better than the Indian microfinance industry, a heady cocktail of entrepreneurship, idealism, a drive to do good for the poor, shrewd business sense, greed and politics.

Roughly, India's two-and-a-half-decade-old microfinance industry is just about half a per cent of the banking industry's loan assets, but when it comes to making noise, nothing can beat the MFIs. In 2006, Krishna district in the coastal region of Andhra Pradesh warned the industry about the pitfalls of heady growth but it refused to see the writing on the wall. Four years later, the southern state passed a law which nearly killed this class of financial intermediaries.

RULES OF THE GAME: Typically, in microfinance, groups are formed to create moral and social pressure for the repayment of loans, even as the group is not responsible if an individual defaults.

The impact of the state law was not uniform, though. A few MFIs got buried under the burden of defaults, some others bounced back to life after being in a coma. At least one of them used the crisis to its advantage and grew phenomenally—it was insulated from the fallout of the Andhra Pradesh law as it did not have any exposure to the entire southern belt. Later, it got a banking licence—the first Indian MFI to enjoy the privilege—and became Bandhan Financial Services Ltd.

The origin of microfinance in India, like elsewhere in the world, is in poverty, and the banking sector's unwillingness to serve the poor, citing reasons ranging from higher transaction costs for smaller loans to a lack of understanding of the rural psyche. Then there are the moneylenders who thrive in every drought and famine, something which Indian farmers are familiar with.

Sometime in the 1830s, British rulers in India forced farmers to pay revenue in cash, replacing the system of paying in kind. The objective was to finance the wars. Bouts of droughts and famines inconvenienced the farmers and they were forced to borrow money from unscrupulous grain traders and moneylenders at high interest rates, which put them in a perpetual debt trap. Before this, land revenue was paid in kind, and indeed there were moneylenders but they never had a roaring business.

There had been droughts in different parts of India periodically, and upheavals by peasants against moneylenders since 1860. The Deccan riots of 1875, around Pune, were a flashpoint caused by agrarian distress. In May–June 1875, peasants in some parts of Pune, Satara and Nagar districts in Maharashtra revolted against increasing agrarian distress. The Deccan riots targeted conditions of *kamiuti*, or debt peonage, or the practice of holding persons in servitude or partial slavery to work off a debt to moneylenders. The rioters' specific purpose was to obtain and destroy the bonds, decrees and other documents in the possession of the moneylenders.[15]

Farmers' inability to pay land revenues in cash forced the British government in India to introduce the so-called *taccavi* loans—loans given to farmers out of the revenue collected in the previous years when they could not pay taxes because of drought or famine. It was actually a system started by the Mughals, and the British rulers adopted it.

[15] https://en.wikipedia.org/wiki/Deccan_Riots.

It is a short-term loan given to poor farmers to purchase seeds, fertilizers, etc. Incidentally, Muhammad Bin Tughlaq was the first Indian ruler in recorded history to advance taccavi loans to villagers for rehabilitation, following a disastrous famine. He also proposed a grand scheme for improving cropping patterns and extending cultivation. However, the experiment did not work well as the selection of farmers was faulty and the implementation was fraught with corruption.

By that time, Germany had introduced a new concept: savings and credit cooperatives. Friedrich Wilhelm Raiffeisen was a German mayor and cooperative pioneer. Several credit union systems and cooperative banks have been named after Raiffeisen, who pioneered rural credit unions. In the 1860s, he founded an agricultural credit union that extended credit to local farmers from savings collected from local communities.

Raiffeisen conceived of the idea of cooperative self-help during his tenure as the mayor of Flammersfeld. Having witnessed the suffering of farmers, who were often in the grip of loan sharks, he was inspired to do something for them. He founded the first cooperative lending bank, in effect the first rural credit union, in 1864. In order to secure the liquidity equalization between the small credit banks, in 1872, Raiffeisen created the first rural central bank at Neuwied, the 'Rheinische Landwirtschaftliche Genossenschaftsbank' (Rhein Agricultural Cooperative Bank).

The British Raj took a leaf out of the Raiffeisen movement and, in 1892, appointed a committee under Fredrick Nicholson, an Indian Civil Service officer, to advise the government on the starting of agricultural banks and land banks in Madras

Presidency. Later, another committee was appointed by Lord Curzon under the chairmanship of Edward Law, another ICS officer.

First Cooperative Arrangement

Both the committees made strong recommendations to introduce rural banks on cooperative lines. Ahead of that, in the erstwhile state of Baroda, Anyonya Sahakari Mandali was organized in 1889, touted to be India's first cooperative arrangement. The Cooperative Societies Bill, based on the recommendations of the two committees, was enacted on 25 March 1904. As the name suggests, the Cooperative Credit Societies Act was restricted to credit cooperatives. India's first urban cooperative credit society was registered in Kanjivaram in Madras Presidency in October 1904. By 1911, there were 5300 societies with more than 3,00,000 members.

The Raiffeisen experiment was replicated in many nations. In France, the Third Republic's desire to attract farmers' votes by supporting small family farms, resulted in the Act of 5 November 1894, which created Crédit Agricole. The Act authorized the creation of Crédit Agricole's local banks by members of farm unions. The banks would be owned by their members, according to the principle of mutuality.

Raiffeisen's concept of the credit cooperative also took deep root in the Netherlands, where the first agricultural cooperative bank appeared in 1895. Following Raiffeisen's model, by the end of the nineteenth century, the first Dutch local banks established two umbrella organizations: the Coöperatieve Centrale Raiffeisen-Bank in Utrecht and the Coöperatieve Centrale Boerenleenbank in Eindhoven.

These two organizations became the central bank for the local banks and played a facilitating role in a number of areas. The two merged in 1972 to become Rabobank Nederland, a cooperative in which all local Rabobanks are members and shareholders. In 1900, the two central institutions had a total of sixty-seven affiliated agricultural cooperative banks. At its high point, in 1955, there were 1324. From that point on, mergers reduced the number of local banks dramatically.

Also, in North America, the Desjardins Group—the largest association of credit unions—was formed, taking a leaf out of the Raiffeisen experiment. It was founded in 1900 in Levis, Quebec, by Alphonso Desjardins.

The India Story

However, unlike in other parts of the world, in India, farmers never used the cooperative platform as a savings vehicle; all along, it has been a credit channel. Even then, fund flow to farmers and small borrowers has been low. The All-India Rural Credit Survey Committee 1951, popularly known as the Gorwala Committee, submitted its report in 1954, in which it observed that large parts of the country were not covered by cooperatives.

Even in those areas where cooperatives existed, a large segment of the agricultural population remained outside their membership. And where membership did exist, the bulk of the credit requirement (75.2 per cent) was met from other sources. The committee headed by Astad Dinshaw Gorwala, an ICS officer, recommended the introduction of an integrated system of rural credit, the partnership of the government in the share capital of the cooperatives and the appointment of government nominees on their boards, thus participating in their management.

ALL SMILES: In microfinance, risk management is all about keeping the loan amounts small, forming a good group and maintaining strong supervision.

The solution, the government thought, would be in the birth of SBI, which was, in fact, a major recommendation of the Gorwala Committee. Imperial Bank of India was rechristened on 30 April 1955 as State Bank of India under an Act of Parliament. Imperial Bank of India had come into existence on 27 January 1921 when the three Presidency banks of colonial India—Bank of Bengal, established on 2 June 1806, Bank of Bombay (incorporated on 15 April 1840) and Bank of Madras (incorporated on 1 July 1843)—were reorganized and amalgamated to form a single banking entity.

On its first day, SBI had 480 offices, including branches, sub-offices and three local head offices; and had a market share of little over a quarter of the Indian banking industry. The government asked it to open 400 branches outside metros immediately to spread banking to the hinterland of India.

Around the same time, quite a few panels focused on the cooperative sector and explored different ways of financing agriculture. For instance, the Agricultural Credit Organization Committee (1947), with Manilal Nanavati as chairman, recommended state assistance in agricultural finance and the conversion of all credit cooperatives into multipurpose cooperatives. It also recommended a three-tier cooperative credit banking system and various subsidies.[16]

The Industrial Policy Resolution of 1956—a resolution adopted by the Indian Parliament in April 1956, the first comprehensive statement on the industrial development of India—emphasized the need for state assistance to enterprises, organized on a cooperative basis for industrial and agricultural purposes, 'to build up a large and growing cooperative sector'.

The Mirdha Committee, in 1965, laid down standards to determine the genuineness of cooperative societies and suggested measures to weed out non-genuine societies, to review the existing cooperative laws and practices, so as to eliminate vested interest. The recommendations of the committee resulted in amendments in the cooperative legislation in most states, which destroyed the autonomous and democratic character of cooperatives.

When the first signs of severe food shortage began showing in 1965, then prime minister Lal Bahadur Shastri

---

[16] http://www.co-op-society.com/history.html.

accorded it high priority, and the first step he took was to create awareness among people. He asked them to participate in the campaign to save food, and attempted to increase grain output by appealing to farmers to grow more than one crop a year. Also, he encouraged people to clean up their backyard and start growing crops and vegetables.

One of the most popular initiatives was the 'miss a meal' campaign. India's newspapers carried a full-page ad saying, 'Today Is a Dinnerless Day,' asking people to skip dinner on Monday evenings.

On 3 December 1965, *Time* magazine wrote:

> REMEMBER! said the three-column ad in Indian newspapers, TODAY is A DINNERLESS DAY. Thus the government one day last week began its campaign to prepare Indians for what has become an annual food crisis. It was bad enough last year when India harvested 88 million tons of grain, far short of the nation's need. This year the harvest is expected to fall below 75 million tons. What with some 12 million more mouths to feed, India faces its severest food crisis in two decades.

Jai Jawan, Jai Kisan

Shastri went on to give more importance to farmers, because they were the real soldiers of the country fighting against food shortages, which had become India's biggest enemy. The slogan *Jai Jawan, Jai Kisan* ('Hail the Soldier, Hail the Farmer') was coined and it was followed by the Green Revolution in

India with the introduction of high-yielding crop varieties and the application of modern agricultural techniques. The focus was on higher-yielding varieties of wheat, developed by many scientists, including American agronomist Dr Norman Borlaug, and Indian geneticist M.S. Swaminathan. The introduction of high-yielding varieties of seeds and the increased use of chemical fertilizers and better irrigation led to the increase in production needed to make India self-sufficient in foodgrains.

Naturally, the input costs rose and agriculture credit became a national imperative. In 1967, 'social control' was introduced to force banks to give loans for the economic development of the nation. The following year, the National Credit Council was set up to assess the demand for bank credit. The finance minister was the chairman, and the governor of RBI was the vice chairman of the council. In 1968, the Banking Laws Amendment Act was passed in Parliament, giving more control to the government over the banking system. All this was a precursor to the nationalization of banks; on 19 July 1969, fourteen private banks were nationalized, and six more on 16 April 1980.

In 1969, the concept of priority sector loans was introduced, and platforms such as the state-level bankers' committees and district-level credit committees were set up for drawing up district credit plans. Under the priority sector norms, banks were required to give 40 per cent of their credit to agriculture and the weaker sections of society. The concept exists even today, although the components of priority loans have been changing over the years.

On 25 June 1975, then prime minister Indira Gandhi declared Emergency in India to take on her political rivals, but an inadvertent victim was rural credit. The 20-Point Programme, which was the bedrock of the Emergency, wanted to attack rural poverty by increasing harvest and pushing for land reforms among others, but this drove moneylenders out of villages, and overnight, all informal windows of credit were shut.

The government had to act fast. A working group was set up under M. Narasimham, who later became the governor of RBI for a few months in 1977, and in the 1990s authored two path-breaking reports, ushering in reforms in the Indian financial sector. Based on his recommendations, the Regional Rural Banks Act was passed in Parliament in 1976. Even before the Act was passed, the first regional rural bank (RRB)—Prathama Grameen Bank—was set up in Moradabad in Uttar Pradesh on 2 October 1975. This could be done by promulgating the Regional Rural Banks Ordinance in September 1975.

This Act allowed the government to set up banks from time to time, wherever it considered necessary. The RRBs were owned by three entities, with their respective shares as follows: central government 50 per cent, state government 15 per cent and the sponsor bank 35 per cent. The regional rural banks were conceived as low-cost institutions with a rural ethos, local feel and pro-poor focus.

Five years later, on 2 October 1980, another Gandhi Jayanti, India launched the Integrated Rural Development Programme (IRDP), the biggest-ever poverty-alleviation programme, to promote sustainable self-employment by offering the poor subsidized bank credit. Five poor families in every village—and India has six lakh villages—were supposed to get bank loans every year: an amount of Rs 10,000, presumably to buy buffaloes or cross-bred cows or goats. The subsidy in the form of margin money was doled out by the government: 25 per cent for the general poor, 33 per cent for scheduled castes and 50 per cent for scheduled tribes. A new agency—District Rural Development Agency (DRDA)—was created for the implementation of the IRDP programme.

The programme was a disaster as banks were under-financed—most of them disbursed the money after netting off the subsidy. And there was massive corruption in the selection of the beneficiaries. By 1989, there were some twenty-five million defaulters and not even 10 per cent of the IRDP beneficiaries were giving back the bank loans. Bankers started interpreting the acronym IRDP in the beginning as *Inko rupaih dena padega* (these people will have to be given money), and after defaults rose, as *Itna rupiah dubana padega* (this much money will have to be sunk).

In 1989, the JD government, a coalition of several parties representing socially underprivileged and lower castes and farmers, floated a loan write-off scheme. The brainchild of then deputy prime minister and minister of agriculture Devi Lal, the Agriculture and Rural Debt Relief Scheme 1990 waived loans up to Rs 10,000 issued to farmers, landless cultivators, artisans and weavers by state-run banks. Till 1992, more than forty-four million farmers benefited from this scheme worth Rs 6000 crore.

End of Social Banking

When India was forced to adopt liberalization in 1991, Narasimham was once again appointed to study the problems of the Indian financial system. Prudential norms were introduced and banks were forced to go on a massive clean-up drive as their balance sheets were full of bad loans. That marked the end of the era of social banking.

The banks turned their backs on the poor and started focusing on profits. Between 1971 and 1990, the share of small loans by amount outstanding (up to Rs 25,000) to total bank credit rose from about 15 per cent[17] to 22 per cent,[18] but the clock reversed post 1991. In the next five years, by 1996, it dropped to 14.2 per cent;[19] and in another ten years, by 2006, it dropped to 4.4 per cent.[20]

One way of addressing the issue was giving money to those at the bottom of the pyramid through SHGs. In the world of finance, it is known as Rotating Savings and Credit Association (ROSCA). This is a group of individuals who agree to meet for a defined period in order to save together in a pool and borrow from it individually as needed—a form of combined peer-to-peer saving and peer-to-peer lending. It's a sort of poor man's bank, where money is not idle for long

---

[17] http://dbie.rbi.org.in/DBIE/dbie.rbi?site=publications#!9, p. 211–14.
[18] https://rbi.org.in/Scripts/PublicationsView.aspx?id=329, p. 254–56.
[19] http://dbie.rbi.org.in/DBIE/dbie.rbi?site=publications#!9, p. 101–06.
[20] https://rbidocs.rbi.org.in/rdocs/Publications/PDFs/64312.pdf.

but changes hands rapidly, satisfying both consumption and production needs.[21]

Within India, it is known as *kuris* in Kerala, *chitty* in Tamil Nadu and *bishy* in Gujarat and many other parts of India. Bishy is, in fact, a coinage of the Hindi word *bis*, which means 'twenty'. Typically, such groups have twenty members.

One of the first organizations to experiment with the use of savings and credit groups was the Village Reconstruction Organization, commonly known as VRO, founded on 6 June 1969 in the wake of the disastrous floods in coastal Andhra Pradesh, especially around Guntur, Krishna and Prakasam districts. It is widely believed that MYRADA pioneered forming SHGs in Karnataka in the 1980s, and got the first loan from NABARD to lend to such groups.

Another NGO, Pradan, linked the first SHG to a bank branch, Punjab National Bank's Khairthal branch, in Alwar district of Rajasthan, in 1987, marking the first SHG–bank linkage. This seed grew into a nationwide tree and, by 31 March 2014, India had 7.43 million SHGs, with about 104 million members, and had banked savings of Rs 9897 crore. Of these, 4.2 million SHGs, or about 40 million women, had bank credit outstanding worth Rs 42,928 crore.[22]

The SHG–bank linkage programme started in 1992 when, in response to advocacy by the pioneer NGOs, RBI approved a pilot project to link 3000 SHGs with bank

---

[21] F.J.A. Bouman, 'Indigenous Savings and Credit Societies in the Developing World', in *Rural Financial Markets in the Developing World*, eds. J.D. von Pischke, Dale W. Adams and Gordon Donald (Washington: Johns Hopkins University Press, 1983).
[22] https://www.nabard.org/Publication/SMFI_2013_14.pdf.

branches all over the country in three years. In 1995, RBI appointed a working group headed by S.K. Kalia, then managing director of NABARD, to study the results of the pilot. The working group commended the SHG–bank linkage model as the right way to extend credit to the rural poor.

It categorically stated that SHGs should not be subjected to registration and regulation but found a way through an inter se agreement to record the name, address, office bearers, members and basic rules of the SHG. Filing of this agreement with the nearby bank branch was enough to open a bank account in the name of the SHG. RBI not only accepted this report but gave NABARD the mandate to scale up this programme nationwide.

The women of Andhra Pradesh were already organized under the banner of the Total Literacy Mission, officially launched in Nellore district in January 1990. Under this mission, women of a neighbourhood often got together and discussed their problems during literacy classes. The binding factor was a common problem most women had at home: alcoholic husbands.

Together, they decided to take a stand against all those who sold the liquor that ruined their families. Gradually, there was a revolt against the local bureaucracy, police officials and the state chief minister. They had one demand: a complete ban on arrack. Their demand was met when N.T. Rama Rao, then chief minister of AP, promulgated prohibition in 1994.

Once their target was achieved, while congratulating the women, the then collector of Nellore, B. Sambasiva Rao, suggested that the anti-arrack campaigners begin a new movement for savings and credit, named Podupu Lakshmi (after the goddess of wealth). The district government staff played a critical role in organizing the women, and Rao's successor in Nellore, K. Raju, built it up further. In his next posting in the district of Kurnool, Rao tried to form a large number of SHGs and link them to banks. Initially, there was resistance from bankers, and only in the southern districts could the SHG model gather some momentum.

By 1997, the combination of the support of Chandrababu Naidu, then chief minister of Andhra Pradesh, the appointment of the able and committed Raju, the initiative of NABARD chairman Kotiah (who was from the same state) and the presence of SHG activists such as Shashi Rajagoplan, C.S. Reddy and Vijay Mahajan made Andhra Pradesh the leading state for the SHG–bank linkage programme. In 2000, AP accounted for over 50 per cent of the SHGs in the country.

While the SHG–bank linkage programme was emerging as a tool to take care of the financial needs of the rural poor, another stream started feeling the pulse of the people: MFIs. Udaia Kumar, young promoter director of Share, an NGO set up as a not-for-profit society in 1989 in Andhra Pradesh, visited Grameen Bank in Bangladesh in 1993, and started a 'Grameen replication' in two branches, one each in Guntur and Kurnool.

The first microfinance institution in India to obtain an NBFC licence was Bhartiya Samruddhi Finance Ltd (BSFL), popularly known by its parent, the Basix Social Enterprise Group, established by Vijay Mahajan in 1996.

For eight years, BSFL was the only for-profit NBFC MFI. Later, Share, Spandana, SKS, Grameen Koota, Gram Vidiyal and Bandhan—all of which ran as NGO MFIs for several years—transferred their portfolio and borrowers to NBFCs with similar names as the NGOs. Through this strategy, all these MFIs, except Basix, were able to meet their costs through grants. All of them remained NGOs even after breaking even and a few of them used the borrower-owned MBTs to funnel the surplus of the NGOs as equity into the NBFCs.

While the SHG model is built on the principle of savings first and credit later, and credit is partly generated from the group's own savings (banks do supplement that), the joint liability group (JLG) model, which is adopted by 95 per cent of Indian MFIs, is only for credit. JLGs are smaller groups, typically of five, where each individual stands as a guarantor for the other four borrowers.

JLG vs SHG

Unlike JLGs, in case of SHGs, the bank's borrower is the group and all transactions by the group with its members are internal. Thus the SHG is its own guarantor. In both cases, however, a degree of peer pressure exists, and neither of them is regulated or registered.

BSFL adopted the JLG model after a 1996 visit to BAAC in Thailand. Set up in 1966, BAAC provides financial assistance to farmers, farmer associations and agricultural cooperatives. About 85 per cent of farmers in Thailand borrow money from BAAC. While BSFL continues to use the original JLG model for male farmers, most Indian MFIs have superimposed the JLG model on the Grameen Bank or ASA Bangladesh models. Here, anywhere from four to eight JLGs, consisting of twenty to forty women borrowers, come together for a meeting at a 'centre'—typically the courtyard of a borrower who is designated as the leader—at a fixed time, usually every week.

A casual visitor may be confused between an SHG meeting and an 'MFI centre' meeting because they see just a group of women sitting and talking about loans (and, of course, the weather, their children's education and the rising prices of dal and other essential commodities). But the difference is enormous. The SHGs are very interactional, with women discussing family and village matters and exchanging notes about business activities. There is no outsider present, nor any hierarchy. The savings and loan transactions are a secondary agenda for an SHG, and the terms of the internal loans are often flexible.

In contrast, at the MFI centres, the meetings are purely transactional, the biggest focus being on ensuring that every member repays the loan instalment due that day, with each member handing over the cash to their JLG leader, and the JLG leader counting it and handing it over to the centre leader, who then counts it again and passes it on to the MFI staff member. Once recovery is 100 per cent, they begin talking about who wants loans for what purpose and how much, but as the terms are fixed by the MFI, it is only a question of whose name comes first.

In essence, the SHG movement, which had RBI's stamp of approval, was patronized by states such as Andhra Pradesh and Tamil Nadu, promoted by NABARD and embraced by the banks as they could meet their priority sector loan target. Within a few years, political leaders like Naidu and Jayalalithaa, the chief minister of Tamil Nadu, realized the potential of using the SHG women as a vote bank.

They began by asking banks to bring down the interest rate of 12 per cent per annum. Before the Andhra Pradesh elections in 2000, Naidu managed to persuade banks to reduce the interest rate to 9 per cent. And in 2004, his arch-rival Y.S. Rajasekhar Reddy, popularly known as YSR, won the elections partly on his promise of *pavala vaddi* (quarter per cent per month or 3 per cent a year as interest) to Andhra Pradesh women on loans to SHGs,[23] with the state government subsidizing the SHGs' interest cost. This was expected to bring down the internal lending rate among SHGs from 24 per cent to at least 18 per cent.

While NABARD was supporting the SHG model as a means of lending money to the poor, SIDBI started helping small entrepreneurs. Brahm Dutt, a joint secretary at the ministry of small-scale industry, who was on the SIDBI board between December 1994 and January 2000, began to promote lending to microenterprises.

SIDBI Foundation for Micro Credit (SFMC) was launched in January 1999 for channelizing funds to the poor. It became the

---

[23] Andhra Pradesh Congress Committee Manifesto 2004. See www. puliveeranna.com/pb/wp_f1ec249b/wp_f1ec249b.html.

apex wholesaler for microfinance in India, providing a complete
range of financial and non-financial services, such as loan funds,
grant support, equity and institution-building support to the
MFIs. The objective was to facilitate their development into
financially sustainable entities, besides developing a network
of service providers for the sector. SIDBI launched SFMC with
a clear focus and strategy to make it the main purveyor of
microfinance in the country; it also played a significant role in
advocating appropriate policies and regulations.

In 1998, Ela Bhatt of SEWA and Vijay Mahajan of
Basix established Sa-Dhan as an 'association of community
development finance institutions'. They organized a meeting in
Ahmedabad in which then RBI governor Bimal Jalan announced
the appointment of a task force on supportive policy and
regulatory framework for microfinance, headed by Y.C. Nanda
of NABARD. The task force submitted its report in October
1999 and RBI acted on its recommendations with alacrity.

A shot in the arm for MFIs came in the form of an RBI
circular on 18 February 2000, which said,

Micro credit extended by banks to individual borrowers
directly or through any intermediary would be reckoned as
part of their priority sector lending . . . The criteria for selection
of micro credit organisations are not being prescribed . . .
Banks may prescribe their own lending norms keeping in
view the ground realities. They may devise appropriate loan
and savings products and the related terms and conditions
including the size of the loan, unit cost, unit size, maturity
period, grace period, margins, etc. The intention is to provide
maximum flexibility in regard to micro lending keeping in

view the prevalent local conditions and the need for provision
of finance to the poor.[24]

For the first time, RBI allowed indirect lending to the small
borrowers to be considered as part of priority loans. At the
same time, the banking regulator also freed interest rates. This
encouraged banks overnight to give money to MFIs to be on-
lent to the rural poor in a big way.

THE SHOW GOES ON: The system has not changed even after Bandhan
became a bank; it still has the same monitoring level and personal touch—
meeting every borrower once a week, fifty-two times a year.

One large private bank entered the arena aggressively and
started giving money to MFIs liberally. In fact, this bank
employed agents to source loans, but RBI was not comfortable
with this model as it was not certain whether these agents
would follow the KYC policy. In January 2006, the regulator

[24] https://rbidocs.rbi.org.in/rdocs/notification/PDFs/11680.pdf.

allowed the agency route for sourcing loans and collection of deposits, and framed rules for business correspondents (then called 'business facilitators').

While NABARD was pumping money into the SHG model, SIDBI and a clutch of banks flooded the MFI turf. Those banks which were sitting on MFI loan applications for months and years started sending faxes (email was not popular then) to MFI offices, sanctioning loans. From zero, bank-lending to the segment rose to Rs 30,000 crore by 2010, when the Andhra Pradesh government clamped down on the industry, almost killing it.

In 2009, in spite of a spirited campaign by Naidu, who even promised a mass loan waiver if elected,[25] the Congress Party was re-elected under YSR, but he died in a helicopter crash on 2 September 2009. He was succeeded by K. Rosaiah, whose government was attacked by YSR's son Y.S. Jagan Mohan, citing Rahul Gandhi as a friend of MFIs. The Congress high command was embarrassed by the charge of being friendly to MFIs and asked Rosaiah to act wisely against MFIs.[26]

In the wake of MFIs using unethical practices to recover the loans which apparently led to suicides by the borrowers, allegations of multiple borrowing and charging high interest rates forced the AP government to promulgate an ordinance in October 2010 to save the borrowers. In December 2010,

---

[25] Telugu Desam Party Election Manifesto, 2009. See also http://www.thehindu.com/todays-paper/tp-national/tp-andhrapradesh/article1204017.ece.

[26] http://indiatoday.intoday.in/story/rahul-dragged-into-ap-microloan-mess/1/118497.html.

the ordinance was enacted as the Andhra Pradesh Microfinance Institutions (Regulation of Moneylending Activities) Act, prohibiting MFIs from collecting repayments from the borrowers' homes or work places, directing them to collect money at public places mentioned in the Act, on a monthly basis, instead of the usual weekly centre meetings.

The Act also required MFIs to take the government's prior approval for each and every new loan, and made the process for that very cumbersome. Use of forceful practices to recover loans was made punishable under the Act.

A 2011 National Council of Applied Economic Research (NCAER) study on 'Assessing the Effectiveness of Small Borrowing in India', sponsored by MFIN in the wake of the AP law, however, did not support the popular criticism of irresponsible lending by MFIs. Nor did it find the interest rate charged by the MFIs excessive compared with that of the SHGs.

The political reality in Andhra Pradesh was different. The Telugu Desam Party, led by Chandrababu Naidu, went around the state saying that MFI borrowers should have been given a loan waiver[27] and asked the people to call the party's workers in case any MFI came for recoveries. The message that was perceived by the borrowers was that they were not required to repay their debt, and in any case, the state government and the Opposition parties were both vying with each other to protect them. The recovery rate plummeted from 99 per cent to 10 per cent.

---

[27] http://archive.indianexpress.com/news/dont-repay-microfinance-loans-tdp/706093/.

An analysis of M-CRIL[28] indicates that the crisis left the MFIs in India with the worst portfolio-quality ratios in the world. Portfolio at risk sprang up from 0.67 per cent (end-March 2010) to 25.5 per cent in 2011. The loans at risk are those that have not been serviced for thirty days.

In his second term, from 2000–04, Naidu drove the SHG movement through the Society for Elimination of Rural Poverty (SERP), an autonomous society of the Government of Andhra Pradesh, chaired by the chief minister with representations from key stakeholders, the government and NGOs. Its precursor was the UNDP-promoted South Asia Poverty Alleviation Program in six mandals of three districts, namely Mahabubnagar, Kurnool and Anantapur. K. Raju, who was earlier the district collector of Nellore, and later Kurnool, was its CEO, and Raju's deputy was T. Vijay Kumar.

SERP's programme, which was called Velugu during Naidu's regime, was renamed Indira Kranthi Patham (IKP) after YSR came to power in 2004. Velugu/IKP was a statewide rural poverty-reduction project to enable the poor to improve their quality of life.

Indeed, SERP has relentlessly worked on a unique structure of community-based organization (CBO) by marshalling 1.14 crore rural women into 10.27 lakh SHGs, 38,646 village organizations, 1098 mandal samakhyas and twenty-two zilla samakhyas. It has established a unique institutional structure for the CBOs.

---

[28] Microfinance Review 2011.

This CBO structure in Andhra Pradesh has facilitated cumulative loans of Rs 34,889 crore from commercial banks to SHG members and collective marketing to the tune of Rs 3925 crore leading to a benefit of Rs 75 to Rs 100 per quintal to the farmers. Pesticide-free cultivation in 23 lakh acres in 2010–11 alone resulted in savings of Rs 3000 to Rs 15,000 per acre for the farmers.[29]

The Politics of Microfinance

Enough has been written on the Andhra Pradesh microfinance crisis in the global media. Its genesis can be traced back to the competition between the two models: SHGs, supported by Velugu/IKP and the NABARD-promoted bank linkage, predominantly by public sector banks, versus the MFI model where the funds came predominantly from SIDBI, and initially also from private banks. The rural women were originally borrowing from local moneylenders. They also started borrowing from their SHGs, which received liberal amounts as 'community investment funds' from Velugu/IKP, which had taken a $600-million loan from World Bank. Then, there were loans to be taken from the SHGs through the bank linkage programme.

On top of this, they were wooed by several MFIs that were competing with each other for expansion. There was no credit bureau system, and it was easy for a woman to take multiple loans. However, when the time came for repayments, they found it difficult, and many complained

[29] www.serp.ap.gov.in.

to their SHG leaders who, in turn, complained to the Velugu/IKP staff, who then took up the matter with the state government.

There was even an allegation that ten people who borrowed from MFIs in Krishna district committed suicide because they were unable to repay the loans taken. SERP's CEO, K. Raju, and deputy CEO, Vijay Kumar, decided to teach the MFIs a lesson, and in March 2006, the Krishna district collector closed down fifty-seven branches of two large MFIs (Share and Spandana Sphoorty) as well as those of a few smaller MFIs. The decision to close down these MFIs was prompted by allegations of unethical collections, illegal operational practices (such as taking savings), usurious interest rates and profiteering.

Representatives of the MFI industry association Sa-Dhan and then RBI governor Y.V. Reddy went to Hyderabad to douse the fire and set up a panel under the chairmanship of Madhava Rao, former chief secretary of Andhra Pradesh and an RBI board member, to investigate the issue. The Rao report, an internal exercise, was never made public, but Reddy's presence there made it clear that both the models, SHG and MFI, had the blessings of the regulator. Former RBI deputy governor Usha Thorat, passionate about spreading finance in the hinterland, told me, 'The SHGs had created the ideal ground for the MFIs to scale up.'

BSFL was the first to get institutional equity in 2001, about Rs 12 crore from ICICI Bank, HDFC Bank, IFC Washington, ShoreBank USA and Triodos Bank, Netherlands. In the next five years, there was no instance of an MFI raising equity as they were all NGO-MFIs. It's only after setting up NBFCs

and transferring the NGO portfolios to the for-profit entities
that equity started coming in. The first instance of a private
equity fund investing in an Indian MFI was when Legatum
put money in Share in 2007.[30] Share had projected a portfolio
of $600 million by 2012. That did not happen but that's a
separate story.

Soon thereafter, JM Financial Fund, and Mauritius-based
microfinance venture capital fund, Lok Capital, put Rs 40
crore and Rs 9.2 crore, respectively, in Padmaja Reddy's
Spandana Sphoorty.

A clutch of private equity funds, led by Kismet
Microfinance, India-focused hedge fund Sandstone Capital,
WestBridge Capital and others picked up stakes in SKS in
2008, the year Compartamos Banco of Mexico made an
initial public offer—the world's first MFI to do so. SKS soon
declared its intent to do the same and, after a long-drawn
process, had a very successful IPO in July 2010.

The fact that SKS Microfinance's Rs 1654 crore IPO
was subscribed 13.69 times[31] and attracted Rs 22,660 crore
from around the world raised a lot of eyebrows about
microfinance becoming a moneymaking game. The financial
hype was accompanied by an increasing outcry against MFIs,
which were expanding recklessly, encouraged not only by a
strong demand for loans from borrowers neglected by the
banking system, but also by investors eager to put money
into the industry at a high valuation. Going by the NCAER

---

[30] http://www.telegraph.co.uk/finance/markets/2809340/Legatum-
in-new-deal.html.

[31] http://www.business-standard.com/article/markets/sks-
microfinance-s-ipo-subscribed-13-69-times-110080300089_1.html.

survey, in the five years between 2005 and 2010, the MFI industry grew at 62 per cent every year in terms of the number of unique clients, and 88 per cent in terms of loan portfolio.

This was short-lived: after allegedly coercive debt-collection practices drove many poor borrowers to suicide, the government of Andhra Pradesh, within three months of the SKS IPO, promulgated the AP MFI ordinance, making it mandatory for MFIs to specify their area of operation, rate of interest and recovery practices, among other things. This was the climax of the fight between two camps: the SHGs, backed by political interests, and the MFIs, backed by profit aspirations. The near-death of the industry and its dramatic bounceback in five years is another story.

The Resurrection

In the five years between 2005 and 2010, the Indian microfinance sector emerged as one of the largest in the world with Andhra Pradesh—dubbed by *The Economist* as 'the state that would reform India'—as its hub. However, the autumn of 2010 changed the face of the industry. The Andhra Pradesh ordinance was a death warrant, and the operations of all MFIs in the state came to a grinding halt. The ripples created by the crisis were felt in almost every state, with bad loans piling up as borrowers refused to pay them back, and banks declining to give loans to MFIs.

In 2010, about 6.5 million borrowers in Andhra Pradesh defaulted in 9.2 million loans from MFIs, the largest number of defaulters in any single location in the world. The state at the time had a population of 48 million (or about 9.6 million households).

THE MAKING OF AN ENTREPRENEUR: From taking loans of Rs 5000, many of the small borrowers have upgraded themselves to taking loans of Rs 1 lakh, and created jobs for others.

The MFI industry's total exposure to Andhra Pradesh was around Rs 7200 crore in 2010 but it was able to collect only 10 per cent of this money from the borrowers. Even MFIs that did not have direct exposure to Andhra Pradesh were shunned by banks. Yes Bank was the first to recall loans given to MFIs. In December 2010, it recalled at least Rs 100 crore. The outstanding loan book of the industry, Rs 30,000 crore in October 2010, had shrunk to half that size in a year.

The crisis triggered a strong response from RBI. Based on the recommendation of a high-powered committee headed by Y.H. Malegam, noted chartered accountant and a member of

the central bank's board then, RBI put in place regulations
for the industry in December 2011. The margin between the
cost of borrowing and the price at which loans were given
was capped, interest rates were regulated and loan norms
were defined. The central government too chipped in by
introducing a bill in Parliament.

The industry has seen many changes, including the creation
of three credit bureaus—Equifax Credit Information Services
Pvt. Ltd, Experian Credit Information Company of India Pvt.
Ltd and CRIF High Mark Credit Information Services Pvt.
Ltd—to help it take appropriate credit decisions and arrest
multiple lending. The bureaus also ensured the introduction
of a code of conduct; diversification of the product basket;
and adoption of new practices to focus on customers' needs.
The code of conduct ensures governance and client protection,
and creates an ethos for responsible lending—something many
MFIs did not do till the crisis broke out. The credit bureaus
are now a repository of at least 100 million loan records. Also,
both MFIN and Sa-Dhan have got the status of self-regulatory
organizations from the banking regulator.

In an interview in January 2011, Malegam had made an
interesting observation on why MFIs charge high rates:

When you are growing at a very fast pace, there is a lot of
development cost which is incurred and that development
cost is reflected in today's cost. You are asking the current
borrower to pay for that development. If you look at any
other industry, no one can do that. There should be some
ways through which you bear that cost and recover it when
you reach a certain size. The whole concept of microfinance
is getting debased because of greed. If you say I am small

and my costs are high and the customer should pay higher interest, then I will tell you to grow larger. Why should a borrower subsidize you?[32]

Since then, MFIs have dropped their interest rates. The industry has also spread to other geographies. The latest regional exposure data, according to MFIN publication *Micrometer* is indicative of the spread, with the south accounting for 36 per cent of the gross loan portfolio (GLP), the west 25 per cent, the north 24 per cent and the east 15 per cent, as on 30 September 2015. Andhra Pradesh did not feature among the top ten states in terms of MFI penetration. The top five states were Tamil Nadu (17 per cent), Karnataka (14 per cent), Maharashtra (12 per cent), Uttar Pradesh (10 per cent) and Madhya Pradesh (8 per cent), accounting for 61 per cent of the GLP.[33]

As of 30 September 2015, MFIs provided microcredit to at least 26.3 million clients. The aggregate GLP of MFIs stood at Rs 36,660 crore, excluding non-performing portfolio or portfolio at risk where repayment was not made for 180 days—as in the case of Andhra Pradesh as well as the loan portfolio of Bandhan, which started its banking operations on 23 August 2015. This exclusion of Bandhan depressed the overall industry numbers by one-fourth, with an even greater impact in states where Bandhan was a significant player. In the April–June quarter of 2015–16, Bandhan accounted for 24 per cent of the industry's gross loan portfolio.

[32] http://www.livemint.com/Politics/eA2GTCGCyxSEFRHcDKKlaM/YH-Malegam-Limit-on-annual-income-can-be-changed.html.
[33] *MFIN Micrometer*, no. 15 (10 November 2015).

In September 2015, the average loan outstanding per client was at Rs 13,901. The MFIs on an aggregated basis had a branch network of 8616 and an employee base of 73,148, of which 62 per cent were loan officers who provided doorstep credit to low-income clients served by MFIs.

Another interesting development was seen at Sa-Dhan's microfinance report in 2015: 'The MFIs have shifted their focus from rural pockets to urban India. For the first time in its 25-year history, Indian MFIs in fiscal year 2015 had more urban clients than rural ones.'

The data, compiled by Sa-Dhan, showed that 67 per cent of the 37 million MFI customers lived in urban India. The share of rural customers was 69 per cent in fiscal year 2012. That dropped marginally to 67 per cent in 2013. In the following two years, the share of rural customers has fallen drastically. In 2014, rural customers constituted 56 per cent of the total. It dropped further to 33 per cent in the following year.[34]

Alok Prasad, former chief executive officer of MFIN, told me, 'We did not waste a good crisis,' on the fifth anniversary of the microfinance crisis that originated in Andhra Pradesh. This statement is generally attributed to Rahm Emanuel, a former White House chief of staff, in response to the Wall Street meltdown, but actually comes from a comment made by Niccolò Machiavelli, a well-known Italian political thinker of the fifteenth century, who wrote, 'Never waste the opportunity offered by a good crisis.' 'That's exactly what the microfinance industry has done. It took a hard look at itself; it reformed and

---

[34] The Bharat Microfinance Report 2015, Sa-Dhan.

moved on, doing what it knows best—providing micro-loans to low-income households,' Prasad said.

The granting of eight licences to MFIs to become small finance banks signals that all is well now with the industry. Indeed, MFIs play a critical role in many countries but nowhere in the world has the industry seen such a dramatic turnaround. Of the eight MFIs that have been given licences, there are two each in Chennai and Bengaluru, and the remaining four are in Guwahati, Navi Mumbai, Ahmedabad and Varanasi—well spread out across India. All eight have over 99 per cent standard assets.

The founders of at least four of them are former bankers: Ramesh Ramanathan of Janalakshmi Financial Services Pvt. Ltd (Citibank), Samit Ghosh of Ujjivan Financial Services Pvt. Ltd (Citibank and HDFC Bank), P.N. Vasudevan of Equitas Holdings Ltd (DCB Bank) and Govind Singh of Utkarsh Micro Finance Pvt. Ltd (ICICI Bank). In the run-up to become a small finance bank, Equitas Holdings's IPO in April 2016 was subscribed over seventeen times, and that of Ujjivan Financial Services forty-one times in the first week of May, demonstrating investors' faith in the MFI business model. Once these eight MFIs become banks, the for-profit MFI industry will shrink by around 40 per cent. But nobody will complain.

Not even Allya Laskar, thirty-four, a mother of three daughters. Laskar, who studied up to Class VIII, lives in Srinagar, Ghutiari Sharif, South 24 Parganas, the hub from where drugs are smuggled into Kolkata by train. In 2007, she was working at a glove-making factory, earning Rs 150 a day. She borrowed Rs 5000 from Bandhan, showing her voter ID card and a photo identification, for a weekly instalment of

Rs 125. She bought a second-hand sewing machine for Rs 3500 and hired a labourer.

In 2015, her eighth loan was Rs 60,000 and her weekly instalment rose to Rs 1440. Twelve people were working at her factory, which had eight sewing machines, producing

TRANSFORMATION: Allya Laskar stocks bottles of water in her fridge as her neighbours love to drink cold water in summer. She has got new friends; her social life has changed.

1000 pairs of gloves a day. She also branched out to selling sarees in 2012 to supplement her income from exporting gloves to the US and a few European markets. In her four-room residence, she has a 22" LG colour TV and a 185-litre grey LG fridge. She keeps ice cream and fruits in the fridge for her children, and fish for her husband. Every Sunday, the Laskar family eats mutton. She keeps bottles of water in her fridge as her neighbours love to drink cold water in the summer. She has new friends; her social life has changed. She is now a customer of Bandhan Bank.

Like Laskar, millions of customers of MFIs will migrate to small banks even as the MFIs will continue to serve many more Laskars, till India's banking system is ready to serve all.

Acknowledgements

The list of people I should thank for their inputs and insight is a long one, and I'm not naming all of them here. They include many from the Bandhan family who patiently answered all my questions, allowing me to get a sense of how the organization was created. I do, however, need to make special mention of Chandra Shekhar Ghosh, Bandhan's founder. He gave me access to employees and the Bandhan archive without any preconditions. He didn't try to influence me or censor anything—this was critical. Even though this is an independent project, I have been associated with Bandhan professionally, and, to that extent, I am an insider.

While all facts and figures were cross-checked with Ghosh, this book is neither a definitive biography of him nor an authoritative account of the Bandhan group.

Quite a few senior RBI executives were gracious enough to talk to me. I respect their desire for anonymity and thank them for their perspectives.

There are others whom I can formally thank. They are Usha Thorat, former deputy governor of RBI; Y.C. Nanda, former chairman of NABARD; Brij Mohan, former executive director of SIDBI; Saneesh Singh, managing director of Dia Vikas Capital Pvt. Ltd; Sushil Roy, Md Enamul Haque and Md Azim Hossain of ASA, Bangladesh; Ajit Maity, chairman of Village Financial Services Pvt. Ltd; Vijay Mahajan, founder and CEO of Basix group; Vikram Akula, chairperson, Vaya Finserv Pvt. Ltd; Alok Prasad, former CEO of Microfinance Institutions Network of India; V. Nagarajan of V. Nagarajan & Co.; and Ragini Bajaj Chaudhary, private sector development advisor at the UK government's Department for International Development.

I have used a few news reports and interviews that appeared in *Mint* and *Business Standard*. These were authored by Aniek Paul, Manish Basu, Romita Datta, Dinesh Unnikrishnan and Surajeet Das Gupta.

I thank Sagnik Gangopadhyay of Ogilvy & Mather in Kolkata for helping us with the cover design.

I am also grateful to four journalist friends for their valuable suggestions—Nabeel Mohideen, Feroze Ahmed Jamal, Somnath Dasgupta and Saisuresh Sivaswamy.

Special thanks to Lohit Jagwani, commissioning editor at Penguin, who went out of his way to try and get to know me better. In past six months, each time I came to Delhi, he would drop in at my hotel and chat with me for hours, asking all kinds of questions. And, of course, thanks to Chiki Sarkar, former publisher at Penguin, who convinced me to come on board and publish this book with them.

I also want to thank my long-suffering wife, Rita, for continually fixing my computer problems and Internet connectivity issues while I was working non-stop on the manuscript.

And finally, my dog, Gogol, for keeping me company through long nights, sitting at my feet, showing signs of approval by wagging his tail, and occasionally, lack of interest, by yawning in the early hours after spending many sleepless nights.

Index

Die Urkraft aus der Natur

Ein alltägliches Phänomen

Der Magnetismus begleitet uns im Alltag auf Schritt und Tritt. Aus dem Büro kennt man ihn von den kleinen Büroklammerdosen, deren Öffnung mit einem Magnetstreifen ausgekleidet ist, damit die metallischen Bürohilfen nicht in alle Winde zerstreut werden, wenn die Dose einmal umkippen sollte.

Im Werkzeugkasten findet man sicherlich den einen oder anderen Schraubenzieher, an dessen Spitze die Schrauben irgendwie »kleben« bleiben, und auch von unserem Kassettenrekorder haben wir schon einmal gehört, dass das Be- und Abspielen seiner Bänder etwas mit Magnetisieren zu tun hat.

Weniger auffällig, dafür aber immerzu präsent, ist die Magnetkraft, die von der Erde ausgeht und die Kompassnadeln dazu veranlasst, in die Richtung der beiden Pole zu zeigen.

Schlechter Ruf

In jüngerer Zeit tritt der Magnetismus allerdings mit eher negativem Image in unser Bewusstsein. Immer wieder ist davon zu lesen und zu hören, dass die elektrischen Magnetwellen, wie sie etwa von Starkstromleitungen ausgesendet werden, möglicherweise gesundheitliche Schäden verursachen können.

Einfluss auf den Menschen

Generell wird es jedoch ausgeschlossen, dass magnetische Wellen unseren Körper auf irgendeine Art und Weise beeinflussen könnten.

In den Schulbüchern liest man, dass unter Magneten jene Körper verstanden werden, die auf Gegenstände aus Eisen, Nickel oder Kobalt eine anziehende Kraft ausüben. Anschließend werden gleich noch Experimente mitgeliefert, in denen man den Magneten mit nicht metallischen Gegenständen wie etwa Papier, Steinen und unseren Fingern in Berührung bringen soll, um festzustellen, dass der Magnet sich offenbar nicht von ihnen angezogen fühlt.

Die Schlussfolgerung, die der Schüler daraus ziehen soll, besteht darin, dass Magnetismus eine Kraft ist, die zwischen bestimmten Metallgegenständen besteht; wir Menschen jedoch, als lebende Organismen, werden nicht durch ihn beeinflusst – es sei denn, wir wohnen beispielsweise unter einer Starkstromleitung und erkranken dadurch möglicherweise an Krebs. Magnetische Wellen haben derzeit also entweder gar keinen, oder aber sogar einen ausgesprochen schlechten Ruf.

Lebensnotwendige Energie
Unumstößliche Tatsache ist jedoch, dass alles Leben den Magnetismus braucht wie die Luft zum Atmen.
In wissenschaftlichen Laborversuchen mit Mäusen, die man in Spezialkäfigen von den Magnetwellen der Erde abschottete, wurde beobachtet, wie den Tieren das Fell ausging und sie immer schwächer wurden, bis sie schließlich dahinsiechten. Das Bindegewebe der Haut sowie das einiger anderer Organe hatte zahllose Wucherungen ausgetrieben; man hätte den Eindruck gewinnen können, dass die Zellen beim Wachstum völlig die Orientierung verloren hatten.

Es ist mittlerweile erwiesen, dass das Erdmagnetfeld das Verhalten einiger Tierarten beeinflusst.

Ähnliches wurde an Pflanzen beobachtet. Auch sie verkümmern, wenn kein Magnetfeld vorhanden ist. Andererseits wuchsen Pflanzen, die mit magnetisiertem Wasser gegossen wurden, deutlich besser.
Auch das Wachstum von Bakterien wird durch Magnetwellen beeinflusst. Wissenschaftler haben entdeckt, dass in Wasser, das mit dem Pluspol eines Magneten behandelt wurde, wenig bis gar keine der Mikroorganismen überleben können. Wird es jedoch mit dem Minuspol eines Magneten behandelt, so kommt es zu einer regelrechten Vermehrungsexplosion der Bakterien. Ein Aspekt, der natürlich auch für unseren täglichen Kampf mit Infektionen von Bedeutung ist.

Das Wesen des Magnetismus

- Magnetismus benötigt für sein Wirken kein Medium, sondern lediglich Raum. Er ist im Weltall genauso präsent wie bei uns auf der Erde.
- Magnetismus ist nur da, wo auch elektrische Energie ist. 1820 legte ein dänischer Forscher zufällig einen Kompass in die Nähe einer elektrischen Leitung. Die Kompassnadel richtete sich sofort dorthin aus. Wurde in der Leitung der Strom abgestellt, wandte sich die Kompassnadel wieder ihrer ursprünglichen Nord-Süd-Richtung zu.
- In der unbelebten Natur sind die Hauptquellen der magnetischen Kraft vor allem Magnete. Dabei können zwei Gruppen unterschieden werden: Dauermagnete und elektronische Magnete. Letztere brauchen für ihre Arbeit die ständige Stromzufuhr.
- In Magneten findet ein geordneter Elektronenfluss statt, d. h., die Elektronen wandern zwischen den einzelnen Atomen organisiert hin und her. In der Folge entstehen an den Magnetenden zielgerichtete Kräfte: Der Nord- bzw. Pluspol und der Süd- bzw. Minuspol. Nur der Nord- und Südpol zweier magnetischer Gegenstände können sich gegenseitig anziehen. Kommen sich die beiden gleichen Pole der Magnete zu nahe, stoßen sie sich ab.
- Magnete können ihre Kraft auf andere Metallgegenstände übertragen. Reibt man einen Eisennagel an einem Magneten, so wird dieser für kurze Zeit auch magnetisch. Durch die Kräfte des Magneten werden die Elektronenwanderungen kurzfristig auf ein organisiertes Niveau gehoben.
- Nicht nur Metallteile können magnetisch sein. Jede lebende Zelle – auch der Mensch – ist von Magnetwellen umgeben. Da Magnetismus das Produkt von Elektrizität und organisierten Elektronenwanderungen ist, und da wir es bei lebendigen Organismen mit einer besonders organisierten Form von Materie zu tun haben, darf es auch nicht verwundern, dass wir hier magnetische Kräfte finden. Das menschliche Gehirn besitzt dabei die kräftigsten Magnetfelder.
- Magnetische Kräfte – wissenschaftlich korrekt als so genannte magnetische Feldstärke bezeichnet – kann man messen. Gebräuchliche Einheiten sind das Tesla und das Gauß. 1 Tesla entspricht 10 000 Gauß. Die magnetischen Feldstärken können stark variieren. In der Magnettherapie werden in der Regel Magnete in Stärken von 250 bis 3000 Gauß eingesetzt.

Die Geschichte der Magnettherapie

Es ist schwer zu sagen, wann dem Menschen die eigentümliche Anziehungskraft von magnetischen Steinen aufgefallen ist und wann man sie das erste Mal nutzte.

Der Legende nach soll ein chinesischer Kaiser vor 5000 Jahren auf seinem Streitwagen eine drehbare Frauenfigur gehabt haben, deren rechter Arm immer in dieselbe Richtung zeigte. Als der Kaiser sich einmal im Nebel verirrte, half ihm die Figur, wieder zu seinem Palast zurückzufinden. Es ist durchaus möglich, dass in dem Frauenarm ein längliches Stück Magnetitgestein verborgen war, das als eine Art Kompassnadel fungierte.

Obwohl der Wahrheitsgehalt dieser Legende fraglich ist, deutet vieles darauf hin, dass es tatsächlich die Chinesen waren, die den Kompass erfanden.

Die medizinischen Ursprünge

Wahrscheinlich waren es auch die Chinesen, die Magnete zum ersten Mal zur Behandlung von Krankheiten einsetzten.

Doch erst in den Hieroglyphen Ägyptens und in den Zeugnissen antiker Gelehrter wurde die Magnettherapie schriftlich festgehalten.

Hippokrates (460–375 v. Chr.) etwa behandelte unfruchtbare Frauen, indem er ihnen mit Muttermilch, Blei und Magnetit aufgeladene Tampons einführte. Der römische Geschichtsschreiber Plinius (23–79 n. Chr.) berichtet von Magneten, die in der Therapie von Augenentzündungen und Brandwunden eingesetzt wurden – ein Einsatzgebiet, das auch aus heutiger Sicht noch Sinn macht. Selbst in der Bibel ist nachzulesen, wie Moses einen Stein in Form einer Schlange auf eine Stange setzte, »und wenn nun die Schlangen einen bissen und er schaute dann die eherne Schlange an, so blieb er am Leben«. Diese eherne Schlange strahlte offenbar eine Art Fluidum ab – und dergleichen gab es damals nur in Form des Magnetismus.

Von Ibn Sina bis Paracelsus

Im Unterschied zu anderen Therapiemethoden wie etwa der Heilpflanzenkunde und der Chirurgie konnten sich die Dauermagnete jedoch nicht durchsetzen. Der arabische Arzt Ibn Sina (980–1037) setzte sie lediglich gegen Depressionen ein. Erst Paracelsus (1493–1541) machte die Magnettherapie zu einer festen Größe in seinem medizinischen System. Für den legendären Schweizer Arzt stand fest: »Der Magnet ist der Monarch aller Geheimnisse.« Er setzte die Magnete bei einer ganzen Reihe von Erkrankungen ein, beispielsweise bei Fallsucht, Krämpfen, Hämorrhoidalleiden, Ausflüssen, Ödemen und Wunden. »Hysterischen« Frauen setzte er ober- und unterhalb der Gebärmutter einen Magneten an, um sie zu beruhigen. Diese Indikation ist heute natürlich nicht mehr aktuell; der Begriff der Hysterie ist weitgehend aus dem Sprachschatz der Medizin verschwunden.

Der entscheidende Schritt zur Wissenschaft

Bei aller Begeisterung war Paracelsus noch weit davon entfernt, das Phänomen des Magnetismus auch nur annähernd verstehen zu können – dazu fehlten ihm die technischen und methodischen Voraussetzungen. Erst William Gilbert (1544–1603), Leibarzt der englischen Königin, versuchte, sich dem Problem

Der islamische Arzt und Philosoph Ibn Sina verbreitete das griechische Denken im Orient.

wissenschaftlich zu nähern. Zwar steckt auch sein Buch »Vom Magneten« noch voller Irrtümer, doch er erkannte bereits, dass man einen Magneten teilen kann und so immer wieder – entsprechend kleinere – Magnete erhält.

Gilberts Ausführungen hatten starken Einfluss auf andere Wissenschaftler. So begann man in Österreich, die Magnete erfolgreich gegen diverse Nervenleiden sowie gegen Krämpfe und Schmerzen einzusetzen. Diese Entwicklung mündete schließlich in den »animalischen Magnetismus« des schwäbischen Arztes und Philosophen Franz Anton Mesmer (1734–1815).

Der Mesmerismus

Seine ersten Magnete bekam Mesmer von einem Astronom und Arzt namens Pater Hell (1720–1792). Dieser hatte bereits per Magnettherapie zwei Patientinnen mit schweren Unterleibskrämpfen therapiert, von denen eine zuvor – ohne Erfolg – lange Zeit von Mesmer behandelt wurde. Mesmer experimentierte mit den Magneten und schaffte es, eine englische Baronin von ihren Unterleibs-

krämpfen zu befreien, die bereits den Status der Unheilbarkeit erlangt hatte. Dieser Heilerfolg erregte in der Öffentlichkeit großes Aufsehen.

Mesmer intensivierte daraufhin seine Arbeit mit den Magneten, um jedoch schon bald feststellen zu müssen, dass seine Heilerfolge weniger auf die strahlenden Metalle in seiner Hand, als auf die Hand selbst zurückzuführen waren. Mesmer vermutete, dass auch zwischen belebten Körpern magnetische Kräfte vorherrschen und dass sie bei einigen Menschen – wie bei ihm selbst – besonders stark sind und deshalb zu Heilzwecken genutzt werden können. Also legte er die Magnete zur Seite, um fortan nur noch durch die Kraft seiner Hände zu heilen.

Offensichtlich konnte Mesmer mit seiner neuartigen Methode einige spektakuläre Erfolge verzeichnen. So heilte er den Sekretär des bayerischen Kurfürsten von seinen nervösen Zuckungen, indem er ihm einfach nur seinen Zeigefinger entgegenhielt. Derartige »Wunderheilungen« gelangen Mesmer wohl öfter, so dass der Kurfürst den Arzt zum Mitglied der Akademie adelte.

Die Anerkennung der Wissenschaft blieb Mesmer jedoch versagt. Man bezichtigte ihn der Scharlatanerie. Mesmer zog sich daraufhin an den Bodensee zurück, um dort fern der Öffentlichkeit weiter zu praktizieren. Es soll hier nicht der Ort sein, über Wert oder Unwert des Mesmerismus zu diskutieren. Festzustellen bleibt jedoch, dass er entscheidend dazu beitrug, das Band zwischen Magnettherapie und Wissenschaft zu lösen. Obwohl sicherlich ein großer Unterschied darin besteht, ob man einen Menschen mit echten Magneten behandelt oder aber nur durch Fingerzeige und Handauflegen – Mesmer sorgte dafür, dass die Magnettherapie von den meisten Schulmedizinern ignoriert wurde und nach wie vor ignoriert wird. Das ist bedauerlich, ist die Magnettherapie mittlerweile doch auch wissenschaftlich untermauert.

Magnettherapie heute

Im 20. Jahrhundert ist viel zum Magnetismus und seinen Einflüssen auf die Gesundheit geforscht worden. Es liegen zahlreiche Labor- und Klinikstudien vor, die deutliche Hinweise darauf geben, dass Magnete bei unterschiedlichen Krankheiten helfen können. In Japan gehört die Magnettherapie denn auch schon zu den etablierten Standardheilverfahren.

Weltweit werden inzwischen jährlich fünf Milliarden Dollar mit Heilmagneten umgesetzt. Der deutsche Anteil daran ist allerdings noch gering. Die hiesige Medizin ruht hauptsächlich auf zwei Säulen: auf der Chirurgie und der Pharmazie.

Wissenschaftliche Anerkennung

Trotz der oftmals stiefmütterlichen Behandlung, die alternative Therapieformen in Europa erfahren, wenden sich immer mehr Menschen diesen Behandlungsformen und damit auch der Magnettherapie zu.

Wie viele dieser Ansätze kann auch die Magnettherapie auf drei Aspekte zurückblicken, die wichtige Qualitätsmerkmale für Heilverfahren bilden. Sie kann anekdotische Heilerfolge, eine lange Tradition und wissenschaftliche Studien aus dem Labor sowie sogar aus der Klinik aufweisen und sollte deshalb unbedingt ernst genommen werden.

Für Körper und Geist

Magnetismus und Krankheit

Nicht nur Magnete können Magnetkräfte aussenden, auch das Leben an sich ist magnetisch. Jede einzelne Zelle in unserem Körper besitzt ein Magnetfeld. Dieses verdankt sie ihrer durchlässigen Membran, durch die zahlreiche Stoffwechselvorgänge und damit auch Elektronenwanderungen reguliert werden. Infolge dieser Aktivitäten kommt es zu magnetischen Feldern, die allerdings deutlich abnehmen können, wenn die Zelle erkrankt. Mit anderen Worten: Nicht wenige Erkrankungen sind von einer Schwäche des Magnetfeldes begleitet, in deren Folge sich der Stoffaustausch durch die Zellwände deutlich verschlechtert. Hierdurch verringern sich auch die Chancen für eine zügige Heilung, denn Zellen mit

Ohne Magnetismus kein Leben

Nicht nur jede einzelne lebende Zelle besitzt ein eigenes Magnetfeld, auch der positive Einfluss äußerer magnetischer Kräfte auf das Leben ist mehrfach dokumentiert.

● Wie bereits geschildert, verloren Mäuse, die in einem Käfig von der Erdmagnetkraft abgeschottet wurden, ihr Fell und gingen schließlich ein. Ihr Bindegewebe zeigte Wucherungen, als hätte es beim Wachstum die Orientierung verloren. Ein Ergebnis, das zu denken geben sollte. Denn wir Menschen zwängen uns recht häufig in Stahlbetonbauten, Autos und andere »Käfige« ein, deren Wände die Magnetkräfte der Erde nur noch eingeschränkt durchdringen können.

● Nicht nur Vögel, auch der Mensch orientiert sich an Magnetfeldern. In einer Studie wurden einer Gruppe von Studenten die Augen verbunden, anschließend verfrachtete man sie in einem Auto zu einer Stelle, die etwa 50 Kilometer von ihrem Ausgangspunkt entfernt war. Dennoch vermochten sie halbwegs sicher zu sagen, wo sie herkamen. Wurde jedoch ein Magnet an ihre Augenbinden gesetzt, verschlechterte sich die Orientierung rapide. Die Studenten zeigten fast alle in die falsche Richtung. Offenbar hatten sie sich zuvor am Magnetfeld der Erde orientiert.

schlechtem Stoffwechsel erholen sich langsamer als andere Zellen. Hier erscheint es dann sinnvoll, das Magnetfeld der erkrankten Zellen mittels der Magnettherapie wieder zu kräftigen.

Im Stärken der geschwächten Magnetfelder, die man oft bei erkrankten Zellen findet, liegt eines der zentralen Argumente für die Magnettherapie. Doch sie kann noch weitaus mehr.

Mit Magnetkräften gegen Infektionen

Ebenso wie andere lebende Organismen, reagieren auch Bakterien sensibel auf Magnetkräfte.

● Magnetisiert man Wasser mit dem Nord-, d. h. Pluspol eines Magneten, so bleibt es erheblich länger keimfrei als unbehandeltes Wasser. Magnetisiert man das Wasser andererseits mit dem Süd-, d. h. Minuspol, so zeigt sich schon bald ein reges Bakterienwachstum. Bei der Magnetbehandlung von Infektionen ist es demnach ganz besonders wichtig, den richtigen Pol einzusetzen.

● Bakterien sind offenbar in der Lage, sich nach magnetischen Feldern zu orientieren, die sie im menschlichen Körper vorfinden.

So suchen sie zielstrebig nach Zellverbänden, deren Magnetfeld geschwächt ist. Insofern diese Zellen in der Regel auch erkrankt sind, bedeutet dies, dass Bakterien aufgrund ihres magnetischen Sinns imstande sind, sich gezielt kranke und geschwächte Zellen für ihre Attacken auszusuchen. Hier ist es sinnvoll, das Magnetfeld der betroffenen Zellen zu stärken.

Entzündungen hemmen, Kortison sparen

In unterschiedlichen Studien konnte beobachtet werden, dass die Magnettherapie entzündungshemmend wirkt. Ursache dafür sind u. a. die Auswirkungen, die die Magnetkräfte auf unseren Hormonspiegel haben. So fand ein Wiener Rheumatologe heraus, dass sich im Blut von Rheumapatienten mehr entzündungshemmendes Kortisol nachweisen lässt, wenn sie mit Magnetfeldern behandelt werden. Auslöser dieses Effekts sind die Wirkungen der Magnete auf die zentrale Hormonsteuerung. Die Mobilisierung der körpereigenen Kortisolproduktion hat erhebliche Auswirkungen auf die Rheumatherapie. Wer viel eigenes Kortisol produziert, braucht weniger externes Kortison, um die Schmerzen und Entzündungen in den Griff zu bekommen. Dadurch senkt sich natürlich das Risiko, an den Nebenwirkungen der Kortisonbehandlung zu erkranken.

Herz und Kreislauf im magnetischen Visier

Wenn es zu einem Herzinfarkt kommt, spielen nicht nur die bekannten Risikofaktoren wie Bewegungsmangel und Rauchen eine Rolle; auch Magnetfeldturbulenzen scheinen einen Einfluss auf Herz-Kreislauf-Erkrankungen zu haben.

Ein Forscherteam registrierte von 1967 bis 1972 alle Patienten, die mit einem Herzanfall in zwei große Krankenhäuser eingeliefert wurden. Sie verglichen die Daten mit den geomagnetischen Aktivitäten zu dieser Zeit. Erstaunlicherweise kamen immer dann die meisten Patienten, wenn das Erdmagnetfeld durch eine Erhöhung der Sonnenaktivität in Turbulenzen geriet.

Da Magnete die Durchblutung verbessern, wirken sie sich positiv auf zahlreiche Erkrankungen aus.

Es bleibt allerdings fraglich, ob umgekehrt Herz-Kreislauf-Erkrankungen durch gezielte Magnetanwendungen geheilt oder verhindert werden können. Aber auch das muss wohl bejaht werden, denn Magnetkräfte beeinflussen auf vielerlei Weise die Aktivität der Blutgefäße.

Der Einfluss auf die Durchblutung

Schon länger ist bekannt, dass Magnetfelder das Fließverhalten salziger Lösungen positiv beeinflussen können. Dieser Umstand legt nahe, dass sie auch den Blut-

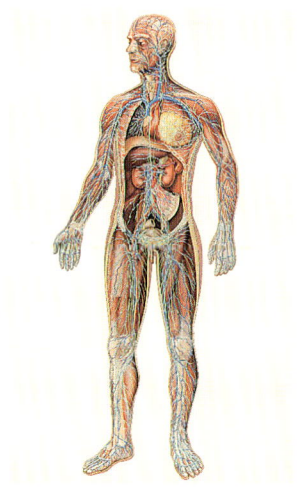

fluss verbessern können, da es sich beim Blutplasma letzten Endes auch um eine Form der salzigen Lösung handelt. In einer Studie des Instituts für Technologie in Cambridge, Massachusetts, konnte diese These kürzlich belegt werden. Demzufolge bringt der Einsatz von Magnetfolien eine Verbesserung des Blutflusses um etwa sieben Prozent.

Dies bringt gleich mehrere Vorteile mit sich. Eine bessere Durchblutung verringert das Risiko eines Blutstaus, der u. a. für Herz- und Venenerkrankungen typisch ist.

Vor allem Magnetfolien mit konzentrisch angeordneten Polen (»Concentric Circle Magnets«) gehören zu den chancenreichen Heilmitteln bei Durchblutungsstörungen wie beispielsweise Krampfadern.

Natürliche Wärmeaggregate

Wer sich Wechselpolmagnetfolien auf die Haut setzt, wird an diesen Stellen schon bald deutliche Erwärmungen spüren. Ursache für dieses Phänomen ist der so genannte Hall-Effekt. Er besteht darin, dass es infolge der magnetischen Wechselpolfelder zu elektrischen Miniwirbelstürmen kommt, in deren Folge Wärme freigesetzt wird. Diese Wärme wiederum führt zu einer Weitstellung der Blutgefäße und damit zu einer verbesserten Durchblutung.

Der Effekt der Gefäßweitstellung und des verbesserten Blutflusses ist vor allem in der Behandlung von Sport- und Unfallverletzungen sowie in der Therapie rheumatischer Erkrankungen erwünscht. Im Unterschied zu anderen – klassischen – durchblutungsfördernden Maßnahmen wie Salben, Gels u. Ä. dringen die Magnetkräfte recht tief ins Gewebe, ohne dass es dabei zu unerwünschten Nebenwirkungen kommt.

Verbesserte Sauerstoffversorgung

Unter dem Einfluss von Magnetkräften verbessert sich auch der Sauerstoffpartialdruck im Blut. Dies bedeutet konkret, dass das Blut leistungsfähiger und somit in die Lage versetzt wird, mehr Sauerstoff in die Zellen des Körpers zu transportieren. Dadurch verbessert sich die Regeneration und letzten Endes auch die Leistungsfähigkeit der Zellen.

Neubildung von Blutgefäßen

Experimente mit so genannten Magnettunneln zeigten, dass Magnetfelder die Neubildung von Blutgefäßen anregen können. Bei den Magnettunneln handelt es sich um Röhren, in denen mittels Strom ein pulsierendes Magnetfeld erzeugt wird. Wenn man nun einen Arm oder ein Bein in diese Röhren legte, zeigten sich dort zahlreiche neue Blutgefäße – und das nicht nur in der Haut, sondern auch an den Knochen. Magnettunnel können dadurch beispielsweise die Heilung von Knochenbrüchen fördern.

Magnete als natürliche Wundheiler

Um den Zusammenhang von Wundheilung und Magnettherapie beurteilen zu können, sind mittlerweile auch in Deutschland einige wissenschaftliche Studien angestellt worden.

Mit Magneten gegen den Schmerz

Die Schmerzbehandlung gehört sicherlich zu den traditionellen Stärken der Magnettherapie.

● Magnetkräfte hemmen den Energiefluss in den Schmerzkanälen. Mit anderen Worten: Die Signale vom Schmerzrezeptor dringen nur noch in reduzierter Form bis zum Gehirn durch, so dass die Schmerzwahrnehmung deutlich verringert wird.

● Magnetkräfte mobilisieren die Ausschüttung von entzündungshemmendem Kortisol. Eine Entzündungshemmung geht jedoch meistens auch mit einer Schmerzhemmung einher.

● Kopfschmerzen und Schmerzen am Bewegungsapparat besitzen oft einen starken Zusammenhang mit muskulären Verspannungen. Diese können allein durch die durchblutungsfördernden Effekte von Magnetfolien wirksam eingedämmt werden.

● Magnetkräfte wirken auf das retikuläre System, einer Region im Gehirn, die sehr urtümlich ist und wesentlich darüber entscheidet, welchen Reizen wir unsere Aufmerksamkeit schenken. Offenbar sind Magnetwellen über ihren Einfluss auf diese Gehirnregion imstande, unsere Schmerzwahrnehmung zu dämpfen.

Am Münchner Klinikum Rechts der Isar etwa wurden mit Hunderten von Patientinnen und Patienten positive Erfahrungen gemacht, wenn es darum ging, mit Magneten den Wundheilungsprozess zu fördern und die Bildung von hässlichen Narben zu verhindern.

Dieser Effekt ist natürlich auch für die kosmetische Chirurgie von Bedeutung. Wunden, die mit einem Magnet verschlossen werden, heilen deutlich schneller und rückstandsloser ab als Wunden, die konventionell vernäht werden.

Behandlung von Narben

Am Wiener Ludwig-Boltzmann-Institut konnte mit Magneten selbst die Ausdehnung und Schmerzentwicklung bereits bestehender Narben verringert werden.

Dabei wurden Magnetpflaster mit einer Stärke von 600 Gauß eingesetzt, deren Nordpol auf die Haut der betreffenden Patienten gesetzt wurde. Selbst ein Patient mit einem nach einer Amputation entzündeten Beinstumpf war nach mehrwöchiger Magnettherapie wieder vollkommen schmerzfrei.

Die beschleunigte und verbesserte Wundheilung durch Magnetkraft ist wahrscheinlich das Resultat zahlreicher Einzeleffekte. So spielen dabei neben Entzündungshemmung und Durchblutungsförderung sicherlich auch die antibiotischen Kräfte der Magnete eine Rolle.

Magnetismus und Schlafstörungen

Es gehört zu den jahrhundertealten Weisheiten der Volksmedizin, dass man besser schläft, wenn das Bett in Nord-Süd-Ausrichtung steht und der Kopf zum Nordpol weist. Ebenfalls bekannt ist, dass Menschen in Holzhäusern und Flachbauten einen erholsameren Schlaf finden als Menschen in mehrstöckigen Betonbauten. Wissenschaftliche Studien konnten diese Phänomene bestätigen, erklären konnten sie sie jedoch lange Zeit nicht. 1992 entdeckte Prof. Joseph Kirschvink vom California Institute of Technology in Pasadena, dass sich im menschlichen Gehirn nicht unerhebliche Mengen an magnetischem Material – nämlich an Magnetit – befinden. Zuvor war nur bekannt gewesen, dass sich dieses Material als

Orientierungshilfe im Gehirn einiger Tierarten (z. B. Tauben) befindet.

Der Mensch greift auf diese inhärente Orientierungshilfe kaum zurück. Er vertraut in erster Linie auf seine Augen und Ohren – und natürlich auf die zahlreichen modernen Messinstrumente, um sich zurechtzufinden. Nichtsdestowweniger bleibt der Magnetitanteil im Gehirn auch heute nicht ohne Wirkung. Es ist davon auszugehen, dass schwache, von außen auf den menschlichen Körper einwirkende Magnetfelder im Magnetit unseres Gehirns gebündelt und dadurch im Inneren des Kopfs verstärkt werden. Mit anderen Worten: Gerade unser Gehirn reagiert aufgrund seines Magnetitanteils besonders sensibel auf Veränderungen, die sich in unserer Umgebung abspielen. Diese Erkenntnis bildet eine solide Basis, um unsere Schlafstörungen im Zusammenhang mit Magnetfeldern zu erklären.

Unser Gehirn wurde über viele Jahrtausende auf das Nord-Süd-Magnetfeld der Erde geeicht. Kommt es nun zu einem Abfall des Magnetfeldes – beispielsweise aufgrund einer Stahl-Beton-Konstruktion, in der wir leben und schlafen –, wird das Gehirn diesen Abfall als Veränderung registrieren und gleichzeitig Probleme bekommen, die Nord-Süd-Ausrichtung des Erdmagnetfeldes wahrnehmen zu können. Beides zusammen wird als Stress empfunden – und Stress ist ein Alarmsignal, das im Schlafzentrum dazu führt, den Schlaf auf Hab-Acht-Stellung und dementsprechend unruhig zu halten. In der Folge kommt es dann zu Schlafstörungen.

Oft reicht es schon aus, das Bett in Nord-Süd-Achse zu bringen und das Kopfende nach Norden auszurichten. Dadurch wird es dem Gehirn leichter gemacht, die verlorene Nord-Süd-Ausrichtung wiederzufinden. Es gibt mittlerweile aber auch Magnetstreifen, die auf den Lattenrost geklebt werden können, und die auf diese Weise den Verlust des Erdmagnetfeldes kompensieren.

Mit Magneten gegen Depressionen

Eine Studie am Technion Israel Institut in Haifa konnte zeigen, dass Magnete die Hirnaktivität stimulieren und so schwere Depressionen lindern können.

Bei dieser Studie wurden insgesamt 67 Patienten entweder mit der transkranialen Magnetstimulation (TMS) behandelt oder mit einer Plazebomethode, bei der die Patienten keine Magnetbehandlung erhielten, aber eine vermuteten. Bei der TMS wird ein Magnetfeld durch eine Spule gezielt in bestimmte Bereiche des Gehirns direkt hinter der Stirn geleitet. Die Behandlung wird in kurzen Abständen wiederholt, sie ist schmerzlos und völlig ohne Nebenwirkungen. Das Ergebnis der Studie: Nach zwei Wochen konnte bei 50 Prozent der mit TMS behandelten Patienten eine deutliche Besserung der Beschwerden erzielt werden. Die sonst üblichen Elektroschockbehandlungen entfielen bei ihnen – im Unterschied zur Plazebogruppe, die weiterhin mit Elektroschocks behandelt werden musste.

Krebswachstum wird gehemmt

Nicht wenige Wissenschaftler sind davon überzeugt, dass auch Krebserkrankungen in einem engen Zusammenhang mit Magnetfeldern stehen. In einem japanischen Versuchslabor wurden krebskranke Ratten mit Magnetfeldern von 50 bis 800 Gauß behandelt. Bereits nach 24 Stunden veränderten sich die Tumore. Zwei Wochen später waren die Krebsherde deutlich kleiner geworden. Diese Ergebnisse wurden durch andere Studien bestätigt – sie dürfen jedoch nicht ohne weiteres auf den Menschen übertragen werden.

Hoffnung für Betroffene

In Anbetracht dessen, was man mittlerweile über Magnetkräfte und ihren Einfluss auf den Körper weiß, ist es dennoch durchaus möglich, dass sie das Wachstum von Tumoren hemmen und vorbeugend die Entstehung von Krebsgeschwüren verhindern können. So ist bekannt, dass im Gegensatz zum gesunden Organismus bei an Krebs erkrankten Patienten der Tumor sauer und das Blut alkalisch ist. Durch eine Magnetbehandlung ließe sich nun diese verkehrte Polung wieder ausgleichen.

Darüber hinaus zeigen Tumorzellen ein anderes Magnetfeld als gesunde Zellen – auch dies könnte durch eine gezielte Anwendung von Magneten wieder korrigiert werden. Ganz zu schweigen von den positiven Einflüssen, die magnetische Felder auf das gesamte Hormongeschehen und damit auf die Immunabwehr haben können.

Das Magnetfeld-Mangelsyndrom

1975 erschütterte Dr. Kyoichi Nakagawa, Direktor des Isuzu-Krankenhauses in Tokio, die medizinische Fachwelt mit seiner Behauptung, dass viele Menschen mit Beschwerden wie Nacken- und Kopfschmerzen, chronischer Erschöpfung, Fibromyalgie und Vergesslichkeit in Wirklichkeit an einem Magnetfeld-Mangelsyndrom (engl. Magnetic-Field-Deficiency-Syndrome, MFDS) leiden.
Nakagawa hatte eine aufwändige Fragebogenaktion mit insgesamt 11 648 Menschen durchgeführt, in der nach den Erfahrungen mit Pflastermagneten gefragt wurde. Demzufolge wurden die Magnete bei folgenden Beschwerden eingesetzt:

- Steifer Nacken   45,2 %
- Hexenschuss   19,0 %
- Neuralgien   13,9 %
- Muskelschmerzen   12,3 %
- Rheumatismus   1,3 %
- Sonstige Beschwerden   6,3 %

Im Durchschnitt bezeichneten 94,3 Prozent der Befragten die Magnetpflaster als wirksam. Eine solche Quote wird nur von den wenigsten Therapieformen erreicht. Viele fühlten sich vor allem in Bezug auf körperliche Arbeit erheblich leistungsfähiger. Bei keinem einzigen hatten die Magnete die Beschwerden verschlimmert oder zu Nebenwirkungen geführt.

Neue Chancen

Die enorm hohe Heilungsquote der Magnetpflaster bei den aufgelisteten Krankheiten führten Nakagawa zu der Überzeugung, dass es sich bei vielen Alltagsbeschwerden und Zivilisationskrankheiten um nichts anderes als das besagte Magnetfeld-Mangelsyndrom handelt.
Im Lauf der letzten 500 Jahre hat die erdmagnetische Strahlung um etwa die Hälfte ihrer Kraft abgenommen, hinzu kommen zahlreiche Isolierfaktoren – wie etwa Autos und Stahlbetonbauten –, die den Menschen vom Erdmagnetfeld abschotten. Diese Entwicklungen kann man nach Nakagawas Ansicht nur durch die gezielte Anwendung von Heilmagneten stoppen.

Klinische Studien

Die Prüfung von Naturheilverfahren

Ein Heilmittel besitzt unter Medizinern umso mehr Anerkennung, je mehr es in klinischen Studien am Menschen erprobt wurde. In diesem Zusammenhang wird es wiederum sehr geschätzt, wenn das Mittel im Plazeboversuch getestet wurde. Plazeboversuch heißt, dass man die Testpersonen in zwei Gruppen einteilt. Die eine Gruppe erhält das Medikament, das getestet werden soll, während die andere lediglich ein unwirksames Scheinmedikament bekommt. Zeigen sich nun am Ende des Versuchs bei der Gruppe, die das richtige Medikament erhielt, deutlichere Besserungen als bei den Plazebopatienten, so ist dies ein deutlicher Hinweis darauf, dass das betreffende Mittel tatsächlich wirkt. Zu natürlichen Heilverfahren existieren in der Regel weniger plazebokontrollierte Studien als zu den Methoden der Schulmedizin. Dies hat mehrere Gründe. Einer der häufigsten ist sicherlich, dass weniger Geld in die Erforschung alternativer Heilverfahren fließt. Dies ist wiederum darin begründet, dass die Schulmedizin ihre Pfründe nicht in Gefahr bringen will. Oft verhält es sich aber auch einfach so, dass Naturheilverfahren mit wissenschaftlichen Methoden nicht unbedingt messbar sind. Man denke nur an die Akupunktur. Sie entzog sich lange Zeit den Tests im Plazeboverfahren, weil es keine Möglichkeit gab, die Behandlung nur scheinbar durchzuführen. Erst vor kurzem entwickelten Forscher Plazebonadeln, bei denen die Testpersonen das Gefühl haben, eine Akupunktur zu erhalten, obwohl die Nadeln gar nicht ins Hautgewebe eindringen. Hiermit können nun auch Plazeboversuche gemacht werden, womit sich die Möglichkeiten zur Erforschung der Akupunktur deutlich erweitert haben.

Heilmagnete im Plazeboversuch

Ähnliche Probleme wie bei der Akupunktur gab es auch bei der Magnettherapie. Zwar war es hier nicht weiter schwierig, Plazebomagnete zu entwickeln, doch es gab immer wieder neugierige Patienten, die ihre Folien oder Pflaster an Metallstücke hielten, um zu testen, ob sie tatsächlich einen echten Magneten am Körper hatten oder nicht. Das bedeutete natürlich das Ende des Plazeboversuchs. Doch auch zu diesem Problem haben Wissenschaftler mittlerweile Lösungen entwickelt. Bei kürzeren Versuchen ist es beispielsweise möglich, die Testpersonen unter ständiger Kontrolle zu halten. Man kann den Patienten auch schwache Magnete als Plazebopflaster geben, die zwar stark genug sind, um Metall anzuziehen, aber zu schwach, um medizinisch wirksam zu sein. Magnetpflaster können beispielsweise auch als Pflaster ausgegeben werden, die mit einem bestimmten Wirkstoff versehen sind, der nach und nach an den Organismus abgegeben wird, ähnlich wie bei Nikotinpflastern. Auf diese Weise kommen die Patienten gar nicht erst auf die Idee, die Pflaster gegen Metall zu halten, um sie zu testen.

Überzeugende Resultate

Auch die Magnettherapie lässt sich also mittlerweile gut erforschen. Und es liegen auch schon einige fundierte Forschungsarbeiten vor. Beeindruckend sind vor allem die Ergebnisse zu den

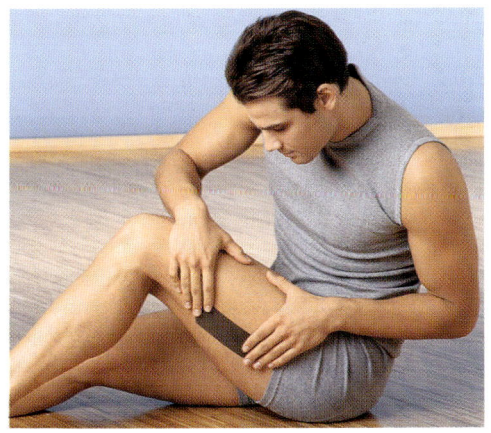

Wissenschaftliche Studien belegen, dass sich Magnetfolien vor allem bei Muskelbeschwerden bewährt haben.

wechselpolaren Magnetfolien. Sie lassen keine Zweifel mehr daran, mit den Folien ein ernsthaftes und chancenreiches Instrument zur Behandlung von Schmerzen gefunden zu haben.

Schulterschmerzen

Zwei japanische Studien aus dem Jahr 1980 untersuchten die Wirkung von Magnetpflastern auf 400 Patienten, die an Schulterschmerzen litten.

Die Patienten wurden in zwei Gruppen unterteilt. Die eine Gruppe erhielt eine Behandlung mit echten Magnetpflastern (Stärke: 800 Gauß), die zweite Gruppe wurde lediglich mit gleich aussehenden, aber sehr schwachen Magnetpflastern (200 Gauß) behandelt. Das Ergebnis: Aus der ersten Gruppe berichteten mehr als 80 Prozent über Besserungen ihrer Beschwerden, in der zweiten Gruppe waren es nur etwa 40 Prozent.

Spontane Schmerzen

Die Studie zu spontanen Schmerzen wurde im Jahr 1983 durchgeführt. Ein amerikanischer Zahnarzt und Kieferchirurg war frustriert darüber, dass er seinen Patienten so viele Spritzen geben musste, die dann zu allem Überfluss auch noch oft wirkungslos blieben. Also klebte er einigen seiner Patienten vor dem Setzen der Injektionen Magnetfolien auf die Wange. Das Resultat: Die Patienten mit kombinierter Magnet-Spritzen-Behandlung litten in der folgenden Behandlung erheblich weniger unter ihren Beschwerden als jene, die nur gespritzt wurden.

Muskel- und Sehnenschmerzen

Eine der wenigen deutschen Studien zur Magnettherapie stammt aus Schaufling in Bayern. Sie wurde 1992 veröffentlicht. Dabei wurde die Wirkung von wechselpolaren Magnetfolien an Patienten untersucht, die an unterschiedlichen Formen von Muskel- und Sehnenschmerzen litten. 50 Patienten wurden mit echten Magnetfolien behandelt, 50 bekamen lediglich Pseudomagnete auf die schmerzenden Stellen geklebt.

Die Ergebnisse: 70 Prozent der Magnetgruppe berichteten von einem deutlichen Nachlassen der Schmerzen, im Unterschied zu 26 Prozent der anderen Gruppe.

In der Magnetgruppe konnte fast die Hälfte der Patienten den Schmerzmittelkonsum verringern, in der Plazebogruppe gelang dies nur einem Zehntel.

Fersenschmerzen

In einer amerikanischen Studie aus dem Jahr 1993 wurde die Wirksamkeit von wechselpolaren Magnetfolien an Patienten erprobt, die an schweren Fersenschmerzen (ausgelöst durch Fersensporn oder Entzündung des Achillessehnenansatzes) litten. Die Patienten wurden wiederum in zwei Gruppen unterteilt: Die eine Gruppe erhielt eine Behandlung mit echten Magnetpflastern (Stärke: 300 Gauß), die andere Gruppe wurde mit Pseudomagnetpflastern behandelt. Das Ergebnis: In der Magnetgruppe berichteten 57,2 Prozent von deutlicher Schmerzlinderung und 77,1 Prozent von deutlichen Besserungen beim Gehen. In der Plazebogruppe berichteten hingegen nur 16,6 Prozent von einer Schmerzlinderung und die gleiche Anzahl von einer Besserung der Schmerzen beim Gehen. Deutlichere Ergebnisse werden auch von anerkannten Schmerzmitteln nicht erreicht.

Gelenkschmerzen

Aus dem Jahr 1997 stammt eine Studie an 50 Postpoliopatienten, die ebenfalls von amerikanischen Forschern durchgeführt wurde. Patienten, die eine Kinderlähmung (Poliomyelitis) durchgemacht haben, leiden oft unter starken bis unerträglichen Schmerzen an Gelenken und Muskeln. Bei der berüchtigten Kinderlähmung wird die Muskelbalance zerstört, was zu schweren Muskelverspannungen und arthritischen Gelenkentzündungen führt. Postpoliopatienten müssen in der Regel hohe Dosierungen an starken Schmerzmitteln einnehmen.

Die Patienten der Studie wurden in zwei Gruppen eingeteilt: Die eine Gruppe erhielt eine Behandlung mit wechselpolaren Magnetpflastern in einer Stärke von 500 Gauß, die andere Gruppe bekam lediglich Pseudomagnete auf die schmerzenden Stellen geklebt. Die Ergebnisse waren eindeutig: 76 Prozent der mit echten Magneten behandelten Patienten berichteten von deutlichen Besserungen, im Unterschied zu lediglich 19 Prozent der mit Plazebomagneten behandelten Vergleichsgruppe.

Karpaltunnelsyndrom

Beim Karpaltunnelsyndrom ist der Handwurzelkanal verengt, durch den die Nervenfasern zu den Fingern verlaufen. Dabei kommt es zu starken Schmerzen, die die Leistungsfähigkeit der Hand einschränken.

Wie wirksam Magnete beim Karpaltunnelsyndrom sein können, zeigt eine Studie des amerikanischen Mediziners Dr. Ronald Lawrence. Er ließ 14 Patienten eine Woche lang Dauermagnete um die Handgelenke tragen. Danach befragte er sie nicht nur nach ihrem Befinden, sondern maß auch, wie schnell die elektrischen Impulse in den Nerven-bahnen der Handgelenke weitergeleitet wurden. Bei Menschen mit Karpaltunnelsyndrom ist die Geschwindigkeit nämlich deutlich gesenkt.

12 der 14 Patienten fühlten sich nach der Magnetbehandlung erheblich besser, bei ihnen wurden auch die Nervenimpulse schneller weitergeleitet. Bei den übrigen Patienten stellten sich keine Besserungen, aber auch keine Verschlimmerungen ein.

Menstruationsschmerzen

Eine Studie der Universität Seoul von 1994 zeigt, dass Magnete bei Menstruationsbeschwerden helfen können.

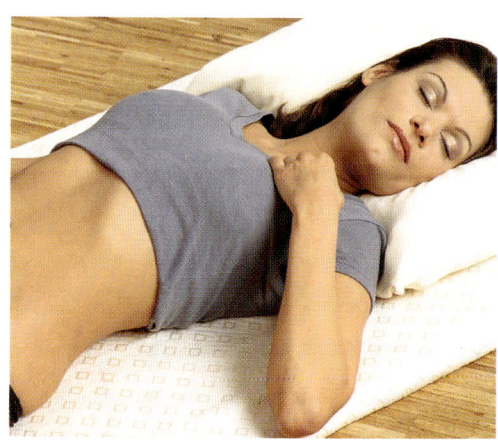

Versuchen Sie, sich bei Menstruationsbeschwerden so weit wie möglich zu entspannen.

Die Wissenschaftler behandelten elf Patientinnen mit Dauermagneten in der Stärke von 800 bis 1200 Gauß, eine zweite Gruppe von zwölf Frauen erhielt Plazebomagnete. Während der Studie und nach Entfernen der Magnete bzw. Pseudomagnete wurden sie zu ihren Beschwerden befragt. Die Frauen mit den echten Magneten berichteten im Gegensatz zur Kontrollgruppe durchweg von erheblichen Besserungen. Das Besondere an dieser Studie ist, dass die Frauen dauerhaft unter Beobachtung standen, so dass sie nicht herausfinden konnten, ob sie einen echten oder einen Plazebomagneten auf dem Körper trugen. Der Test zeigte außerdem, dass Magnete ihre schmerzlindernden Kräfte innerhalb weniger Stunden entfalten können.

Rückenschmerzen

Wie bei allen Heilverfahren, so existieren auch zur Magnettherapie Studien, in denen keine sonderlichen Wirkungen beobachtet wurden. Die wohl aussagekräftigste Studie stammt aus dem Jahr 2000. Sie wurde in der Fachzeitschrift *JAMA* veröffentlicht. Hier erhielten 20 Patienten mit Rückenschmerzen abwechselnd Plazebo- und echte Magnete, die sie auf ihrem Rücken tragen sollten.

Das Ergebnis: Den Patienten ging es nach Versuchsende im Durchschnitt etwas besser, allerdings war dies unabhängig davon, ob sie Plazebomagnete oder echte Magnete erhielten. Wenn aber ein Medikament nicht deutlich besser abschneidet als ein Plazebo, so sind natürlich Zweifel an seiner Wirksamkeit angebracht.

Ungeeignete Versuchsbedingungen

Zu dieser Studie muss jedoch einiges angemerkt werden. Sie wurde mit bipolaren Magnetpflastern durchgeführt, die mit der Nordpolseite zur Haut aufgeklebt werden. Von diesen Pflastern heißt es in der Naturmedizin, dass sie in erster Linie kühlend wirken. Kühleffekte sind jedoch bei Rückenschmerzen eher sinnlos, hier kommt es mehr darauf an, mit Wärme und durchblutungsfördernden Methoden zu arbeiten.

Mit anderen Worten: Die besagte Studie wurde mit Magnetpflastern durchgeführt, deren Chance bei Rückenschmerzen im Vornherein als gering eingestuft werden mussten. Viel interessanter wäre eine dementsprechende Studie mit wechelpolaren Magnetfolien, bei denen nicht nur der Nord-, sondern auch der Südpol – und zwar im kreisförmig angeordneten Wechsel zum Nordpol – zum Einsatz kommt. Diese Magnetfolien fördern die Durchblutung und erzeugen Wärme, was im Hinblick auf Rückenschmerzen als erheblich wirkungsvoller einzustufen ist.

Durchblutungsstörungen

Bei einer Studie US-amerikanischer Wissenschaftler aus dem Jahr 1999 wurden Diabetiker als Testpersonen ausgewählt, die aufgrund ihrer Stoffwechselkrankheit an schmerzhaften Durchblutungsstörungen an den Füßen litten. Unter den einen Fuß erhielten sie Einlegesohlen, in die Magnete eingearbeitet waren, der andere Fuß wurde mit einer magnetfreien Einlegesohle ausgestattet.
Die Patienten wurden nicht darüber informiert, dass sie im Rahmen einer wissenschaftlichen Studie die Wirkung der Magnettherapie testen sollten.

Das Ergebnis war eindeutig. Während die Füße mit den normalen Einlegesohlen nur geringfügige Besserungen zeigten, ging es den mit Magneten behandelten Füßen erheblich besser. Dort hatten die Schmerzen deutlich nachgelassen. Ein weiterer Hinweis darauf, dass Magnete gerade bei Durchblutungsstörungen hilfreich sein können.

Schwindel und Tinnitus

Zwei Studien aus dem Jahr 1983 befassen sich mit der Wirkung von Dauermagneten auf Menschen, die infolge einer Schädelverletzung unter starken Schwindelattacken leiden. Auch hier zeigte sich eine deutlichere Wirksamkeit der echten Magnete gegenüber einer Scheintherapie mit Plazebomagneten. Die Verfasser der Studien kamen zu dem Schluss, dass Magnete bei Durchblutungsstörungen im Innenohrbereich (z. B. bei Tinnitus, Hörsturz und Vertigo) echte Therapiechancen besitzen.

Kaum Nebenwirkungen

Die magnetischen Felder von Starkstromleitungen oder Elektrogeräten haben nicht unbedingt den besten Ruf. So stehen sie beispielsweise in dem Verdacht, Krebs erregend zu sein. Von den Magneten, die in der Therapie eingesetzt werden, sind jedoch derartige Wirkungen nicht zu befürchten, vor allem dann, wenn es sich um Dauermagnete handelt, die keinerlei Stromzufluss brauchen:

● Bereits Mitte der 1960er Jahre kam ein Artikel der Fachzeitschrift *Nature* zu dem Schluss, dass von Magneten mit einer Stärke bis zu 5000 Gauß keinerlei negative Effekte zu befürchten sind.

● Auch die WHO (Weltgesundheitsorganisation) stellte in einer Studie von 1987 fest, dass in den letzten vier Jahrzehnten nichts gefunden wurde, was auf einen schädlichen oder gar Krebs erregenden Effekt der Dauermagnete hinweisen würde. Im Gegenteil: Laborexperimente an Zellkulturen geben sogar konkrete Hinweise darauf, dass Magnete das Wachstum bestimmter Krebsgeschwüre hemmen.

Vorsicht bei Herzpatienten

Generell wird jedoch Menschen mit Herzrhythmusstörungen oder Herzschrittmachern von einer Magnettherapie abgeraten. Elektronische Herzschrittmacher und Aktivitäten des Herzmuskels (die ja auch von körpereigener Elektrizität gesteuert werden) können durch Magnetwellen möglicherweise irritiert werden. Konkrete Belege, ob diese These auch für die schwachen Therapiemagneten gilt, existieren allerdings nicht.

Andere Wechselwirkungen

Schwangeren Frauen bis zum sechsten Monat wird ebenfalls von der Anwendung der Magnete abgeraten, da noch zu wenig über die Wirkungen von Magnetkräften auf das ungeborene Leben bekannt ist. Negative Berichte zu Heilmagneten und der Entwicklung von Embryos gibt es bislang aber ebenfalls nicht.

Für die oft geäußerte Einschränkung schließlich, wonach Epileptiker keine Magnete auf ihren Körper setzen dürften, gibt es noch nicht einmal Verdachtsmomente, die eine solide medizinische oder physikalische Grundlage hätten.

Fazit: Die Magnettherapie ist im Vergleich zu schulmedizinischen Therapieformen absolut arm an Nebenwirkungen.

Heilmagnete richtig anwenden

Zwischen Medizintechnik und Naturheilverfahren

Da die Magnettherapie eine lange Geschichte hinter sich hat, hat sie in ihrer Anwendung mittlerweile auch zahlreiche Ausprägungen erfahren.

Grundsätzlich kann zwischen Dauer- und Strommagneten unterschieden werden. In jüngerer Zeit wurden Strommagnete mit ausgeklügelten Systemen entwickelt, wie etwa das Quantron-Resonanz-System, das beachtliche Erfolge bei Migräne und anderen Kopfschmerzen erzielen soll. Diese Form der Magnettherapie hat jedoch nichts mehr mit natürlichen Heilverfahren zu tun. Es handelt sich vielmehr um teure Medizintechnik auf höchstem Niveau, die sicherlich ihre Heilungschancen besitzt, aber mit der Magnettherapie als preiswerter alternativer Heilmethode nichts mehr gemein hat.

Unverstärkte Dauermagnete

Die klassische Magnettherapie setzt vielmehr auf Dauermagnete, die keinen Strom für ihre Arbeit benötigen. Natürlich hat auch bei ihnen die Entwicklung nicht Halt gemacht, so dass es mittlerweile zahlreiche Formen von Dauermagneten gibt. Der ursprünglich naturheilkundliche Gedanke – mit einer natürlichen Urkraft ohne elektrische Verstärkung den menschlichen Organismus zu unterstützen – blieb jedoch erhalten.

Bipolare Magnetpflaster

Bipolare Magnetpflaster repräsentieren die klassische Magnettherapie, wie sie in Japan entwickelt wurde, also die Lehre des »Taiki«. Es handelt sich dabei um Blockmagnete, die unter einem kleinen Klebestreifen eingelassen sind. In der Regel werden sie mit dem Nordpol zur Haut aufgesetzt. Ihre Stärke liegt meistens bei 800 Gauß. Naturärzte schätzen die kleinen Magnetpflaster, weil sie einen kühlenden Effekt haben und auf diese Weise bei Entzündungen mit starker Rötung und Hitzeentwicklung angezeigt sind. Bei Krankheiten jedoch, bei denen eine Verstärkung der Durchblutung gefordert ist, scheinen sie wirkungslos sein. Eine Studie mit bipolaren Magnetpflastern an

Patienten mit Rückenbeschwerden brachte jedenfalls keine positiven Ergebnisse.

Wechselpolare Magnetfolien

Im amerikanischen Sprachraum werden diese Magnete als Concentric Circle Magnets bezeichnet. Dieser Begriff bringt die Struktur der Magnete recht gut zum Ausdruck. Auf den Magnetfolien sind die Pole konzentrisch aneinander gereiht. In der Mitte sitzt der Nordpol, dann folgt ein Südpolring, dann wieder ein Nordpolring usw. Der Vorteil der wechselpoligen Magnetfolien liegt darin, dass die konzentrische Anordnung der Pole gewährleistet, dass viele Blutgefäße angesprochen werden. Eine solche Reaktion wird sonst nur von elektrisch betriebenen Spulen erreicht.

Das Magnetmaterial besitzt eine Dicke von 0,75 bis 1,0 Millimeter. In Fällen von besonders starken Schmerzen können auch bis zu 1,5 Millimeter dicke Magnete angebracht werden.

Die wechselpolaren Magnetfolien bilden eine Synthese aus alter Heiltradition und moderner Fertigungstechnik. Die Erfolge

scheinen dieser Kombination Recht zu geben. Zwar sind die wechselpolaren Magnetfolien teurer als einfache Magnetpflaster, doch dafür zeigen wissenschaftliche Studien der letzten Zeit, dass wir mit ihnen eine wirksame Waffe gegen den Schmerz gefunden haben.

Ein weiterer Vorteil der Magnetfolien besteht darin, dass man sie mittlerweile auch in gut sortierten Apotheken erhält. Ihre Hauptanwendungsgebiete sind Muskelkater, Muskelzerrungen, Muskelsteifheit, Nacken-Schulter-Syndrom, Spannungskopfschmerzen, Hexenschuss, Rückenschmerzen, Wadenkrämpfe, Prellungen, Verstauchungen, Arthritis, Menstruationsbeschwerden, Tennisarm, Narbenschmerzen und Verstopfungen.

Große Blockmagnete

Magnete gibt es in Form von großen und kleinen Scheiben, Blöcken, Zylindern, Ringen und Hufeisen.

Die Anwendung von Blockmagneten ist heute nicht mehr üblich. Sie werden dementsprechend kaum noch im Handel angeboten. Einige Therapeuten setzen allerdings die großen

Magnetklötze noch ein, um den ganzen Körper zu behandeln. Es steht hier also nicht die gezielte Therapie eines bestimmten Körperteils im Vordergrund, sondern die so genannte systemische Therapie. Diese Behandlungsform empfiehlt sich beispielsweise bei niedrigem oder erhöhtem Blutdruck sowie Müdigkeit, Impotenz, Erschöpfung und Konzentrationsschwäche.

Magnetische Unterbetten, Matratzen und Kissen

Diese Ausstattung soll für einen erholsamen Schlaf sorgen, bei bettlägerigen Patienten hilft sie auch gegen Wundliegen. In Japan zählen magnetische Matratzen zur Standardausrüstung im Schlafzimmer. Es wird geschätzt, dass jeder achte Japaner auf einer magnetischen Matratze schläft.

In Deutschland werden mittlerweile ebenfalls magnetische Unterbetten verkauft. Besonders wirkungsvoll sind sie, wenn sie mit wechselpolaren Magnetfolien ausgerüstet wurden.

Magnetisiertes Wasser

Magnetisiertes Wasser hat einen stark erhöhten pH-Wert, es ist also weniger sauer als normales Wasser. Es soll die Entstehung von Krebserkrankungen hemmen. Die Magnetisierung erfolgt am besten dadurch, dass man ein

---

Wichtige Regeln für die Anwendung von Magnetfolien und Pflastermagneten

● Vor dem Auflegen der Magnete die Haut sorgfältig reinigen.

● In ganz seltenen Fällen kommt es zu allergischen Reaktionen auf die Pflaster- bzw. Klebstoffe der Magnete. Hier ist von der Anwendung von Pflaster- und Folienmagneten abzuraten.

● Die Behandlung sollte den Zeitraum von 30 Tagen nicht überschreiten.

● Ihre stärkste Wirkung erzielen Magnetfolien und -pflaster zwischen dem zweiten und fünften Tag. Ist nach zwei Wochen keine spürbare Besserung der Beschwerden eingetreten, sollte die Behandlung abgebrochen werden.

Wichtig: Wenn die Beschwerden abgeklungen sind, die Folien oder Pflaster nicht sofort abnehmen, sondern noch zwei weitere Tage tragen, um den Erfolg zu stabilisieren!

großes Glas Wasser 24 Stunden zwischen zwei große Blockmagnete (Magnetkraft zwischen 5000 und 7000 Gauß) stellt.

Magnetische Einlegesohlen

Am besten wirken die Einlegesohlen, wenn sie mit wechselpolaren Magnetfolien ausgestattet sind. Sie fördern die Durchblutung der Füße und sind hilfreich bei kalten Füßen im Winter. Ihre Wärmeentwicklung kann allerdings auch die Schweißbildung anregen und dadurch das Risiko von Fußpilz erhöhen.

Magnetschmuck

Ein Magnet an der Halskette kann bei Husten und Kloß im Hals hilfreich sein, ein magnetischer Armreif hilft möglicherweise bei Entzündungen im Handgelenk. Ansonsten ist aber der Magnetschmuck eher als kosmetisches denn als medizinisches Instrument einzuschätzen.

Die richtige Polung

Lediglich bei den wechselpolaren Magnetfolien braucht sich der Patient keine Gedanken darüber zu machen, mit welchem Ende des Magneten er eigentlich arbeiten will. Bei allen anderen Magneten ist es jedoch von größter Wichtigkeit, die Pole zu kennen. Denn Nord- und Südpol haben ganz unterschiedliche Wirkungen. So wirkt der Nordpol eher kühlend und energieraubend, er eignet sich dadurch beispielsweise zur Behandlung von schmerzhaften Entzündungen und fiebrigen Erkrankungen. Der Südpol wirkt hingegen wärmend und energiespendend, er ist daher angezeigt bei Beschwerden wie niedrigem Blutdruck, Müdigkeit und Konzentrationsschwäche.

Normalerweise sind die jeweiligen Pole bei den Heilmagneten markiert. Falls nicht: Hier ein Trick, wie sie die richtigen Polzuordnungen finden. Nehmen Sie einen Kompass, und stellen Sie ihn so auf, dass die schwarze Nadelspitze nach Norden zeigt. Bringen Sie nun das eine Ende Ihres Magneten in die Nähe der schwarzen Nadelspitze. Bleibt die Position der Nadel unverändert, handelt es sich um den Nordpol des Magneten (denn bei der schwarzen Nadelspitze handelt es sich um einen Südpol). Dreht sich jedoch die Nadel um, handelt es sich bei dem Magnetende um den Südpol.

Beschwerden lindern von A bis Z

Die Anwendung der traditionsreichen Magnettherapie hat sich bislang vor allem bei der Behandlung von Krankheiten bewährt, die mit Entzündungen und Durchblutungsstörungen einhergehen. Die besten Erfahrungen wurden dabei mit den wechselpolaren Magnetfolien gemacht. Hier sind die Plus- und Minuspole in wechselnden Kreisen aneinander gereiht. Diese Anordnung hat die größte Wirkung auf die Blutgefäße und das Fließverhalten des Bluts – größer als das Anbringen der reinen Süd- und Nordpolseiten der Magnete.

Die Anwendung der Magnete ist heute wesentlich leichter als früher, als noch mit großen, teilweise kiloschweren Metallklötzen gearbeitet wurde. Die modernen Pflaster und Folien wiegen nur noch wenige Gramm, sie lassen sich problemlos auf der Haut befestigen und unter der Kleidung verstecken.

Arthritis

○ Symptome

Arthritis kann sich u. a. durch Gelenkschmerzen (meist mit Schwellungen), Morgensteifigkeit und Rheumaknoten an den Gelenken, Knochenvorsprüngen und Sehnen bemerkbar machen.

○ Ursachen

Arthritis gehört zu den Autoimmunkrankheiten, bei denen sich der Körper buchstäblich gegen sich selbst wendet. Das Immunsystem verliert die Orientierung und richtet sich nicht nur gegen die Parasiten im Gelenk, sondern auch gegen die körpereigenen, gesunden Zellen der Gelenkinnenhaut. Dort führen sie zu Entzündungen und Wucherungen. Als Ursachen werden Infektionen, aber auch psychische Einflüsse vermutet. Viele Arthritiker gehen davon aus, dass Nahrungsmittel wie Fleisch, Wurst, Alkohol, Süßigkeiten und Weißmehlprodukte die Beschwerden verstärken. Dies ist jedoch wissenschaftlich nicht bewiesen. Es ist vielmehr so, dass das Immunsystem am häufigsten durch Milch- und Getreideprodukte irritiert wird.

Eine große Rolle spielt bei Arthritispatienten die Psyche. Sie haben meist Probleme, mit ihren Aggressionen umzugehen und verdrängen ihre Gefühle. Sie lenken ihre zerstörerischen Energien auf sich selbst – genauso, wie die Immunabwehr sich gegen die Gelenkzellen ihres eigenen Körpers richtet. Gegenüber ihren Mitmenschen sind Arthritispatienten oft schüchtern, aufopfernd und mitfühlend. Interessant ist in diesem Zusammenhang, dass Frauen dreimal so häufig unter rheumatoider Arthritis leiden wie Männer.

○ Mit Magneten heilen

Magnete lindern die Entzündungserscheinungen und fördern die Durchblutung. Sie führen in einigen Fällen bereits nach wenigen Stunden zu einer deutlichen Schmerzlinderung.
Im Gegensatz zu vielen traditionell verwendeten Salben haben Magnete außerdem den Vorteil, dass sie nicht chemisch durch Gewebeschichten dringen müssen, um das betroffene Gelenk zu erreichen. Hautreizungen mit Jucken oder Brennen sind deshalb bei der Magnettherapie überaus selten anzutreffen.

⊙ Begleitende Maßnahmen

Werden Sie egoistischer! Arthritiker leiden oft unter dem Samaritersyndrom. Sie denken nur an andere und sind übermäßig hilfsbereit. Versuchen Sie, diese Einstellungen zugunsten einer positiven, egoistischeren Haltung abzubauen. Hängen Sie Fotos in Ihrer Wohnung auf, die nur Sie zeigen. Seien Sie mutiger, oder besuchen Sie einen Rhetorikkurs, um sich in Disputen besser behaupten zu können.

Basische Salze Basische Mischungen aus Natriumkarbonat, Kaliumkarbonat, Kalziumzitrat und anderen Salzen können die Therapie sinnvoll unterstützen, da Übersäuerung und die Entstehung von Arthritis in der Regel Hand in Hand gehen. Die basischen Salzprodukte erhält man in Apotheken, Drogerien und Reformhäusern. Die genaue Anwendung entnehmen Sie den Packungsaufschriften oder den Packungsbeilagen.

Die Anwendung

Die Magnete sollten die ganze Nacht sowie für mindestens vier Stunden am Tag um die betroffenen Gelenke getragen werden. Die Anwendung kann auf zweierlei Weise erfolgen:

● Die Magnete können in mehreren konzentrischen Folien rund um das betroffene Gelenk angebracht werden. Der Nachteil dieser Methode besteht darin, dass man je nach Gelenk mit recht vielen Magnetfolien und auch dementsprechend viel Klebematerial arbeiten muss. Durch die Bewegungen im Gelenk kann es außerdem immer wieder passieren, dass sich die eine oder andere Folie löst.

● Im Handel erhält man mittlerweile Magnetmanschetten für die unterschiedlichen Gelenke. Am Anfang fühlt man sich durch sie etwas in der Bewegungsfreiheit eingeschränkt, doch dieses Gefühl legt sich in der Regel bereits nach wenigen Stunden.

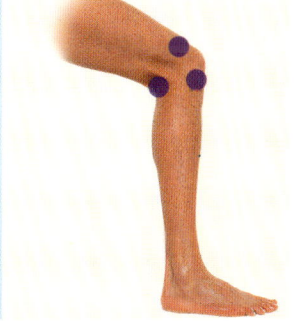

Arthrose

○ Symptome

Die Erkrankung befällt vornehmlich die Knie- und Hüftgelenke und macht sich zunächst durch Spannungsgefühle und Knirschen bei der Bewegung bemerkbar. Im späteren Verlauf kommen Schmerzen und Schwellungen hinzu, die sich im so genannten aktivierten Arthroseschub bis zur Unerträglichkeit steigern können. Der Patient hat Schwierigkeiten beim Laufen, Treppensteigen und beim Heben von Lasten. Im Spätstadium der Arthrose kommt es zu Verformungen im Gelenk mit starken Bewegungseinschränkungen. Die daraus resultierenden Fehlbelastungen versucht der Patient mit einer Kippung und Verdrehung in der Wirbelsäule auszugleichen. Hierdurch kommt es schließlich auch zu schmerzhaften Rückenverspannungen.

○ Ursachen

Bezüglich ihrer Entstehungsart werden zwei Formen der Arthrose unterschieden.
Die primäre Arthrose ist Resultat des Alterns oder einer Überbeanspruchung der Gelenke.

Die sekundäre Arthrose entsteht infolge von angeborenen Gelenkveränderungen, Erkrankungen (z. B. rheumatische Erkrankungen und Diabetes mellitus) oder Unfällen.

○ Mit Magneten heilen

Magnete verbessern die Durchblutung in den betroffenen Gelenken; Entzündungen und Schmerzen werden gelindert. Besonders groß sind die Chancen bei Gelenkarthrose, die mit starken Schmerzen, aber mit relativ geringer Schwellung einhergeht. Der Patient sollte sich allerdings immer vor Augen halten, dass Magnetkräfte nicht die physiologischen Veränderungen (vor allem den Knorpelverschleiß) aufheben können, die infolge der Erkrankung aufgetreten sind.

○ Begleitende Maßnahmen

Unterstützende Ernährungsumstellung Arthrosepatienten haben einen erhöhten Bedarf an Kalzium und den Vitaminen C, E, B1, B6 und B12. Stellen Sie daher Ihren Speiseplan auf Obst, Käse und Vollkornprodukte um. Essen Sie weniger Rind- und Schweinefleisch, stattdessen mehr Fisch (aber keinen Aal!)

und Geflügel. Außerdem sollten Sie sich regelmäßig Bierhefepulver (für die Vitamin-B-Versorgung) über Ihr Mittagessen streuen.

Teufelskrallenwurzel (Harpagophytum procumbens) Die traditionsreiche Heilpflanze besitzt schmerz- und entzündungshemmende Eigenschaften und ist darüber hinaus praktisch nebenwirkungsfrei. Dies ist durch mehrere wissenschaftliche Studien mittlerweile belegt. Teufelskrallenwurzel ist als Präparat in der Apotheke erhältlich. Die Dosierung richtet sich nach den jeweiligen Packungsbeilagen.

Brennnesselblätter (Urticae herba) Die Wirkstoffe der Brennnesselblätter greifen in den Schmerzstoffwechsel ein und hemmen die Ausschüttung von Substanzen, die unsere Schmerzfühler sensibilisieren.

Die Anwendung erfolgt am besten über Extrakte und Säfte aus dem Reformhaus und aus der Apotheke. Die Dosierung richtet sich nach den jeweiligen Packungsbeilagen.

Wichtig: Der Einsatz von Teufelskrallenwurzel und Brennnesselblättern gemeinsam ist überflüssig. Entscheiden Sie sich für eine der beiden Heilpflanzen.

Die Anwendung

Die Magnete sollten die ganze Nacht sowie für mindestens vier Stunden am Tag um die betroffenen Gelenke getragen werden. Die Anwendung kann auf zweierlei Weise erfolgen:

● Die Magnete können in mehreren konzentrischen Folien rund um das betroffene Gelenk angebracht werden. Der Nachteil dieser Methode besteht darin, dass man je nach Gelenk mit recht vielen Magnetfolien und auch dementsprechend viel Klebematerial arbeiten muss. Durch die Bewegungen im Gelenk kann es außerdem immer wieder passieren, dass sich die eine oder andere Folie löst.

● Im Handel erhält man Magnetmanschetten für die unterschiedlichen Gelenke. Sie empfehlen sich vor allem bei den großen Gelenken in Hüfte und Knie. Am Anfang fühlt man sich durch sie etwas in der Bewegungsfreiheit eingeschränkt, doch dieses Gefühl legt sich in der Regel bereits nach wenigen Stunden.

Asthma bronchiale

◦ Symptome

Typisch für einen Asthmaanfall sind die »giemende« Atmung (stoßartige Atemzüge, das entspannte Ausatmen bleibt aus), ein Enge- und Druckgefühl in der Brust und ein krampfartiger Husten. Er ist oft von starken Ängsten begleitet. Die Symptome können sich nach wenigen Minuten schon wieder gelegt haben, halten aber oft auch mehrere Stunden oder Tage an.

◦ Ursachen

Bei Patienten bis zu 40 Jahren wird das Asthma zu 90 Prozent aller Fälle durch eine Allergie verursacht. Bei Patienten über 40 entsteht es oft in Begleitung von Emphysemen und anderen Lungenkrankheiten.
Asthma bronchiale gehört – ebenso wie einige Arten von Allergien – außerdem zu den psychosomatischen Krankheiten; asthmatische Anfälle treten unter Stress und seelischer Belastung besonders häufig auf. In der Psychosomatik wird der Asthmaanfall oft als ein unterdrücktes Weinen bezeichnet.

Während des Schlafs sorgt das Nervensystem für eine Engstellung der Bronchien, weil zu dieser Zeit nur wenig Luft benötigt wird. Diese Engstellung hält auch noch eine gewisse Zeit nach dem Aufwachen an, obwohl eigentlich schon wieder mehr Luft benötigt wird. Aus diesem Grund geschehen Asthmaanfälle meistens in den frühen Morgenstunden. Die Magnete sollten daher besonders zur Nacht aufgelegt werden.

◦ Mit Magneten heilen

Über ihren Einfluss auf die Durchblutung entspannen Magnete die Atemwegsmuskeln. Magnetkräfte sorgen außerdem über ihre Wirkung auf die Ionenladung von Blütenpollen und Staubpartikeln dafür, dass weniger Allergene in die Atemwege gelangen.

◦ Begleitende Maßnahmen

Die richtige Sitzposition Bei einem plötzlich auftretenden Anfall möglichst gerade auf einen Stuhl setzen, der Bauch sollte locker nach vorne durchgewölbt werden, um dem Zwerchfell – einem der wichtigsten Atemmuskeln – die Arbeit zu erleichtern.

Kaffee Wenn das Inhalations-spray nicht gleich zur Hand ist, wenn ein Anfall kommt, kann ersatzweise zu Kaffee gegriffen werden. Koffein wirkt der Verkrampfung der Atemwegsmuskeln entgegen. Die Mindestdosis beträgt 2 Tassen.

Lernen Sie weinen Egal ob Frust, Trauer oder Wut – alles, was den Druck in den Tränensäcken erhöht, sollte nicht verdrängt, sondern herausgelassen werden. Suchen Sie sich einen Platz, an den Sie sich zurückziehen und an dem Sie ungestört Ihren Gefühlen nachgeben können.

Vorsicht bei Kälte Akute Kältereize führen zur spontanen Engstellung der Bronchien. Ziehen Sie sich im Winter einen Schal über Mund und Nase.

Nasenatmung Bei der Atmung durch die Nase wird die Luft vor dem Eintritt in die Bronchien gereinigt und erwärmt.

Richtige Stressatmung Legen Sie, wenn Sie unter Stress stehen, die Hand auf Ihren Bauch, und spüren Sie, wie das Zwerchfell die Bauchdecke auf- und abbewegt. Solche Übungen sind unauffällig, man kann sie auch in der Öffentlichkeit durchführen.

Die Anwendung

Befestigen Sie ein bis zwei rechteckige konzentrische Magnetfolien (Größe 50 mal 120 oder 90 mal 150 Millimeter) in Längsrichtung zur Luftröhre. Die oberste Folie kommt auf die Kuhle zwischen den beiden Schlüsselbeinenden, die nächste Folie folgt darunter über dem Brustbein. Die Folien sollten während der gesamten Nacht und am besten auch während des gesamten Tages getragen werden.

Allergiker sollten in der Nacht zusätzlich eine runde konzentrische Magnetfolie auf der Nasenwurzel zwischen den Augenbrauen befestigen (ausnahmsweise mit dem aktiven Magnetfeld nach oben!), um die Pollen- und Staubbelastung für die Atemwege zu verringern.

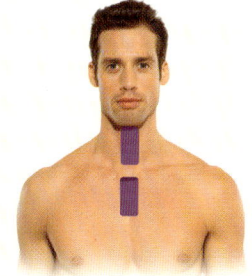

Blasen-entzündung

Symptome

Die Blasenentzündung kommt in der Regel plötzlich und zeigt sich durch zunehmenden Harndrang, obwohl nur kleine Harnmengen abgegeben werden, Schmerzen beim Harnlassen und eine trübe, manchmal auch blutige Verfärbung des Urins. Typisch ist der starke krampfartige Schmerz nach dem Ablassen des Urins.

Ursachen

Da die weibliche Harnröhre sehr viel kürzer ist als die männliche und entzündungsauslösende Keime somit auch schneller in die Blase gelangen können, erkranken etwa 50-mal mehr Frauen als Männer an den unangenehmen Blasenentzündungen. Bei einem Drittel der erkrankten Frauen besteht außerdem von Geburt aus eine stark ausgeprägte Neigung der Haut- und Schleimhautzellen, Bakterien festzuhalten. Dies bedeutet konkret, dass die Keime mit dem Urin nicht einfach fortgespült werden, sondern sie erhalten die Chance, sich sozusagen in den Harnwegen zu verstecken.

Eine Blasenentzündung kann auch durch Geschlechtsverkehr übertragen werden. Dabei liegen die Ursachen für den Harnwegsinfekt meist beim Partner. Empfängnisverhütende Spiralen und Kondome können hier einen wirksamen Schutz aufbauen, andere Verhütungsmittel wie das Diaphragma verändern jedoch das Scheidenmilieu und können dadurch sogar das Risiko einer Harnwegsinfektion erhöhen. Auslösender Keim der Blasenentzündung ist in 80 Prozent aller Fälle die Bakterie Escherichia coli. Sie zählt eigentlich zu unseren Nutzkeimen. Normalerweise ist sie im menschlichen Darm zu Hause, wo sie uns beim Verdauen hilft. Gelangt der Colikeim aber von dort aus in die Harnröhre, so kann er zu einem echten Problem werden.

Mit Magneten heilen

Magnete wirken durchblutungsfördernd und hemmen außerdem das Wachstum der Bakterien in den Harnwegen.

Begleitende Maßnahmen

Teebaumöl Das Öl konnte in mehreren Studien seine antibiotischen Kräfte unter Beweis stellen. Setzen Sie Ihrem Badewasser etwa 10 Tropfen des Öls zu, es dringt von selbst in die tieferen Gewebeschichten ein.

Pflanzliche Heilmittel Zu den phytotherapeutischen Mitteln der ersten Wahl zählen Zubereitungen aus Bärentrauben- und Goldrutenblättern. Die Wirkstoffe der Bärentraube hemmen das Wachstum der Bakterien, die der Goldrute wirken keim- und entzündungshemmend und sorgen als Harntreiber außerdem für eine zusätzliche Spülung der Harnwege. Die Anwendung erfolgt am besten über Präparate aus der Apotheke.

Nehmen Sie ausreichend Flüssigkeit zu sich Sie sollten mindestens 2 Liter pro Tag trinken, im Sommer kann es auch erheblich mehr werden. Trinken Sie auch dann, wenn Sie kein Durstgefühl verspüren.

Die richtige Vorbeugung
- Setzen Sie sich nicht auf kalte Bänke oder Stühle.
- Achten Sie auf trockene Kleidung. Wechseln Sie nach dem Schwimmen die Badekleidung.
- Gehen Sie nach dem Geschlechtsverkehr auf die Toilette, um möglicherweise eingedrungene Keime auszuspülen.
- Frauen sollten nach dem Stuhlgang immer in Richtung After abwischen, damit die Keime nicht zum Blaseneingang transportiert werden.
- Härten Sie Ihren Körper mit Wechselduschen, Trockenbürsten und viel Bewegung an der frischen Luft ab.

Die Anwendung

Die Anwendung erfolgt über wechselpolare, rechteckige Magnetfolien (die Größe beträgt etwa 90 mal 150 Millimeter), die im spitzen Winkel zueinander zwischen Bauchnabel und Schambein aufgebracht werden. Ergänzend dazu kann Wasser getrunken werden (etwa einen halben Liter pro Tag), das per Nord-, d. h. Pluspolmagnet magnetisiert wurde.

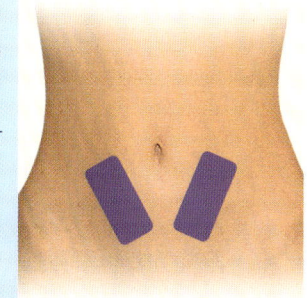

Fibromyalgie

○ Symptome

Wissenschaftler schätzen, dass etwa drei Prozent der Bundesbürger an Fibromyalgie leiden. Die betroffenen Patienten beschreiben ihre Beschwerden oft mit Sätzen wie »Mir tut alles weh«; in bayerischen Kliniken sprach man deshalb früher auch scherzhaft vom Ois-ziagt-Syndrom, vom Alles-zieht-Syndrom. Damit wurde zum Ausdruck gebracht, dass man die Beschwerden eher mit einer wehleidigen bis hypochondrischen Einstellung als mit einer ernst zu nehmenden Erkran-kung in Verbindung brachte.

Tatsache ist jedoch, dass die Fibromyalgie zu den rheumatischen Erkrankungen gehört und ihre Schmerzen durchaus real sind. Sie treten nur in der Muskulatur auf und können daher – im Unterschied zu den Gelenkerkrankungen – weitflächig verteilt sein und komplette Körperteile treffen. Dies kann schließlich zu einer starken Beeinträchtigung der Beweglichkeit führen. Einige Körperstellen, die so genannten Tenderpunkte, reagieren überdurchschnittlich sensibel auf Fingerdruck. Sie sind typisch für die Fibromyalgie und können dem Arzt dazu dienen, die Diagnose abzusichern.

○ Ursachen

Die Ursachen der Fibromyalgie sind bis jetzt noch unklar. Einige Wissenschaftler vermuten hinter den Schmerzen mikroskopische Schäden in der Muskulatur, andere vermuten die Ursachen in einer Störung der Botenstoffe im zentralen Nervensystem.

Auch die Psyche spielt bei der Krankheitsentstehung eine Rolle. Doch die oft geäußerte These, nach der alle Fibromyalgiepatienten depressiv sind, ist nicht haltbar. Depression und Fibromyalgie sind zwei unterschiedliche Krankheitsbilder, die sich nur äußerlich ähneln. Bei der Depression fehlen die Tenderpunkte, wie sie für die Fibromyalgie typisch sind. Allerdings können die enormen Belastungen durch die rheumatische Erkrankung durchaus in ein psychisches Tief münden.

○ Mit Magneten heilen

Klinische Studien zur Wirksamkeit von Magneten bei der Behandlung der Fibromyalgie existieren bislang noch nicht. Es gibt jedoch zahlreiche Berichte von betroffenen Patienten, die durch Magnete Erleichterung bekommen haben. Darüber hinaus sprechen Fibromyalgiepatienten traditionell gut auf Akupunktur an, und deren Effekte werden laut einer japanischen Studie bei Muskelschmerzen durch die Magnetbehandlung oftmals noch übertroffen.

Fazit: Die Magnettherapie ist für den Fibromyalgiekranken in jedem Fall einen Versuch wert, allein aufgrund ihrer absoluten Risikolosigkeit. Falls bereits eine medikamentöse Therapie vorgenommen wird, braucht diese wegen der Magnete auch nicht unterbrochen zu werden.

Die Anwendung

Befestigen Sie wechselpolare Magnetfolien auf Ihren Tenderpunkten, also auf jenen Stellen, wo der Schmerz besonders stark ist. Verwenden Sie möglichst große Folien, um die betreffenden Zonen großflächig abzudecken.

Tragen Sie die Folien auf jeden Fall nachts, möglichst aber auch ein paar Stunden am Tag.

○ Begleitende Maßnahmen

Muskelentspannung Bei Fibromyalgie haben sich Entspannungstechniken oft als hilfreich erwiesen. Besonders bewährt haben sich autogenes Training und Biofeedback sowie die Muskelrelaxation nach Jacobson. Nachteil des Biofeedbacks ist, dass man einen erheblichen technischen Aufwand benötigt. Das autogene Training wiederum sorgt zwar für eine tiefe Entspannung, doch bis dahin muss konsequent und lange trainiert werden. Leichter zu erlernen ist sicherlich das Programm nach Jacobson, außerdem besitzt es einen eindeutigeren Bezug zur Muskelarbeit als die beiden anderen Entspannungstechniken. Dieser Effekt ist gerade für den Fibromyalgiepatienten mit seinen Muskelschmerzen von Bedeutung. Zum Vertiefen des Entspannungsgrades kann man später immer noch auf andere Entspannungstechniken umsteigen. Kurse zum Jacobsontraining werden mittlerweile preiswert und leicht zugänglich an fast allen Volkshochschulen angeboten. Dort laufen sie oft auch unter dem Terminus »Tiefenentspannungstraining«.

Finger- und Armschmerzen

○ Symptome

Die Symptome sind taube Finger, Nadelstiche in der Haut, schmerzende Unterarmsehnen und Handgelenke, die in manchen Fällen sogar alltägliche Handlungen wie das Zähneputzen zur Tortur werden lassen. Im Fachjargon werden die Beschwerden unter RSI zusammengefasst (Repetitive Strain Injury, Verletzung durch wiederholte Belastungen). Deutsche Wissenschaftler haben RSI lange Zeit ignoriert, obwohl die Krankheit bereits in den 1980er Jahren in Australien und den USA ausgiebig diskutiert wurde. In Australien sind etwa 22 Prozent der Bildschirmarbeiter betroffen, in den USA ist RSI mit 48 Prozent der häufigste Grund für die Anzeige einer am Arbeitsplatz entstandenen Gesundheitsstörung.

○ Ursachen

20 bis 25 Prozent aller Computerarbeitskräfte leiden an RSI. Besonders betroffen sind jene, die schnell schreiben müssen (über 300 Anschläge pro Minute). Neben der Schnelligkeit des Schreibens ist auch die Tastenbelegung an den Keyboards schuld am RSI-Syndrom. Dort findet man immer noch die QWERT-Belegung der alten Remington-Schreibmaschine, bei der Mittel- und Zeigefinger überdurchschnittlich belastet werden. Mittlerweile gibt es Tastaturen mit anderen Belegungen im Handel, bei der die Computerarbeitskräfte allerdings ihr 10-Finger-System umstellen müssen. Nicht zu vergessen ist schließlich die Tatsache, dass Berufskrankheiten oftmals Menschen treffen, die an ihrem Beruf keinen Spaß haben und sich deshalb verkrampfen oder Krankheiten als willkommene Gelegenheit sehen, eine Pause einzulegen. Beim RSI-Syndrom ist genau das Gegenteil der Fall. Laut Untersuchungen der Technischen Hochschule in Darmstadt trifft es ausgerechnet die hoch motivierten Leistungsträger in den Betrieben.

○ Mit Magneten heilen

Gerade bei entzündlichen Prozessen an Sehnen und Muskeln besitzen Magnete große Heilungschancen. Sie fördern die Durchblutung und erzeugen eine angenehm lockernde Wärme.

Mitunter stellen sich die Heilerfolge von Magnetbehandlungen schon recht früh ein. Im Fall von chronischen Sehnenentzündungen in der Hand muss man sich jedoch in Geduld üben. Die ersten Fortschritte werden hier meist erst nach zwei bis drei Wochen erzielt.

◒ Begleitende Maßnahmen

Tragen Sie elastische Handschuhe Dehnbare Handschuhe wirken bei geschädigten Finger- und Armsehnen wie ein elastischer Druckverband, der die Durchblutung fördert, eine angenehme Wärme erzeugt und Schwellungen verhindert.

Eine neue Tastatur Wer sich aus alter Gewohnheit gegen ein Keyboard mit neuer Tastenbelegung sträubt, kann mittlerweile auch auf Tastaturen zurückgreifen, bei denen die Tastenblöcke in zwei Tastengruppen unterteilt sind. Dadurch verändert sich der Winkel in den Handgelenken, und die Belastung der Unterarmsehnen wird reduziert.

Pausen entspannen die verkrampfte Muskulatur Legen Sie an Ihrem Computerterminal öfter mal kleine Arbeitsunterbrechungen ein. Machen Sie jede Stunde eine Pause von drei bis fünf Minuten, in denen Sie Ihre Finger etwas dehnen.

Die Anwendung

Einige Hersteller führen mittlerweile spezialangefertigte Magnethandschuhe im Sortiment. Sie haben den Vorteil, die magnetischen Kräfte gut über die gesamte Hand zu verteilen.

Ansonsten kann die Anwendung auch über die normalen Magnetfolien erfolgen. Deren Befestigung auf Rücken und Innenfläche der Hand ist in der Regel kein Problem, das Anbringen an den Fingern erfordert jedoch viel Geschick. Auch gelangen ihre Magnetkräfte nicht in sämtliche Bereiche der entzündeten Hand, problematische Zonen wie etwa an den Fingerbeugen werden nicht erreicht.

Tragen Sie Magnethandschuhe oder Magnetfolien so lange wie möglich, auf jeden Fall die ganze Nacht über. Während der Computerarbeit können sie nicht getragen werden, da hierdurch die Beweglichkeit der Finger doch deutlich eingeschränkt wird.

Frostbeulen

○ Symptome

Frostbeulen zeigen sich als meist rötliche oder bläuliche Hautverfärbungen, die schließlich teigig anschwellen und zu einem schmerzhaften Knoten auswachsen können.

Die Mangeldurchblutung in den Frostbeulen führt zunächst dazu, dass dort kein Schmerz mehr empfunden wird. Sie können sich also entwickeln, ohne dass wir es bemerken.

Frostbeulen sind die Vorstufe einer Erfrierung, die ernsthafte Folgen wie Operationen und komplette Finger- oder Zehenverluste haben kann. Die Erfrierung zeigt sich daran, dass die Haut kalt, hart, weiß und gefühlsunempfindlich ist. Bei Erwärmung verfärbt sie sich tiefblau oder purpurrot. Mit Erfrierungen müssen Sie unbedingt einen Arzt aufsuchen!

○ Ursachen

Die Frostbeulen tragen eigentlich einen falschen Namen. Am häufigsten entstehen sie bei nasskaltem Wetter mit Temperaturen von 1 bis 4 °C. Besonders gefährdet sind Frauen; etwa jede dritte

Frau zieht sich im Winter Frostbeulen zu, weil sie sich nicht witterungsgerecht kleidet.

○ Mit Magneten heilen

Frostbeulen sind ein Schutzmechanismus unseres Körpers. Wenn es kalt wird, drosselt er an besonders exponierten Stellen (Fuß, Hände, Nase) die Durchblutung, um die Körpertemperatur halten zu können. Längerfristige Blutdrosselungen führen zu Sauerstoffmangel im Gewebe, zu Frostbeulen und im schlimmsten Fall zu akuten Erfrierungen mit kompletten Gewebeuntergängen. Magnete verbessern die Durchblutung und dadurch die Sauerstoffversorgung im betroffenen Hautgewebe.

○ Begleitende Maßnahmen

Homöopathie Auch das homöopathische Mittel Abrotanum Pentarkan hilft. Die Dosierung beträgt 3-mal täglich 15 Tropfen.

Teebaumöl Das Öl des australischen Teebaums wirkt desinfizierend und verbessert die Hautdurchblutung. Bereiten Sie sich Ihre eigene Ölmischung nach dem folgenden Rezept. 2 Teelöffel Olivenöl mit 4 Tropfen Teebaumöl mischen und diese

Die Anwendung

Die Anwendung sollte nur durch wechselpolare Magnetfolien erfolgen, insofern diese die größte Hautwärme und damit den besten Durchblutungseffekt erzeugen. Die nach wie vor erhältlichen nordpolaren Magnetpflaster haben keinen Sinn, sie sorgen sogar noch für eine unerwünschte Drosselung der Blutzufuhr.

Kleben Sie die Magnetfolien für mehrere Stunden täglich und über die ganze Nacht auf die betroffenen Hautstellen. Wichtig: Falls sich nach 24 Stunden keine deutlichen Besserungen zeigen, müssen Sie den Arzt aufsuchen. Dann handelt es sich möglicherweise um eine Erfrierung, bei der bereits größere Gewebeanteile abgestorben sind.

Wer immer wieder unter kalten Extremitäten leidet, sollte sich Magnetfolien zur Vorbeugung aufkleben. Aber Vorsicht: Natürlich ersetzt auch Magnetkraft keine warme Bekleidung.

Mischung auf die erkrankten Stellen tupfen. Teebaumöl eignet sich auch zur Behandlung von eitrigen Frostbeulen sowie zur Vorbeugung.

Die richtige Vorbeugung – so schützen Sie sich vor Frostbeulen

● Behindern Sie nicht die Blutzirkulation an den gefährdeten Hautstellen. Achten Sie auf weites und wärmendes Schuhwerk, auch die Socken sollten nicht den Fuß abschnüren. Keine hochhackigen Schuhe oder dünne, flache Slipper. Auch die Hände sollten gut geschützt werden.

● Wer schon häufiger Frostbeulen oder sogar schon Erfrierungen hatte, sollte die Haut mit Magneten schützen. Für die Füße und Hände gibt es mittlerweile auch magnetische Handschuhe, Manschetten und Einlegesohlen. Diese sind in der Anwendung weitaus unproblematischer als die üblichen Folien oder Pflaster.

● Die Luft ist umso kälter, je windiger es ist. Eine Außentemperatur von 0 °C beispielsweise wirkt bei Windstärke 5 bereits 5 °C kühler; bei einer Windstärke von 10 Meter pro Sekunde wirkt sie sogar wie –15 °C. Meiden Sie daher im Winter böige und zugige Plätze, oder schützen Sie sich mit einer speziellen Wind abweisenden Kleidung.

Gallenblasen-entzündung

○ Symptome

Die Gallenblasenentzündung zeigt sich im akuten Stadium durch Fieber, Schüttelfrost, vorübergehende Gelbsucht, Erbrechen und Schmerzen im rechten Oberbauch. Die chronische Verlaufsform der Erkrankung verursacht in der Regel keine Beschwerden, kann aber im Endstadium zur Schrumpfgallenblase führen. Im Laborbefund zeigt sie sich durch eine erhöhte Konzentration der weißen Blutkörperchen und einer Erhöhung der Blutsenkungsgeschwindigkeit.

○ Ursachen

Zu den klassischen Auslösern der Gallenblasenentzündung zählen vor allem Gallensteine, deren Entstehung wiederum durch Stress und eine falsche Ernährung (zu viele tierische Fette) gefördert wird. Die Steine können zu einem Abknicken des Verbindungsstrangs (Ductus cysticus) führen, an dem die Gallenblase befestigt ist. Durch dieses Hindernis dickt sich die Gallenflüssigkeit ein, und der Inhalt der Gallenblase staut sich auf. Infolge dieses Staus wird die Gallenblase überdehnt, und die Schleimhaut an ihren Innenwänden entzündet sich. Mitunter kommen auch noch bakterielle Infektionen hinzu.

○ Mit Magneten heilen

Magnete verbessern den Gallenfluss, entkrampfen die Gallenwege und fördern die Durchblutung der Gallenblase. Nicht zu vergessen schließlich sind die leicht antibiotischen Wirkungen, die das Entstehen von Infekten in den Gallenwegen verhindern können.

Gerade bei chronischen Gallenblasenentzündungen sind Magnete hilfreich. Die erkrankte Gallenblase wird selbst in leichteren Fällen oft von Ärzten herausoperiert, oft mit der Begründung, dass dieses Organ ohnehin keine sonderlichen Funktionen erfülle. Tatsache ist jedoch, dass die Gallenblase weit mehr als nur ein Zwischenbehälter für die Gallenflüssigkeit aus der Leber ist. In ihr wird die Gallenflüssigkeit präzise konzentriert und dosiert, um für einen reibungslosen Verlauf der Fettverdauung zu sorgen. Sie ist also durchaus ein wertvolles Organ.

Die Anwendung

Am besten befestigen Sie rechteckige, wechselpolare Magnetfolien in einer Größe von 50 mal 120 Millimeter oder 90 mal 150 Millimeter auf der schmerzenden Stelle. Das Anbringen einer solchen Folie bildet auch eine wirksame erste Hilfe bei der berüchtigten Gallenkolik. Nichtsdestoweniger muss in diesem akuten Stadium unbedingt der Arzt hinzugezogen werden. Ihre großen Stärken zeigt die Magnettherapie sicherlich bei der chronischen Gallenblasenentzündung. Im Unterschied zu den üblichen medikamentösen Behandlungsformen dieser Krankheit ist sie absolut risikoarm (Magnetkräfte führen zu keiner chemischen Belastung des Körpers). Außerdem entstehen – langfristig gesehen – erheblich geringere Kosten.

☙ Begleitende Maßnahmen

Kurkuma Zu den wichtigsten Wirkstoffen des Kurkumawurzelstocks gehören die gelben Farbstoffe Kurkumin, Mono- und Bisdesmethoxykurkumin sowie die ätherischen Öle Tumeron, Borneol und Cineol. Die gelben Farbstoffe sind in jüngerer Zeit von Wissenschaftlern ausführlich untersucht worden. Demzufolge regen sie die Entleerung der Gallenblase an und schützen die in unserem Organismus vorhandenen Fette vor dem Angriff aggressiver Sauerstoffmoleküle. Auch die ätherischen Öle greifen in die Fettverdauung ein, indem sie die Produktion fettverarbeitender Galle aus den Leberzellen anregt. Darüber hinaus schützen sie die Arterien vor schädlichen Fettablagerungen.

Die Anwendung erfolgt entweder über Präparate aus der Apotheke (Choldestal Krugmann Kapseln und Lösung, Bilagit Mono Kapseln) oder aber in Kombination mit Schöllkraut und Pfefferminze über einen Gallenblasentee nach dem folgenden Rezept.

Je 20 Gramm Pfefferminzblätter, Schöllkraut und Kurkumapulver gut miteinander vermischen. 2 Teelöffel der Mischung mit 1 Tasse heißem Wasser übergießen, 10 Minuten ziehen lassen, anschließend abseihen. Die Dosierung beträgt 3 Tassen pro Tag, jeweils zu den Mahlzeiten getrunken. Anstelle des Schöllkrauts können Sie auch Kamille verwenden.

Hexenschuss

○ Symptome

Der Schmerz »schießt« regelrecht ins Kreuz, die Lendenwirbelsäule blockiert, die Hautpartie des unteren Rückens fühlt sich kalt an. Der Betroffene ist nicht mehr in der Lage, sich z. B. aus seiner gebückten Position zu erheben. Sein Körper nimmt eine vornübergebeugte Schonhaltung ein. Beim Hexenschuss beschränken sich die Beschwerden auf den unteren Bereich der Lendenwirbelsäule. Sie strahlen – im Unterschied zum Ischiasleiden – nicht in die Beine aus.

○ Ursachen

Fast alle Schädigungen der Wirbelsäule können zu einem Hexenschuss führen. Typisch ist die schockartige Verspannung der tiefen Rückenmuskeln. Dieser Reflex schützt einerseits die Wirbelsäule vor weiteren Schäden, andererseits verringert er jedoch die Durchblutung und führt zu starken Schmerzen. Zu den klassischen biologischen Ursachen zählen:
● Kälte im Rückenbereich, etwa durch offene Fenster und Türen oder durchgeschwitzte Kleidung

● Langes Sitzen, da auch hierdurch die Durchblutung verschlechtert wird
● Heben von Lasten mit vornübergebeugtem Rücken oder spontane Drehungen der Wirbelsäule

○ Erste Hilfe

Gehen Sie in die Psoashaltung
Legen Sie sich auf den Rücken, die Beine werden im 90-Grad-Winkel gebeugt und auf einem Stuhl oder einer Bank abgelegt. Versuchen Sie, aus dem Bauch, also unter Einsatz Ihres Zwerchfells, zu atmen. Zusätzlich können Sie sich an der inneren Fußsohlenkante in der Nähe der Ferse massieren lassen; dort sitzen die Akupressurpunkte zur Entspannung der tiefen Rückenmuskeln.

Vorsicht vor Muskelrelaxanzien
Ärzte verschreiben oft so genannte Relaxanzien, um die verspannte Muskulatur zu lösen. Doch so schmerzhaft ein Hexenschuss auch ist: Bei dieser Methode wird sicherlich mit Kanonen auf Spatzen geschossen. Die meisten Relaxanzien gehören zu derselben Medikamentengruppe wie das hochwirksame Schlafmittel Valium,

mit einer ähnlich langen Liste von Risiken und Nebenwirkungen. Die Magnettherapie ist hier – bei keinesfalls geringerer Wirksamkeit – sicherlich risikoloser.

◔ Mit Magneten heilen

Die Wirksamkeit von Dauermagneten bei plötzlich »einschießenden« Schmerzen wie dem Hexenschuss ist wissenschaftlich gut dokumentiert. Offenbar greifen Dauermagnete direkt in die Schmerzübertragung ein, außerdem entspannen sie die verkrampfte Muskulatur.

◔ Begleitende Maßnahmen

Homöopathische Mittel

● Arnica D6 sollte unmittelbar nach Auftreten des Hexenschusses zur Anwendung kommen. Die Dosierung beträgt am Anfang 2 Tabletten pro Stunde, später 1 bis 2 Tabletten pro Tag.

● Rhus toxicodendron D6 ist besonders dann angezeigt, wenn der Hexenschuss wie ein Dolch zugestoßen hat und es zu einer starken Steife im Lendenwirbelbereich gekommen ist. Die Dosierung beträgt je nach Bedarf 3-mal täglich 1 bis 2 Tabletten.

Die Anwendung

Am besten helfen großflächige Magnetfolien (Magnetdurchmesser etwa 90 Millimeter, Stärke des Magnetmaterials extra dick, also mindestens 1,5 Millimeter) mit Wechselpolfeldern, da sie die Durchblutung in den verkrampften Muskeln optimal fördern. Sie werden paarig auf den schmerzenden Rückenpartien aufgebracht, die Einzelstücke jeweils links und rechts der Wirbelsäule. Sie sollten tagsüber und nachts getragen werden. Wer häufiger von der »Hexe« heimgesucht wird, sollte die Anschaffung einer magnetisierten Rückenmanschette (mittlerweile als »Deluxe Lumbar« bei einigen Fachhändlern erhältlich) in Erwägung ziehen. Sie eignet sich auch zur Vorbeugung, allerdings sollte sie in diesem Fall nur tagsüber getragen werden.

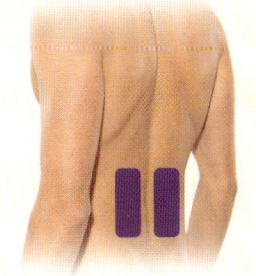

Husten

○ Symptome

Reizhusten zeigt sich durch ein Kribbeln im Hals und ist typisch für Empfindlichkeit gegenüber Kaltluft. Er kündigt oft eine nahende Erkältung an.

Das nervöse Hüsteln oder Räuspern ist in der Regel psychosomatisch bedingt.

Ein tief sitzender Husten mit Schleimauswurf zeigt eine ernsthafte Erkrankung der oberen Luftwege an, während ein kratzender und krampfartiger Husten vor allem bei asthmatischen Erkrankungen und Keuchhusten auftreten kann.

Husten kann ein Symptom für zahlreiche Erkrankungen sein. Gehen Sie auf jeden Fall zum Arzt, wenn Sie die folgenden Symptome beobachten können:

● Farbiger, d. h. gelblich grüner oder roter Auswurf
● Starke Schmerzen
● Rasseln und Pfeifen während des Hustens oder wenn der Husten chronisch geworden ist

○ Ursachen

Unabhängig von Art, Ursache und Ausmaß des Hustens, geht es bei fast jedem Husten darum,

Fremdkörper aus den Atemwegen zu entfernen. Eine Ausnahme bildet das psychosomatische Räuspern.

Der Hustenreflex wird durch zahlreiche Sinneszellen in der Bronchialschleimhaut und den Atemwegen ausgelöst. Bei Reizung dieser Rezeptoren (z. B. durch Gase, Kälte oder Fremdkörper) werden Signale an das Gehirn weitergeleitet, von wo aus schließlich gezielte Befehle an die Muskeln des Oberkörpers (vor allem Rücken- und Bauchmuskeln) geschickt werden.

○ Mit Magneten heilen

Erkrankungen der Bronchien reagieren in der Regel gut auf Magnetkräfte. In einer klinischen Studie an Patienten mit chronischer Bronchitis zeigte sich, dass niedrig-frequente Magnetfelder die Muskeln der Bronchien entspannen und dadurch das Atmen erleichtern. Darüber hinaus wird der Schleim gelöst, der Patient kann besser abhusten.

○ Begleitende Maßnahmen

Inhalationen mit Kamille und Thymian 3 bis 4 Liter Wasser in einem Topf zum Kochen bringen. 2 Esslöffel Kamillenblüten

Die Anwendung

Die Therapie erfolgt am besten über wechselpolare Magnetfolien, die entlang der Luftröhre von der Kuhle zwischen den Schlüsselbeinen bis zur Mitte des Brustbeins aufgelegt und befestigt werden. Die Anzahl der Folien richtet sich nach der Größe des Patienten. Sie sollten am besten ohne Unterbrechung, Tag und Nacht, getragen werden.

In dieser Form auf den Körper gelegte Magnetfolien können auch bei Raucherhusten hilfreich sein.

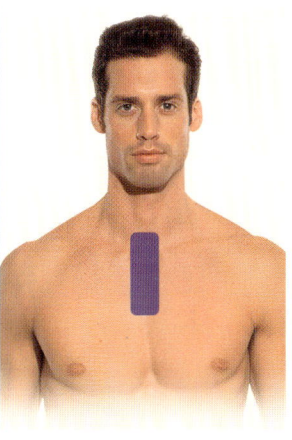

und Thymiankräuter hinzufügen. 10 Minuten ziehen lassen, anschließend zum Inhalieren in eine große Schüssel geben. Atmen Sie langsam und tief ein, wechselweise durch Mund und Nase; das Atmen muss angenehm sein, der Dampf darf nicht in den Atemwegen oder auf der Haut brennen. Die Dauer der Anwendung beträgt mindestens 8, höchstens 15 Minuten.

Akupressur »Cha-ba-Es« – dieser Punkt liegt zwischen den Schlüsselbeinenden über dem Brustbein. Drücken Sie diesen Punkt mit mittelstarkem, gleich bleibendem Druck, wenn Sie einen akuten Hustenanfall haben.

Lu 5, der »Ellbogenteich«, liegt in der Ellbogenfalte auf der dem Daumen zugewandten Seite. Sie spüren ihn bei gebeugtem Arm deutlich als Kuhle neben der Sehne des Bizepsmuskels. Massieren Sie diesen Punkt in kreisenden Bewegungen, mindestens 1 Minute lang, 4-mal täglich, erst rechts, dann links.

Vorsicht bei reizlindernden Medikamenten Hustenreiz ist lästig, aber in vielen Fällen unverzichtbar, um die Bronchien von Fremdkörpern zu reinigen. Greifen Sie nur dann zu Medikamenten, wenn es sich nicht um eine entzündliche Erkrankung der Atemwege handelt.

Ischiasleiden

○ Symptome

Beim Ischiasleiden werden Nervenwurzeln des Ischiasnervs an der Wirbelsäule gequetscht. Je nachdem, welche Wurzel getroffen ist, zeigt sich der Schmerz im Gesäß, an der Vorderseite des Oberschenkels, seitlich oder hinten am Bein; er kann sogar bis in die Fußspitzen ausstrahlen. Ein erfahrener Arzt kann aus einer präzisen Schmerzbeschreibung bereits schließen, an welcher Stelle der Wirbelsäule es zur Nervenquetschung kam. Eine seltenere Form des Ischiasleidens ist das Kaudasyndrom, das sich durch Lähmungs- und Taubheitserscheinungen in den Beinen bemerkbar macht. Es kann auch zu Impotenz führen. Hier sollte sofort ein Arzt aufgesucht werden.

○ Ursachen

Hauptursache für das Ischiasleiden sind Abnutzungen der unteren zwei Bandscheiben. Die Bandscheiben bilden gewissermaßen den Stoßdämpfer zwischen den einzelnen Wirbelkörpern. Sie nutzen sich jedoch nicht durch Bewegung ab, sondern durch lang andauerndes Sitzen und Bewegungsmangel. Regelmäßige, rückenfreundliche Sportarten tragen im Gegenteil sogar dazu bei, dass die Regenerationskräfte der Bandscheibe mobilisiert werden.

Wenn Sie akute Ischiasschmerzen haben, empfehlen sich auch hier – ähnlich wie beim Hexenschuss – die Psoashaltung und eine entspannende Fußmassage als Erste-Hilfe-Maßnahmen (siehe Seite 50).

○ Mit Magneten heilen

Spontane Schmerzen wie beim Ischiasleiden reagieren recht zuverlässig auf Magnete; dies ist auch wissenschaftlich gut dokumentiert. Demzufolge fördern Dauermagnete nicht nur die Durchblutung und Entkrampfung der schmerzenden Muskeln rund um die betroffenen Bandscheiben, sie greifen auch direkt in die Schmerzübertragung ein.

○ Begleitende Maßnahmen

Homöopathische Mittel

● Arnica D6 ist angezeigt, wenn der Patient den Eindruck hat, dass sich eine Klemme in seinen Rücken geschoben hat. Die Dosierung beträgt 2 Tabletten pro Stunde, im weiteren Verlauf der Erkrankung 1 bis 2 Tabletten pro Tag.

● Bryorheum hilft bei Rückenschmerzen, die sich bei Kälte verschlimmern. Die Dosierung beträgt 4-mal täglich 10 Tropfen.

● Nux vomica D6 hilft bei brennenden Schmerzen, die am Abend besser werden, in den frühen Morgenstunden jedoch am schlimmsten sind. Die Dosierung beträgt 1 bis 2 Tabletten 3-mal täglich.

Hilfe aus der Pflanzenkunde Die schmerzlindernde Wirkung der Teufelskrallenwurzel (Harpagophytum procumbens) ist wissenschaftlich belegt. Sie greift direkt in den Schmerz- und Entzündungsstoffwechsel ein.

Man kann sich Harpagophytum als Tee zubereiten, der jedoch außerordentlich bitter und streng schmeckt. Gaumenfreundlicher sind die modernen Harpagophytumpräparate aus der Apotheke.

Die richtige Vorbeugung

● Treiben Sie regelmäßig Sport, z. B. Gymnastik, Krafttraining oder auch Aquajogging.

● Heben Sie Lasten nicht »aus dem Kreuz«, gehen Sie möglichst in die Hocke. Sollte die vornübergebeugte Haltung nicht zu vermeiden sein (wenn man beispielsweise etwas aus dem Kofferraum holt), achten Sie darauf, dass Ihre Beine etwas gebeugt sind und die Rückenmuskeln voll unter Spannung stehen.

Die Anwendung

Am besten helfen großflächige Magnetfolien (Magnetdurchmesser etwa 90 Millimeter, Stärke des Magnetmaterials extra dick, also mindestens 1,5 Millimeter) mit Wechselpolfeldern, da sie die Durchblutung in den verkrampften Muskeln optimal fördern. Sie werden paarweise auf den schmerzenden Rückenpartien aufgebracht, die Einzelstücke jeweils links und rechts der Wirbelsäule. Sie sollten tagsüber und nachts getragen werden.
Wer häufiger von Ischiasbeschwerden heimgesucht wird, sollte die Anschaffung einer magnetisierten Rückenmanschette (mittlerweile als »Deluxe Lumbar« bei einigen Fachhändlern erhältlich) in Erwägung ziehen. Sie eignet sich auch zur Vorbeugung, allerdings sollte sie in diesem Fall nur tagsüber getragen werden.

Kalte Füße und kalte Hände

○ Symptome

Viele Menschen haben nicht nur im Winter kalte Hände und Füße. Ob in beheizten Räumen, unter der Daunenbettdecke oder an einem lauen Sommertag, es will ihnen einfach nicht gelingen, warme Extremitäten zu bekommen, obwohl der Rest des Körpers eigentlich wohl temperiert ist.

○ Ursachen

Warme Hände und Füße sind nicht selbstverständlich. Die durchschnittliche Körpertemperatur von 37 °C wird von der Hautoberfläche bei weitem nicht erreicht. Je weiter sich das Blut vom Körperinneren entfernt, desto mehr kühlt es sich ab. In der Haut beträgt die Temperatur noch knappe 30 °C, das Hautgewebe selbst erreicht gerade noch 25 °C.

Darüber hinaus haben Hände und Füße eine sehr exponierte Lage und sind dadurch den kühlen Witterungen schutzloser ausgesetzt als die übrigen Körperteile. Schließlich muss das Blut zu den Füßen den längsten Weg zurücklegen. Dies erklärt, warum die ausgekühlten Füße selbst dann nicht sofort warm werden, wenn sie in eine Wolldecke eingewickelt werden. Der Körper braucht einfach eine gewisse Zeit, bis er genügend Blut in die Füße transportiert hat.

Auch psychische Reize wie Angst und Stress wirken abkühlend auf die Haut, insofern sie dort für eine Drosselung der Blutzufuhr sorgen. Dieser Mechanismus kann sogar zu einer eigenständigen Krankheit werden, nämlich dem Raynaudsyndrom, das erstmals von dem französischen Arzt Maurice Raynaud (1834–1881) beschrieben wurde. Es äußert sich als anfallartige Durchblutungsstörung in den Fingern und in den Rückenflächen von Hand und Fuß. Die betroffenen Stellen werden zunächst bleich und kalt, um sich dann blau zu verfärben und heftig zu schmerzen. Es besteht bei den Wissenschaftlern kein Zweifel mehr an dem Zusammenhang des Raynaudsyndroms mit chronischen Ängsten und Überforderungsgefühlen.

Auch Hormone spielen bei der Entstehung der Krankheit eine wichtige Rolle. So tritt das Raynaudsyndrom bei Frauen ungefähr viermal häufiger auf als bei Männern.

○ Mit Magneten heilen

Bei kalten Händen und Füßen besitzen Magnete gute Therapiechancen. Ihr durchblutungsfördernder Effekt sorgt schon bald für eine spürbare Erwärmung. Im Unterschied zu durchblutungsfördernden Salben haben sie den Vorteil, dass ihre Kraft nicht nachlässt.

○ Begleitende Maßnahmen

Trainieren Sie Ihre Hautblutgefäße! Gehen Sie in ein Zimmer mit angenehmer Temperatur, und legen Sie die Hände für 3 bis 5 Minuten in einen Behälter mit kaltem Wasser. Danach gehen Sie in einen kühlen Raum (Keller oder Badezimmer) und legen die Hände wiederum für etwa 3 bis 5 Minuten in warmes Wasser.

Homöopathie Calcium carbonicum Hahnemanni D6 hilft, wenn der Betroffene nicht nur unter kalten Extremitäten leidet, sondern auch noch viel und säuerlich schwitzt, leicht ins Frieren gerät und oft erkältet ist. Die Dosierung beträgt 3-mal täglich 1 bis 2 Tabletten.
Chininum arsenicosum D4 hilft bei kalten Füßen und Händen, die durch ständige Nervosität und allgemeine Schwäche begleitet werden.
Nux vomica D6 ist angezeigt bei reizbaren Menschen. Die Dosierung beträgt 3-mal täglich 1 bis 2 Tabletten.

Die Anwendung

Prinzipiell kann die Anwendung über normale wechselpolare Magnetfolien erfolgen. Sie haben allerdings den Nachteil, nicht alle Hautbereiche von Füßen und Händen bedecken zu können, vor allem Finger und Zehen werden nicht 100-prozentig abgedeckt. Im Fachhandel erhält man allerdings mittlerweile Handschuhe und Einlegesohlen, die mit wechselpolaren Magneten bestückt werden. Die Sohlen passen in fast jeden Schuh, und die Handschuhe können im Winter unter Fäustlingen versteckt werden. Wer immer wieder mit kalten Füßen und Händen zu kämpfen hat, sollte sich deren Anschaffung sicherlich überlegen.

Karpaltunnel-syndrom

○ Symptome

Das Karpaltunnelsyndrom macht sich durch Taubheit und Schwäche von Daumen, Zeige- und Mittelfinger bemerkbar. Die Hand kribbelt, in schweren Fällen kommt es auch zu starken Schmerzen, die bis in die Schulter ausstrahlen können und in der Nacht besonders stark sind.

○ Ursachen

Hauptursache des Karpaltunnelsyndroms ist eine Verengung des so genannten Handwurzelkanals, durch den die Nervenfasern zu den Fingern verlaufen. Diese Verengung wird ausgelöst durch Wasseransammlungen (Ödeme) im Bereich des Handgelenks, die bei Übergewicht, Stoffwechselstörungen und während der Schwangerschaft vorkommen. Zu den weiteren Auslösern der Erkrankung zählt das längere und wiederholte Arbeiten mit gebeugten Fingern bei angewinkeltem Handgelenk, da auch hierdurch der Handwurzelkanal verengt wird und es zu einer Druckerhöhung an den Fingernerven kommt.

○ Mit Magneten heilen

Das Einreiben mit entzündungshemmenden Salben hilft beim Karpaltunnelsyndrom nur wenig, da sie mit ihren Wirkstoffen nicht tief genug ins Gewebe eindringen können. Die Magnettherapie dagegen entfaltet ihre Energie auch in tieferen Gewebeschichten – und das, ohne dabei das darüber liegende Gewebe zu reizen.

Magnete wirken schmerz- und entzündungshemmend und fördern außerdem im betroffenen Handgelenk den Abtransport überschüssiger Wassermengen. Wie bereits erwähnt (siehe Seite 24), belegt die Studie des amerikanischen Mediziners Dr. Ronald Lawrence eindeutig, wie wirksam die Behandlung mit Dauermagneten bei Patienten mit Karpaltunnelsyndrom ist.

Die Zahl der amerikanischen Golfspieler, die mit Hilfe von Dauermagneten ihre Handgelenkprobleme in den Griff bekommen haben, ist mittlerweile ebenfalls unüberschaubar. Nichtsdestoweniger darf nicht übersehen werden, dass die Magnettherapie lediglich symptomatisch greift. Eine letztendliche Lösung des Karpaltunnelproblems setzt voraus, dass vor allem die Ursachen – z. B. Übergewicht, Überlastung des Handgelenks, falsche Grifftechniken beim Golf- und Tennisspielen – beseitigt werden.

◐ Begleitende Maßnahmen

Homöopathie Arnica D6 ist angezeigt, wenn die Schwellung im Vordergrund steht. Die Dosierung beträgt 3-mal 1 Tablette pro Tag. Rhus toxicodendron D6 hilft (3-mal täglich 1 Tablette), wenn das Gelenk steif ist und sich der Anfangsschmerz bei fortgesetzter Bewegung verbessert.

Vitamin B6 (Pyridoxin) Das Vitamin konnte in einer klinischen Studie an 20 Testpersonen seine Wirkung beim Karpaltunnelsyndrom unter Beweis stellen. Als Stoffwechsel- und Nervenvitamin dämpft es die Übertragung von Schmerzsignalen und hilft beim Abbau von Ödemen. Wissenschaftler empfehlen eine Tagesdosis von 200 Milligramm. Eine solche Menge an Vitamin B6 kann nicht über die Nahrung aufgenommen werden, man muss wohl oder übel auf die Präparate aus der Apotheke oder der Drogerie zurückgreifen.

Die Anwendung

Befestigen Sie wechselpolare Magnetfolien ober- und unterhalb des betroffenen Handgelenks. Die Größe der Folien richtet sich nach der Größe des Handgelenks. Im Fachhandel gibt es aber auch schon spezielle Magnetbandagen für das Karpaltunnelsyndrom (»Thumb & Wrist«, »Wrist Splint«). Sie schränken die Beweglichkeit nur unwesentlich ein, sind aber natürlich nicht ohne weiteres unter einem Hemd zu verstecken.
Die Magnete sollten so lange und so oft wie möglich getragen werden, am besten auch während der Tätigkeit, die zu den Problemen im Handgelenk geführt haben. In jedem Fall sollte man die Magnetfolien in der Nacht anlegen.

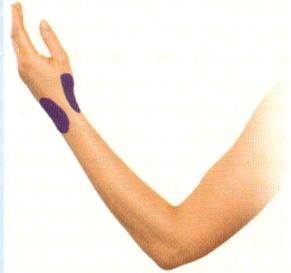

Katerkopf-schmerzen

○ Symptome

Zu den typischen Symptomen eines Katers gehören Übelkeit, Kopfschmerzen sowie Licht- und Geräuschempfindlichkeit. Es kann auch zu Erbrechen und Schwindelanfällen kommen. Die kognitiven Funktionen des Gehirns sind dabei deutlich eingeschränkt, was bis zu 48 Stunden andauern kann – selbst dann, wenn im Blut gar kein Alkohol mehr nachweisbar ist.

○ Ursachen

Von möglichen anderen Ursachen abgesehen, spielt Alkohol natürlich die entscheidende Rolle beim Entstehen der Katerkopfschmerzen. Er destabilisiert die Zellmembranen und den Serotoninspiegel und greift damit direkt in die Schmerzregulierung ein. Darüber hinaus beeinträchtigt er den Schlaf, was das Schmerzempfinden ebenfalls deutlich erhöht.

○ Mit Magneten heilen

Der durch Alkohol verstärkte Mineralienentzug führt auch zu einer Störung des Magnetfeldes in den Zellen. Mit Hilfe von Magneten kann hier wirksam gegengesteuert werden. Auch verkrampften Magenwänden helfen die Magnete auf die Sprünge.

○ Begleitende Maßnahmen

Magnesium und Vitamin E Durch hohen Alkoholkonsum werden die Membranen in den Zellen durchlässiger für Kalzium, das dadurch aus den Zellorganen in das Zellplasma eindringen kann. Infolgedessen wird die Zelle mit Kalzium überladen und gerät in einen Schmerz auslösenden Reizzustand. Magnesium arbeitet nun als Gegenspieler von Kalzium und drückt es gewisser-

Die Anwendung

Die Anwendung erfolgt über zwei wechselpolare, kreisrunde Magnetfolien, jeweils eine auf jede Schläfe. Bei Übelkeit kann ergänzend noch eine rechteckige Folie mit einem kräftigen Magneten (Mindestdicke 1,5 Millimeter) auf den Oberbauch gesetzt werden. Hilfreich können auch die magnetischen Augenmasken (»Eye Masks«) sein, die es mittlerweile im Fachhandel gibt.

maßen wieder zurück in die Zellorgane. Der zelluläre Stress verschwindet und damit auch der Schmerzreiz.

Alkohol sorgt des Weiteren dafür, dass der Organismus verstärkt unter dem Beschuss aggressiver Moleküle – den freien Radikalen – steht. Insofern macht es auch Sinn, ihm einen hochaktiven Radikalefänger wie Vitamin E zuzuführen.

Nehmen Sie noch am Abend nach der Party ein Magnesium-Vitamin-E-Präparat mit mindestens 500 Milligramm Magnesium zu sich (z. B. Bilatin Magnesium + Vitamin E, Buer Vitamin E + Magnesium, Elex Verla 500). Am Morgen wiederholen Sie die Einnahme.

Viel Wasser trinken Alkoholexzesse bringen unseren Wasser- und Mineralienhaushalt durcheinander. Trinken Sie daher so viel Mineralwasser wie möglich, am besten beginnen Sie mit Ihrer Wasserkur schon direkt am Abend der Party.

Ingwer und Koriander Beide Gewürze sind alte Hausmittel gegen Katerkopfschmerzen. Ingwer besitzt ähnlich schmerzstillende Wirkungen wie ASS (in Aspirin), wobei er allerdings schonender für die Magenwände ist. Koriandersamen erhöhen die Aktivität der Entgiftungsenzyme, die dringend für den Alkoholabbau benötigt werden.

1 Teelöffel frisches Ingwerpulver und 1 Teelöffel gemahlene Koriandersamen mit 1 Tasse kochendem Wasser überbrühen. Zugedeckt 10 Minuten ziehen lassen, anschließend abseihen. Trinken Sie 2 Tassen des Ingwer-Koriander-Tees in kleinen Schlucken.

Vergessen Sie alte Vorurteile! Die oft zitierten Sätze »Wein auf Bier, das rat ich dir« und »Bier auf Wein, das lass sein« sind wissenschaftlich so nicht zu halten. Wer seinen alkoholischen Getränkeplan am Abend einer Party fleißig mischt, d. h., wer viel durcheinander trinkt, wird wahrscheinlich am nächsten Morgen leiden müssen – unabhängig von der Reihenfolge der genossenen alkoholischen Getränke.

Das alte Antikaterfrühstück, am Morgen danach einen Salzhering oder einen Rollmops zu essen, bringt nichts. Im Gegenteil: Insofern der Alkohol die Magenwände gereizt hat, sollte man sie jetzt nicht auch noch durch schwer verdauliche Speisen zusätzlich belasten.

Knie-entzündungen

◌ Symptome

Knieentzündungen machen sich durch Schmerzen u. a. im vorderen Kniebereich bemerkbar, die sich verschlimmern, wenn man einige Zeit mit angewinkelten Beinen sitzt. Manchmal hat man auch ein Gefühl der Sperre, dass irgendetwas »im Gelenk steckt«. Bewegt man die Kniescheibe bei entspanntem Knie mit der Hand, ist ein Knirschen spürbar.

◌ Ursachen

Die häufigste Ursache für Kniebeschwerden ist Knorpelverschleiß an der Kniescheibe. Die Kniescheibe liegt an der Vorderseite des Knies in der Sehne des großen Oberschenkelmuskels. Bei Bewegungen des Beins gleitet sie über das Kniegelenk. Um hier einen reibungslosen Verlauf zu gewährleisten, ist sie an ihrer Rückseite mit Knorpelsubstanz überzogen. Bei vielen Menschen ist jedoch die Oberschenkelmuskulatur an der Außenseite stärker ausgeprägt als innen. In der Folge gleitet die Kniescheibe unsymmetrisch über das Gelenk, der Knorpel wird

abgeschliffen, und es kommt zu einer Entzündung – oft mit Reizerguss, der dann die Ursache für die »Beinsperre« ist.

◌ Mit Magneten heilen

Gegenüber den gängigen Rheumasalben besitzt die Magnettherapie den Vorteil, in tiefe Gewebezonen vordringen zu können, ohne dabei die oberen Gewebeschichten zu reizen.

Eine israelische Studie von 1996 konnte zeigen, wie hilfreich Magnete in der Behandlung von Knieentzündungen sind. Die Forscher erzeugten bei 20 Testratten durch ein Spezialverfahren eine Kniegelenkentzündung. Daraufhin wurden zehn Tiere dem Kraftfeld eines Dauermagneten ausgesetzt, zehn Tiere blieben als Kontrollgruppe ohne Behandlung. Eine Woche später zeigten nur zwei der behandelten Tiere noch Entzündungen am Kniegelenk, gegenüber acht in der Kontrollgruppe. Die kranken Tiere der Kontrollgruppe zeigten außerdem deutliche Tendenzen zur Arthritis.

Dennoch setzen Magnete nicht an den Ursachen der Krankheit an, die meist durch eine muskuläre Dysbalance ausgelöst wird.

Die Anwendung

Die Anwendung erfolgt mit wechselpolaren Magnetfolien, die auf der schmerzenden Zone des Kniegelenks befestigt werden. Kleben Sie die Folien am besten bei halb gebeugtem Gelenk auf. Damit wird erreicht, dass Sie beim Strecken und Beugen des Knies von den Magneten nur wenig behindert werden. Die Folien sollten auf jeden Fall nachts, am besten aber auch mehrere Stunden am Tag getragen werden.

Ein weitere Möglichkeit besteht darin, sich im Fachhandel spezielle Magnetmanschetten für das Kniegelenk zu besorgen. Ihr Vorteil: Die Magnetkräfte werden gleichmäßig im Kniegelenk verteilt, außerdem verrutschen sie nicht so leicht wie die Einzelmagnete. Ihr Nachteil: Sie schränken die Bewegungsfreiheit doch erheblich ein – ein Effekt, der gerade bei Kniegelenkentzündungen unerwünscht ist.

Hier muss in jedem Fall zusätzlich ein spezielles Krafttraining durchgeführt werden.

◑ Begleitende Maßnahmen

Muskeltraining Setzen Sie sich auf einen hohen Stuhl oder eine Tischkante. Strecken Sie wechselweise die Beine in die Waagrechte, wobei die Fußspitze extrem nach außen gedreht wird. Führen Sie bei dieser Übung 3-mal 20 Wiederholungen auf jeder Seite aus. Sie können den Trainingsreiz erhöhen, indem Sie Gewichtmanschetten um die Fußgelenke legen.

Homöopathische Mittel Arnica D6 unmittelbar nach dem sportlichen Training oder Wettkampf verhindert die spontan eintretenden Reizergüsse im angeschlagenen Kniegelenk. Die Dosierung beträgt 1 bis 2 Tage lang 3-mal 2 Tabletten täglich.

Calcium fluoratum D6 kräftigt den Kniescheibenknorpel. Die Dosierung beträgt 3-mal täglich 1 bis 2 Tabletten.

Die richtige Vorbeugung Sparen Sie nicht am Schuhwerk! Achten Sie bei Sport- und Straßenschuhen auf bequemen Sitz, Stabilität und ein gutes Fußbett.

Weiche Waldböden eignen sich zum Joggen besser als harter Asphalt. Am schlimmsten für die Gelenke ist jedoch, wenn man beim Laufen ständig den Laufbelag wechselt.

Knochenhaut-entzündung

○ Symptome

Bei einer Knochenhautentzündung treten vor allem unter körperlicher Belastung Schmerzen z. B. an der Innenseite des Schienbeins auf. Wenn man mit dem Finger über die Innenkante des Schienbeins wandert, bemerkt man Unebenheiten und einen Druckschmerz.

○ Ursachen

Die Knochenhaut am Schienbein wird von zahlreichen Blutgefäßen und Nervenenden durchzogen. Aus diesem Grund reagiert sie sehr empfindlich auf mechanische Belastungen. Knochenhautentzündungen treffen vor allem Sportler, die häufig den Bodenbelag wechseln. Die Entzündungen bereiten vor allem beim Laufen große Schmerzen. Dadurch verstärkt sich beim Sportler die Neigung, den Fuß mehr auf der Außenkante aufzusetzen, um die Belastung des Schienbeins zu verringern. In der Folge kommt es jedoch zu riskanten Fehlbelastungen im Kniegelenk, mit dementsprechenden Risiken.

○ Mit Magneten heilen

Magnetfolien besitzen bei der Knochenhautentzündung recht große Heilungschancen, da die Knochenhaut nur dünn mit Gewebeschichten bedeckt ist und dadurch für die Magnetkräfte gut erreichbar ist.
Die Folien verbessern die Durchblutung und stabilisieren das Magnetfeld des erkrankten Gewebes. Erste Schmerzlinderungen stellen sich schon nach wenigen Stunden ein, der Heilungsverlauf der Entzündung insgesamt dauert jedoch auch unter Magnettherapie recht lange.

Die Anwendung

Für die Anwendung nimmt man länglich-rechteckige Folien mit wechselpolarem Magnetfeld, die in Längsrichtung auf dem schmerzenden Schienbein befestigt werden. Sie sollten möglichst durchgehend Tag und Nacht aufgeklebt bleiben.
Die Heilung einer Knochenhautentzündung kann lange dauern, mitunter bis zu sechs Wochen. Nach Abklingen der Beschwerden sollte der Einsatz der Folien außerdem noch für ein paar Tage fortgesetzt werden.

☉ Begleitende Maßnahmen

Möglichst früh mit der Therapie beginnen Knochenhautentzündungen sind außerordentlich hartnäckig und haben schon so manche Sportkarriere zur Tortur gemacht. Die Therapiechancen sind am größten, je früher mit der Behandlung begonnen wird.

Fangopackungen Die Packungen lindern den Schmerz und fördern die Heilung, sollten aber nur zum Abend angewandt werden. Legen Sie den Fango direkt auf die betroffene Stelle, und bedecken Sie ihn mit einem Leinen- und einem Handtuch. Die Anwendung sollte mindestens 1 Stunde dauern. Man spürt eine deutliche Erwärmung und Schmerzlinderung. Entfernen Sie schließlich die Packung, und legen Sie sich danach noch für 30 Minuten ins warme Bett.

Ruhe! Eine Trainings- bzw. Laufpause von mindestens 1 Woche ist bei einer Knochenhautentzündung unvermeidbar. Sie können sich mit gelenkschonenderen Sportarten wie Radfahren, Schwimmen, Gymnastik oder Krafttraining in Form halten.

Homöopathische Mittel Arnica D6 mindert die Schwellung und sollte möglichst unmittelbar nach dem Training oder Wettkampf eingenommen werden. Die Dosierung beträgt 3-mal 5 bis 10 Tropfen täglich.

Ruta D6 hilft bei Knochenschmerzen und Entzündungen, deren Schmerzen sich unter Bewegung verschlimmern, und ist daher bei Knochenhautentzündungen ein Mittel der ersten Wahl. Die Dosierung beträgt täglich 3-mal 1 bis 2 Tabletten.

Übergewicht oder Plattfuß? Die meisten Sportler hören es nicht gerne, wenn man ihre Knochenhautschmerzen mit Übergewicht oder Plattfüßen in Verbindung bringt. Nichtsdestoweniger erledigt sich so manches Schienbeinproblem von selbst, wenn das Gewicht reduziert oder das Schuhwerk mit Einlagen unterstützt wird.

Die richtige Vorbeugung Sparen Sie auch hier nicht am Schuhwerk. Weiche Waldböden eignen sich zum Joggen besser als harter Asphalt. Am schlimmsten für die Gelenke ist aber der ständige Wechsel im Laufbelag. Versuchen Sie, den Wechsel nicht abrupt zu vollziehen, sondern geben Sie Ihren Schienbeinen die Chance, sich langsam an die neuen Beläge zu gewöhnen.

Läuferknie

○ Symptome

Das Läuferknie zeigt sich durch Schmerzen im Außenbereich des Kniegelenks, und zwar am Oberschenkelknochen auf Höhe der Kniescheibe. Der Schmerz tritt vor allem bei längeren Läufen auf und kann so heftig sein, dass der Athlet den Lauf unterbrechen muss. Der Schmerz lässt dann zwar nach, doch beim Weiterlaufen kehrt er sofort wieder zurück.

○ Ursachen

Der Sportler läuft zu sehr auf den Außenkanten seiner Füße. Dadurch reibt sich das so genannte iliotibiale Band (es erstreckt sich an der Oberschenkelaußenseite von der Hüfte bis zum Kniegelenk) am Oberschenkelknochen, und es kommt zu einer Entzündung.

Die Schmerzen beim Laufen können den Sportler dazu veranlassen, das betroffene Knie in einer Schonhaltung beim Laufen vorwärts zu führen. Dadurch verändern sich die orthopädischen Verhältnisse im Bewegungsapparat jedoch endgültig zu ihrem Nachteil. Schwere Schäden (vor allem an Kniekapsel und Meniskus) können die Folge sein.

○ Mit Magneten heilen

Zu den Erfolgen der Magnettherapie bei Sportverletzungen und chronischen Entzündungen existieren zahlreiche Fallberichte. Die Magnetkräfte fördern die Durchblutung, hemmen Entzündungen und lindern – oft bereits nach wenigen Stunden – die Schmerzen.

Dennoch bekämpfen die Magnete lediglich die schmerzhaften Entzündungen am Kniegelenk, die Ursachen der Krankheit (meistens eine Dysbalance in der Wadenmuskulatur) werden hingegen nicht behandelt. Hier muss in jedem Fall zusätzlich ein spezielles Krafttraining durchgeführt werden.

○ Begleitende Maßnahmen

Weniger ist mehr Senken Sie die Laufbelastung. Versuchen Sie, Ihre Ausdauer beispielsweise mit Fahrradfahren aufzubauen.

Kräftigung der Muskeln auf der Wadenaußenseite Setzen Sie sich auf einen Stuhl, die Beine im rechten Winkel, die Knie sind etwa 20 Zentimeter voneinander

Die Anwendung

Die Anwendung erfolgt mit wechselpolaren Magnetfolien, die auf der schmerzenden Zone des Kniegelenks (meistens auf der Außenseite) befestigt werden. Kleben Sie die Folien am besten bei halb gebeugtem Gelenk auf. Damit wird erreicht, dass Sie beim Strecken und Beugen des Knies von den Magneten nicht behindert werden. Die Folien sollten auf jeden Fall nachts, am besten aber auch während des Lauftrainings getragen werden. Der Fachhandel bietet zwar mittlerweile auch Magnetmanschetten für das Knie, doch die darin angeordneten Magnete treffen meistens nicht die Zonen, die beim Läuferknie betroffen sind. In diesem Fall sind daher die Einzelmagnete sinnvoller. Sie lassen dem Athleten außerdem viel Bewegungsfreiheit, ganz zu schweigen davon, dass sie unter jeder Trainingshose versteckt werden können, ohne aufzufallen.

entfernt. Pressen Sie die Knie für 10 bis 15 Sekunden kräftig gegeneinander, wobei die Fußinnenseiten auf dem Boden bleiben und der Außenrist deutlich angehoben wird. Machen Sie diese Übung mindestens 5-, besser 10-mal pro Tag. Man kann sie auch bequem und zu jeder Zeit im Bürostuhl durchführen. **Homöopathische Mittel** Arnica D6 ist ein bewährtes Mittel bei allen Verletzungen infolge von Überanstrengung. Die Dosierung beträgt 3-mal täglich 1 bis 2 Tabletten. Bryonia D6 hilft gegen Schmerzen, die nur bei Bewegung schlimmer werden. Die Dosierung beträgt 3-mal täglich 10 Tropfen.

Die richtige Vorbeugung Nehmen Sie sich Zeit für den Kauf Ihres Laufschuhs, und sparen Sie nicht am Geld. Der richtige Schuh muss nicht nur bequem sein; er soll außerdem das Außenkantenlaufen des Fußes so weit wie möglich verhindern. Lassen Sie sich von einem erfahrenen Läuferkollegen beim Schuhkauf begleiten, der Sie mit den verschiedenen Schuhen beim Laufen beobachtet.

Meiden Sie Bergabläufe. Sie bringen nichts für die Kondition und belasten die Gelenke unnötig. Versuchen Sie, nur auf einem Belag zu laufen. Häufige Belagwechsel fördern Entzündungen an Sehnen und Gelenken.

Magen-schmerzen

○ Symptome

Magenschmerzen beschränken sich auf den oberen Bauchbereich und sind oft von einem Druckgefühl begleitet. Halten sie länger an, sollte der Hausarzt konsultiert werden.
Wenn die Bauchschmerzen plötzlich und heftig auftreten und mit Erbrechen, starkem Aufgeblähtsein, Fieber, keuchender Atmung oder rasendem Puls einhergehen, sollte auf jeden Fall der Notarzt gerufen werden.

○ Ursachen

Die häufigste Ursache ist ein überforderter Magen nach zu vielen, zu fetten oder verdorbenen Speisen.

Die Funktionen der Magenwände stehen außerdem in engem Kontakt zur Psyche. Situationen, die einen Geborgenheitsverlust beinhalten, ein Zuwachs an Verantwortung oder unterdrückte Aggressionen gehören zu den typischen psychischen Belastungssituationen, die auf den Magen schlagen.

○ Mit Magneten heilen

Magnetfelder entspannen die Magenwände und schaffen außerdem ungünstige Lebensbedingungen für parasitäre Bakterien. Ein weiterer Vorteil der Magnete besteht darin, dass sie die Fett- und Muskelschichten im Bauch durchdringen und dadurch keine Probleme haben, ihre heilenden Energien auch im Magen selbst zu entfalten.

Die Anwendung

Die Anwendung erfolgt über wechselpolare Magnetfolien, die eine möglichst große Oberfläche (mindestens 50 mal 120 Millimeter) haben sollten. Befestigen Sie diese Folien auf einer gedachten Senkrechtlinie zwischen Bauchnabel und Brustbein, die Unterkante liegt etwa zwei Finger breit über dem Nabel.

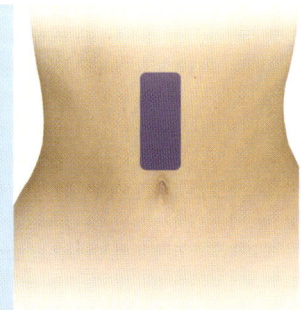

◐ **Begleitende Maßnahmen**

Kamille, Minze und Melisse Kamille wirkt entzündungshemmend, außerdem schützt und stärkt sie die Schleimhäute. Minze setzt die Empfindlichkeit der Magenschleimhaut gegen Übelkeit auslösende Reize herab. Außerdem hat sie desinfizierende Eigenschaften. Bei Melisse steht schließlich die beruhigende und krampflösende Wirkung auf die Magenwände im Vordergrund. Brauen Sie sich einen Tee nach folgendem Rezept. Jeweils 1 Teelöffel Kamillenblüten, Pfefferminzblätter und Melissenblätter mit 1/4 Liter kochendem Wasser übergießen, 10 Minuten ziehen lassen, abseihen und zu den Mahlzeiten in kleinen Schlucken trinken.

Homöopathie Nux vomica D6 hilft bei Sodbrennen, Völlegefühl und Schmerzen im Oberbauch. Die Dosierung beträgt 3-mal täglich 1 bis 2 Tabletten vor den Mahlzeiten.

Magnesium phosphoricum D6 ist angezeigt bei Krämpfen im Bauch, die durch Druck und Wärme nachlassen, und bei starken Blähungen. Die Dosierung beträgt stündlich 1 Tablette bis zum Abklingen der Schmerzen.

Ignatia D6 wirkt bei Beschwerden infolge von seelischen Belastungen wie z. B. Trauer und Kummer, die auf den Magen geschlagen sind. Die Dosierung bei Ignatia D6 beträgt 3-mal täglich 1 bis 2 Tabletten.

Carbo vegetabilis Pentarkan hilft bei plötzlich auftretenden Magenkrämpfen, die von Aufstoßen oder Blähungen begleitet werden. Die Dosierung beträgt stündlich 1 Tablette bis zum Abklingen der Beschwerden.

Staphisagria D6 ist besonders geeignet für introvertierte Menschen, die angestauten Ärger und Konflikte im Magen »verarbeiten«. Die Dosierung beträgt 3-mal täglich 1 bis 2 Tabletten.

Die richtige Vorbeugung Machen Sie Ihren Aggressionen, Ihrem Ärger und anderen angestauten Gefühlen richtig Luft, anstatt sie in sich hineinzufressen.

Achten Sie auf eine magenfreundliche Ernährung. Trinken Sie viel (mindestens 2 Liter Flüssigkeit pro Tag), und meiden Sie fetthaltige Speisen. Ballaststoffe (in Vollkornreis, Getreideprodukten, Schwarz- und Knäckebrot) und basische Kost (z. B. Kartoffeln und Möhren) eignen sich gut bei Magenbeschwerden.

Menstruations-beschwerden

○ Symptome

Zu den Menstruationsbeschwerden gehören eine starke Blutung und krampfartige Schmerzen im Unterleib. Als mögliche Komplikationen können sich eine schleichende Blutarmut mit Konzentrations- und Kreislaufschwäche einstellen.

○ Ursachen

Menstruationsbeschwerden können durch ungewöhnliche Gewebebildungen in der Gebärmutter, Hormonschwankungen oder auch durch bestimmte Verhütungsmittel wie das Intrauterinpessar (»Spirale«) und die Antibabypille verursacht werden.
Oft spielen aber auch psychische Faktoren eine Rolle. Auch heute noch wird die Regelblutung von vielen Frauen schamhaft verschwiegen – mit der Folge, dass Körper und Psyche verspannen und mit starken Menstruationsbeschwerden reagieren.

○ Mit Magneten heilen

Menstruationsbeschwerden haben immer etwas mit Verkrampfungen und Verspannungen zu tun. Hierbei können Magnete hilfreich sein. Wie hilfreich, zeigt eine wissenschaftliche Studie der Universität Seoul. Elf Frauen, die unter starken Regelschmerzen litten, wurden mit Dauermagneten in einer Stärke von 800 bis 1200 Gauß behandelt. Eine zweite Gruppe von zwölf Frauen mit gleichem Krankheitsbild erhielt lediglich Plazebomagnete.

Drei Stunden nach Beginn der Magnetbehandlung und anschließend noch einmal drei Stunden nach Entfernen der Magnete bzw. Plazebomagnete wurden die behandelten Frauen zu ihren Beschwerden befragt. Die erste Gruppe berichtete im Gegensatz zur Kontrollgruppe durchweg von erheblichen Besserungen.

Das Besondere an dieser Studie ist, dass die Frauen unter dauerhafter Beobachtung standen, so dass sie nicht über irgendeinen Test herausfinden konnten, ob sie einen echten oder nur einen scheinbaren Magneten an ihrem Körper trugen.

Weiterhin wurde durch den Test bewiesen, dass Magnete ihre schmerzlindernden Kräfte bereits innerhalb weniger Stunden entfalten können.

Die Anwendung

Die Anwendung erfolgt über großflächige wechselpolare Magnetfolien, die auf dem unteren Bauchbereich aufgeklebt werden. Am besten sollten sie schon kurz vor dem erwarteten Regeltermin zum Einsatz kommen.

◔ Begleitende Maßnahmen

Frauenmanteltee (Alchemilla vulgaris) Die Heilpflanze hilft bei Menstruationsbeschwerden, die von starken Krämpfen begleitet werden. Längerfristig stärken Kuren aus Frauenmantel die Gebärmutter, wodurch bei den Monatsblutungen weniger Blutverluste und Schmerzen auftreten. Trinken Sie 3 Tassen Frauenmanteltee pro Tag. Bei starken Unterleibskoliken beginnen Sie mit der Anwendung etwa 3 Tage vor Beginn der Monatsregel. 2 Teelöffel getrocknete Frauenmantelblätter mit 1 Tasse kochendem Wasser überbrühen. 10 Minuten ziehen lassen und anschließend abseihen.

Gänsefingerkraut (Potentilla anserina) Die traditionsreiche Heilpflanze ist auch unter dem Namen »Krampfkraut« bekannt.

Kaum eine andere Pflanze wirkt besser bei Krämpfen während der Menstruation. Beginnen Sie mit der Gänsefingerkur (3 Tassen Gänsefingerkrauttee pro Tag) etwa 3 Tage vor dem erwarteten Regeltermin.

1 Esslöffel getrocknetes Gänsefingerkraut mit 1 Tasse heißem Wasser überbrühen. 10 Minuten zugedeckt ziehen lassen, anschließend abseihen.

Eine weitere wirksame Anwendungsmöglichkeit ist die Zubereitung mit Milch.

1 1/2 Teelöffel getrocknetes Gänsefingerkraut mit 1 Glas Milch aufkochen, 10 Minuten ziehen lassen und abseihen. So heiß wie möglich trinken.

Schafgarbe (Achillea millefolium) Die Schafgarbe enthält neben entkrampfenden ätherischen Ölen und Flavonoiden das natürliche Schmerzmittel Salizylsäure. Sie wirkt recht schnell und kann daher auch zum Einsatz kommen, wenn die Regel bereits begonnen hat. Am schnellsten wirkt ein Schafgarbenbad.

1 Hand voll des getrockneten Krauts mit einem Leinensäckchen ins Badewasser geben. Die Badedauer sollte 10 bis 15 Minuten nicht überschreiten.

Migräne

○ Symptome

Die Migräne ist ein meistens
halbseitig auftretender Kopf-
schmerz. Als Begleitsymptome
können sich Übelkeit, Erbrechen, Lichtscheu, Sehstörungen
(z. B. Augenflimmern) und
Sprachstörungen einstellen.
Bei einigen Patienten kündigt
sich die eigentliche Schmerz-
attacke vorher durch eine Aura
an: Sternchen vor den Augen,
Einschränkungen des Gesichts-
felds, Schwindel, Hautkribbeln
oder auch Sprachprobleme.

○ Ursachen

Bei Erwachsenen sind es vor
allem kopfgesteuerte Menschen
mit einem übersteigerten Hang
zum »Zerdenken«, die von Migräne heimgesucht werden.
Dafür sprechen auch die Beobachtungen von Physiologen,
die beim Gehirn von Migränepatienten ein überdurchschnittlich aktives EEG (Elektroenze-
phalogramm) messen konnten.
Migränepatienten stehen sozusagen fortwährend unter Strom.
Die Migräne bei Kindern wird
hauptsächlich durch Überlastungen wie langes Fernsehen und
Computerspielen ausgelöst. Häufiger Ärger und Stress in Schule
und Familie können ebenfalls zu
Migräne führen.
Wenn Kinder fast täglich unter
Migräneattacken leiden, kann
auch eine Unverträglichkeit in
Bezug auf bestimmte Nahrungsmittel vorliegen. Besonders Kon-
servierungs- und Lebensmittel-
farbstoffe, die sich in Limonade
oder Colagetränken verbergen,
Süßigkeiten wie Gummibärchen
und Schokolade sowie Fertigge-
richte sind klassische Migräne-
auslöser. Hier kann eine Ernährungsumstellung hilfreich sein.

○ Mit Magneten heilen

In der japanischen Medizin wird
über Therapieerfolge mit Dauermagneten (mit nordpolaren Magnetpflastern) berichtet. Als wissenschaftlich gesichert gilt, dass
Dauermagnete die Spannung in
den Blutgefäßwänden und damit
den Blutfluss beeinflussen – ein
Faktor, der für die Migräne von
großer Bedeutung sein kann.

○ Begleitende Maßnahmen

Pestwurz (Petasites hybridus)
Pestwurz konnte in einer Studie
die Zahl der Migräneattacken
und Migränetage pro Monat um

56 Prozent senken. Als Teeaufguss eignet die Pflanze sich aufgrund ihrer giftigen Alkaloide jedoch nicht! Verwenden Sie nur Extrakte, bei denen die Alkaloide durch flüssiges Kohlendioxid herausgewaschen wurden. Richten Sie sich bei der Dosierung nach der Packungsbeilage.

Die Anwendung anderer Schmerzmittel sollte während der Pestwurzanwendung unterbrochen oder zumindestens stark reduziert werden. Die Kombination von Magnettherapie und Pestwurz ist jedoch unproblematisch und kann ausgesprochen hilfreich sein.

Die Anwendung

Laut japanischer Magnetlehre erfolgt die Anwendung am besten über nordpolare Magnetpflaster, die auf den klassischen Akupunkturpunkten der Migräne befestigt werden. Eine andere Möglichkeit besteht darin, mit den Nordpolmagneten die betreffenden Punkte für einige Minuten zu massieren. Auf diese Weise werden Magnettherapie und Akupressur miteinander kombiniert. Die einzelnen Punkte sind:

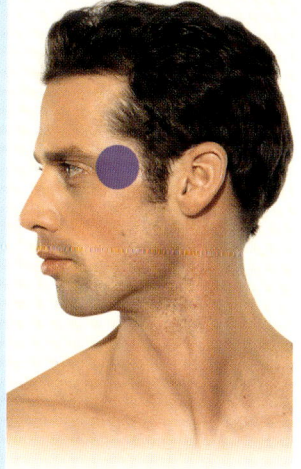

- Tai Yang (»Die Sonne«). Er liegt etwa eineinhalb Finger breit hinter und knapp unterhalb des äußersten Endes der Augenbrauen. Suchen Sie diesen Punkt mit Hilfe eines Spiegels. Sie befinden sich an der richtigen Stelle, wenn Sie eine Vertiefung in der Schläfe spüren.
- Pian Tou Dian. Dieser Punkt liegt am Mittelgelenk des Ringfingers, und zwar auf der dem kleinen Finger zugewandten Seite.
- LU 7. Dieser Akupunkturpunkt liegt auf der Innenseite des Unterarms, etwa zwei Finger breit vor dem Handgelenk und direkt neben den Sehnen auf der Daumenseite.

Muskel-hartspann

○ Symptome

Als Symptome zeigen sich vor allem morgens und abends harte und verspannte Muskeln.

○ Ursachen

Die Muskeln brauchen eine gewisse Zeit, um sich nach einer intensiven Belastung wieder zu erholen. Wird diese Zeit unterschritten, kommt es zum Mangel an wichtigen Substanzen wie Kalium und zu einer Ansammlung von Stoffwechselzwischenprodukten wie Milchsäure. Das Gehirn reagiert auf diese Veränderungen damit, dass es die Muskeln unter hohe Spannung setzt, um sie vor weiteren Überlastungen zu schützen.
Es sind nicht nur Sportler, die ihren Muskeln oftmals zu wenig Pausen gönnen. Auch im Büroalltag werden viele Muskeln zu lange belastet. Dazu gehören vor allem die Muskeln im Nackenbereich, in den Hüftbeugen, in den Unterarmen und die tiefen Rückenmuskeln.
Muskelhärten können aber auch psychischen Ursprungs sein. Die Muskelspannung wird vom zentralen Nervensystem kontrolliert und reagiert sehr sensibel auf psychische Belastungen.
Angst z. B. führt zu einer starken Spannung in all den Muskeln, die zu einer raschen Flucht benötigt werden. Dazu gehören vor allem die Muskeln in den Hüftbeugen, auf der Rückseite der Oberschenkel und den Waden.

○ Mit Magneten heilen

Magnete lösen die Muskelspannung, fördern die Durchblutung und unterstützen dadurch den Abtransport von Stoffwechselzwischenprodukten und geschädigtem Zellmaterial aus den verhärteten Muskeln. Darüber hinaus wirken Magnete auch schmerzhemmend.

Die Anwendung

Die Anwendung erfolgt am besten über großflächige Folien (50 mal 120 Millimeter) mit wechselpolarem Magnetfeld. Befestigen Sie diese Folien direkt über dem schmerzhaften Muskelbereich. Sie sollten möglichst lange, also Tag und Nacht, getragen werden. Nach ein bis zwei Tagen sollten erste Besserungen eintreten.

⟡ Begleitende Maßnahmen

Homöopathie Rhus toxicodendron D6 verbessert die Muskelversorgung und eignet sich vor allem bei Muskelhartspann infolge von sportlicher Überanstrengung. Die Dosierung beträgt 3-mal täglich 1 bis 2 Tabletten. Plantival ist ein Kombinationspräparat, das sich besonders bei Versagensängsten mit psychisch bedingtem Hartspann eignet. Die Dosierung beträgt 4-mal täglich 1 Dragee.

Fangopackungen Der Mineralschlamm lindert den Schmerz und verbessert die Muskeldurchblutung; er sollte aber nur abends angewendet werden. Legen Sie den Fango direkt auf die betroffene Stelle, und bedecken Sie ihn mit einem Leinen- und einem Handtuch. Die Anwendung sollte mindestens 1 Stunde dauern. Legen Sie sich anschließend für 30 Minuten ins warme Bett.

Aromatherapie Düfte wirken stark auf die unbewussten Steuerungsmechanismen unserer Muskelspannung. Bei angst- und stressbedingtem Hartspann eignen sich vor allem die Düfte von Lavendel, Neroli, Weihrauch und Ysop. Bringen Sie ein paar Tropfen des jeweiligen Öls auf einen Duftstein in Ihrem Wohnzimmer. Sie können auch die besonders harten Muskelpartien direkt mit dem Öl beträufeln, bevor Sie zur Arbeit gehen. Die Öle verbreiten ein angenehmes Aroma und werden Ihre Kollegen nicht stören.

Die richtige Vorbeugung Machen Sie nicht den Fehler, Ihre Ängste krampfhaft verstecken zu wollen. Wer sie verbirgt, verdrängt sie ins Unbewusste, und von dort aus senden sie ständig Signale an Ihre Muskeln. Seien Sie vor allem sich selbst gegenüber ehrlich, was Ihre Schwächen und Ängste angeht.

Gönnen Sie Ihren Muskeln ausreichend Pausen zur Erholung. Bei der Arbeit sollten Sie 5 Minuten pro Stunde für Bewegung und Entspannung aufwenden, und wenn es nur der Gang zum Kaffeeautomaten oder zur Toilette ist.

Auch beim Sport sollten Sie sich nicht überanstrengen. Trainieren Sie nicht über Ihren Muskelkaterschmerz hinweg! Vermeiden Sie außerdem Trainingsbelastungen, bei denen gezielt nur einzelne Muskelgruppen beansprucht werden.

Muskelkater

Symptome

Der typische Schmerz bei Muskelkater tritt erst etwa 24 bis 36 Stunden nach einer intensiven sportlichen Belastung auf und erstreckt sich über relativ große Muskelflächen. Er setzt deshalb so spät ein, weil die Muskelfasern in ihrem Inneren keine Sinneszellen besitzen, die das Gehirn über Schäden informieren können. Die Sinneszellen befinden sich am Faserrand, was die Informationsübertragung entsprechend verzögert.

Ursachen

Der Muskelkater ist die schmerzhafte Folge von mikroskopisch kleinen Verletzungen. Diese Schäden werden durch nachgebende Bewegungen (z. B. beim Liegestütz und Bergabwandern) und durch hohe Milchsäurekonzentrationen provoziert, die aufgrund zu hoher Belastungen oder bei schlecht Trainierten auftreten.

Mit Magneten heilen

Magnete fördern die Durchblutung und unterstützen dadurch den Abtransport von Stoffwechselzwischenprodukten und geschädigtem Zellmaterial aus den »verkaterten« Muskeln. Darüber hinaus wirken sie schmerzhemmend.

Insofern Magnete die Durchblutung fördern, kann es sinnvoll sein, sie als Muskelkaterprophylaxe anzuwenden. Wer also ein hartes Training plant, bei dem er mit Muskelkater rechnet, sollte sich – wenn es das Training zulässt – zur Vorbeugung einige Magnetfolien auf die Muskeln kleben. Aber Vorsicht: Die Durchblutung durch ein intensives Aufwärmprogramm kann ein Magnet nicht ersetzen!

Begleitende Maßnahmen

Aromatherapie Bestimmte Düfte lindern den Schmerz und entspannen den Muskel. Hierzu gehören Kamille, Lavendel, Majoran und Wacholder. 5 bis 8 Tropfen des jeweiligen Öls in eine Duftschale oder Duftlampe träufeln, die im Wohn- oder Schlafzimmer aufgestellt wird.

Massagen mit Johanniskrautöl Diese Massagen wirken schmerzlindernd und entspannend. Hochwertiges Johanniskrautöl erhalten Sie in Reformhäusern und in Drogerien.

Die Anwendung

Die Anwendung erfolgt am besten über großflächige Magnetfolien (mindestens 50 mal 120 Millimeter) mit wechselpolarem Magnetfeld. Befestigen Sie diese Folien direkt über dem schmerzhaften Muskelbereich. Sie sollten möglichst lange, also Tag und Nacht, getragen werden. Nach ein bis zwei Tagen sollten die Schmerzen verschwunden sein.

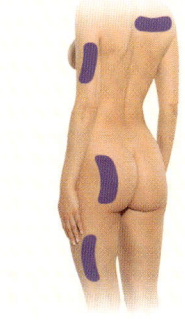

Einige Tropfen des Öls auf die Haut träufeln und mit kreisenden Bewegungen sorgfältig einmassieren. Der Massagedruck sollte nicht schmerzhaft sein. Die Anwendung kann nach ein paar Stunden wiederholt werden. Sie eignet sich vorzüglich zur Ergänzung der Magnettherapie. Die Magnete müssen natürlich während der Massage entfernt werden.

Homöopathische Mittel Arnica D6 lindert die beim Muskelkater auftretenden Schwellungen. Am besten nehmen Sie die ersten 2 Tabletten unmittelbar nach der sportlichen Tätigkeit ein, wenn Sie einen Muskelkater befürchten. Anschließend sollten Sie 3 Tage lang 3-mal 2 Tabletten einnehmen.

Rhus toxicodendron D6 hilft gegen Schmerzen, die bei Bewegung besser und bei Berührung schlimmer werden. Die Dosierung des Präparats beträgt 3-mal täglich 2 Tabletten.

Die richtige Vorbeugung Trainieren Sie regelmäßig. Ein gut trainierter Körper kann auf nachgebende Muskelbelastungen besser reagieren und produziert weniger Milchsäure.

Darüber hinaus sollten Sie sich vor dem Training mindestens 20 Minuten lang aufwärmen. Nach besonders harten Belastungen empfiehlt sich eine Cool-down-Phase, die den Abtransport der Milchsäure vorantreibt. In der Regel reicht dazu ein gemächliches Jogging schon vollkommen aus.

Muskelkrämpfe

○ Symptome

Der Muskel verharrt in einem schmerzhaften Spannungszustand, der vom Betroffenen durch eigenen Willen nicht mehr gelöst werden kann.

○ Ursachen

Meistens sind eine Unterversorgung des Muskels mit Flüssigkeit, ein Mineralienmangel, Überanstrengung, psychische Blockaden oder ein Kälteschock die Ursachen; aber auch Diabetes mellitus oder Erkrankungen der Wirbelsäule können zu Muskelkrämpfen führen.

Am häufigsten sind Waden- und Zehenmuskeln von Krämpfen betroffen. Auf ihnen lastet ein Großteil des Körpergewichts. Der Wadenmuskel zieht sich außerdem über zwei Gelenke, wobei er auf das erstgenannte streckend, auf das letztere beugend wirkt. Bei bestimmten Bewegungsabläufen (wie etwa beim Brustschwimmen, wo das Kniegelenk mit angezogenen Füßen ständig gebeugt und gestreckt wird) wird er deshalb schlecht durchblutet und kann schließlich verkrampfen.

Auch die Psyche spielt bei Krämpfen eine große Rolle. Je weniger wir psychisch hinter einer Bewegung stehen, desto mehr neigen die an ihr beteiligten Muskeln zum Krampf.

○ Erste Hilfe

Setzen Sie den verkrampften Muskel unter kräftige, aber nicht ruckartige Dehnung. Den Wadenmuskel dehnen Sie am besten in Rückenlage bei gebeugtem Kniegelenk, die Fußspitzen werden dabei behutsam nach oben gezogen. Der Wadenkrampf verschwindet schneller, wenn Sie sich vor der Dehnung für 5 bis 10 Sekunden einen Beutel Eis in die Kniekehle drücken. Im Anschluss an diese spontane Kühlung kommt es schlagartig zu einer Erweiterung der Blutgefäße in Richtung Unterschenkel.

○ Mit Magneten heilen

Heilmagnete verbessern die Durchblutung und fördern die Regeneration des verkrampften Muskels. Außerdem wirken sie krampflösend und schmerzhemmend. Durch regelmäßige Magnetanwendungen lässt sich insgesamt die Krampfneigung der Muskulatur verringern.

Begleitende Maßnahmen

Homöopathie Cuprum metallicum C200 wirkt gegen den akuten Krampfanfall. Die Dosierung bei einem Krampf beträgt eine einmalige Gabe von 5 Tropfen. Cuprum aceticum D6 hilft längerfristig bei immer wiederkehrenden Krämpfen in der Wade. Die Dosierung beträgt täglich 3-mal 1 bis 2 Tabletten. Zincum valerianicum D3 hilft bei Krämpfen, die nachts auftreten. Die Dosierung beträgt 2 Tabletten vor dem Schlafengehen.

Die Anwendung

Nach einem akuten Krampf befestigen Sie eine oder mehrere großflächige Wechselpolmagnetfolien (mindestens 50 mal 120 Millimeter) auf der schmerzenden Stelle (sofern die Größe des Muskels dies zulässt). Die Magnetbehandlung sollte nach Abklingen der Beschwerden prophylaktisch noch einige Tage fortgesetzt werden. Überhaupt empfiehlt es sich zur Vorbeugung weiterer Krämpfe, die gefährdeten Muskelzüge nachts und auch einige Stunden am Tag mit wechselpolaren Magnetfolien zu behandeln.

Die richtige Vorbeugung Achten Sie auf eine ausreichende Zufuhr an den Mineralien Magnesium und Kalium.
Bei starker Hitze und großem Flüssigkeitsverlust sollten Sie ruhig zu dementsprechenden Präparaten greifen (beispielsweise Magnesium Tonil, Magnesium Verla oder Eunova forte). Ansonsten finden sich beide Mineralien vor allem in Gemüse und Nüssen. Es gibt auch einige Mineralwässer, die überdurchschnittlich viel Kalium und Magnesium enthalten; achten Sie auf die Flaschenaufschriften. Trinken Sie vor allem im Sommer mehr, als Ihr Durstgefühl eigentlich verlangt (mindestens 2, besser 3 Liter pro Tag). Das Durstgefühl ist gewissermaßen ein physiologischer Spätzünder, es stellt sich erst dann ein, wenn im Körper bereits ein starker Flüssigkeitsmangel vorherrscht. Achten Sie auch bei Ihrer Kleidung darauf, dass das Blut ungehindert im Körper fließen kann. Socken mit eng anliegenden Bündchen beispielsweise schnüren die Blutzufuhr zu den Zehen ab, wo es dann zu ärgerlichen und vor allem schmerzhaften Krämpfen kommen kann.

Muskelzerrung

⊙ Symptome

Zunächst ist nur ein leichtes Ziehen im Muskel spürbar. Schon bald kommt es jedoch zu Verkrampfungen, und nach einigen Stunden kann sich sogar eine Verfärbung an der gezerrten Stelle zeigen. Wenn auch eine Unterbrechung im Muskelverlauf spürbar sein sollte, muss der Arzt hinzugezogen werden.

Bei der Zerrung handelt es sich um einen Muskelfaserriss ersten Grades, d. h., dass weniger als fünf Prozent der Muskelfasern gerissen sind. Demgegenüber sind bei einem Muskelfaserriss zweiten Grades mehr als fünf Prozent der Fasern durchtrennt; oftmals ist im Muskel eine deutliche Lücke zu spüren.

⊙ Ursachen

Zerrungen treten besonders häufig bei Muskeln auf, die über mehrere Gelenke ziehen (wie etwa die Waden-, Oberschenkel- und Oberarmmuskeln). Ein ungenügendes Warm-up, kalte Umgebungstemperaturen, Stress, bestehende Infekte und Muskelkater begünstigen die Entstehung von Zerrungen.

⊙ Erste Hilfe

Kältekompressen Kalte Kompressen verhindern Schwellungen und lindern den ersten Schmerz. Wickeln Sie ein paar Eiswürfel in ein Handtuch, und pressen Sie es auf die schmerzende Stelle. Die Kälteanwendung sollte mindestens 30 Minuten dauern und auch später immer wieder für längere Zeit wiederholt werden. Als Alternative kommen kommerzielle Kältekompressen aus der Apotheke infrage. Deren Anwendung entnehmen Sie bitte der Packungsbeilage.

⊙ Mit Magneten heilen

Magnete fördern die Durchblutung des gezerrten Muskels und unterstützen dadurch den Abtransport von Stoffwechselzwischenprodukten und geschädigten Zellen. Darüber hinaus lindern sie den Schmerz. Magnetfolien können auch zur Therapie von Muskelfaserrissen eingesetzt werden.

⊙ Begleitende Maßnamen

Homöopathie Arnica D6 lindert die bei Muskelzerrungen auftretenden Schwellungen. Die Dosierung beträgt 3-mal 2 Tabletten pro Tag.

Die Anwendung

Die Anwendung erfolgt über großflächige wechselpolare Magnetfolien, die über dem schmerzenden Muskelgebiet aufgeklebt werden. Bei akuten Muskelverletzungen gilt, dass die Magnettherapie frühestens 36 Stunden nach Verletzungseintritt zum Einsatz kommen sollte. Der Grund: Erst nach diesem Zeitraum ist die Akutphase der Verletzung abgeschlossen, und die körpereigene Heilung ist so weit fortgeschritten, dass sie mit wärmenden bzw. durchblutungsfördernden Maßnahmen unterstützt werden kann. Die Folien sollten durchgehend Tag und Nacht auf der Haut bleiben, bis der Muskel wieder voll belastbar ist.

Rhus toxicodendron D6 hilft gegen Schmerzen, die sich bei Bewegung bessern und bei Berührung verschlimmern. Die Dosierung beträgt 3-mal täglich 2 Tabletten.

Calcium carbonicum Hahnemanni D6 empfiehlt sich zur Nachbehandlung, wenn nach dem Verschwinden der Schmerzen ein Schwächegefühl im Muskel geblieben ist. Die Dosierung beträgt 3-mal täglich 1 bis 2 Tabletten.

Gymnastik Etwa 48 Stunden nach der Verletzung sollten Sie mit einer statischen Dehnung (d. h. ohne Wippen oder Federn) des betroffenen Muskels beginnen. Halten Sie den Muskel für 10 bis 15 Sekunden in einer Dehnung, die ohne Schmerzen für Sie erträglich ist.

No sports! Im Profisport ist es üblich, einen Athleten auch noch mit einer Zerrung im Wettkampf zu belassen. Ein riskantes Unterfangen, da der gezerrte Muskel besonders anfällig für kräftigere Faserrisse ist und aufgrund der von ihm ausgehenden Schmerzen den gesamten Bewegungsablauf behindert. Der Hobbysportler sollte von derartigen Experimenten die Finger lassen.

Die richtige Vorbeugung Trainieren Sie nicht weniger als zweimal wöchentlich. Ein gut trainierter Muskel besitzt mehr Blutgefäße und ist dadurch besser vor Verletzungen geschützt. Darüber hinaus sollte der Sportler sich vor dem Training mindestens 20 Minuten lang aufwärmen. Gut geeignet sind lockeres Laufen und Radfahren.

Nacken-verspannungen

○ Symptome

Die Nackenmuskeln sind verspannt und anfällig für Schmerzen, die bis in den Kopf hinauf- oder in die Arme hinabziehen.

○ Ursachen

Hauptursache sind Überanstrengung und Durchblutungsstörungen in den Nackenmuskeln, die durch Zugluft, ständige Anspannung (etwa durch Starren auf den Computerbildschirm), ruckartige Bewegungen und Ängste hervorgerufen werden können. Darüber hinaus ist die Nackenpartie durch einige muskuläre Besonderheiten gekennzeichnet, die sie für Verspannungen anfällig macht. So ist der wichtigste und größte Muskel im Nackenbereich der dreigeteilte Kapuzenmuskel. Der untere Teil setzt an der Wirbelsäule an und zieht sich fächerartig nach oben zum Schulterblatt. Der mittlere Teil zieht quer von der Wirbelsäule zum oberen Schulterblattrand, und der obere bildet die seitliche Kontur des Halses nach und zieht abwärts von der Halswirbelsäule zum äußeren Schlüs-

selbeindrittel. Bei solch unterschiedlichen Faserverläufen muss der Kapuzenmuskel auch viele Aufgaben übernehmen:

● Er stabilisiert und zieht die Schultern nach oben, ist also wesentlich beim Tragen von Koffern und Taschen beteiligt.

● Der quer verlaufende Teil zieht die Schultern nach hinten, mit der Folge, dass er bei vorwiegend sitzender Tätigkeit im Büro unter ständiger Dehnung gehalten wird.

● Der obere Teil stabilisiert und zieht den Kopf nach hinten, mit der Folge, dass er bei konzentriert-starrender Tätigkeit am Bildschirm unter ständiger Anspannung steht.

Die einzelnen Muskelteile werden also sehr einseitig belastet. Dabei kommt es zu Ermüdung und Durchblutungsmangel, die längs verlaufenden Teile des Muskels verspannen sich, während die quer verlaufenden an Spannung verlieren.

Hartnäckige Verspannungen in der Nackenmuskulatur haben jedoch auch psychische Ursachen. Unter Angst und Wut nämlich veranlasst unser Nervensystem speziell die Nackenmuskeln dazu, sich in gewissermaßen permanenter Hab-Acht-Stellung anzuspannen, um möglichst schnell auf eventuelle Angriffe reagieren zu können.

◯ Mit Magneten heilen

Magnete fördern die Durchblutung und lösen die Verspannungen in der Muskulatur. Die Heilwirkung von Magnetfeldern bei Nackenschmerzen wurde durch eine klinische Untersuchung bestätigt. Die Anwendungsdauer betrug in dieser Studie drei Wochen.

◯ Begleitende Maßnahmen

Aromatherapie Bestimmte Düfte lindern den Schmerz und entspannen die Muskeln. Hierzu gehören Kamille, Lavendel, Majoran und Wacholder. 5 bis 8 Tropfen des jeweiligen Öls in eine Duftschale oder Duftlampe träufeln, die Sie nach Belieben im Wohn- oder Schlafzimmer aufstellen können.

Johanniskrautöl Das alte Heilöl lindert Muskelschmerzen. Massieren Sie es sich mehrmals täglich in die Nackenpartie ein.

Homöopathie Rhus toxicodendron D6 hilft gegen Nackenbeschwerden nach Überanstrengung oder einer ruckartigen Bewegung oder Verrenkung. Die Dosierung beträgt 3-mal täglich 10 Tropfen.
Bryorheum ist bei steifem Hals durch Kälte oder Zugluft angezeigt. Die Dosierung beträgt 3-mal täglich 10 Tropfen.

Die Anwendung

Bei Nackenschmerzen helfen wechselpolare Magnetfolien, die auf die betroffenen Nackenmuskeln gesetzt werden. Bei Beschwerden direkt über der Halswirbelsäule empfiehlt sich die Anwendung einer länglichen Magnetfolie, die entlang der Wirbelsäule aufgeklebt wird.
Tragen Sie die Folien durchgehend Tag und Nacht, über einen Zeitraum von mindestens zwei Wochen.

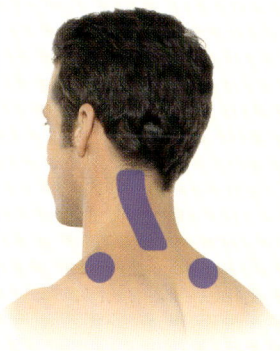

Narben

◌ Symptome

Narben bestehen aus stabilem, aber gefäßarmem Gewebe. Sie enthalten keine Pigments und Haarwurzeln, weswegen sie kahl bleiben und stets ihre blass-rötliche Farbe behalten.

◌ Ursachen

Narben werden durch großflächige Verletzungen der Haut verursacht. Bei der Wundheilung bildet sich zunächst so genanntes Granulationsgewebe, das die verletzte Stelle als eine Art Kruste schützt. Dieses zell- und blutgefäßreiche Granulationsgewebe wird dann allmählich in ein zell- und blutgefäßarmes, dafür aber faserreiches und stabiles Narbengewebe umgewandelt. Je schneller dieser Prozess vor sich geht, desto kleiner wird die Narbe.

◌ Mit Magneten heilen

Bei frischen Narben machen Magnete das Gewebe weicher, die Schmerz- und Entzündungsanfälligkeit rund um die Narbe geht dadurch deutlich zurück. Ältere Narben lassen sich durch Magnetanwendungen nicht mehr beeinflussen.

◌ Begleitende Maßnahmen

Die Narbe akzeptieren Wenn eine Narbe erst einmal voll entwickelt ist, kann sie nur noch schwer beeinflusst werden. Bei großen, entstellenden Narben greift die Schulmedizin mitunter zu speziellen Gels, Steroiden, Operationen oder sogar zu Röntgenstrahlanwendungen. Es ist jedoch praktisch unmöglich, ein fertiges Narbengewebe zum Verschwinden zu bringen. Es ist daher in jedem Fall ratsam, sich mit der Narbe als einem neuen Teil des Körpers abzufinden.

Die Narbe vor Sonnenlicht und mechanischen Reizen schützen Narbengewebe reagiert am Anfang noch recht empfindlich auf Berührungen; es sollte daher nicht zu stark belastet werden. Außerdem besitzt es keine Pigmente. Schützen Sie es daher mit starken Lichtschutzcremes, bei kleineren Narben verwenden Sie am besten die Lichtschutzstifte für die Lippen.

Der Vitamin-E-Trick Der Radikalefänger Vitamin E, der Zellwände versiegeln kann, vermag dramatische Erfolge bei der Wundheilung zu erzielen. Wenn Vitamin E jedoch oral eingenommen wird, erreicht es die Wunde nur

Die Anwendung

Die Anwendung sollte am besten über wechselpolare Magnetfolien erfolgen. Die Größe der Folien richtet sich dabei nach dem jeweils betroffenen Narbenbereich.

Achten Sie bei der Anwendung besonders darauf, dass die Klebestreifen der Magnetfolien nur auf der gesunden und keinesfalls auf der verletzten Haut befestigt werden. Lediglich die Magnete haben Kontakt zur Narbe. Die Magnetfolien sollten nachts und auch einige Stunden am Tag zum Einsatz kommen.

stark verdünnt und verspätet. Brechen Sie daher ein oder zwei Vitamin-E-Kapseln so auf, dass ihr Öl auf die noch blutende oder frisch vernarbte Wunde träufelt. In vielen Fällen kann hierdurch eine Narbenbildung komplett verhindert werden.

Die richtige Vorbeugung Wird eine Narbe sozusagen prophylaktisch, d. h. sofort nach Eintritt der Verletzung, behandelt, kann das Schlimmste meist noch verhindert werden.

● Alle offenen Wunden müssen innerhalb der ersten sechs Stunden gereinigt werden. Am besten suchen Sie dazu einen Arzt auf. Als Erste-Hilfe-Maßnahme zu Hause sollte die Wunde nach Möglichkeit vorsichtig und äußerst sorgfältig gesäubert und anschließend mit einer sterilen Kompresse abgedeckt werden.

Kleinere Abschürfungen heilen am besten, wenn man sie gut säubert und danach in Ruhe lässt. Bei Kindern empfiehlt sich ein Pflaster oder ein Verband allerdings auch bei kleineren Verletzungen, damit sie während des Heilungsprozesses nicht in Versuchung geraten, die juckende Blutkruste aufzukratzen.

● Bei tiefen und stark blutenden Wunden sollte die Wundversorgung komplett dem Arzt überlassen werden.

● Behandeln Sie Wunden nicht mit Jod. Denn das tut nicht nur höllisch weh, sondern behindert außerdem den natürlichen Heilungsverlauf. Mittlerweile gibt es genug Desinfektionsmittel im Handel, die den Bakterien den Garaus machen, ohne dass der Verletzte dabei die Zähne zusammenbeißen müsste.

Neuralgien

○ Symptome

Neuralgien sind heftige Schmerz-
schübe, die am betroffenen Nerv
entlangführen. Am häufigsten ist
die Trigeminusneuralgie. Hier ist
der Gesichtsnerv betroffen, wodurch es zu Schmerzanfällen in
einer der beiden Gesichtshälften
kommt. Oft ist dabei auch das
Sehvermögen eingeschränkt.

○ Ursachen

Nervenschmerzen können durch
eine Reizung oder Schädigung
der Nerven entstehen. Stoff-
wechselkrankheiten wie Gicht
und Diabetes mellitus, die das
Säure-Basen-Gleichgewicht in
das saure Milieu verschieben,
können ebenfalls in eine Neural-
gie münden.
Oft sind Neuralgien jedoch psy-
chosomatischer Natur. Einige
Psychotherapeuten und Ärzte
interpretieren vor allem die Trigeminusneuralgie dementsprechend. Wer seelisch angespannt
ist, neigt auch dazu, das Gesicht
zu verspannen, was wiederum
Neuralgien auslösen kann. Nicht
umsonst sind Trigeminusneural-
gien bei depressiv veranlagten
Menschen besonders häufig.

○ Mit Magneten heilen

In mehreren Laborstudien
konnte gezeigt werden, dass
Magnetfelder die Regeneration
von geschädigten Nerven anregen. Die Studien wurden zwar
mit elektromagnetischen Feldern
durchgeführt, doch ihre Ergebnisse sind teilweise – aufgrund
der Frequenzen der aufgebauten
Felder – durchaus auf Dauermagnete übertragbar.

○ Begleitende Maßnahmen

Homöopathie Aconitum D6 hilft,
wenn die Schmerzen durch kalten Wind ausgelöst wurden. Das

Die Anwendung

Die Anwendung erfolgt über
wechselpolare Magnetfolien, die
auf den schmerzenden Stellen
befestigt werden.
Bei der Trigeminusneuralgie
steht man natürlich vor dem
Problem, dass die Magnete im
Gesicht befestigt werden müssen. Die Anwendung bleibt daher
wohl oder übel auf die Nacht
beschränkt. Wer allerdings zu
Hause arbeitet, oder wenn die
Beschwerden im Urlaub auftreten, sollte die Magnetfolien auch
tagsüber tragen.

Gesicht fühlt sich an, als würde es von heißen Drähten durchzogen. Die Dosierung beträgt 5 Globuli (Kügelchen) etwa alle 30 Minuten, bis sich die Beschwerden deutlich bessern. Magnesium phosphoricum D6 ist angezeigt, wenn die Gesichtsschmerzen schießend oder krampfartig kommen. Die Dosierung beträgt 5 Globuli (Kügelchen) alle 30 Minuten, bis die Beschwerden sich deutlich gebessert haben.

Spigelia D12 hilft vor allem dann, wenn die Schmerzen morgens beginnen und am Mittag besonders stark sind. Sie sind stechend, brennend, reißend oder schießend und konzentrieren sich vor allem auf den Augenbereich. Die Dosierung beträgt 5 Globuli alle 30 Minuten, bis die Beschwerden sich deutlich bessern.

Johanniskraut (Hypericum perforatum) Johanniskraut verbessert die Stimmungslage des Patienten. Als wirksames Antidepressivum befreit es ihn von dem Gefühl, das »Gesicht zu verlieren« und verletzt zu werden. Auf der anderen Seite wirkt Johanniskraut direkt auf die Signalübermittlungen im Nervensystem. Es unterstützt vor allem die Arbeit der hemmenden Botenstoffe, und dies bedeutet konkret, dass Johanniskraut wie ein Filter wirkt, der das Nervensystem vor schmerzhaften Übererregungen schützt.

Trinken Sie täglich 2 bis 3 Tassen Johanniskrauttee: 1 gehäuften Teelöffel Johanniskraut mit 1 Tasse kochendem Wasser überbrühen, 12 Minuten ziehen lassen und anschließend abseihen.

Als Alternative kommen auch Hypericumpräparate aus der Apotheke infrage. Die Dosierung liegt bei 1 Milligramm Gesamthyperizin pro Tag. Zusätzlich können Sie am Morgen und Abend auch einen Umschlag auf die schmerzende Stelle legen, der zuvor mit einer Mischung aus 1 Teil Johanniskrauttinktur und 2 Teilen Wasser getränkt wurde.

Vorsicht bei Schmerzmitteln! Neuralgien bereiten starke Schmerzen, und das erhöht natürlich die Gefahr des Schmerzmittelmissbrauchs. Dabei wirken die handelsüblichen Schmerzmittel viel zu langsam, als dass sie direkt auf einen aktuellen Neuralgieanfall reagieren könnten.

Prellungen

○ Symptome

Prellungen sind durch bläuliche Verfärbung der Haut gekennzeichnet, die meistens mit einer Schwellung verbunden sind. Die blauen Flecken können – vor allem unter Druckeinwirkung – sehr schmerzempfindlich sein. Prellungen am Schädel können große Beulen bilden, da die Schwellung aufgrund des darunter liegenden Schädelknochens nur nach außen, in Richtung Haut, abgeleitet werden kann. Sie sind daher kein Hinweis auf schwere Verletzungen wie etwa eine Gehirnerschütterung. Kommt es jedoch im Anschluss an Prellungen im Kopfbereich zu Schwindelanfällen, Übelkeit oder Erbrechen, muss der Verletzte umgehend ins Krankenhaus gebracht werden.

○ Ursachen

Prellungen zeigen sich als blaue Flecken, die Ausdruck für eine Blutung unterhalb des Hautgewebes sind. Die wiederum ist das Resultat einer Verletzung an Bändern, Sehnen, Muskeln oder Knochen, meistens verursacht durch Gewalteinwirkungen von außen. Besonders schmerzhaft sind Prellungen, bei denen es zu Quetschungen des Muskelgewebes kommt, beispielsweise durch einen Tritt auf den Oberschenkel oder einen Fausthieb auf den Oberarm.

Bei Verletzungen, die tief unten im Gewebe stattgefunden haben, kann der blaue Fleck erst einige Stunden oder sogar einige Tage später an die Oberfläche dringen. Für eine sinnvolle erste Hilfe ist es dann jedoch zu spät. Nach schmerzhaften Stößen, Schlägen, Stürzen u. Ä. sollte man deshalb grundsätzlich kühlende Maßnahmen einleiten, auch wenn es noch nicht zu einer Verfärbung gekommen ist.

○ Erste Hilfe

Lang andauerndes Kühlen als Erste-Hilfe-Maßnahme lindert Schmerzen und schließt die verletzten Blutgefäße. Prellungen an Knochen oder Gelenken sollten mindestens 30 Minuten, Verletzungen im Muskelbereich sogar 45 Minuten lang gekühlt werden. Zur Kühlung verwendet man am besten Eiswürfel, die in ein dickes Handtuch eingerollt wurden. Ist kein Eis vorhanden, sollte das betroffene Körperteil wenigstens für 15 Minuten unter fließendes kaltes Wasser gehalten werden.

◌ Mit Magneten heilen

Magnetfolien fördern die Durchblutung und unterstützen dadurch den Abtransport von verletzten Gewebeteilen und geronnenem Blut. Die Magnettherapie darf allerdings erst etwa 36 bis 48 Stunden nach Verletzungseintritt erfolgen, da eine verstärkte Durchblutung erst nach Abklingen der Akutsymptome Sinn macht.

Die Anwendung

Auf die blauen Flecken bzw. Prellungen werden wechselpolare Magnetfolien in entsprechender Größe aufgeklebt. Das Klebematerial sollte nur in Kontakt mit gesunden Teilen der Haut kommen, die Prellung selbst sollte nur vom Magneten bedeckt sein. Tragen Sie die Magnete am besten durchgehend Tag und Nacht. Für das berüchtigte »blaue Auge« kommen als Alternative auch magnetische Augenmanschetten infrage, die mittlerweile im Fachhandel angeboten werden.

◌ Begleitende Maßnahmen

Homöopathie Arnica D6 begrenzt die Schwellung und den Umfang der blauen Flecken, weil es den Abtransport von Gewebeflüssigkeit und ausgetretenem Blut unterstützt. Die Dosierung beträgt 3-mal täglich 1 bis 2 Tabletten, in akuten Fällen 1 Tablette stündlich.

Hypericum D6 wirkt schmerzlindernd und eignet sich vor allem beim »blauen Auge«. Die Dosierung beträgt 3-mal täglich 1 bis 2 Tabletten.

Die richtige Vorbeugung Treten die blauen Flecken meist infolge von Sportverletzungen auf, sollte die Warm-up-Phase verlängert werden. Achten Sie beim Sport auch auf die richtige Schutzbekleidung (Helm, Schienbeinschoner, Schulterpolster).

Bei Kindern sind blaue Flecken eine Art »Erziehungsinstrument«. Beim Fahrradfahren sollten sie natürlich einen Helm tragen, ansonsten ist es jedoch falsch, sie von verletzungsgefährlichen Orten wie dem Abenteuerspielplatz oder von Treppen fernzuhalten. Durch harmlose blaue Flecken lernen Kinder, sich richtig zu bewegen und vorsichtiger beim Spielen zu sein.

Reizmagen

○ Symptome

Bei Reizmagen stellen sich die folgenden Beschwerden ein, die nach eiweiß- und fetthaltigen Mahlzeiten zunehmen: Schmerzen, Druck- und Völlegefühl im Oberbauch sowie Sodbrennen, Appetitlosigkeit und Übelkeit.

○ Ursachen

Der Reizmagen wird durch Störungen in der Magenmuskulatur verursacht, die wiederum durch Stress, Bewegungs- und Schlafmangel sowie opulente Speisen mit viel Fett, Eiweiß oder Gewürzen hervorgerufen werden. Außerdem nimmt mit zunehmendem Alter die Funktionsfähigkeit unserer Muskeln ab. Das gilt auch für die Muskulatur in den Magenwänden. Dies wird jedoch von vielen älteren Menschen vergessen, die ihren Magen überfordern.

Der Reizmagen steht schließlich auch in engem Zusammenhang mit psychischen Belastungen. Angst, Wut, unerfüllte Wünsche und depressive Gedanken blockieren die Tätigkeit der Magenmuskulatur. Die Nahrung verbleibt dadurch länger im Magen,

was spätestens bei der nächsten Nahrungsaufnahme zum Problem wird.

○ Mit Magneten heilen

In ihrer entspannenden Wirkung auf die Muskeln liegt eine große Stärke der Magnettherapie. Magnetkräfte können außerdem problemlos die Muskeln und das Fett der Bauchdecke durchdringen. Nichtsdestoweniger hat die Magnettherapie auch dort ihre Grenzen. Gegen ein Bombardement aus Fetten, Alkohol und Nikotin kann auch sie nichts ausrichten. Hier muss letzten Endes eine Nahrungs- oder Lebensumstellung des Patienten erfolgen.

○ Begleitende Maßnahmen

Heilerde Die Mischung aus Löss und Lehm besänftigt den Magen und begünstigt den Aufbau einer gesunden Darmflora. Eine Therapie mit Heilerde eignet sich also generell zur längerfristigen Beseitigung von Verdauungsbeschwerden. 1 Teelöffel zur innerlichen Anwendung geeignete Heilerde in stillem Mineralwasser oder Kräutertee (am besten Kamillentee) aufschwemmen und jeweils nach dem Mittag- und Abendessen in kleinen Schlucken trinken.

Die Anwendung

Die Magnetkräfte müssen durch mehr oder weniger dicke Gewebeschichten dringen, um zum gereizten Magen gelangen zu können. Deshalb empfiehlt sich die Anwendung besonders kräftiger wechselpolarer Magnetfolien (»forte«, Stärke des Magnetmaterials 1,5 Millimeter). Eine rechteckige Folie mit möglichst großem Durchmesser wird in Längsrichtung auf dem Oberbauch befestigt. Sie sollte am Tag getragen werden, zur Nacht wird sie abgesetzt.

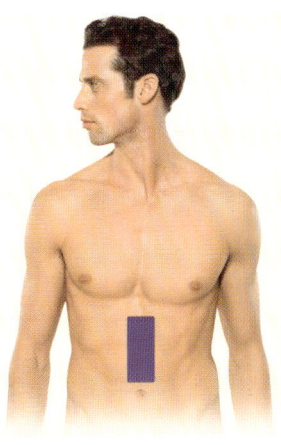

Rollkur Die Rollkur ist ein altes und bewährtes Hausmittel. Sie beginnt am Abend. 2 Esslöffel Kamillenblüten mit 1/2 Liter kochendem Wasser übergießen, 10 Minuten ziehen lassen, abseihen. Am Morgen nach dem Aufwachen trinken. Danach für jeweils 5 Minuten auf den Rücken, auf die rechte Seite, auf den Bauch und schließlich auf die linke Seite rollen. Ihr Magen ist jetzt bereit für die alltäglichen Belastungen.

Kü-Ka-Lei-Wa-Gemüsesuppe

2 bis 3 ungeschälte und klein geschnittene Kartoffeln sowie je 2 Teelöffel Leinsamen und Kümmelfrüchte in 2 Liter Wasser kochen. Die Suppe über den Tag verteilt in kleinen Schlucken bei lauwarmer Temperatur trinken. Die erste Portion am besten schon morgens vor dem Frühstück zu sich nehmen.

Das alte asiatische Rezept verbindet die traditionellen Verdauungshilfen Kartoffelstärke, Leinsamen und Kümmel sinnvoll miteinander und hat sich bei empfindlichem Magen bestens bewährt.

Reduzieren Sie Ihr Esstempo

Nehmen Sie sich ausreichend Zeit für das Essen. Kauen Sie ausgiebig, und verteilen Sie das Essen auf 5 kleinere Mahlzeiten pro Tag.

Rücken-
schmerzen

○ Symptome

Die chronischen, bisweilen auch akuten Schmerzen im gesamten Rückenbereich können in Nacken und Kopf ausstrahlen. Mitunter kommt es zu Schwindel.

○ Ursachen

Im Alter nimmt die Elastizität der Bandscheiben ab, die Pufferung zwischen den Wirbelkörpern wird somit immer schwächer. Infolgedessen nimmt der Verschleiß an den Wirbelkörpern immer mehr zu.

Gefördert wird dieser natürliche Verschleiß vor allem durch Bewegungsmangel und ein unausgewogenes Muskelgerüst. Bei den meisten Menschen sind die tiefen Rückenmuskeln im Verhältnis zur Bauchmuskulatur zu stark ausgebildet; auch sind die hinteren Schultermuskeln oft schwächer als ihre Gegenspieler, die Brustmuskeln. Dadurch wird die Stabilität des Rückens empfindlich gestört. Als erste Symptome zeigen sich in der Regel Muskelverspannungen im Lenden-, Schulter- und Nackenbereich, später kommen Verschleiß-

erscheinungen und dementsprechende Beschwerden an der Wirbelsäule hinzu.

Umstritten ist, ob so genanntes falsches Sitzen die Entstehung von Rückenschmerzen begünstigt. Denn ein »richtiges« Sitzen auf einem Stuhl oder auf einem Sessel gibt es nicht. Alle Arten des Sitzens stellen für unseren Rücken eine unphysiologische Belastung dar, gleichgültig, wie orthopädisch hochwertig das betreffende Möbelstück ist. Wer also weniger Rückenbeschwerden haben will, muss entweder weniger sitzen oder seine Position beim Sitzen möglichst oft verändern.

Gesichert ist, dass Rückenschmerzen auch psychosomatische Hintergründe haben. Angst, unterdrückte Aggressionen, Hektik, aber auch Hoffnungslosigkeit und Starrköpfigkeit können Rückenschmerzen begünstigen.

○ Mit Magneten heilen

Magnete gehören gerade bei diffusen Rückenschmerzen zu den Mitteln der ersten Wahl. Über ihren entspannenden Effekt auf die verhärtete Rückenmuskulatur hinaus, wirken sie schmerz- und entzündungshemmend.

Gegenüber anderen Heilmitteln bei Rückenschmerzen besitzt die Magnettherapie eine Reihe von Vorteilen. So dringt sie recht tief in das erkrankte Gewebe vor, ohne dabei das umliegende Gewebe zu reizen – ganz im Unterschied zu den herkömmlichen Salben, die erst diverse Zellschichten chemisch durchdringen müssen, um überhaupt in die Nähe der Wirbelsäule zu kommen.

Darüber hinaus kann man Magnete gezielt dort aufsetzen, wo es wehtut. Dieser Aspekt unterscheidet die Magnete wiederum von den traditionellen schulmedizinischen Schmerzmitteln, die sich – gleichgültig ob sie als

Die Anwendung

Die Anwendung erfolgt über wechselpolare, rechteckige Magnetfolien (die Größe beträgt etwa 90 mal 150 Millimeter), die im spitzen Winkel zueinander zwischen Bauchnabel und Schambein aufgebracht werden. Ergänzend dazu kann Wasser getrunken werden (durchschnittlich 1/2 Liter pro Tag), das per Nord-(d. h. Plus-)polmagnet magnetisiert wurde.

Tablette geschluckt oder als Spritze injiziert werden – im gesamten Körper verteilen.

○ Begleitende Maßnahmen

Teufelskralle Die Wurzeln der Teufelskralle enthalten den Wirkstoff Harpagosid, der gezielt in den Arachidonsäurestoffwechsel eingreift und die Produktion von schmerz- und entzündungsfördernden Substanzen blockiert. Ein weiterer Vorteil von Harpagosid ist, dass er von unserem Körper überdurchschnittlich gut aufgenommen wird.

Untersuchungen an der Universitätsklinik Frankfurt ergaben, dass mit Hilfe der Teufelskralle Rückenschmerzen teilweise effektiver bekämpft werden konnten als mit herkömmlichen Rheumamitteln. Die Nebenwirkungen waren in jedem Fall geringer. Auch die Kosten betrugen gerade mal ein Drittel der herkömmlichen Therapie.

Teufelskrallenpräparate (Arthrosetten H Kapseln, Dolo-Arthrodynat, Doloteffin, Harpagoforte ASmedic, Herbadon, Jucurba, Teufelskralle Kapseln R und Kai Fu) sind in der Apotheke erhältlich. Die Dosierung richtet sich nach den Packungsbeilagen.

Schlafstörungen

⊙ Symptome

Bei Schlafstörungen unterscheidet man Einschlaf-, Durchschlaf- und Ausschlafstörungen. Alle drei Typen können auch in Kombinationen auftreten, doch dass jemand in der Nacht »kein Auge zukriegt« – wie oft behauptet wird –, ist überaus selten.

⊙ Ursachen

Nicht immer ist Stress die Hauptursache für Schlafstörungen, auch wenn dies von den Betroffenen oft so empfunden wird. Japanischen Untersuchungen zufolge begünstigt die Abschottung vom Erdmagnetfeld, wie sie in unserem »Betonzeitalter« zu beobachten ist, Schlafstörungen enorm. Diesen Mangel kann man durch Dauermagnete beheben, beispielsweise in Form magnetisierter Unterbetten. Auf der anderen Seite reagieren manche Menschen sensibel auf elektromagnetische Felder, wie sie z. B. von elektronischen Weckern oder anderen Geräten ausgesendet werden. Manchmal hilft es, wenn man das Schlafzimmer komplett von elektronischen Geräten befreit.

Auch manche Krankheiten gehen mit Schlafstörungen einher. Dazu gehören Herzerkrankungen, Bluthochdruck, Asthma bronchiale und Erkrankungen des rheumatischen Formenkreises. Bestimmte Medikamente wie Beta-Blocker, Antibiotika, Aufputschmittel und Hormonpräparate (also auch die Antibabypille) können ebenfalls Schlafprobleme fördern, genauso wie der übermäßige Genuss von Alkohol und Zigaretten. Auch ein opulentes Mahl vor dem Zubettgehen beansprucht Magen und Kreislauf auf Kosten der Tiefschlafphasen.

Es kann auch vorkommen, dass Schlafstörungen bereits in der Kindheit verwurzelt sind. Wenn Eltern ihr Kind ins Bett schicken, wenn es ihnen lästig wird, kann dies zu einem verhängnisvollen Mechanismus der Schlaflosigkeit führen. Denn Befehle führen nicht selten zu Trotzreaktionen, und so kann es vorkommen, dass das Kind wohl ins Bett geht, dort aber mit allen Kräften wach zu bleiben versucht. Dieser Mechanismus kann sich bis ins Erwachsenenalter fortsetzen und dann zu schweren, chronischen Schlafstörungen führen.

◗ Mit Magneten heilen

Viele Schlafstörungen haben ihre Ursache darin, dass der Schlafsuchende vom Erdmagnetfeld abgeschottet ist, beispielsweise durch Stahlbetonbauten. Hier kann die Anschaffung magnetischer Unterbetten sinnvoll sein, die es mittlerweile im Fachhandel zu kaufen gibt.

Manchmal können Schlafstörungen auch behoben werden, wenn das Bett in eine Achse mit den beiden Erdpolen gestellt wird, wobei das Kopfteil nach Norden zeigen muss. Den Erdnordpol finden Sie problemlos mit dem Kompass heraus.

◗ Begleitende Maßnahmen

Akupressur Massieren Sie die folgenden Punkte jeweils 1 Minute pro Seite sanft mit Zeige- und Mittelfinger:

● »Das göttliche Tor«. Er liegt an der mittleren Handgelenkfalte unter dem Kleinfingerballen. Sie können ihn deutlich als Kuhle spüren.

● »Punkt der drei Yin«. Er liegt 5 Zentimeter oberhalb des inneren Fußknöchels. Massieren Sie diesen Punkt nur leicht, da die Knochenhaut dort sehr sensibel sein kann.

● »Schlaflosigkeit«. Dieser Akupressurpunkt sitzt in der Fersenmitte, etwa 1 Zentimeter vom hinteren Fersenrand entfernt.

Aromatherapie Schaffen Sie ein beruhigendes Raumklima – mit Duftölen wie Geranium, Kamille, Melisse, Sandelholz oder Ylang-Ylang. Sie können diese Düfte entweder im Raum versprühen (5 bis 8 Tropfen mit destilliertem Wasser vermischt), oder Sie können die ätherischen Öle in eine Duftlampe bzw. auf einen Duftstein geben.

Die fünf goldenen Schlafregeln

● Stehen Sie immer zur gleichen Zeit auf, und gehen Sie immer zur gleichen Zeit ins Bett. Halten Sie dieses Ritual möglichst auch am Wochenende ein.

● Schaffen Sie sich günstige Schlafbedingungen. Halten Sie das Schlafzimmer dunkel und ruhig, schaffen Sie sich ein genügend großes Bett an.

● Verzichten Sie auf Mittagsschlaf und Nickerchen.

● Schalten Sie ab, bevor Sie ins Bett gehen, d. h., vermeiden Sie am späten Abend geistige oder körperliche Kraftakte.

● Verzichten Sie nach Möglichkeit auf Alkohol, Zigaretten und Aufputschmittel.

Schnupfen

○ Symptome

Zu den typischen Schnupfen-
symptomen zählen eine trop-
fende Nase, Niesen sowie leichte
Hals- und Rachenschmerzen.
Gelegentlich kommt es auch zu
Husten. Kommt noch Fieber
hinzu, spricht man von einem
grippalen Infekt.

○ Ursachen

Erkältungen sind die Folge einer
Virusinfektion der oberen Atemwege. Sie ist ansteckend, d.h.,
die Viren werden über Niesen,
Husten oder Hautkontakt übertragen. Prinzipiell kann man zu
jeder Jahreszeit eine Erkältung
bekommen, doch im Winter ist
die Ansteckungsgefahr besonders
hoch. In den kalten Monaten
kommt es öfter zu Unterkühlun-
gen an den Füßen, woraufhin
das vegetative Nervensystem die
Durchblutung in den Atem-
wegen drosselt. Dadurch sinkt
die Abwehrfähigkeit der dortigen
Schleimhäute und die Schnup-
fenerreger haben es leichter, in
den Organismus vorzudringen.
Darüber hinaus steigt die Wahr-
scheinlichkeit, einen Schnupfen
zu bekommen, unter längeren

psychischen Belastungen um das
Doppelte, da durch ständigen
Stress das Immunsystem eben-
falls geschwächt wird.

○ Mit Magneten heilen

Magnetfelder wirken entzündungshemmend, durchblutungsfördernd und schwach antibiotisch. Das Ein- und Ausatmen
sowie das Abhusten von Schleim
kann durch Magnetkräfte deutlich erleichtert werden.

○ Begleitende Maßnahmen

Schniefen statt Schnäuzen Wer
kennt sie nicht, die Mahnung,
beim Schnupfen nicht die Nase
hochzuziehen, sondern brav ins
Taschentuch zu schnauben?
Außerdem, so der weit verbreitete Tenor, werde beim Schnäuzen der Schleim besser gelöst.
Doch das Gegenteil ist der Fall.
Während beim Hochziehen ein
Unterdruck entsteht, der das
Sekret aus den Nebenhöhlen
saugt, wird es beim Schnäuzen
direkt in die Kieferhöhlen gedrückt. Also: Besser unschick-
lich schniefen, als unmedizinisch
schnäuzen! Dieser Rat gilt vor
allem für Menschen, die bereits
Probleme mit den Nebenhöhlen
haben.

Die Anwendung

Sie benötigen insgesamt zwei bipolare Magnete (mit der Nordseite zur Haut), die auf die Kuhle zwischen den inneren Schlüsselbeinenden und dem Brustbein gesetzt werden. Sie verbleiben Tag und Nacht auf der Haut. Zur Nacht sollte noch ein weiterer Magnet zwischen den Augenbrauen auf die Stirn geklebt werden.

Als durchblutungsfördernde und antibiotische Maßnahme besitzen die Heilmagnete auch eine große Chance bei der Vorbeugung von Erkältungskrankheiten. Tragen Sie die Magnete an den oben angegebenen Stellen für ein bis zwei Stunden pro Tag, und den Viren und anderen Krankheitserregern wird es schwer gemacht, sich in den Atemwegen festzusetzen.

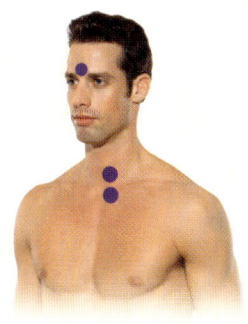

Homöopathie Aconit D30 hilft am besten zu Beginn der Erkältung. Es ist allerdings ein Erstmittel, darf also nicht zu lange verabreicht werden. Die ideale Dosierung beträgt 3-mal 5 Kügelchen im Abstand von 2 Stunden, und danach nichts mehr. In der Regel reicht diese Behandlung zusammen mit den Magneten – für eine normale Erkältung vollkommen aus.

Viel trinken! Der Wasserbedarf ist bei Erkältungskrankheiten deutlich erhöht. Trinken Sie viel und regelmäßig, also auch dann, wenn Sie keinen Durst haben.

Am besten eignen sich hierfür Kräutertees oder ein Gemisch aus stillem Mineralwasser und Fruchtsaft in einem Mischungsverhältnis von 4:1.

Teebaumöl Das australische Öl bekämpft die Erkältungserreger und aktiviert in Gestalt einer Aromatherapie das Immunsystem. 3 bis 5 Tropfen des Öls auf ein Taschentuch geben und mehrmals täglich zum Inhalieren an die Nase halten. Für die Nachtruhe können Sie 5 Tropfen Teebaumöl auf Ihr Kopfkissen geben, wenn Ihnen der Duft des Öls nicht unangenehm ist.

Schulter-schmerzen

○ Symptome

Schmerzen im Schulterbereich werden durch Bewegungen des Schultergelenks meist verstärkt. Mitunter ist in den Schultergelenken auch ein Knacken zu hören.

○ Ursachen

Die Schultergelenke reagieren sehr empfindlich auf häufiges Arbeiten über Kopf, wenn also die Arme über der Kopflinie bewegt werden müssen. Darüber hinaus treten auch häufig Dysbalancen zwischen den vorderen (Brust-)Muskeln und den hinteren (Schulterblatt-)Muskeln auf. Dadurch kommt es zu Fehlbelastungen im Schultergelenk. Außerdem gehören Schulterschmerzen neben Nackenbeschwerden zu den häufigsten Symptomen des Magnetfeld-Mangelsyndroms (»Magnetic-Field-Deficiency-Syndrome«, siehe Seite 19).

○ Mit Magneten heilen

Zwei japanische Studien von 1980 untersuchten die Wirkung von Magnetpflastern auf etwa 400 Patienten, die an Schulterschmerzen litten. Die Patienten wurden in zwei Gruppen unterteilt: Die eine Gruppe erhielt eine Behandlung mit echten Magnetpflastern mit einer Stärke von 800 Gauß, die zweite Gruppe wurde lediglich mit gleich aussehenden, aber sehr schwachen Magnetpflastern (200 Gauß) behandelt.

Das Ergebnis: Aus der ersten Gruppe berichteten über 80 Prozent über Besserungen ihrer Beschwerden, in der zweiten Gruppe waren es hingegen nur etwa 40 Prozent.

○ Begleitende Maßnahmen

Borretschöl Borretschöl enthält große Mengen an Gamma-Linolensäure, die durch ihren Einfluss auf den Prostaglandinspie-

Die Anwendung

Testen Sie, welche Punkte im Schulterbereich besonders druckempfindlich sind. Genau auf diese Punkte werden dann wechselpolare Magnetfolien geklebt. Als Alternative kommen noch magnetische Schultermanschetten in Betracht, die es mittlerweile im Fachhandel zu kaufen gibt.

gel entzündliche Prozesse unterdrücken kann. In der Naturheilkunde wird die traditionsreiche Heilpflanze außerdem eingesetzt, um die Nebennierenfunktionen nach einer Kortisonbehandlung wiederherzustellen. Dadurch stellt Borretschöl eine wirksame Ergänzung zu den üblichen Heilmethoden bei Gelenkschmerzen dar, insofern es zumindestens einen Teil der Nebenwirkungen von Kortisonmedikamenten zu puffern vermag.

Borretschöl kommt am besten in Form von Präparaten aus der Apotheke zum Einsatz. Beachten Sie bei der Anwendung die Vorschriften auf den jeweiligen Packungsbeilagen.

Brennnesselblätter (Urticae herba) Das Brennnesselkraut enthält Substanzen, die gezielt in Schmerz- und Entzündungsprozesse eingreifen. Es eignet sich zur Kombination mit nicht steroidalen Schmerzmitteln wie ASS (Azetylsalizylsäure) und Diclofenac, um deren Dosis zu senken. Dies hat sich bei vielen Gelenkerkrankungen, insbesondere aber bei Arthritis, bewährt.

● Tee: 2 Teelöffel der getrockneten Brennnesselblätter mit 1 Tasse kochendem Wasser überbrühen. 12 Minuten ziehen lassen, anschließend abseihen. Etwa 3 Tassen täglich trinken. Als Alternative kommen Extrakte und Säfte aus dem Reformhaus und der Apotheke infrage. Die Dosierung richtet sich nach den jeweiligen Packungsbeilagen.

● Brennnesselsuppe (für 2 Personen): 4 Hand voll frische und junge Brennnesseltriebe waschen und in 300 Milliliter Rinderbrühe 10 Minuten lang bei mittlerer Hitze kochen lassen. Anschließend abseihen, den Sud beiseite stellen und die gekochten Brennnesseltriebe pürieren. 1/2 Zwiebel klein schneiden und in 1 Esslöffel erhitzter Butter glasig werden lassen. 1 Esslöffel Mehl hinzufügen und zu einer hellen Mehlschwitze anrühren. Mit 1/4 Liter kalter Milch aufgießen und glatt rühren. Den Brennnesselsud dazugeben und noch einmal 15 Minuten bei mittlerer Hitze kochen lassen. Anschließend die pürierten Brennnesseln in die Suppe geben. Vor dem Servieren mit etwas Salz und frisch gemahlenem schwarzen Pfeffer abschmecken und mit frischer Petersilie sowie 1 Esslöffel saurer Sahne garnieren.

Sehnen-entzündung

◌ Symptome

Sehnenentzündungen entwickeln sich schleichend und oft ohne sichtbaren Grund (wie etwa als Folge eines Unfalls). Die Sehne ist berührungsempfindlich und schmerzt vor allem dann, wenn sie nach einiger Zeit der Ruhe wieder belastet wird. Im fortgeschrittenen Stadium ist die Haut über der entzündeten Sehne deutlich gerötet.

◌ Ursachen

Sehnen übertragen die Kraft des Muskels auf die Knochen. Sie reagieren jedoch weitaus langsamer als die Muskeln auf Trainingsreize. Deshalb kommt es bei Sportarten mit relativ schneller Muskelentwicklung – z. B. Bodybuilding, Krafttraining, Gewichtheben, aber auch Tennis oder Leichtathletik – häufig zu einer Überlastung und infolgedessen auch zu einer Entzündung der Sehnen. Sehnenentzündungen sind sehr schmerzhaft. Dadurch beeinträchtigen sie den Bewegungsablauf, was wiederum die Verletzungsanfälligkeit erhöht.

◌ Mit Magneten heilen

Sehnen – vor allem große Sehnen wie am Fuß und in der Schulter – sind relativ schlecht durchblutet. Dies erklärt, warum Sehnenentzündungen in diesem Bereich so hartnäckig sind und sich nur schwer beeinflussen lassen. Darüber hinaus entzieht sich das kompakte Sehnengewebe den herkömmlichen durchblutungsfördernden Gels und Salben.

Magnete haben es demgegenüber leichter. Ihre Kräfte durchdringen auch das Sehnengewebe, ohne dabei jedoch andere Gewebeteile zu reizen.

Die Heilwirkung von Magnetkräften bei Sehnenentzündungen ist klinisch belegt; allerdings wurde die betreffende Studie mit elektrischen Magnetfeldern durchgeführt.

◌ Begleitende Maßnahmen

Ruhe! Das betroffene Körperteil muss so lange ruhig gestellt werden, bis die Beschwerden deutlich nachgelassen haben. Das kann einige Wochen dauern. Danach sollten die durch die Ruhigstellung verkürzten Muskeln durch sanfte Gymnastik wieder elastisch gemacht werden.

Die Anwendung

Die Anwendung erfolgt am besten über wechselpolare Magnetfolien, die auf der schmerzenden Sehne befestigt werden. Bei besonders kompaktem und massigem Gewebe wie etwa der Achillessehne empfiehlt sich eine Stärke des Magnetmaterials von mindestens 1,5 Millimeter (»forte«). Tragen Sie die Magnete so oft und so lange wie möglich, auch während der sportlichen Belastung!

Sportartwechsel Bei chronischen Sehnenbeschwerden hilft oft ein Wechsel zu einer Sportart mit anderen Bewegungsschwerpunkten. Das Interessante dabei ist, dass dieser Wechsel nicht dauerhaft sein muss. So gibt es Fußballspieler, die wegen Schmerzen an der Achillessehne zum Radfahren wechselten und ein Jahr später wieder Fußball spielten – ohne Probleme mit der Achillessehne. Das Fersensehnengewebe hatte durch die gleichförmigen Belastungen beim Radfahrtritt offenbar die notwendige Widerstandskraft bekommen, um auch beim Fußballspielen bestehen zu können.

Homöopathische Mittel Apis mellifica D6 hilft bei besonders hartnäckigen Entzündungen. Die Dosierung beträgt 3-mal täglich 1 bis 2 Tabletten.
Rhus toxicodendron D6 ist angezeigt, wenn der Schmerz bei Bewegung schwächer wird. Die Dosierung beträgt 3-mal täglich 1 bis 2 Tabletten.
Ruta D6 wirkt, wenn Verschlimmerungen der Beschwerden bei Feuchtigkeit, Kälte, Ruhe, im Stehen, Liegen und nachts auftreten. Die Dosierung beträgt 3-mal täglich 1 bis 2 Tabletten.

Die richtige Vorbeugung Grundsätzlich gilt für Sehnenentzündungen dasselbe wie für alle Sportverletzungen: Das Verletzungsrisiko sinkt, je besser der Sportler aufgewärmt ist.
Sorgen Sie für eine Grundlagenkondition (vor allem Kraft, Beweglichkeit und Ausdauer), bevor Sie mit einer technischen Disziplin beginnen.
Erlernen Sie die Bewegungsabläufe einer Sportart gewissenhaft und peinlich genau.
Tragen Sie keine Schuhe mit hohen Absätzen, da diese zur Verkürzung der Achillessehnen beitragen und dadurch das Entzündungsrisiko erhöhen.

Sehnenscheiden- entzündung

○ Symptome

Die Sehnenscheidenentzündung ist eine typische Sportverletzung (Tennis, Badminton, Squash) der Unterarmsehnen. Im ersten Stadium schmerzt die Sehne nur nach schwerer und langer Anstrengung. In Ruhe verschwindet der Schmerz langsam. Im zweiten Stadium treten die Schmerzen vor allem zu Beginn sportlicher Bewegungsabläufe auf. Nach einer gewissen Aufwärmphase werden sie schwächer, doch nach Beendigung des Sports und in der Nacht verschlimmern sie sich. Im dritten Stadium werden die Schmerzen chronisch und halten auch noch tagelang nach dem Sport an.

○ Ursachen

Bei der Sehnenscheide handelt es sich um einen Röhrenschutz für besonders stark beanspruchte und häufig geknickte Sehnen. Ihr Außenteil besteht aus einem spröden Gewebering, ihr Innenteil sondert einen Schleim ab, damit die Sehne besser gleiten kann. Die Sehnenscheide ist ein Schutzorgan. Ist sie verletzt, ist dies ein deutlicher Hinweis auf starke Überlastungen und falsche Bewegungsabläufe. Sehnenscheidenentzündungen im Stadium 2 und 3 sind sehr schmerzhaft. Dadurch beeinträchtigen sie wiederum den Bewegungsablauf, was sie zu einem großen Risiko für andere Verletzungen macht.

○ Mit Magneten heilen

Magnete haben bei der Sehnenscheidenentzündung in allen Stadien gute Chancen. Sie verringern die Schwellung in der Sehnenscheide und sorgen auf diese Weise dafür, dass die Sehne wieder besser gleiten kann. Die Zahl der Squash-, Tennis- und Golfspieler, die mit Magneten ihre Unterarmprobleme in den Griff bekommen haben, ist unüberschaubar. Die Wirksamkeit von Magnetfeldern auf den Heilungsverlauf von Sehnen- und Sehnenscheidenentzündungen ist aber auch klinisch belegt.

○ Begleitende Maßnahmen

Ruhe! Eine Ruhigstellung, bis die Beschwerden deutlich nachgelassen haben, ist sehr wichtig. Das kann bei Sehnenscheidenentzündungen, die das 2. oder

Die Anwendung

Befestigen Sie eine oder zwei wechselpolare Magnetfolien genau dort, wo die Sehne schmerzt. Als Alternative kommen aber auch magnetische Unterarmmanschetten in Betracht, die der Fachhandel mittlerweile zu bieten hat (»Elbow Support« oder – etwas kleiner – »Universal Elbow«; für das Handgelenk »Wrist Splint«).

das 3. Stadium erreicht haben, durchaus einige Wochen dauern. Starten Sie nach der Pause zunächst einmal mit Gymnastik, um die durch die Ruhigstellung verkürzten Muskeln wieder elastisch zu machen.

Bewegungstest Überprüfen Sie Ihre Bewegungsabläufe. Gerade bei Golf- und Tennisspielern werden Sehnenscheidenentzündungen oft durch falsche Bewegungsabläufe verursacht.

Homöopathische Mittel Apis mellifica D6 hilft bei besonders hartnäckigen Entzündungen. Die Dosierung beträgt 3-mal täglich 1 bis 2 Tabletten.

Arnica D6 mindert die Schwellung und sollte möglichst unmittelbar nach dem Training oder Wettkampf eingenommen werden. Die Dosierung beträgt 3-mal täglich 5 bis 10 Tropfen. Rhus toxicodendron D6 ist angezeigt, wenn der Schmerz bei Bewegung schwächer wird. Die Dosierung beträgt 3-mal täglich 1 bis 2 Tabletten.

Ruta D6 wirkt, wenn sich die Sehne anfühlt, als wäre sie verkürzt. Die Dosierung beträgt 3-mal täglich 1 bis 2 Tabletten.

Die richtige Vorbeugung Grundsätzlich gilt für Sehnenscheidenentzündungen dasselbe wie für alle Sportverletzungen: Das Verletzungsrisiko sinkt, je besser der Sportler aufgewärmt ist.

Eine gute Kondition ist die Grundlage für saubere Bewegungsabläufe. Wer zehn Jahre lang keinen Sport mehr gemacht hat, sollte sich erst eine konditionelle Grundlage (vor allem Kraft, Beweglichkeit und Ausdauer) verschaffen, bevor er mit technischen Disziplinen beginnt.

Erlernen Sie die Bewegungsabläufe einer Sportart gewissenhaft und peinlich genau. Wer sich Tennis, Squash, Badminton u. Ä. nach dem Prinzip »Hauptsache, es funktioniert« beibringt, wird schon bald Sehnenprobleme bekommen.

Spannungs-kopfschmerzen

○ Symptome

Der Schmerz verteilt sich vom Hinterkopf aus diffus über die gesamte Schädeldecke. Nachts lassen die Schmerzen nach.

○ Ursachen

Spannungskopfschmerzen haben meistens psychische Ursachen. Die Betroffenen machen für ihre Beschwerden häufig den beruflichen Stress verantwortlich – eine Einschätzung, die auch wissenschaftlich gestützt wird. Termindruck, Angst vor Kündigung oder Konflikte mit Kollegen setzen Stressreaktionen in Gang, die u. a. auch darin münden können, die Nackenmuskulatur fortwährend anzuspannen. Diese chronische Anspannung führt schließlich zu schmerzhaften Muskelhärten, die sich bis zum Kopf erstrecken können. Außerdem verschlechtert der dauernde Muskeldruck die Durchblutung in Richtung Kopf.

○ Mit Magneten heilen

Die Behandlung von Spannungskopfschmerzen gehört zu den Stärken der Magnettherapie. Sie sorgt für eine Entspannung der problematischen Muskeln und dämpft den Durchfluss von Schmerzsignalen in den Nervenbahnen. Es gibt auch zahlreiche wissenschaftliche Belege zur Wirksamkeit magnetischer Felder auf Spannungskopfschmerzen; sie wurden allerdings mit elektronischen Magnetsystemen durchgeführt.

○ Begleitende Maßnahmen

Haltungskorrekturen Neben Magnetanwendungen sollten im Arbeitsalltag Haltungskorrekturen vorgenommen werden, um die Muskeln im Nacken- und Kopfbereich vor einseitigen Belastungen zu schützen. So sollte man während körperlich monotoner Arbeiten häufiger eine Pause einfügen. Darüber hinaus empfiehlt sich die Anschaffung eines Stuhls mit dynamischer Rückenlehne – auch wenn er teuer ist und vom Arbeitgeber nicht bezahlt wird. Bei Arbeiten über Kopf sollte eine Leiter oder ein Hocker benutzt werden. Bei notwendigen Drehbewegungen ist es besser, sich mit dem ganzen Körper zu drehen. Abrupte Bewegungen des Kopfes sollten vermieden werden.

Die Anwendung

Die Behandlung erfolgt über wechselpolare Magnetfolien, die auf beiden Seiten oberhalb des Schläfenknochens, etwa zwei Finger breit neben den Augen, aufgesetzt werden. Zusätzlich ist es sinnvoll, zwei wechselpolare Magnetfolien auf die Nackenmuskeln zu setzen. Die Folien am Nacken verbleiben Tag und Nacht auf der Haut, die Folien am Kopf werden nachts abgenommen.

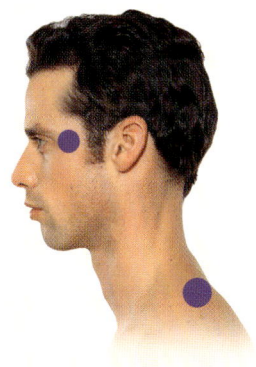

Automatische körperliche Ausgleichsreaktionen wie Gähnen, Zukneifen der Augen oder Streckbewegungen sollten nicht aufgrund falsch verstandener Disziplin unterdrückt, sondern bewusst zugelassen werden. Wer beruflich häufiger anderen Menschen gegenübersitzen muss, kann mit dem richtigen »Gesprächswinkel« wirksame Kopfschmerzprophylaxe betreiben. Der Besucher wird hierzu nicht frontal gegenüber platziert, sondern im 90-Grad-Winkel am Schreibtischrand. Dadurch wird die mimische Muskulatur entlastet, und die Halsmuskulatur bekommt durch abwechselnde Rotationsbewegungen die Chance, sich zu entspannen.

Pfefferminzöl Jüngste Untersuchungen der Universität Kiel zeigen, dass Pfefferminzöl – oberhalb der Schläfen mehrmals täglich leicht einmassiert – Kopfschmerzattacken lindert. In seiner Wirksamkeit reicht das Öl dabei sogar an die bekannten Schmerzmittel ASS und Parazetamol heran.

Homöopathie Nux vomica D6 hilft bei Kopfschmerzen, die durch Stress verursacht werden, und bei Kopfschmerzen, die durch starken Nikotinkonsum ausgelöst werden. Nehmen Sie stündlich 5 Globuli (Kügelchen) oder 1 Tablette, bis eine deutliche Besserung der Beschwerden eintritt. Die Präparate erhalten Sie in Apotheken.

Tennisellbogen

○ Symptome

Beim Tennisellbogen handelt es sich um eine Entzündung am Ansatz der Unterarmmuskulatur am Ellbogengelenk. Die Entzündung kann sich auf die dortigen Sehnen oder Sehnenscheiden beschränken, sie kann aber auch auf den angrenzenden Schleimbeutel ausstrahlen.

Die Schmerzen strahlen in den Unterarm am äußeren Ellbogen aus. Der Unterarm kribbelt, die Muskulatur wird relativ schnell müde; sogar Tätigkeiten wie das Schreiben werden als Belastung empfunden.

○ Ursachen

Verursacht werden diese Veränderungen meistens durch eine falsche Spieltechnik beim Tennis oder durch eine Überlastung. Der Tennisellbogen kann auch erfahrene Tennisspieler treffen, die beim Spielen verkrampfen. Die Hände greifen den Schläger fester als sonst und setzen dadurch die Sehnen einer stärkeren Belastung aus.

Neben Tennisspielern werden vor allem Hausfrauen, Kfz-Mechaniker und Golfspieler vom Tennisellbogen heimgesucht. Manchmal wird die Krankheit auch durch eine Entzündung an einer anderen Stelle im Körper (z. B. an den Zähnen) verursacht.

○ Mit Magneten heilen

Der Tennisellbogen hat aufgrund seiner Hartnäckigkeit schon so manchen Tennis- und Golfspieler zur Verzweiflung gebracht. Mit der Magnettherapie hat man hier eine echte Behandlungsalternative. Die Magnetkräfte wirken auch auf jene Gewebeteile im Ellbogen (Sehnen und Sehnenansätze), die für Salben oder Gels unerreichbar sind. Sie fördern die Durchblutung und wirken schmerz- und entzündungshemmend.

Gerade professionelle Tennis- und Golfspieler, die Ellbogen- und Unterarmprobleme hatten, haben den derzeitigen Magnetboom in den USA ausgelöst. Sie sind gewissermaßen die »Gewährsleute der ersten Stunde« in der Geschichte der modernen Magnettherapie.

○ Begleitende Maßnahmen

Homöopathie Apis mellifica D6 hilft bei besonders hartnäckigen Entzündungen. Die Dosierung

Die Anwendung

Befestigen Sie eine oder zwei wechselpolare Magnetfolien genau dort, wo der Ellbogen schmerzt. Als Alternative kommen auch magnetische Unterarmmanschetten in Betracht, die der Fachhandel mittlerweile zu bieten hat (»Elbow Support« oder – etwas kleiner – »Universal Elbow«).

beträgt 3-mal täglich 1 bis 2 Tabletten. Rhus toxicodendron D6 ist angezeigt, wenn der Schmerz bei Bewegung schwächer wird. Die Dosierung beträgt 3-mal täglich 1 bis 2 Tabletten.

Bienengiftsalbe und Eisabreibung
Bienengiftsalbe zieht die Entzündung aus dem Körper, die anschließende Eisabreibung »versiegelt« die gereizten Blutgefäße und Nerven.

Bestreichen Sie die schmerzende Stelle mit Bienengiftsalbe (aus der Apotheke), und wickeln Sie einen wärmenden Verband um den Ellbogen. Nach etwa 30 Minuten entfernen Sie den Verband mitsamt der Salbe. Reiben Sie den Ellbogen dann 10 Minuten lang mit Eis ab – am besten, indem Sie Wasser in einem Joghurtbecher einfrieren und das Eis – wie bei einem Lippenstift – langsam aus dem Becher herausdrücken. Wiederholen Sie die Anwendung mindestens 2-mal pro Tag.

Die richtige Vorbeugung Die Bespannung und Griffstärke Ihres Schlägers sollte genau zu Ihren individuellen Bedürfnissen passen. Mindestens genauso wichtig ist aber, sich von falschen Vorbildern zu verabschieden. Die einhändige, durchgezogene Rückhand von Boris Becker beispielsweise ist für normale, untrainierte Anfänger eher ungeeignet; da ist die beidhändige »Schieberückhand« des Olympiasiegers Miloslav Mecir gelenkschonender und möglicherweise genauso effektiv.

Erlernen Sie die Bewegungsabläufe einer Sportart gewissenhaft und peinlich genau. Wer sich Tennis, Squash, Badminton u. Ä. nach dem Prinzip »Hauptsache, es funktioniert« beibringt, wird schon bald Sehnenprobleme bekommen.

Bleiben Sie bei Ihren Leisten! Erst müssen Sie das Grundlinienspiel beherrschen, bevor Sie gelegentlich einen Ausflug zum Volleyspiel ans Netz machen dürfen.

Tinnitus

○ Symptome

Ohne äußeren Anlass stellen sich im Ohr Geräusche ein, die in Klang und Lautstärke sehr unterschiedlich sein können. Mitunter ist auch die Klangwahrnehmung verzerrt. Büßt der Betroffene außerdem noch einen Teil seines Hörvermögens ein, liegt möglicherweise ein Hörsturz mit Tinnitus vor.

○ Ursachen

Als gesichert gilt mittlerweile, dass Tinnitus mit einer Schädigung der Sinneszellen – der so genannten Haarzellen – beginnt. Die Betroffenen büßen also mehr oder weniger große Anteile ihres Hörvermögens ein. Im Gegensatz zum Hörsturz sind diese Anteile beim Tinnitus in der Regel eher klein. Sie reichen aber aus, um in den Schallverarbeitungsstellen des Gehirns Reaktionen in Gang zu setzen, die zum Ohrensausen führen. Für die Schädigungen am Innenohr kommen die unterschiedlichsten Ursachen infrage. Sie reichen von Infektionen über Bluthochdruck bis zu Halswirbelblockaden oder schlichtem Lärm.

○ Mit Magneten heilen

Magnetkräfte verbessern die Versorgungssituation im Innenohr. Außerdem sind sie teilweise in der Lage, die Übertragung überflüssiger Signale zum Gehirn zu unterdrücken. Studien mit elektrischen Magnetfeldern ergaben bei chronischen Tinnituspatienten in 70 Prozent der Fälle eine deutliche Besserung. Allerdings können diese Beobachtungen nicht ohne weiteres auf Dauermagnete übertragen werden. Die Chancen der Magnettherapie sind dann am größten, wenn der Tinnitus noch nicht länger als ein halbes Jahr andauert und möglicherweise eine verbesserte Durchblutung im Innenohr helfen kann. Bei länger anhaltendem Tinnitus ist das Tinnitus-Retraining als chancenreicher einzuschätzen.

○ Begleitende Maßnahmen

Das tägliche Tinnitus-Retraining
Das Grundprinzip des Tinnitus-Retrainings besteht darin, unsere Ohren möglichst lange mit unkorrelierten, d. h. bedeutungslosen Reizen zu stimulieren. Auf diese Weise soll das Gehirn wieder lernen, die Tinnitustöne herauszufiltern.

Die Anwendung

Die Anwendung erfolgt über wechselpolare, möglichst kleine Magnetfolien,
die nicht größer als 50 Millimeter sind
und direkt vor dem Gehörgang befestigt werden. Tagsüber werden Sie die
Magnetfolien aus optischen Gründen
kaum tragen können. Legen Sie die
Magnete also überwiegend nachts an,
und versuchen Sie darüber hinaus
dennoch, die Folien auch für mehrere
Stunden am Tag zu tragen.

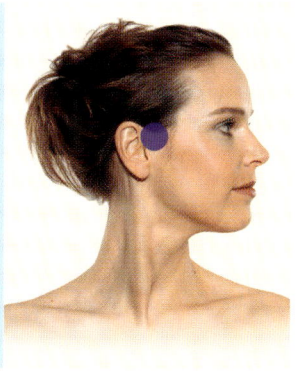

Wichtig ist, dass die Beschallung,
die aufgebaut wird, deutlich lei-
ser ist als das Ohrensausen. Der
Kampf zwischen dem Tinnitus
und den Schallreizen aus der
Umwelt muss geführt werden,
damit das Gehirn auch wirklich
umdenken lernt. Es geht also
nicht darum, den Tinnitus mit
anderen Geräuschen zu mas-
kieren. Es reicht aus, wenn die
Beschallung gerade noch für uns
hörbar ist.
Außerdem müssen die Geräusche möglichst monoton klingen,
so dass sie uns wohl beruhigen,
ansonsten aber für unser Gehirn
eher uninteressant sind. Einige
Musikrichtungen wie etwa gre-
gorianische Gesänge oder chine-
sische bzw. indische Musik mit

Harfen oder dergleichen erfüllen
dieses Kriterium. Optimal ist
aber das Plätschern eines Zim-
merspringbrunnens, das Rau-
schen eines belaubten Baums,
die nahe Meeresbrandung, das
ferne Säuseln einer gut befahre-
nen Straße oder ein auf Rau-
schen eingestelltes Radio.
Wichtig ist weiterhin, dass die
Beschallung möglichst konstant
aufgebaut wird. Am Anfang sollten es sechs Stunden pro Tag,
später können es auch vier Stunden sein. Da es sich dabei nicht
um konzentriertes Arbeiten handelt, sondern lediglich darum,
das Gehirn durch Hintergrund-
geräusche zu überlisten, ist das
Training auch mehrere Stunden
am Tag möglich.

Venen-
erkrankungen

○ Symptome

Die Beine sind geschwollen und fühlen sich schwer an, bei oberflächlichen Venen zeigt sich eine Rötung und Entzündung der Haut. Typisch ist das Brennen in den Beinen, vor allem nach längerem Stehen.

40 Prozent aller Männer und über 50 Prozent aller Frauen haben kranke Venen, bei 15 Prozent lassen sich ausgeprägte Krampfadern feststellen. Der unauffällige Beginn der Erkrankungen bringt es mit sich, dass die Betroffenen oft zu spät gegensteuern. Dadurch kann es zu ernsthaften Problemen wie Wasseransammlungen in Unterschenkeln und Knöcheln oder zu offenen Unterschenkelgeschwüren kommen.

○ Ursachen

Die bisherige medizinische Lehrmeinung lautet, dass Venenerkrankungen durch eine Überfüllung des Venensystems in den Beinen hervorgerufen werden. Nach heutiger wissenschaftlicher Erkenntnis müssen bei Venenerkrankungen aber auch die aktiven Leistungen der Gefäßwand selbst betrachtet werden. Hier steht vor allem die Gefäßinnenwand, das so genannte venoläre Endothel, im Blickpunkt. Es kontrolliert normalerweise den Stoffaustausch zwischen dem venösen Blut und dem umliegenden Gewebe. Doch die Endothelschicht – vor allem in den kleinen Venen – ist überaus anfällig für Gifte, Infekte und andere störende Einflüsse. Dadurch wird sie immer wieder durch Zellen des Immunsystems attackiert. Es kommt zu Entzündungen und Schädigungen, die Kontrollfunktionen der Gefäßinnenwand werden stark eingeschränkt. Die Folge ist, dass der Stoffaustausch aus dem Gleichgewicht gerät. Aus dem venösen Blut wird Wasser in das umliegende Gewebe gedrückt, und die Fließeigenschaft des Bluts wird derart nachteilig beeinflusst, dass schließlich auch die großen Venen Probleme bekommen, es abzutransportieren.

Eine sinnvolle Therapie sollte bei Venenerkrankungen also über die klassischen Behandlungsmethoden (Kompressionsstrümpfe, Operationen) hinausgehen und auch die geschädigten Veneninnenwände stabilisieren. Gerade dabei haben Magnete große Therapiechancen.

○ Mit Magneten heilen

Heilmagnete hemmen Entzündungen und wirken der Ausbildung von Wasseransammlungen im Gewebe entgegen. Außerdem verbessern sie die Funktionstüchtigkeit der Venenwände. In einer Laborstudie konnte ferner gezeigt werden, dass Dauermagnete die Fließeigenschaften des Bluts verbessern.

Schon wenige Tage nach Beginn der Magnetanwendung ist ein deutliches Nachlassen der Spannung im geschwollenen Gewebe zu spüren. Bereits bestehende Krampfadern können mit Magneten natürlich nicht mehr beeinflusst werden.

Die Anwendung

Die Therapie erfolgt über wechselpolare Magnetfolien, die auf die schmerzenden Stellen gesetzt werden. Aufgrund des meist länglichen Entzündungsverlaufs empfehlen sich rechteckige Folienformen. Die Magnete sollten möglichst Tag und Nacht getragen werden.

○ Begleitende Maßnahmen

● Viel Laufen, Gehen, Treppensteigen in zügigem Tempo, damit die Blutzirkulation wieder in Gang kommt und die Muskeln das Blut aus den Adern pressen (Stimulation der so genannten Muskelpumpe). Dynamische Ausdauersportarten wie Schwimmen und Joggen sollten gegenüber Kraftsportarten wie Bodybuilding bevorzugt werden.

● Langes Stehen und Sitzen mit übergeschlagenen Beinen vermeiden. Öfter die Beine hochlegen – auch nachts! Bei längerem Sitzen Beine und Füße bewegen und zwischendurch immer wieder einmal aufstehen.

● Beine täglich kalt duschen, und in kaltem Wasser in der Dusche oder Badewanne treten.

● Übergewicht langsam, aber stetig reduzieren.

● Stützstrümpfe tragen, wann immer es möglich ist.

● Es ist wissenschaftlich belegt, dass Extrakte aus Rosskastanien und Schnurbaum die Venenwände stabilisieren. Man erhält die Präparate in der Apotheke. Zunächst sollte aber der Versuch gemacht werden, die Venenwände ausschließlich mit Hilfe der Magnete zu stabilisieren.

Zahnschmerzen

○ Symptome

Der pochende Schmerz an einem oder mehreren Zähnen verstärkt sich meist beim Kontakt mit heißen oder kalten Speisen.

○ Ursachen

Hauptursache sind Karieslöcher im Zahnschmelz. Aber auch Zahnfleischschwund, eingeklemmte Essensreste sowie entzündete oder überempfindliche Zahnnerven können Schmerzen verursachen. Dauern Zahnschmerzen länger als drei Tage an, sollten Sie auf jeden Fall einen Zahnarzt aufsuchen.

○ Mit Magneten heilen

Die lindernde und wohltuende Wirkung von Dauermagneten bei Zahnschmerzen konnte in einer wissenschaftlichen Studie belegt werden. Nach dem heutigen Wissensstand deutet vieles darauf hin, dass Magnete direkt in die Reizübermittlung unserer Schmerzwahrnehmung eingreifen. Nichtsdestoweniger sollten ihre Möglichkeiten im Hinblick auf Zahnschmerzen nicht überschätzt werden. Karieslöcher können selbst Magnete nicht

zum Verschwinden bringen. Hier ist ein Besuch beim Zahnarzt leider unvermeidlich.

○ Begleitende Maßnahmen

Salzwasserspülungen 1 Teelöffel Speisesalz in 1 Glas Wasser (etwa 200 Milliliter) rühren und mit dieser Lösung mehrmals täglich den Mund ausspülen. Diese Anwendung sollte vor allem nach den Mahlzeiten erfolgen; dadurch werden mögliche Essensreste aufgeweicht und fortgespült. Das Salz wirkt außerdem keimtötend und auch leicht entzündungshemmend.

Nelkenöl Das Öl der Gewürznelke wirkt antibiotisch sowie schmerz- und entzündungshemmend. Die entsprechenden Präparate erhalten Sie in der Apotheke. Bevorzugen Sie Produkte, in denen das Nelkenöl als Mono-

Die Anwendung

Befestigen Sie eine runde wechselpolare Magnetfolie genau auf jener Stelle der Wange, unter der es schmerzt. Die Magnetkräfte haben keine Probleme, durch die Wangenmuskeln bis zum kranken Zahn durchzudringen.

substanz enthalten ist und nicht mit anderen Heilpflanzen kombiniert wurde.

Verstreichen Sie das Nelkenöl mit einem Wattestäbchen auf den schmerzenden Stellen. Bei schweren Schmerzen können Sie das Öl auch direkt auf den Zahn träufeln.

Eisakupressur Reiben Sie einen Eiswürfel an der Stelle der Hand, an der sich Daumen- und Zeigefingerknochen treffen. Die Dauer der Anwendung beträgt etwa 5 Minuten.

Eine kanadische Studie fand heraus, dass diese Eisakupressur bei Zahnschmerzen eine Erfolgsquote von 60 bis 90 Prozent hat, weil sie genau den Nervenweg betäubt, auf dem normalerweise auch der Zahnschmerz »transportiert« wird.

Die richtige Vorbeugung

● Pflegen Sie Ihre Zähne. 2-mal Zähneputzen pro Tag (nach den Mahlzeiten) ist ein absolutes Muss, besser ist 3-mal. Wichtig ist, dass die Zeit fürs Zähneputzen insgesamt 7 Minuten pro Tag beträgt. Zusätzlich sollte 1- bis 2-mal pro Woche auch Zahnseide zum Einsatz kommen, um Essensreste zischen den Zähnen zu beseitigen.

● Gehen Sie 2-mal pro Jahr zum Zahnarzt – zur Kontrolle und um sich den Zahnstein entfernen zu lassen.

● Essen Sie weniger zuckerreiche Speisen. Wenn Sie es doch nicht lassen können, feiern Sie wenigstens echte Orgien: Eine Tafel Schokolade auf einmal setzt Ihre Zähne weniger unter Zuckerbeschuss als viele kleine Schokosnacks über den Tag verteilt.

● Benutzen Sie fluoridhaltige Zahnpasten, da diese den Zahnschmelz kräftigen. Trinken Sie außerdem grünen oder schwarzen Tee – diese Teesorten enthalten erheblich mehr Fluor als etwa Kaffee.

● Zuckerfreie Kaugummis fördern die Produktion von desinfizierendem Speichel und entfernen Essensreste.

● Für den Zahnaufbau bei Kindern bietet sich eine homöopathische Kur an. Morgens 1 Messerspitze Apatit-D6-comp.-Pulver und abends 1 Messerspitze Conchae-Pulver 5 % (natürliches Kalziumkarbonat) einnehmen. Nach einer Einnahme von 4 Wochen und anschließenden 3 Wochen Pause beginnt die Anwendung von neuem.

Über den Autor

Dr. Jörg Zittlau hat Philosophie, Biologie und Sportmedizin studiert und arbeitet heute als freier Wissenschaftsjournalist mit den Schwerpunkten Alternativmedizin, Psychologie und Ernährung.

Hinweis

Das vorliegende Buch ist sorgfältig erarbeitet worden. Dennoch erfolgen alle Angaben ohne Gewähr. Weder Autor noch Verlag können für eventuelle Nachteile oder Schäden, die aus den im Buch gemachten praktischen Hinweisen resultieren, eine Haftung übernehmen.

Bezugsquellen

• BIO-PAINflex® Medical Magnetics Deutschland GmbH, Heidkämpe 15, 28816 Stuhr, Tel. und Fax: 07 00/72 46 35 39; Freecall: 08 00/72 46 35 39 (Bestellservice und Informationen)
• Galerie fit & gesund, Mittelweg 19, 20148 Hamburg, Tel. und Fax: 0 40/4 10 65 19.
• PAINflex®-Magnete sowie wechselpolare Magnetfolien sind außerdem in Apotheken erhältlich.

Literatur

Hannemann, Holger: Energiemedizin. Ariston Verlag. München 1995

Rickert, Ulrich: Magnete besiegen den Schmerz. Goldmann Verlag. München 1986

Stiftung Warentest: Handbuch – Die andere Medizin. Berlin 1996

Tierra, Michaela: Heilen mit Magneten. Windpferd Verlag. Aitrang 1998

Zittlau, Dr. Jörg: Schmerzen lindern mit Magneten. Südwest Verlag. München 2000

Zittlau, Dr. Jörg: Schmerzmittelersatzstoffe. Südwest Verlag. München 1998

Bildnachweis

AKG, Berlin: 5, 8; Jump, Hamburg: 32 (Kristiane Vey); Südwest Verlag, München: Titel (Ute Schönenburg), 13 (N.N.), 21, 24 (Susanne Kracke), 35, 39, 41, 51, 53, 59, 68, 73, 77, 83, 91, 97, 105, 109 (Michael Nagy)

Impressum

© 2000 Südwest Verlag, München, in der Econ Ullstein List Verlag GmbH & Co. KG, München

Redaktion und Projektleitung: Dr. Ulrike Kretschmer

Redaktionsleitung und medizinische Fachberatung: Dr. med. Christiane Lentz

Bildredaktion: Gabriele Feld, Tanja Nerger

Produktion: M. Metzger (Leitung), A. Aatz

Umschlag: Matthias Liesendahl, München

Satz/DTP: Matthias Liesendahl

Druck und Bindung: Druckerei Uhl, Radolfzell

Gedruckt auf chlor- und säurearmem Papier

ISBN 3-517-06387-8